Essays on
German Theater

The German Library: Volume 83

Volkmar Sander, General Editor

ESSAYS ON
GERMAN THEATER

Edited by Margaret Herzfeld-Sander
Foreword by Martin Esslin

CONTINUUM • NEW YORK

1985

The Continuum Publishing Company
370 Lexington Avenue, New York, NY 10017

The German Library
is published in cooperation with Deutsches Haus,
New York University
This volume has been supported by a grant
from The Marie Baier Foundation, Inc.

Library of Congress Cataloging in Publication Data

Main entry under title:

Essays on German theater.

The German Library ; v. 83)
1. Drama—Addresses, essays, lectures.   2. Theater—
Addresses, essays, lectures.   3. Theater—Germany—
Addresses, essays, lectures.   4. German drama—History
and criticism—Addresses, essays, lectures.   5. Dra-
matic criticism—Germany—Addresses, essays, lectures.
   I. Herzfeld-Sander, Margaret.   II. Series.
PN1621.E85   832'.009   85-14889
        ISBN 0-8264-0296-8
        ISBN 0-8264-0297-6 (pbk.)

Acknowledgments will be found on pages 355ff.,
which constitute an extension of this page.

Contents

v

Contents · vii

Foreword

In the center of most major—and many minor—cities of the German-speaking world the traveler will, on his exploratory walks, inevitably find himself in front of a monumental public building as sumptuous and palatial as any town hall or cathedral: the local municipal or (in the capitals of the Länder) state theater. The grandeur of their architecture, whether in a classical or Renaissance idiom, or (in the buildings replacing those destroyed in World War II) in the most daring modernistic styles, the spaciousness of their entrance halls and foyers, clearly indicate that such buildings are not merely places of amusement, vulgar emporia of an entertainment industry run by businessmen bent on a quick return on their investment, but, indeed, veritable "Temples of the Muses." The audiences that fill them in the evenings, arrive in their Sunday best, in a mood of solemn determination to be edified, educated, and elevated into communion with the most sublime blessings of art and culture.

In the German Federal Republic alone no fewer than seventy-five cities boast of such theaters. Indeed, any self-respecting city that wants to be more than a mere village or country town *has* to have its own publicly financed theater. In many of the larger centers these institutions provide opera and operetta, classical and contemporary drama, as well as avant-garde experimental theater in several separate auditoria. They have not only their permanent ensembles of actors and singers, but their own orchestras, ballet companies, choruses, all on long-term contracts. And the civic or state authorities are prepared to pay for all this on a lavish scale: on average only twenty percent of the running costs of such subsidized theaters is recovered at the box office.

For the theater is an institution central to the national ethos and self-image; theatergoing throughout the German-speaking world is an integral part of "Culture." To be a regular theatergoer is a status symbol, a sign that one is a person with *Bildung* (which does mean more than merely "education" but implies a certain moral stature, a completely formed personality, an individual with dignity and independence of mind).

The theater as a mere source of entertainment exists, but it is of a much lower status and despised as mere *Boulevardtheater,* a reference to the commercial theater of the Parisian boulevards (in that sense "Broadway" is the boulevard par excellence). No more damning verdict can be pronounced on a play than that it is *Boulevard.* For the theater, in the eyes of German *Bildung,* must be more than merely amusing; it has a moral, an intellectual mission and function; it forms part of the higher things in life.

The reason for this special status of the theater in German life and culture—and the German pattern has become the model for the culture of most of the nations of Central and Eastern Europe— lies in the part drama and the theater have played in the struggle for national identity and unity.

At the beginning of the eighteenth century, Germany was slowly recovering from the devastation of the Thirty Years' War. Politically the German-speaking world was fragmented into a multitude of larger and smaller sovereign states, kingdoms, principalities, and dukedoms. The rulers of these states imitated the court of Versailles; the more educated people at their courts tended to speak French to show their superiority over the German-speaking common people. (Even late into the eighteenth century, Frederick the Great, king of Prussia, the most powerful German ruler, preferred to speak French and to write his literary works in that language.) The theaters, which each of these sovereign states, from the largest to the most ludicrously small, simply had to have in emulation of the Comédie Française, mostly performed French plays and Italian operas in their original language.

There was German-speaking theater as well—strolling players who had developed their own coarse type of drama: bombastic heroic-sentimental plots interspersed with the most drastic comedy derived from the commedia dell'arte and performed to a large extent extempore with improvised jests by comic characters called Hans Wurst (Johnnie Sausage) Pickelhaering (Pickled Herring) and other variations on the Italian Arlecchino, Brighella, and Truffaldino. This was a vigorous folk theater of immense vulgarity, regarded by the rising bourgeoisie as utterly shameful and obscene.

That rising bourgeoisie, as it gained strength and influence, began to strive for national unity and political as well as cultural independence. The only basis for political unity was the fact that the German language was spoken throughout a large area between the North Sea and the Baltic in the North, the Alps in the South, the Rhine in the West, and the fluctuating borders of the Slav world in the East. Thus the reestablishment of the German language as one of the great idioms of Europe, focal point and unifying bond of a great nation, became the central concept of these political strivings.

The forging of a generally accepted standard German, the establishment of the principles of German poetics, and, above all, the creation of a German literature that could rival that of the established great national languages of Europe—French (with Racine, Corneille, and Moliere), Italian (with Dante and Petrarch), Spanish (with Calderon, Lope de Vega, and Cervantes) English (with Shakespeare and Milton)—thus emerged as the most urgent political task for the future. As Aristotle had proclaimed tragedy the highest form of poetry, the creation of a national drama, a national theater inevitably became one of the top priorities of this struggle.

In 1737 the Professor of Poetry at Leipzig University, Johann Christoph Gottsched (1700–1766), had persuaded the principal of a leading troupe of strolling players, Caroline Neuber, to perform an important symbolic act, the solemn banishment of the Hanswurst, and of coarse improvised dialogue, from her stage. The subsequent passionate debate about the models to be followed by German drama—Racine vs. Shakespeare—became one of the central themes of German cultural history of the period. Eventually Gotthold Ephraim Lessing (1729–1781), a great critic, polemicist, and playwright who became the resident literary adviser, or *Dramaturg,* of the first German "national theater," which civic-minded burghers had started in Hamburg in 1767, secured victory for the Shakespearean model over the advocates of the regularities of the French "unities." And by the end of the century a number of dramatists of world stature had emerged: Schiller and Goethe established the claim of German drama, and hence German literature, to be the equal of the other great national literatures of Europe.

This is the reason why drama and theater are of such decisive importance in the genesis of German national identity and political unity: only after the claim that Germany was one of the major cultural forces of Europe had been triumphantly established could the efforts for political unity gain credibility and ultimately result in the establishment of the Bismarckian Reich in 1871. (This pattern was closely followed by the emerging nationalisms in Central and Eastern Europe—the establishment of claims to political independence in the Czech, Slovak, Slovene, Croat, Serbian, Hungarian, and Rumanian-speaking areas was always closely linked with the creation of national theaters and national dramatic literatures. A parallel phenomenon was the link between Irish nationalism and the creation of the Abbey Theatre on the western fringe of Europe.)

Paradoxically, the existence of so many court theaters—originally devoted to French plays and Italian opera in the many major and minor residences and capital cities of the fragmented country—contributed to the acceptance of drama as a central element in German society: the court theater had been the hallmark of a "capital" city, a major or minor metropolis. Now that the theater had become the symbol of the superior national culture, the former court theaters, "democratized" as municipal or state theaters, continued to function as a status symbol for their locality (analogous, in some ways, to the way in which the possession of a local major baseball or football team confers status on a city in the United States).

The debates of the eighteenth century on the right model for a German national drama, and the rigorous striving to make the German theater a respectable, intellectually superior cultural institution, not only made theoretical talk about drama one of the most fruitful and widespread topics of public debate, it also established the theater as a central domain of the nation's *Bildung*. An educated German of respectable social status goes to the theater as to a shrine of the national identity, an institution designed to provide spiritual and intellectual nourishment. The repertoire of the state or municipal theater, moreover, is regarded as a source of information about the latest trends in the arts and philosophy. The *Intendant* (administrative head) and the *Dramaturg* (literary manager) of such a theater see it as their duty to keep their public abreast of all that is important and new in national and international dramatic literature, as well as providing constant access to the major classical works that are the source of the national culture, so that they can be seen at regular intervals, in up-to-date interpretations. No young person aiming to become a person of *Bildung*, it is argued, should be deprived of growing up without having seen the major works of Goethe, Schiller, Sophocles, Shakespeare, Ibsen, or Brecht in exemplary productions. To achieve this objective, the theaters of this type provide a true repertoire, carefully planned in the long term, with different plays on subsequent days, so that a visitor spending a week in the city can see at least two or three different productions.

In such a culture the theater is perceived as part of the educational infrastructure, on a level with museums, libraries, and universities, and accordingly under the ultimate supervision and administration of the ministries of culture of the Länder; and theatergoing is regarded as an intellectual pursuit. Theater criticism thus also becomes, above all, an exercise of scholarship. Even newspaper critics devote most of their space to an intellectual analysis of the play's message and philosophy. The theatergoer sees his objective as primarily on a par with that of his reading of the latest literary masterpieces or works of sociology and philosophy. The theaters provide, for each production, a program brochure which contains some sixty pages of background information about the play and its history, as well as discussions of its philosophical and sociocultural implications. These program brochures are avidly read and pondered by the members of the audience before the rise of the curtain and in the intermissions.

It is in the light of these facts that the importance of the critical literature on drama in the German-speaking world must be seen: in the formation of the national consciousness, the nation's claim to political identity and independence, theoretical writings about drama have played a central and vital part. The debate about whether to adhere to the "unities" prescribed by the French academy or to follow the example of the irregular but emotionally true tragic structures of Shakespeare, had deep political and philosophical overtones. All major philosophers had to take positions on the aesthetics of drama: Kant, Hegel, Schopenhauer, Nietzsche; even Marx and Engels engaged in passionate debate about the political implications of a play, Ferdinand Lassalle's *Sickingen,* which set the tone for the subsequent Marxist aesthetics of drama. Brecht felt called upon to develop a completely new aesthetics of drama, because he had become convinced that the traditional, "Aristotelian" theory was in contradiction to dialectical materialism.

Indeed, no self-respecting playwright could forego taking up a theoretical position, whether romantic, realistic, naturalistic, symbolist, expressionist, neo-romantic, anti-Aristotelian/Brechtian or surrealist. From Hebbel to Arno Holz, from Georg Kaiser to Piscator, from Hofmannsthal to Brecht, playwrights simply had to demonstrate and explain the aesthetic philosophy behind their practice. The debate about the aesthetics of theater, its theory and practice, mirrors the major trends in *Weltanschauung* throughout the centuries and decades. Journalistic and academic critics constantly intervene in this rich stream of argument by interpreting the views of the major creative figures and, in turn, opening new philosophical and sociological lines of debate.

The historical origin of the culturally respectable, "artistic" theater from an effort to distance it from the vulgar and "obscene" popular theater has—as in other areas of German literary culture— led to a rigid division between the "higher" and the "trivial" spheres, the intellectual and the commercial sectors within the different genres, a division much less noticeable in, say, the French or English-speaking cultures, where writers like Feydeau or P. G. Wodehouse, comedians like Chaplin or the Marx Brothers, can lay claim to being great artists as well as commercial and popular successes.

In the German-speaking world the contempt of the intellectuals for the theater as mere entertainment, the "boulevard theater," as well as the remnants of genuine folk theater (as in the Bavarian and Austrian *Bauerntheater*), leads to the somewhat paradoxical consequence that even efforts to heal the division between the "intellectually respectable" and the despised "folk" theater—such as Brecht's assault on the "classical," "Aristotelian" position—of necessity also take the form of highly theoretical and intellectual debate. There seems to be no way out of that dilemma: once sophistication and intellectual awareness have led to a loss of innocence, naivety cannot be reconstituted by theoretical ratiocination. These have been the stumbling blocks to the attempts by Brecht and his East German followers (Peter Hacks, Heiner Müller) at a truly proletarian theater of high artistic sophistication as well as to the West German avant-garde's efforts to create an anti-bourgeois, socially conscious theater for audiences that would consist of more than just the usual bourgeois subscribers in their Sunday suits and evening gowns. Yet it is against this background of the theater's high prestige as a forum for ideas; as the summit of the literary arts; as the place where all the arts can coalesce in a Wagnerian *Gesamtkunstwerk* or dialectically oppose and ironize each other in Brechtian epic "alienation"; of the drama as a method of thought, of concrete philosophizing, that the astonishing wealth of critical and theoretical writings about drama and theater that the German-speaking world has produced over the last two hundred and fifty years must be seen and appreciated. If Schiller spoke of the theater as a "moral institution"; if Goethe made his Wilhelm Meister embark on his path to self-knowledge and self-realization by joining a troupe of strolling actors and playing Hamlet; if Nietzsche started his work as a philosopher with an inquiry into the origins of tragedy and spent much of his life as an advocate and later as an antagonist of Wagner; if Ibsen and Strindberg found their spiritual home in the German theater; if Piscator and Brecht wanted to make the theater the fountainhead of social and political revolution; and if, indeed, after the Second World War Germany's theaters were reopened and rebuilt before even the most urgent needs of housing had been tackled—all this reflects the pivotal position that drama, and thinking and writing about drama, has occupied and still occupies in the consciousness of the German-speaking world.

MARTIN ESSLIN

Introduction

The reader of German essays on drama and the theater will notice the close connection between discussions of the literary genre, the function of the theater, and the steady production of theoretical texts by dramatists, philosophers, and critics through the ages. The question may then be raised as to why a volume like this neglects to consider writings before Lessing's *Letters Concerning the Newest Literature* (1759–65) and *The Hamburg Dramaturgy* (1767–69). After all, Martin Opitz established guidelines for German writers in his *Book of German Poetics* (1624), stressing the need to follow the rules of Aristotle's *Poetics* and the exemplary plays of ancient Greek dramatists. A century later Johann Christoph Gottsched, a contemporary of Lessing, published *Attempt at Critical Poetics for German* (1730). He wanted to create a theater that was to instruct and improve society. While tragedy, as the highest form of art, was to be addressed to the courts, rational and satirical comedies were the means to educate the emerging middle class. He laid the foundation for a new public theater. But his strict adherence to Aristotelian rules and his recommendation to emulate the classic French writers Corneille and Racine with their stiff Alexandrinian verse, instead of Shakespeare's iambic meter, passionate characters, and lifelike actions, placed him in opposition to a generation best represented by Lessing. It was Lessing who became the most vociferous and revered writer of the Age of Enlightenment, who gave a new direction to playwriting and dramaturgy. Deploring the frenchified theatre in Germany as unsuited to German thinking, he praised the English plays of Jonson, Beaumont and Fletcher, and above all Shakespeare as sources of inspiration. Lessing's own observations on literature and dramatic theory in turn developed into a manifesto for future playwrights. He recognized the need to help the emerging bourgeois class to become less dependent on the courts. He argued that modern drama and theater, as the most public forms of literary discourse, could improve the taste and attitude of a middle class audience that still attended performances out of mere idle curiosity and boredom. A vision of a modern theater like his had to include a receptive and enlightened spectator. Lessing's laments about the lack of firmly established public theaters, actors, and a knowlegeable and sensitive audience, help to explain the utopian quality of his writings, which were meant to instigate the establishment of a bourgeois art and of reasoned public discourse about it. From now on, any reflection on the composition and substance of drama had to include a familiarity with the stage and its social function. Germany, split into innumerable feudal territories, was for decades to come a "belated nation." However, when social changes shifted the balance from the courts to the public sphere, new bourgeois values gave an impetus to the arts.

This was by no means a one-way street. The written word contributed to forming a body of thought inspired by the ideas of freedom, justice, equality, and the ideal of the brotherhood of men. In the new dialectical relationship between art and society, theater had an important role in creating an awareness that the advancement of society necessitated the inclusion of the general public. Beginning with Lessing, a constant output of theoretical essays and plays tried to clarify the formal and human dimensions of dramatic literature and the question of how the modern human condition could be represented on the stage. Thus Lessing fittingly leads the list of writers dealing with aesthetic and conceptual questions in German dramatic literature.

As there is no shortage of critical material, a choice had to be made in order to offer what, it is hoped, is a representative sampling. As a basic principle, an historic-chronological arrangement of texts was followed, in order to make it possible for the reader to pursue the inner logic of reflections on this subject matter as it developed over time and also to provide an historic orientation. In some instances original versions had to be shortened so as to give an overview of the total body of dramatic theories. The majority of these excerpts were included because they reveal the essential ideas of a given era and communicate the spirit of cultural and aesthetic debate up to the present time. A few statements by such dramatists as Grillparzer, Hauptmann, Sternheim, are included in lieu of the more specific dramatic conceptions embodied in their plays.

An alternate way of grouping the texts might have been to organize the material according to thematic criteria. This might have offered enlightenment about commonly shared values and viewpoints and illuminated the radical intellectual changes involved in the transition from a semifeudal to a democratic and pluralistic society. However, that would have resulted in too much overlapping. For a thematic rather than a chronological reading of the material, the following topics are suggested: 1. The Reception of Shakespeare in Germany. 2. The Theater as an Instrument of Enlightenment. 3. The Greek Mind and the Modern Age. 4. The Relationship between the Historian, the Playwright, and the Critic. 5. The Merging of the Sister Arts. 6. The Search for a New Theater. 7. Contemporary Pluralism. These issues may provide some insight into common bonds among the texts without glossing over their individual differences. In German writings on the theater there have always been strong connections to other literatures of the world. The scope of references today has become global. The range is from Aristotle and ancient Greek dramatists to the Elizabethan theater, Shaw, and Bond; from Molière and Diderot to Artaud, Ionesco, and Beckett; from Gorki, Stanislavski, and Meyerhold to Grotowski; from the Chinese theater to the Living Theater.

The Reception of Shakespeare

English theatrical companies traveling on the continent first introduced rather crude versions of Shakespeare's plays. A few German playwrights became familiar with them after they were translated into German, *The Absurda Comica, or Master Peter Squentz,* a play written in 1648 by Andreas Gryphius, was probably influenced by Shakespeare's *A Midsummer Night's Dream.* But Shakespeare's influence was overshadowed by Greek, Latin, and classical French theater, until Lessing started to promote him. Under the spell of Johann Gottfried Herder's treatise on Shakespeare (*On the German Mind and Art,* printed in 1773), the young Goethe's hymnic lecture "For Shakespeare's Birthday" (1771) praised the poetic genius of the dramatist who had offered mankind the history of the world and life itself. Neither this essay nor Goethe's later, more detailed study *Shakespeare and No End* (1813, 1816) are presented here in order to make room for Goethe as commentator on the essence of drama and the task of the dramatist. Instead there is a short excerpt from *Notes on the Theater* by J. M. R. Lenz which in its aphoristic manner and evocative tone embodies the theatrical vision of the Storm and Stress generation and their enthusiasm for Shakespeare. Writers of the Romantic Era also had a sensitive affinity with Shakespeare. W. A. Schlegel and Ludwig Tieck provided imaginative, poetic translations that became extremely popular with the German public. Schlegel's own critical writings express the desire for a fusion of the poetic and the theatrical in modern plays that would be comparable to Shakespeare's theater.

The most frequently discussed play is *Hamlet.* Hegel sees in Hamlet the epitome of the romantic protagonist placed in a range of external circumstances and torn by the inner conflict of his soul. In Freytag's notes on the structure of drama, definitions of dramatic characterization and action are illustrated by references to the structure of *Hamlet.* The popularity and influence of Shakespeare's plays were extraordinary. In the nineteenth and twentieth centuries historic distance brought about a more dispassionate, analytic reception. But Shakespeare's works continue to be a source of inspiration even today. It was only recently that Heiner Müller saw in Hamlet the quintessential German soul. Adaptations and reinterpretations of his plays by Brecht (*Coriolanus* 1951/52), Müller (*Macbeth* 1971, *Hamletmaschine* 1977, *Anatomy Titus The Fall of Rome A Shakespeare Commentary* 1985), and Botho Strauss (*The Deerpark,* 1983) reflect in their treatment of the subject matter the historic changes from Shakespeare to modern times. The German theater of ideas and Shakespeare's plays have an equal attraction today. Brecht and Shakespeare are the most frequently performed playwrights in the German repertory theaters.

The Theater as an Instrument of Enlightenment

The decisive, programmatic essay on the role of the theater in society is Schiller's *The Stage Considered as a Moral Institution*. This text was chosen instead of his aesthetic writings *On Naive and Sentimental Poesy* (1795) or *On the Sublime* (1801), which actually better explains his general views on drama, because the ideas on the possibilities of the theater expressed in this essay mark the beginning of an ongoing debate in German-speaking countries on the function of the theater as a public art form. The importance of Schiller's argument that the stage be considered a moral institution is that it postulates the symbiosis of the aesthetic and moral sense in the dramatic genre which needs the stage to open the sphere of the spirit to the audience. Ever since Schiller aspired to enhance the cultivation of the human mind through the art of the theater, the instructive and civilizing effect of the stage were to become crucial features in defining the relationship between playwright and theater. As the stage, beyond its value of amusing the public, must have an enlightening, moral, and political function, critics starting with Schiller and continuing to the present have maintained that it would be a major loss if the theater and the public were to become separated from each other.

Georg Lukács sees the failure of the theater in the fact that the former unity between relevant drama, the stage and the audience has been disrupted in modern times. Increased individuation and subjectivity have led to esoteric, elitist products and the public appeal of the theater has therefore lost much of its force. What is known today as the crisis in the theater is the dilemma of an institution in search of an audience.

The experimental character of finding new formal devices in order to persuade the public to participate in the theatrical experience is demonstrated in a number of essays: Piscator's call for political theater, Toller's political commitment, and Brecht's demand for a radical new drama. And there is the unending debate in the post-modernist era on how to keep the theater alive as a meaningful public forum.

One of the major questions is raised by Friedrich Dürrenmatt. It is the question regarding the effectiveness of the theater. His argument deals with the problem of whether the contemporary world can be reproduced by means of the theater at all. The issue was taken up by many contemporary playwrights, including Brecht, Hochhuth, Hacks, Kipphardt, Weiss, Frisch and Walser, all of whom are included in this collection. The public theaters Lessing wanted to see established as institutions of enlightenment have become a reality today in both East and West Germany, Austria, and Switzerland. In the West alone there are over two hundred heavily subsidized stages. Houses are efficient, equipped with the most modern technological machinery. The repertory system offers international playbills. But this is not enough. Martin Walser once again speaks of a division between art and life, between the theater and the public. His polemic is directed against both the sterility of the new architecture and the social irrelevance of theatrical representations. Reminiscent of Lessing's indictment of the spectators at his time, Walser also criticizes the conservative mentality of the bourgeois audience. Thus a theater of enlightenment, now also referred to as emancipatory theater, is still under the obligation to look for the play that will lure the audience away from illusionary distractions and have it confront the problems of the age. The excerpts in this volume, from Schiller to Walser, are an introduction to this continuing debate.

The Greek Mind and the Modern Age

Since Lessing, a deeper critical understanding of Aristotle's *Poetics* and the structure and meaning of ancient Greek plays has taken root. During the nineteenth century the critical dialogue about classic Greek drama that had been initiated by Lessing, Goethe, and Schiller, is resumed by Grillparzer. His plays and reflections on drama are a last commitment to the tragic spirit. In his view, the principle of world justice is man's destiny. However, Fatum is replaced by what he calls the unknown quantity that is the final cause of all action. Destiny is but an opaque perception and the spectator will have to decide whether the tragic disposition of the modern play grows out of the unpredictable course of life or emanates from a hidden power. It is Hegel who adds a new historic quality to an understanding of the Greek mind by exploring the cardinal differences between classical and modern ideological and dramatic perceptions. The consciousness about the importance of historic transformations and the waning of the tragic spirit permeates his reflections and can no longer be banished from future inquiries into the origin and death of tragedy.

After studying Hegel, Friedrich Hebbel claimed the tragic sense to be an outcome of the historic process itself, a manifestation of the will in history. He deduces the possibility of dramatic tragedy not by looking into man's inner being, his passions and actions, or his external social world, but by placing the tragic in the idea itself. The total disappearance of tragedy, however, remains a possibility. The knowledge of the end of Greek tragedy is then displayed in Nietzsche's *The Birth of Tragedy*. Yet for clarification of the modern mind and the formulation of novel dramatic forms, many writers today still resort to a confrontation with ancient drama. Ultimately Dürrenmatt's concept of tragi-comedy (cf. his seminal essay "Problems of the Theater" in volume 89 of The German Library), as well as the principles of Brecht's Epic Theater still stem from this dialogue with the Aristotelian theater. In the nineteenth century tragedy is replaced by the bourgeois drama which appropriates social circumstances. Hence critical studies add a sociological perspective to the humanistic tradition.

The Relation between the Historian, the Playwright, and the Critic

The reader will find statements by playwrights on the varying tasks of the historian and the poet in writing about history. Critics trace the development of the dramatic genre by linking it to historic economic changes. German dramatists have shown a predilection for historical and revolutionary drama. This preoccupation with history and ideological concepts, frequently called the theater of ideas, may be understandable by looking at the devastating events in the country's history, the unfulfilled dreams of the French Revolution, and last but not least the precept of history as idea, force or process.

Goethe makes the distinction between the historian, who must be faithful to facts, and the poet who makes use of them in the poetic treatment of historic subject matter. It would have been beyond the scope of this volume to include the extensive remarks by Schiller the historian and the dramatist. However, Büchner's short statement that the poet as writer of history is superior to the historian but that he too must be concerned with authenticity and not morality, had an influence on authors of historical and revolutionary dramas. Plays by Brecht, Weiss, and Kipphardt show the rational, materialist viewpoint in the tradition of Georg Büchner.

History as the very essence of dramatic art still informs the recent plays of Heiner Müller. In his essays he rejects the progressive, linear development of history and the liberating forces of revolution. The writer has to "look history in the eye, which could mean the end of politics and the beginning of human history." History and revolution for Müller have choked on their own contradictions, which lie in the discrepancy between humane objectives and actual bloody violence and death. Müller's plays as well as his dramaturgical reflections have been haunted by the image of modern man surrounded by the debris of history.

Dramaturgy as a reflection of historic consciousness has its parallel development in critical essays in this volume. The letters of Marx and Engels commenting on a contemporary historical drama by Lassalle place emphasis on realistic instead of idealistic treatment of historic subject matter. Corresponding in its dramatic realization to the advanced historic consciousness of the era in which it originates, historical drama surpasses the purely affirmative character of literature; therefore, its nature is directive. In this manner the essays "The Sociology of Modern Drama" by Lukács and "The Origins of Domestic Drama" by Hauser have become classic examples of literary studies within a historic-sociological matrix. Brecht's "Shouldn't We Abolish Aesthetics?" is an outspoken attack on traditional aesthetic judgment proposing a new sociological approach instead.

The Merging of the Sister Arts

Connections between language and music, dance and music, and the fusion of the epic, lyric, and dramatic in a work of art are proof that neither the arts nor the modes of expression were ever rigidly separated. "The Art Work of the Future," according to Wagner, will unite the sister arts into a collective whole in the drama of the stage. It will be fully realized through the fellowship of all artists. Noteworthy is the extent to which the concept of the collective art work was being transformed on the modern stage. The Epic Theater, a rejection of the culinary arts, found its first application in Piscator's political theater as a collective effort of playwrights, technicians, and various participating experts. The new theater deliberately separated the arts, reassembling them in a montage to achieve the shock value needed to gain the audience's attention. Brecht perfected in his dramaturgy what had started as an experiment. Recently Peter Weiss, influenced by Brecht's theater, further expanded it by including elements of Antonin Artaud's "Theater of Cruelty." The unified work of art may have found its best modern expression in the total theater of *Marat/Sade*. The most recent attempt of a collective effort is the work by Robert Wilson with the collaboration of Heiner Müller and a host of artists and playwrights to contribute to the monumental spectacle *CIVILwarS*.

The Search for a New Theater

There are two writers who deal specifically with the form, substance, and influence of Expressionist drama, Toller in his essay "Remarks Concerning German Post-War Drama" and Brecht in "On Experimental Theater." Before the turn of the century, Frank Wedekind had already broken with the Naturalist drama in *Spring's Awakening* (1898). In its fragmentary style this play foreshadowed much of the explosiveness of the expressionist playwrights. The conflict between generations and the aggressive provocation of bourgeois morality lead directly to Sternheim, Toller, and Kaiser. The dissonance between the generations and the clash between individuals and institutions had emerged in the plays of Storm and Stress, but, as Toller argues in his essay, never with such force and intensity. The theater had the task of showing the proletarian as a rebel and the stage as the site of the struggle for a new order. Political drama received its persuasive power through expressionist techniques and the documentary style of Piscator's stage. It culminates in the Brechtian rejection of the old individualist drama "which is beyond redemption." In any case, the objectives were once more to close the gap between art and reality, between stage and audience. The denunciation of political theater as propaganda was countered by Toller and others as a misunderstanding of the nature of political drama and by his proposition that all art forms are by necessity ideological statements. At the same time Horváth, in search of a new audience in Vienna, revived and transformed the folk-play, which had become a cheap piece of entertainment. The theater, however, has to provoke the audience by exposing on the stage the self-righteous members of the middle class. The aim must be to demask the faulty values of the petit bourgeois. In its own way it is as political a theater as that of Piscator in Berlin. Marieluise Fleisser, whose plays had a great impact on contemporary playwrights like Franz Xaver Kroetz and Martin Sperr, eliminated the tradition of dramatic eloquence and contributed to the new genre of the folk-play by replacing the sentimental tone with a laconic discourse. The folk-play genre, once "crude and humble" was then completely remodeled by Brecht. Brecht, indeed, is also the key figure when, at the height of Expressionism, the scientific age demanded what came to be called New Objectivity [*Neue Sachlichkeit*] in literature. Brecht's assertion that the old drama is beyond repair and needs radical reform was no idle talk: it was accompanied by playwrighting, practical work in the theater, and theoretical writings. Drawing on the literatures of the world and the German literary tradition, Brecht devised a theatrical style to rearrange life itself in modern society. His "Anti-Aristotelian Theater of Dialectics" changes Schiller's idea of the theater as a moral institution to an emancipatory theater and thus continues a tradition initiated by Lessing in the Age of Enlightenment. In anticipation of the last part of this introduction, it is safe to say that no other playwright since Aristotle has had such a decisive influence on contemporary German drama and theory in the years following the end of World War II in 1945. Brecht is the strongest link between modern and post-modern theater. Only with the re-establishment of an uncensored theater after the Hitler years could the innovations and ideas of the twenties and thirties come to fruition.

Contemporary Pluralism

The great importance the theater still has today in the German-speaking countries is reflected in each text of the post-Brechtian decades in this collection. Present-day writers commenting on the theater vary in their interpretations of the world and their dramatic methods. Influenced by the respective socio-political climate, there is also a noticeable shift in outlook from the fifties and sixties to the seventies and eighties. Nobody claims today that there is only one all-embracing and valid mode of artistic expression. However, regardless of how different the theories, there is a shared belief in the social function of the theater in counteracting the popularity of commercial entertainment. Many also agree that the playwright must again struggle with the audience to win it over.

There still remains hope of broadening the appeal and attracting those who have never attended theaters. When dramatic literature reappeared after 1945, one of the urgent tasks was to come to terms with recent history. Every single dramatist, German, Swiss, and Austrian, was affected by the power and destructiveness of Fascism. This fact may explain the serious mood of many plays written in the fifties and sixties.

In Germany the Theater of the Absurd never became as trend-setting as in France. In the fifties Ionesco and Beckett were enthusiastically received, but only Hildesheimer identified with them in his early plays and in his theoretical writings. His text, reprinted here, has become a classic. After the war the Swiss writers Frisch and Dürrenmatt were the first to bring to the stage a theatrical reality reflecting the historic and contemporary world. Frisch, after having dealt with Fascism and anti-Semitism in his plays, speaks about the possibility of overcoming historical reality and enlarging life by surpassing the limits of time and space and by reinventing the real. Dürrenmatt's Dramaturgy of Invention sounds very much like Frisch's views, but he has his own philosophical interpretation of man's position in modern times. His use of the grotesque in form and apperception is also an antipode to the Absurd Theater (see his *Problems of the Theater* in volume 89 of The German Library). The lecture on Schiller informs the reader about Dürrenmatt's view concerning how the world can still be produced on the stage today.

The hope that a moral or a political theater might help people come to terms with recent German history is expressed in three representative texts by Rolf Hochhuth, Peter Weiss and Heinar Kipphardt. Their concern is the documentary theater which has many faces. Hochhuth was the first playwright to revive the documentary theater by making use of historic documents of the Hitler era to create his play *The Deputy* (1963). His conceptual approach is, however, traditional. He rejects Brechtian models and follows Schiller in placing the individual and the question of man's responsibility in the center of the documentary play. Peter Weiss' dramaturgical notes have become the base of the political and revolutionary documentary play. But contrary to Piscator's dictum that the aesthetic quality is less important than the political thrust, Weiss and Kipphardt make it clear that the documentary drama and the theater as art-products are no substitute for political action and hence need the aesthetic dimension.

The younger generation strikes out in different directions. They are troubled by the increasing affluence of middle-class society, a lingering Fascist mentality, and human and social indifference. Franz Xaver Kroetz shows in his folk-plays the socially damaged lives of people at the fringes of society, unable to articulate their plight, and the working-class people struggling to reach consciousness. But according to Handke, "politically committed theater does not take place in theater rooms," but elsewhere, in lecture halls or in the streets. Even Martin Walser, initially propagating realism on the stage, turns his back on the realist political theater of the sixties and commends a Theater of Consciousness, which should once again show the individual sensibilities of dramatic characters. Tankred Dorst follows the argument by expressing the desire to portray in the theater the individual's moral accountability. This is a noticeable change from political commitment to individual concerns.

In conclusion, the texts of Peter Hacks and Heiner Müller are to inform the reader about some of the developments in the German Democratic Republic. After their early plays, indebted to Brecht, both Hacks and Müller move toward new positions. Hacks revives classical myth to master modern reality and Heiner Müller's recent plays and dramaturgical statements speak of power, of the victims of history, of destruction and death. Further deconstructing the dramatic forms of the Epic Theater, Müller deconstructs history itself. It is a post-Brechtian theater unable to offer solutions. But post-modernism will one day become superfluous as "literature participated in history by participating in the movement of language first evident in common language and not on paper. In this sense literature is *an affair of the people* and the illiterate are the hope of literature." Thus Heiner Müller's theory in its speculative manner has a utopian quality lacking in his plays.

As in all anthologies, there are omissions in this collection. Schiller's great essays have already been mentioned, but there are others. A case could be made for inclusion of more discussions on tragedy, from Arthur Schopenhauer's *The World as Will and Idea* (1818) to Walter Benjamin's *Origin of German Tragedy* (1928). There might be more about Wagner's *Gesamtkunstwerk*, Kleist's *Marionettentheater*, Brecht's "Epic Theater." Certainly the most important essay in German criticism of recent times besides those of Brecht is Dürrenmatt's *Problems of the Theater* (1954). The main reason for not including them here is that they can be found elsewhere in this series. Nevertheless, I think that this volume provides a representative selection of German writings on the theater. All the more so, since quite a few of the texts are made available here in English for the first time.

M. H. S.

Gotthold Ephraim Lessing

The Seventeenth Letter Concerning the Newest Literature

February 16, 1759

"Nobody," say the authors of the *Bibliothek,*[1] "will deny that the German stage owes a large part of its initial improvement to Professor Gottsched."[2]

I am this Nobody; I deny it straightaway. One might wish that Mr. Gottsched had never been involved in the theater. His supposed improvements concern either dispensable trivialities or are positively harmful.

When Mrs. Neuber[3] flourished, and so many felt the calling to serve her and the stage, things looked very miserable indeed for our dramatic poesy. No one had heard of rules; no one paid attention to models. Our historical and heroic tragedies were full of nonsense, bombast, smut and low humor. Our comedies consisted of disguises and magic; and brawls were their wittiest inspirations. It did not take the keenest and greatest mind to see that things were in a state of degradation. Nor was Mr. Gottsched the first to perceive this; he was only the first who believed himself possessed of enough ability to remedy the situation. And how did he go about doing this? He understood a little French and began to translate; he also encouraged anyone else to translate who could rhyme and understand "Oui, Monsieur." He put together his *Cato,* as a Swiss critic says,[4] with "paste and scissors." *Darius* and the *Austern* (The Oysters), *Elise* and the *Bock im Prozesse* (The Billy-Goat on Trial), *Aurelius* and the *Witzling* (The Wit), *Banise* and the *Hypocondrist* he had assembled without paste and scissors. He

1

put his curse on extemporizing. He had Harlequin ceremoniously driven from the theater, which was itself the biggest harlequinade that has ever been played. In short, he wanted not so much to improve our old theater as to be the creator of a completely new one. And what kind of a new theater? A frenchified one, without considering whether this frenchified theater were suited to the German manner of thinking or not.

He should have been able to tell well enough from our old works, which he has cast aside, that we take our cue more from the taste of the English than the French; that we want more to see and think about in our tragedies than the timid French tragedy gives us to see and think about; that the Grand, the Terrifying, the Melancholy, have a greater effect on us than the Mannered, the Tender, the Infatuated; that too much simplicity tires us more than too much complexity, etc. He should, therefore, have stayed on this track, and it would have led him directly to the English theater.—And don't say that he also sought to use the English, as his *Cato* supposedly shows. For the very fact that he considered Addison's *Cato* to be the foremost English tragedy shows clearly that he looked only through the eyes of the French and at that time had not heard of Shakespeare, Jonson, Beaumont and Fletcher, etc., whom he now at this later point, out of pride, still does not want to hear about.

The results would have been better, I'm sure of it, if the masterpieces of Shakespeare had been translated for our Germans, with a few modest alterations, than what happened as a result of acquainting them so well with Corneille and Racine. First, people would have found the former much more to their taste than they have—that is, have not—found the latter; and second, the former would have inspired quite a different sort of mind among us than we have seen hailed in the wake of the latter. For a genius can only be sparked by another genius; and most easily from such as one who seems to owe all to nature and who is not intimidated by the demanding exigencies of art.

Even if one judges by the models of the ancients, Shakespeare is a far greater tragic poet than Corneille—though the latter knew the ancients very well and the former hardly at all. Corneille comes closer to them in the mechanical arrangement, Shakespeare in the essentials. The Englishman almost always reaches the goal of tragedy, even if he chooses unusual paths known only to him; the Frenchman almost never reaches it, even though he treads the beaten paths of the ancients. Next to Sophocles's *Oedipus,* there can be no work that has more power over our passions than *Othello,* or *King Lear,* or *Hamlet,* etc. Does Corneille have a single tragedy that could have moved you even half as much as Voltaire's *Zaire?* And Voltaire's *Zaire,* how inferior is that work to the *Moor of Venice,* of which it is a weak copy, and from which the character of Orosman is wholly taken?

But that our old works really do have much of the English to them, this I could amply prove to you with but a little effort. To name only the best known of them: *Doctor Faust* has many scenes that only a Shakespearean genius could have conceived. And how much was Germany, and is it still in part, in love with its *Doctor Faust!* . . .

Translated by David Coons

Notes

1. *Bibliothek der schönen Wissenschaften,* vol. 3, no. 1, p. 85.
2. Johann Christoph Gottsched (1700–1766), professor of poetics in Leipzig, leading theater critic, author, and translator of French plays.
3. Leading German actress of her time and director of a theater company.
4. Johann Jakob Bodmer (1698–1783), Gottsched's major critic before Lessing.

From *The Hamburg Dramaturgy*

1

. . . If heroic sentiments are to arouse admiration, the poet must not be too lavish of them, for what we see often, what we see in many persons, no longer excites astonishment. Every Christian in *Olindo and Sophronia*[1] holds being martyred and dying as easy as drinking a glass of water. We hear these pious bravadoes so often and out of so many mouths, that they lose all their force.

The second remark concerns Christian tragedies in particular. Their heroes are generally martyrs. Now we live in an age when the voice of healthy reason resounds too loudly to allow every fanatic who rushes into death wantonly, without need, without regard for all his citizen duties, to assume to himself the title of a martyr. We know too well to-day how to distinguish the false martyr from the true, but despise the former as much as we reverence the latter, and at most they extort from us a melancholy tear for the blindness and folly of which we see humanity is capable. But this tear is none of those pleasing ones that tragedy should evoke. If therefore the poet chooses a martyr for his hero let him be careful to give to his actions the purest and most incontrovertible motives, let him place him in an unalterable necessity of taking the step that exposes him to danger, let him not suffer him to seek death carelessly or insolently challenge it. Else his pious hero becomes an object of our distaste, and even the religion that he seeks to honour may suffer thereby. . . .

2

. . . The first tragedy that deserves the name of Christian has beyond doubt still to appear. I mean a play in which the Christian interests us solely as a Christian. But is such a piece even possible? Is not the character of a true Christian something quite untheatrical? Does not the gentle pensiveness, the unchangeable meekness that are his essential features, war with the whole business of tragedy that strives to purify passions by passions? Does not his expectation of rewarding happiness after this life contradict the disinterestedness with which we wish to see all great and good actions undertaken and carried out on the stage?

Until a work of genius arises that incontestably decides these objections,—for we know by experience what difficulties genius can surmount,—my advice is this, to leave all existent Christian tragedies unperformed. This advice, deduced from the necessities of art, and which deprives us of nothing more than very mediocre plays, is not the worse because it comes to the aid of weak spirits who feel I know not what shrinking, when they hear sentiments spoken from the stage that they had only expected to hear in a holier place. The theatre should give offence to no one, be he who he may, and I wish it would and could obviate all preconceived offence. . . .

. . . I know full well that the sentiments in a drama must be in accordance with the assumed character of the person who utters them. They can therefore not bear the stamp of absolute truth, it is enough if they are poetically true, if we must admit that this character under these circumstances, with these passions could not have judged otherwise. But on the other hand this poetical truth must also approach to the absolute and the poet must never think so unphilosophically as to assume that a man could desire evil for evil's sake, that a man could act on vicious principles, knowing them to be vicious and boast of them to himself and to others. Such a man is a monster as fearful as he is uninstructive and nothing save the paltry resource of a shallow-head that can deem glittering tirades the highest beauties of a tragedy. . . .

9

It is right and well if in every-day life we start with no undue mistrust of the character of others, if we give all credence to the testimony of honest folk. But may the dramatic poet put us off with such rules of justice? Certainly not, although he could much ease his business thereby. On the stage we want to see who the people are, and we can only see it from their actions. The goodness with which we are to credit them, merely upon the word of another, cannot possibly interest us in them. It leaves us quite indifferent, and if we never have the smallest personal experience of their goodness it even has a bad reflex effect upon those on whose faith we solely and only accepted the opinion. Far therefore from being willing to believe Siegmund[2] to be a most perfect and excellent young man, because Julia, her mother, Clarissa and Edward declare him to be such, we rather begin to suspect the judgment of these persons, if we never see for ourselves anything to justify their favourable opinion. It is true, a private person cannot achieve many great actions in the space of four-and-twenty hours. But who demands great actions? Even in the smallest, character can be revealed, and those that throw the most light upon character, are the greatest according to poetical valuation. . . .

11

Very good then; all antiquity believed in ghosts. Therefore the poets of antiquity were quite right to avail themselves of this belief. If we encounter ghosts among them, it would be unreasonable to object to them according to our better knowledge. But does this accord the same permission to our modern poets who share our better knowledge? Certainly not. But suppose he transfer his story into these more credulous times? Not even then. For the dramatic poet is no historian, he does not relate to us what was once believed to have happened, but he really produces it again before our eyes, and produces it again not on account of mere historical truth but for a totally different and a nobler aim. Historical accuracy is not his aim, but only the means by which he hopes to attain his aim; he wishes to delude us and touch our hearts through this delusion. If it be true therefore that we no longer believe in ghosts; and if this unbelief must of necessity prevent this delusion, if without this delusion we cannot possibly sympathise, then our modern dramatist injures himself when he nevertheless dresses up such incredible fables, and all the art he has lavished upon them is vain.

Consequently?—It is consequently never to be allowed to bring ghosts and apparitions on the stage? Consequently this source of terrible or pathetic emotions is exhausted for us? No, this would be too great a loss to poetry. Besides does she not own examples enough where genius confutes all our philosophy, rendering things that seem ludicrous to our cooler reason most terrible to our imagination? The consequence must therefore be different and the hypotheses whence we started false. We no longer believe in ghosts? Who says so? Or rather, what does that mean? Does it mean: we are at last so far advanced in comprehension that we can prove their impossibility; that certain incontestable truths that contradict a belief in ghosts are now so universally known, are so constantly present even to the minds of the most vulgar, that everything that is not in accordance with these truths, seems to them ridiculous and absurd! It cannot mean this. We no longer believe in ghosts can therefore only mean this: in this matter concerning which so much may be argued for or against, that is not decided and never can be decided, the prevailing tendency of the age is to incline towards the preponderance of reasons brought to bear against this belief. Some few hold this opinion from conviction, and many others wish to appear to hold it, and it is these who raise the outcry and set the fashion. Meanwhile the mass is silent, and remains indifferent, and thinks now with one side, now with the other, delights in hearing jokes about ghosts recounted in broad daylight and shivers with horror at night when they are talked of.

Now a disbelief in ghosts in this sense cannot and should not hinder the dramatic poet from making use of them. The seeds of possible belief in them are sown in all of us and most frequently in those persons for whom he chiefly writes. It depends solely on the degree of his art whether he can force these seeds to germinate, whether he possesses certain dexterous means to summon up rapidly and forcibly arguments in favour of the existence of such ghosts. If he has them in his power, no matter what we may believe in ordinary life, in the theatre we must believe as the poet wills. . . .

14

Domestic tragedies found a very thorough defender in the person of the French art critic who first made *Sara*[3] known to his nation. As a rule the French rarely approve anything of which they have not a model among themselves.

The names of princes and heroes can lend pomp and majesty to a play, but they contribute nothing to our emotion. The misfortunes of those whose circumstances most resemble our own, must naturally penetrate most deeply into our hearts, and if we pity kings, we pity them as human beings, not as kings. Though their position often renders their misfortunes more important, it does not make them more interesting. Whole nations may be involved in them, but our sympathy requires an individual object and a state is far too much an abstract conception to touch our feelings.

"We wrong the human heart," says Marmontel,[4] "we misread nature, if we believe that it requires titles to rouse and touch us. The sacred names of friend, father, lover, husband, son, mother, of mankind in general, these are far more pathetic than aught else and retain their claims forever. What matters the rank, the surname, the genealogy of the unfortunate man whose easy good nature towards unworthy friends has involved him in gambling and who loses over this his wealth and honour and now sighs in prison distracted by shame and remorse? If asked, who is he? I reply: He was an honest man and to add to his grief he is a husband and a father; his wife whom he loves and who loves him is suffering extreme need and can only give tears to the children who clamour for bread. Show me in the history of heroes a more touching, a more moral, indeed a more tragic situation! And when at last this miserable man takes poison and then learns that Heaven had willed his release, what is absent, in this painful terrible moment, when to the horrors of death are added the tortures of imagination, telling him how happily he could have lived, what I say is absent to render the situation worthy of a tragedy? The wonderful, will be replied. What! is there not matter wonderful enough in this sudden change from honour to shame, from innocence to guilt, from sweet peace to despair; in brief, in the extreme misfortune into which mere weakness has plunged him!"

19

Now Aristotle has long ago decided how far the tragic poet need regard historical accuracy: not farther than it resembles a well-constructed fable wherewith he can combine his intentions. He does not make use of an event because it really happened, but because it happened in such a manner as he will scarcely be able to invent more fitly for his present purpose. If he finds this fitness in a true case, then the true case is welcome; but to search through history books does not reward his labour. And how many know what has happened? If we only admit the possibility that something can happen from the fact that it has happened, what prevents us from deeming an entirely fictitious fable a really authentic occurrence, of which we have never heard before? What is the first thing that makes a history probable? Is it not its internal probability? And is it not a matter of indifference whether this probability be confirmed by no witnesses or traditions, or by such as have never come within our knowledge? It is assumed quite without reason, that it is one of the objects of the stage, to keep alive the memory of great men. For that we have history and not the stage. From the stage we are not to learn what such and such an individual man has done, but what every man of a certain character would do under certain given circumstances. The object of tragedy is more philosophical than the object of history, and it is degrading her from her true dignity to employ her as a mere panegyric of famous men or to misuse her to feed national pride.

29

Comedy is to do us good through laughter; but not through derision; not just to counteract those faults at which it laughs, nor simply and solely in those persons who possess these laughable faults. Its true general use consists in laughter itself, in the practice of our powers to discern the ridiculous, to discern it easily and quickly under all cloaks of passion and fashion; in all admixture of good and bad qualities, even in the wrinkles of solemn earnestness. Granted that Molière's Miser never cured a miser; nor Regnard's Gambler, a gambler; conceded that laughter never could improve these fools; the worse for them, but not for comedy. It is enough for comedy that, if it cannot cure an incurable disease, it can confirm the healthy in their health. The Miser is instructive also to the extravagant man; and to him who never plays the Gambler may prove of use. The follies they have not got themselves, others may have with whom they have to live. It is well to know those with whom we may come into collision; it is well to be preserved from all impressions by example. A preservative is also a valuable medicine, and all morality has none more powerful and effective, than the ridiculous. . . .

33

. . . I have further expressed my views that characters must be more sacred to a poet than facts. For one reason, because if characters are carefully observed in so far as the facts are a consequence of the characters, they cannot of themselves prove very diverse; while the self-same facts can be deduced from totally different characters; secondly, because what is instructive is not contained in the mere facts but in the recognition that these characters under these circumstances would and must evolve these facts. . . .

. . . It is certainly open to the poet, as a poet, to choose which form he wills. Whether that which history ratifies or any other, according as it be suited to the moral intention he has in his play. Only if he chooses other and even opposed characters to the historical, he should refrain from using historical names, and rather credit totally unknown personages with well-known facts than invent characters to well-known personages. The one mode enlarges our knowledge or seems to enlarge it and is thus agreeable. The other contradicts the knowledge that we already possess and is thus unpleasant. We regard the facts as something accidental, as something that may be common to many persons; the characters we regard as something individual and intrinsic. The poet may take any liberties he likes with the former so long as he does not put the facts into contradiction with the characters; the characters he may place in full light but he may not change them, the smallest change seems to destroy their individuality and to substitute in their place other persons, false persons, who have usurped strange names and pretend to be what they are not.

34

. . . Now a character in which the instructive is lacking, lacks purpose.

To act with a purpose is what raises man above the brutes, to invent with a purpose, to imitate with a purpose, is that which distinguishes genius from the petty artists who only invent to invent, imitate to imitate. They are content with the small enjoyment that is connected with their use of these means, and they make these means to be their whole purpose and demand that we also are to be satisfied with this lesser enjoyment, which springs from the contemplation of their cunning but purposeless use of their means. It is true that genius begins to learn from such miserable imitations; they are its preliminary studies. It also employs them in larger works for amplification and to give resting-places to our warmer sympathy, but with the construction and elaboration of its chief personages it combines larger and wider intentions; the intention to instruct us what we should do or avoid; the intention to make us acquainted with the actual characteristics of good and bad, fitting and absurd. It also designs to show us the good in all their combinations and results still good and happy even in misery; the bad as revolting and unhappy even in happiness. When its plot admits of no such immediate imitation, no such unquestionable warning, genius still aims at working upon our powers of desire and abhorrence with objects that deserve these feelings, and ever strives to show these objects in their true light, in order that no false light may mislead us as to what we should desire, what we should abhor.

45

. . . What good does it do the poet, that the particular actions that occur in every act would not require much more time for their real occurrence than is occupied by the representation of each act; and that this time, including what is absorbed between the acts, would not nearly require a complete revolution of the sun; has he therefore regarded the unity of time? He has fulfilled the words of the rule, but not their spirit. For what he lets happen in one day, can be done in one day it is true, but no sane mortal would do it in one day. Physical unity of time is not sufficient, the moral unity must also be considered, whose neglect is felt by every one, while the neglect of the other, though it generally involves an impossibility, is yet not so generally offensive because this impossibility can remain unknown to many. If, for instance, in a play a person must travel from one place to another and this journey alone would require more than a day, the fault is only observed by those who know the distance of the locality. Not everybody knows geographical distances, while everybody can feel in him for what actions he would allow himself one day, for what several. The poet therefore who does not know how to preserve physical unity of time except at the expense of moral unity, who does not hesitate to sacrifice the one to the other, consults his own interests badly and sacrifices the essential to the accidental.

46

It is one thing to circumvent the rules, another to observe them. The French do the former, the latter was only understood by the ancients.

Unity of action was the first dramatic law of the ancients; unity of time and place were mere consequences of the former which they would scarcely have observed more strictly than exigency required had not the combination with the chorus arisen. For since their actions required the presence of a large body of people and this concourse always remained the same, who could go no further from their dwellings nor remain absent longer than it is customary to do from mere curiosity, they were almost obliged to make the scene of action one and the same spot and confine the time to one and the same day. They submitted *bonâ fide* to this restriction; but with a suppleness of understanding such that in seven cases out of nine they gained more than they lost thereby. For they used this restriction as a reason for simplifying the action and to cut away all that was superfluous, and thus, reduced to essentials, it became only the ideal of an action which was developed most felicitously in this form which required the least addition from circumstances of time and place.

The French on the contrary, who found no charms in true unity of action, who had been spoilt by the wild intrigues of the Spanish school, before they had learnt to know Greek simplicity, regarded the unity of time and place not as consequences of unity of action, but as circumstances absolutely needful to the representation of an action, to which they must therefore adapt their richer and more complicated actions with all the severity required in the use of a chorus, which however they had totally abolished. When they found however, how difficult, nay at times how impossible this was, they made a truce with the tyrannical rules against which they had not the courage to rebel. Instead of a single place, they introduced an uncertain place, under which we could imagine now this, now that spot; enough if the places combined were not too far apart and none required special scenery, so that the same scenery could fit the one about as well as the other. Instead of the unity of a day they substituted unity of duration, and a certain period during which no one spoke of sunrise or sunset, or went to bed, or at least did not go to bed more than once, however much might occur in this space, they allowed to pass as a day.

Now no one would have objected to this, for unquestionably even thus excellent plays can be made, and the proverb says; cut the wood where it is thinnest. But I must also allow my neighbour the same privilege. I must not always show him the thickest part, and cry, "There you must cut! That is where I cut!" Thus the French critics all exclaim, especially when they speak of the dramatic works of the English. What an ado they then make of regularity, that regularity which they have made so easy to themselves! But I am weary of dwelling on this point!

As far as I am concerned Voltaire's and Maffei's *Merope* may extend over eight days and the scene may be laid in seven places in Greece! if only they had the beauties to make me forget these pedantries! . . .

48

O ye manufacturers of general rules, how little do ye understand art, how little do ye possess of the genius that brought forth the masterpieces upon which ye build and which it may overstep as often as it lists!—My thoughts may appear as paradoxical as they like, yet so much I know for certain, that for one instance where it is useful to conceal from the spectator an important event until it has taken place there are ten and more where interest demands the very contrary. By means of secrecy a poet effects a short surprise, but in what enduring disquietude could he have maintained us if he had made no secret about it! Whoever is struck down in a moment, I can only pity for a moment. But how if I expect the blow, how if I see the storm brewing and threatening for some time about my head or his? For my part none of the personages need know each other if only the spectator knows them all. Nay I would even maintain that the subject which requires such secrecy is a thankless subject, that the plot in which we must have recourse to it is not as good as that in which we could have done without it. It will never give occasion for anything great. We shall be obliged to occupy ourselves with preparations that are either too dark or too clear, the whole poem becomes a collection of little artistic tricks by means of which we effect nothing more than a short surprise. If on the contrary everything that concerns the personages is known, I see in this knowledge the source of the most violent emotions. Why have certain monologues such a great effect? Because they acquaint me with the secret intentions of the speaker and this confidence at once fills me with hope or fear. If the condition of the personages is unknown, the spectator cannot interest himself more vividly in the action than the personages. But the interest would be doubled for the spectator if light is thrown on the matter, and he feels that action and speech would be quite otherwise if the personages knew one another.

Many hold pompous and tragic to be much the same thing. Not only many of the readers but many of the poets themselves. What! their heroes are to talk like ordinary mortals! What sort of heroes would those be? "Ampullae et sesquipedalia verba," sentences and bubbles and words a yard long, this constitutes for them the true tone of tragedy.

Diderot says,[5] "We have not omitted anything that could spoil the drama from its very foundations." (Observe that he speaks especially of his countrymen.) "We have retained the whole splendid versification of the ancients that is really only suited to a language of very measured quantities and very marked accents, for very large stages and for a declamation fitted to music and accompanied with instruments. But its simplicity in plot and conversation and the truth of its pictures we have abandoned."

Diderot might have added another reason why we cannot throughout take the old tragedies for our pattern. There all the personages speak and converse in a free public place, in presence of an inquisitive multitude. They must therefore nearly always speak with reserve and due regard to their dignity; they cannot give vent to their thoughts and feelings in the first words that come, they must weigh and choose them. But we moderns, who have abolished the chorus, who generally leave our personages between four walls, what reason have we to let them employ such choice stilted rhetorical speech notwithstanding? Nobody hears it except those whom they permit to hear it; nobody speaks to them but people who are involved in the action, who are therefore themselves affected and have neither desire nor leisure to control expressions. This was only to be feared from the chorus who never acted, however much they might be involved in the play, and always rather judged the acting personages than took a real part in their fate. It is as useless to invoke the high rank of the personages; aristocratic persons have learned how to express themselves better than the common man, but they do not affect incessantly to express themselves better than he. Least of all in moments of passion; since every passion has its own eloquence, is alone inspired by nature, is learnt in no school and is understood by the most uneducated as well as by the most polished.

There never can be feeling with a stilted, chosen, pompous, language. It is not born of feeling, it cannot evoke it. But feeling agrees with the simplest, commonest, plainest words and expressions. . . .

75

For it is certainly not Aristotle who has made the division so justly censured of tragic passions into terror and compassion. He has been falsely interpreted, falsely translated. He speaks of pity and *fear*, not of pity and *terror;* and his fear is by no means the fear excited in us by misfortune threatening another person. It is the fear which arises for ourselves from the similarity of our position with that of the sufferer; it is the fear that the calamities impending over the sufferers might also befall ourselves; it is the fear that we ourselves might thus become objects of pity. In a word this fear is compassion referred back to ourselves.

78

. . . When Aristotle maintains that tragedy excites pity and fear
to purify pity and fear, who does not see that this comprehends
far more than Dacier has deemed good to explain? For according
to the different combinations of these conceptions he who would
exhaust Aristotle must prove separately—1. How tragic pity purifies
our pity. 2. How tragic fear purifies our fear. 3. How tragic pity
purifies our fear. 4. How tragic fear purifies our pity. Dacier rested
at the third point only and he only explained this badly and
partially. For whoever has endeavoured to arrive at a just and
complete conception of Aristotle's doctrine of the purification of
the passions will find that each of these four points includes in it
a double contingency, namely, since (to put it briefly) this purification rests in nothing else than in the transformation of passions
into virtuous habits, and since according to our philosopher each
virtue has two extremes between which it rests, it follows that if
tragedy is to change our pity into virtue it must also be able to
purify us from the two extremes of pity, and the same is to be
understood of fear. Tragic pity must not only purify the soul of
him who has too much pity, but also of him who has too little;
tragic fear must not simply purify the soul of him who does not
fear any manner of misfortune but also of him who is terrified by
every misfortune, even the most distant and most improbable.
Likewise tragic pity in regard to fear must steer between this too
much and too little, and conversely tragic fear in regard to pity.

80

To what end the hard work of dramatic form? Why build a
theatre, disguise men and women, torture their memories, invite
the whole town to assemble at one place if I intend to produce
nothing more with my work and its representation, than some of
those emotions that would be produced as well by any good story
that every one could read by his chimney-corner at home?

The dramatic form is the only one by which pity and fear can
be excited, at least in no other form can these passions be excited
to such a degree. Nevertheless it is preferred to excite all others
rather than these;—nevertheless it is preferred to employ it for any
purpose but this, for which it is so especially adapted.

The public will put up with it; this is well, and yet not well. One has no special longing for the board at which one always has to put up with something.

It is well known how intent the Greek and Roman people were upon their theatres; especially the former on their tragic spectacles. Compared with this, how indifferent, how cold is our people towards the theatre! Whence this difference if it does not arise from the fact that the Greeks felt themselves animated by their stage with such intense, such extraordinary emotions, that they could hardly await the moment to experience them again and again, whereas we are conscious of such weak impressions from our stage that we rarely deem it worth time and money to attain them. We most of us go to the theatre from idle curiosity, from fashion, from ennui, to see people, from desire to see and be seen, and only a few, and those few very seldom, go from any other motive.

I say we, our people, our stage, but I do not mean the Germans only. We Germans confess openly enough that we do not as yet possess a theatre. What many of our critics who join in this confession and are great admirers of the French theatre think when they make it I cannot say, but I know well what I think. I think that not alone we Germans, but also that those who boast of having had a theatre for a hundred years, ay, who boast of having the best theatre in all Europe, even the French have as yet no theatre, certainly no tragic one. The impressions produced by French tragedy are so shallow, so cold. . . .

81

Of the two it is Corneille who has done the greatest harm and exercised the most pernicious influence on these tragedians. Racine only seduced by his example, Corneille by his examples and doctrines together, the latter especially, which were accepted as oracles by the whole nation (excepting one or two pedants, a Hédelin, a Dacier who however did not know themselves what they desired) and followed by all succeeding poets. I would venture to prove bit by bit that these doctrines could produce nothing but the most shallow, vapid, and untragical stuff. . . .

1. Aristotle says tragedy is to excite pity and fear, Corneille says

oh, yes, but as it happens, both together are not always necessary, we can be contented with one of them, now pity without fear, another time fear without pity. Else where should I be, I the great Corneille with my Rodrigue and my Chimène? These good children awaken pity, very great pity, but scarcely fear. And again where should I be with my Cleopatra, my Prusias, and my Phocas? Who can have pity on these wretches? but they create fear. So Corneille believed and the French believed it after him.

2. Aristotle says tragedy should excite pity and fear, both, be it understood, by means of one and the same person. Corneille says: if it so happens very good. It is not however absolutely necessary and we may employ two different persons to produce these two sensations as I have done in my *Rodogune*. This is what Corneille did and the French do after him.

3. Aristotle says by means of the pity and fear excited in us by tragedy our pity and our fear and all that is connected with them are to be purified. Corneille knows nothing of all this and imagines that Aristotle wished to say tragedy excites our pity in order to awaken our fear, in order to purify by this fear the passions which had drawn down misfortunes upon the person we commiserate. I will say nothing of the value of this aim, enough that it is not Aristotle's and that since Corneille gave to his tragedies quite another aim they necessarily became works totally different from those whence Aristotle had abstracted his theories, they needs became tragedies which were no true tragedies. And such not only his but all French tragedies became because their authors did not think of the aim of Aristotle, but the aim of Corneille. . . .

101–104

But it is possible to study until one has studied oneself deep into error. What therefore assures me that this has not happened to me, that I do not mistake the essence of dramatic art is this, that I acknowledge it exactly as Aristotle deduced it from the countless masterpieces of the Greek stage. I have my own thoughts about the origin and foundation of this philosopher's poetics which I could not bring forward here without prolixity. I do not however hesitate to acknowledge (even if I should therefore be laughed to scorn in these enlightened times) that I consider the work as infallible as the Elements of Euclid. Its foundations are as clear and definite, only certainly not as comprehensible and therefore more exposed to misconstruction. Especially in respect to tragedy, as that concerning which time would pretty well permit everything to us, I would venture to prove incontrovertibly, that it cannot depart a step from the plumbline of Aristotle, without departing so far from its own perfection.

In this conviction I set myself the task of judging in detail some of the most celebrated models of the French stage. For this stage is said to be formed quite in accordance with the rules of Aristotle, and it has been particularly attempted to persuade us Germans that only by these rules have the French attained to the degree of perfection from which they can look down on all the stages of modern peoples. We have long so firmly believed this, that with our poets, to imitate the French was regarded as much as to work according to the rules of the ancients.

Nevertheless this prejudice could not eternally stand against our feelings. These were fortunately roused from their slumbers by some English plays, and, we at last experienced that tragedy was capable of another quite different effect from that accorded by Corneille and Racine. But, dazzled by this sudden ray of truth, we rebounded to the edge of another prejudice. Certain rules with which the French had made us acquainted, were too obviously lacking to the English plays. What did we conclude thence? This, that without these rules the aim of tragedy could be attained, ay, that these rules were even at fault if this aim were less attained.

Now even this deduction might have passed. But with these rules we began to confound all rules, and to pronounce it generally as pedantry to prescribe to genius what it must do or leave alone. In short we were on the point of wantonly throwing away the experience of all past times and rather demanding from the poet that each one should discover the art anew.

I should be vain enough to deem I had done something meritorious for our theatre, if I might believe that I have discovered the only means of checking this fermentation of taste. I may at least flatter myself that I have worked hard against it, since I have had nothing more at heart than to combat the delusion concerning the regularity of the French stage. No nation has more misapprehended the rules of ancient drama than the French. They have adopted as the essential some incidental remarks made by Aristotle about the most fitting external division of drama, and have so enfeebled the essential by all manner of limitations and interpretations, that nothing else could necessarily arise therefrom but works that remained far below the highest effect on which the philosopher had reckoned in his rules. . . .

1767–1769   *Translated by Helen Zimmern*

Notes

1. Play by J. F. v. Cronegk (1757).
2. Character in a play by Heufeld based on Rousseau's *La Nouvelle Héloïse.*
3. Lessing's own play *Miss Sara Sampson.*
4. Jean François Marmontel (1713–1799), French writer and encyclopedist; quoted from his *Poétique française* (1763), II, 10.
5. Denis Diderot (1713–1784), philosopher, essayist, playwright, principal author of the *Encyclopédie;* quoted from the second conversation following "The Natural Son."

GOTTHOLD EPHRAIM LESSING, 1729–1781, dramatist, critic, and theologian. Together with his contemporary Immanuel Kant (1724–1804), he represents the high point of German Enlightenment. His plays *Miss Sara Sampson* (1755), *Minna von Barnhelm* (1767), *Emilia Galotti* (1772), and *Nathan the Wise* (1799) ushered in a new era in German drama. His theoretical writings *Laokoön* (1766), *Anti-Goetze* (1778), and the two from which excerpts are printed here established him as one of the greatest and most influential critics of the eighteenth century.

Jakob Michael Reinhold Lenz

From *Notes on the Theater*

... I made the observation that the essence of poetry is imitation and what a fascination it is for us—we are, or at least want to be, the first rung on the ladder of independent creatures who act freely, and since we see around us a world that is proof of a being that acts with infinite freedom, the first impulse we feel in our soul is the desire to imitate him; since, however, the world has no bridges and we must simply be content with the things that are there, we feel at least an augmentation of our existence in imitating him and bliss in creating his work in miniature. ...

Our soul is a thing whose effects are successive, one after the other, like those of the body. The origin of that—so much is certain—is what our soul wholeheartedly wishes neither successively to know nor to want. With one glance we would like to penetrate the innermost nature of all creatures, receive with sensitivity all the delight that is in nature, and unite it with us. ...

All of us like to reduce our aggregated concepts to simplicity, and why so? Because it is then possible to embrace them more quickly—and more simultaneously. But we would be inconsolable if, because of them, we were to lose the sight and presence of these perceptions, and I make the assumption that the second source of poetry is the enduring attempt again to dismantle all our collected concepts and to see through them, making them vivid and present. ...

The true poet does not include in his imagination, according to whim, what gentlemen choose to call beautiful nature, which, by your leave, is nothing but nature gone awry. He takes a position—

and must then make the connection accordingly . . . It would be possible to confuse his painting with the thing itself. . . .

In the course of phlegmatic reflection about these two sources I have hence discovered that the latter, in common with all the fine arts, should be imitation, but that the former, in common with all sciences without exception, should to some extent be observation. In this respect poetry seems differentiated from all arts and sciences in that it unites these two sources, having keenly thought through, investigated, and seen through everything, and then produced them again in exact imitation. . . .

Probably no one will contest my statement that drama requires an imitation, consequently a poet. Even in daily life (let us ask the rabble, whose humor is not yet so mean as to recoin words) a skillful imitator is considered a good comedian, and if drama were anything other than imitation, it would soon lose its thrill. . . .

The issue now is: In drama, what is actually the main subject of imitation—man or man's fate? This is the knot, the origin of two such different fabrics as the plays of the French (should we mention the Greeks?) and of the English at an earlier period, or even more so of all the older Nordic countries, which were not shackled by the Greek. . . .

And hang it all! If nature was a genius, did it seek advice from Aristotle?

I must still fire back at one of his fundamental laws which makes so much noise simply because it is so small, and that is the dreadfully and lamentably famous edict of the three unities. And what, my dears, are the names of these three unities? Is it not the one we seek in all subjects of knowledge, the one that provides us with the point of view from which we are able to embrace and survey the whole? What more do we want, or what less do we want? . . .

What are the names of the three unities? I want to mention to you a hundred unities, all of which, however, always remain the one. Unity of country, unity of language, unity of religion, unity of morals—well, what is it going to be? Always the same, always and eternally the same. The poet and the public must feel but not classify the one unity. God is only one in all his works, and so too must the poet be, regardless of how large or small his area of influence. . . .

Aristotle. Unity of action. *"Fabula autem est una, non ut aliqui putant, si circa unum sit."*[1] He always separates the action from the main character taking action who, *bongré malgré,*[2] must fit into the plot like a hawser into a needle's eye. Among the ancient Greeks it was the action that the people gathered together to see. Among us it is the series of actions, one supporting and lifting the others which follow one another like claps of thunder and must coalesce into a large whole that subsequently amounts to nothing more and nothing less than the main character who, like them, stands out among the entire group of his associates. Among us, therefore, *fabula est una si circa unum sit.* What can we do about the fact that we no longer find enjoyment in fragmented actions but have become old enough to desire a whole? Or the fact that we wish to see a human being, whereas the former saw only unchangeable fate and its secret influences? Or, dear sirs, do you shy away from seeing a human being?

Unity of place—or would you prefer to say unity of the chorus, for what else was it? After all, in Greek theater the people come forth as if summoned and ordered, and nobody takes offense. . . .

Unity of time, wherein Aristotle establishes the essential difference between the tragedy and the epos. . . . But is not ten years, which the Trojan War lasted, just as much definite time as *unus solis ambitus?*[3] Where to, dear art judge, with this *differentia specifica?* It is absolutely clear that in the epos the poet himself appears, but in the drama his heroes appear. . .

Since we justifiably must fear that the fundament of Aristotelian drama is somewhat broken down, we want to attempt it at the other end, climb onto the roof of the French structure, and consult our sound reason and feeling.

What did the top students bring us from the Jesuit colleges? Masters? We want to see if that is so. The Italians had a Dante, the English a Shakespeare, the Germans a Klopstock, each of whom already regarded the theater from his own point of view, not through Aristotle's prism. No turning up your nose that Dante's epos occurs here. Everywhere I see theater in it—scenery, heaven and hell analogous to the eras of monks . . . We all know what Shakespeare and Klopstock did in their *bardiets,*[4] but the French are frightened by all such nonsense. . . .

Not much time is needed to prove that French plays accord with

Aristotle's rules; they have exaggerated them to a point that causes extreme anxiety in anyone of sound mind. Nowhere in the world is there such a ponderous observer of the three unities: the arbitrary knot of the action has been processed to such perfection by the French thread weavers that one is in fact obliged to admire their wit, which knows how to confuse the simplest and most natural incidents in such curious ways that there was never a good comedy written outside the country that was not produced, repeatedly in a different form, by fifty of their best talents. Like Aristotle, they believe the utter uniqueness of the drama is that it take place within twenty-four hours . . . They are indifferent about narration in the tragedy and epos and, like Aristotle, not only do they make the characters incidental, they do not even want to tolerate them in tragedies . . . But what is the source of this glowing poverty? The wit of a Shakespeare is never exhausted, regardless of how many plays he wrote. The poverty comes—permit me to tell you, Messrs. Aristotelians—it comes from the similarity of the acting characters, *partium agentium;* the manifoldness of characters and psychologies is the storehouse of nature, only here does the divining rod of genius tap. And nature alone determines the infinite manifoldness of actions and events in the world. . . .

1771   *Translated by Martha Humphreys*

Notes

1. Aristotle, *Poetics* 8, 1: "The fable is one, not like some believe, when it is centered upon one [person or thing]."
2. Willy-nilly.
3. One revolution of the sun.
4. Term used by Klopstock for a patriotic play interspersed with songs.

JAKOB MICHAEL REINHOLD LENZ, 1751–1792, representative of the Storm and Stress period, author of *Der Hofmeister* (The Tutor, 1773), and *Die Soldaten* (The Soldiers, 1775). The disruptedness and inner strife of his life became the subject of Georg Büchner's tale *Lenz* (1836).

Friedrich Schiller

The Stage Considered as a Moral Institution

The stage owes its origin to the irresistible attraction of things new and extraordinary, to man's desire for passionate experience, as Sulzer[1] has observed. Exhausted by the higher efforts of the mind, wearied by the monotonous and frequently depressing duties of his profession, satiated with sensuality, man must have felt an emptiness in his nature that was at odds with his desire for constant activity. Human nature, incapable either of remaining forever in an animal state or of devoting itself exclusively to the more subtle work of the intellect, demanded a middle condition which would unite these two contradictory extremes; a condition that would ease the hard tension between them and produce a gentle harmony, thereby facilitating the mutual transition from one to the other. This function is performed by the aesthetic sense or the appreciation of beauty.

Since it must be the first aim of the wise legislator, when faced with two effects, to choose the higher, he will not be content merely to have disarmed the impulses of his people. He will also endeavor, if possible, to use these tendencies as instruments for higher plans and convert them into sources of happiness. To this end he selected the stage as the best means of opening an endless sphere to the spirit thirsting for action, of feeding all spiritual powers without straining any, and of combining the cultivation of the mind and the emotions with the noblest entertainment.

The man who first made the statement that *religion* is the strongest pillar of the state; that without religion law itself would be deprived of its force, has, perhaps, unknowingly supplied the stage with its noblest defense. The very inadequacy and unreliability of political laws that make religion indispensable to the state also determine the moral influence of the stage. This man meant to imply that, while laws revolve around negative duties, religion extends her demands to positive acts. Laws merely impede actions that might cause the disintegration of society. Religion prescribes actions that tend to consolidate the structure of society. Laws control only the external manifestations of the will; actions alone are subject to them. Religion extends her jurisdiction to the remotest corners of the heart and traces thought to its deepest source. Laws are smooth and flexible, as changeable as mood and passion. The bonds of religion are stern and eternal.

Even if we assume, as indeed we cannot, that religion possesses this great power over every human heart, will it, or can it bring to perfection all of human culture? On the whole, religion (I am separating here the political aspect from the divine) acts mainly on the sensual part of the people. It probably has an infallible effect only by way of the senses. It loses its power if we take this away. And how does the stage achieve its effect? Religion ceases to be anything for most men if we remove its images, its problems, if we destroy its pictures of heaven and hell. And yet they are only fantasy pictures, riddles without a solution, terrifying phantoms and distant allurements.

What strength religion and law can gain when they are allied with the stage, where reality can be viewed as living presence, where vice and virtue, happiness and misery, folly and wisdom pass in review before man in thousands of true and concrete pictures, where Providence solves her riddles, ties her knots before our eyes; where the human heart, on the rack of passion, confesses its subtlest stirrings; where every mask is dropped, every painted cheek is faded, and truth, like Rhadamanthus,[2] sits incorruptibly in judgment.

The jurisdiction of the stage begins where the domain of secular law comes to an end. When justice is blinded by gold and revels in the wages of vice; when the crimes of the mighty scorn her impotence and the dread of human power has tied the hands of legal authority, then the stage takes up the sword and the scales and drags vice before a dreadful tribunal. The entire realm of fantasy and history, the past and the future are at its beck and call.

Bold criminals, who have long since turned to dust, are summoned to appear before us by the all-powerful voice of poetry and to re-enact their shameful lives for the instruction of a horrified posterity. Like impotent shadow figures in a concave mirror, they unfold before our eyes the terrors of their own century, and we heap imprecations upon their memory in an ecstasy of horror. Even when morality is no longer taught, even when there is no longer any faith in religion, even when law has ceased to exist, we will still shudder at the sight of Medea as she staggers down the palace steps, the murder of her children having taken place. Humanity will tremble with wholesome horror and each man will secretly congratulate himself on his own good conscience when he sees that frightful sleepwalker, Lady Macbeth, washing her hands and hears her challenge all the perfumes of Arabia to obliterate the loathsome smell of murder. . . . As surely as a visual representation has a more powerful effect than a dead text or a cold narrative, so the stage exercises a more profound and lasting influence than morality and law.

Here, however, the stage merely assists human justice. A still wider field is open to it. A thousand vices that are tolerated by justice are punished in the theater. A thousand virtues ignored by human law are recommended on the stage. Here it serves as a companion to wisdom and religion. It draws its teachings and examples from this pure source and clothes stern duty in a charming and alluring garb. What glorious emotions, resolutions, passions well up in our souls, and with what godlike ideals it challenges our ambitions! When gracious Augustus, magnanimous like his gods, holds out his hand to the traitor Cinna who already imagines he sees the death sentence on his lips, and says: "Let us be friends, Cinna,"[3]—who among us, at this moment, would not gladly clasp the hand of his mortal enemy in order to emulate the divine Roman? When Franz von Sickingen,[4] on his way to punish a prince and to fight for alien rights, happens to look back and see the smoke rising from the castle occupied by his helpless wife and children, continues on his journey to keep his word—then, how great man rises before me, how small and contemptible the dread power of insuperable destiny!

Vice, as reflected in the mirror of the stage, is made as hideous as virtue is made desirable. When the helpless, childish Lear, out in a stormy night, knocks in vain on his daughters' door; when, his white hair streaming in the wind, he describes the unnatural conduct of his daughter Regan to the raging elements; when at last he pours out his unbearable suffering in the words: "I gave you everything!": how abominable ingratitude seems to us, how solemnly we promise respect and filial love! . . .

But the sphere of influence of the stage extends still farther. The theater continues to work for our development even in those areas where religion and law will not stoop to follow human sentiments. The happiness of society is as much disturbed by folly as by crime and vice. Experience as old as the world teaches us that in the web of human events, the heaviest weights are often suspended by the most delicate threads; and in tracing actions to their source, we have to smile ten times before revolting in horror once. My list of criminals grows shorter every day of my life, but my list of fools becomes more complete and longer. If the moral guilt of one class of people stems from one and the same source; if the appalling extremes of vice that have stigmatized it are merely altered forms, higher degrees of a quality which in the end provokes only smiles and sympathy, why should not nature have adopted the same course in the case of the other class? I know of only one method of guarding man against depravity, and that is to guard his heart against weaknesses.

We can expect the stage to serve this function to a considerable degree. It is the stage that holds the mirror up to the great class of fools and shames the manifold forms of their folly with wholesome ridicule. The effect it produced before by means of terror and pity, it achieves here (and perhaps more speedily and infallibly) by wit and satire. If we were to judge comedy and tragedy on the basis of their effectiveness, experience would probably decide in favor of the former. Loathing may torture a man's conscience, but he suffers more keenly when his pride is wounded by derision and contempt. Our cowardice causes us to recoil from what is frightening, but this very cowardice exposes us to the sting of satire. Law and conscience often protect us from crime and vice; the ludicrous demands a peculiarly fine perception which we exercise nowhere more than in front of the stage. We may allow a friend to attack our morals and our emotions, but we find it hard to forgive him a single laugh at our expense. Our transgressions may tolerate a mentor and judge, our bad habits hardly a witness. The stage alone is permitted to ridicule our weaknesses because it spares our sensibilities and does not care to know who is the guilty fool. Without blushing we can see our own mask reflected in its mirror and are secretly grateful for the gentle rebuke.

But the stage's broad scope by no means comes to an end here. The stage, more than any other public institution, is a school of practical wisdom, a guide through social life, an infallible key to the most secret passages of the human soul. Self-love and a callous conscience, admittedly, often neutralize its effect. A thousand vices brazenly persist despite its castigations. A thousand good feelings meet with no response from the cold heart of the spectator. I myself am of the opinion that perhaps Molière's Harpagon[5] has never reformed a single usurer, that the suicide of Beverley[6] has saved very few of his brothers from the abominable addiction to gambling, that Karl Moor's[7] unfortunate brigands' story will not make the highroads safer for travelers. But even if we set limits to *this effect* of the stage, even if we are so unjust as to discount it altogether, is not what remains of its influence still vast enough? Even if the stage neither augments nor diminishes the total number of vices, has it not acquainted us with them? We have to live with these profligates and fools. We must either avoid them or put up with them, undermine their influence or succumb to it. But now they no longer surprise us. We are prepared for their assaults. The stage has revealed to us the secret of finding them out and rendering them harmless. It is the stage that has lifted the mask from the hypocrite's face and exposed the net in which cunning and cabal have entangled us. It has dragged deception and falsehood from their labyrinthine dens and made them show their horrid countenances to the light of day. The dying Sarah[8] may not frighten a single debauchee. All the pictures of the dreadful fate in store for the seducer may not quench his fire. The artful actress herself may be contriving to prevent her artistry from having this effect. Nevertheless we can be thankful that his snares have been revealed to unsuspecting innocence, and that it has been taught by the stage to mistrust his promises and tremble at his vows of love.

The stage not only makes us aware of men and human character, but also of the grim power of destiny, and teaches us the great art of bearing it. In the web of life chance and design play an equal role. The latter we can direct, to the former we must submit blindly.

We have already gained much if an inevitable fate does not find us wholly unprepared, if our courage and our prudence have already been exercised in similar circumstances and if our hearts have been steeled for the blow. The stage presents us with many varied scenes of human woe. It involves us artificially in the troubles of strangers and rewards us for the momentary pain with pleasurable tears and a magnificent increase of courage and experience. It escorts us with the forsaken Ariadne through the echoing passages of Naxos. It descends with us to Ugolino's[9] tower of starvation. In its company we ascend the steps of the frightful scaffold and witness the solemn hour of death. What we have experienced in our souls only as a vague presentiment, we hear on the stage loudly and incontrovertibly corroborated by nature taken by surprise. In the Tower dungeon the queen withdraws her favor from the deceived favorite. In the face of death, the treacherous sophistry of the frightened Moor deserts him. Eternity releases a dead man in order to reveal secrets which cannot be known to the living. The confident villain loses his last ghastly refuge because even the tomb can speak.

But the stage not only familiarizes us with the fate of mankind, it also teaches us to be more just toward the unfortunate and to judge him more leniently; for it is only when we know the full measure of his suffering that we are permitted to pronounce sentence upon him. No crime is more dishonorable than that of a thief, but, even as we condemn him, can we refrain from shedding a tear of compassion for Eduard Ruhberg[10] when we have shared with him the dreadful agony that drives him to commit the deed? Suicide is usually regarded as a crime; but when Mariana,[11] overwhelmed by the threats of an irate father, by her unhappy love and by the terrifying prospect of the convent walls, drains the poisoned cup, who would be the first to condemn this victim of an infamous maxim? Humanity and tolerance are becoming the ruling principles of our age. Their rays have penetrated to our courts of justice and even to the hearts of our princes. How great a share in this divine work belongs to our theaters? Is it not the theater that makes man known to man and discloses the secret mechanism that controls his conduct?

One noteworthy class of men has more cause to be grateful to the stage than any other. It is only here that the great of the world hear what they rarely if ever hear elsewhere: the truth. Here they see what they scarcely ever see: man.

While man's moral development has greatly benefited, and in a variety of ways, from the higher order of drama, his intellectual enlightenment is no less indebted to it. It is in this higher realm that the great mind, the warm-hearted patriot uses it to the best advantage.

Surveying the human race as a whole, comparing nations with nations, centuries with centuries, he sees how the majority of people are chained like slaves to prejudice and opinion which forever deter them from finding happiness, and that the pure rays of truth illumine only a few isolated minds which had perhaps expended their entire lives in order to purchase their little gain. How can a wise legislator enable his people to share in these benefits?

The stage is the common channel in which from the thinking, better part of the people the light of wisdom flows down, diffusing from there in milder rays through the entire state. More correct ideas, purified principles and feelings flow from thence through all the vein of all the people. The mists of barbarism, of gloomy superstition disappear. Night yields to victorious light.

Among the many magnificent fruits of the better stage, I would like to single out two. How universal has the tolerance of religious sects become in recent years! Even before Nathan the Jew and Saladin the Saracen[12] shamed us and preached the divine doctrine that submission to the will of God is not dependent upon our misconceptions of Him; even before Joseph II battled with the dreadful hydra of pious hatred,[13] the stage was engaged in planting the seeds of humanity and gentleness in our hearts. The shocking pictures of heathenish, priestly fanaticism taught us to avoid religious hatred. In this frightful mirror Christianity cleansed itself of its stains.

Errors in *education* might be combated in the stage with equal success. We are still awaiting the play that will deal with this significant subject. Because of its effects, no subject is of more importance to the state than this, and yet no institution is so at the mercy of the illusions and caprices of the citizenry as education. The stage alone could pass in review the unfortunate victims of careless education in a series of moving, upsetting pictures. Our fathers might learn to abandon their foolish maxims; our mothers might learn to love more wisely. The best-hearted teachers are led astray by false ideas. It is still worse when they pride themselves on a certain method and systematically ruin the tender young plant in philanthropinums and hothouses. . . .

Likewise the chiefs and guardians of the state—if they knew how to do it—could use the stage to correct and enlighten popular opinion of government and the governing class. The legislating power might speak to those subject to it in foreign symbols, might defend its actions before they had time to utter a complaint, might silence their doubts without appearing to do so. Even industry and inventiveness might draw inspiration from the stage if the poets thought it worth while to be patriotic and if princes would condescend to hear them.

I cannot possibly overlook the great influence that a good permanent theater would exercise on the spirit of a nation. By national spirit I mean opinions and tendencies which are common to the people of one nation and differ from those of other nationalities. Only the stage can produce this accord to so great a degree because it takes all human knowledge as its province, exhausts all situations of life, and sheds light into every corner of the human heart; because it unites all sorts and conditions of people and commands the most popular road to the heart and understanding.

If a single characteristic predominated in all of our plays; if all of our poets were in accord and were to form a firm alliance to work for this end; if their work were governed by strict selection; if they were to devote their paintbrushes to national subjects; in a word, if we were to see the establishment of a national theater: then we would become a nation. What linked the Greek states so firmly together? What drew the people so irresistibly to the stage? It was the patriotic subjects of their plays. It was the Greek spirit, the great and consuming interest in the republic and in a better humanity that pervaded them.

The stage has another merit which I especially delight in mentioning, because the stage now seems to have won its case against its persecutors. The influence upon morals and enlightenment that we have so far claimed for it has been doubted. But even its enemies have admitted that it is to be preferred to all other luxuries and forms of public entertainment. Its services in this respect, however, are more important than is usually conceded.

Human nature cannot bear the constant, unrelenting grind of business. Sensual delight dies with gratification. Man, surfeited with animal pleasures, weary of long exertion, tormented by an unceasing desire for activity, thirsts for better and finer amusement. If he does not find it, he will plunge headlong into debauchery which hastens his ruin and destroys the peace of society. Bacchanalian carousings, the ruinous games of chance, a thousand revelries hatched by idleness become inevitable unless the legislator knows how to guide these tendencies in his people. The businessman is in danger of becoming a miserable hypochondriac in return for a life he has generously devoted to the state. The scholar is likely to sink into dull pedantry, the common man becomes a brute.

The stage is an institution where pleasure is combined with instruction, rest with exertion, amusement with culture. Not a single faculty is strained to the detriment of another, no pleasure is enjoyed at the expense of the whole. When grief gnaws at our hearts, when melancholy poisons our solitary hours, when the world and business have become repulsive to us, when our souls are oppressed by a thousand burdens and the drudgery of our profession threatens to deaden our sensibilities, the stage welcomes us to her bosom. In the dreams of this artificial world, we can forget the real one. We find ourselves once more. Our feeling reawakens. Wholesome passions stir our slumbering nature and the blood begins to circulate in our veins with renewed vigor. Here the unhappy man dispels his sorrow in weeping over that of another. The happy become more sober and the over-confident more cautious. The sensitive weakling learns to stand up to the tough demands of manhood. The unfeeling brute experiences human feeling for the first time.

And finally, what a triumph for you, oh nature—nature so often trampled underfoot, who has just as often risen again—when men from all corners of the earth and every walk of life, having shed their shackles of affectation and fashion, torn away from the insistent pressure of fate, united by the all-embracing bond of brotherly sympathy, resolved in one human race again, oblivious of themselves and of the world, come closer to their divine origin.

Each enjoys the raptures of all, which are reflected on him from a hundred eyes in heightened beauty and intensity, and in his breast there is room for only one sensation: the awareness that he is a human being.

1784   *Translated by Jane Bannard Greene*

Notes

1. Johann Georg Sulzer (1720–1779); reference is to his main work *Allgemeine Theorie der schönen Künste* (1771).
2. In Greek mythology one of the judges in Hades.
3. In Corneille's *Cinna*.
4. Anonymous drama of 1783. Franz von Sickingen led the knights of southwest Germany in the so-called Knights' War of 1522–1523. See also Marx's and Engels's letters to Ferdinand Lassalle in this volume.
5. In *L'Avare*.
6. *Beverley oder der englische Spieler*, play by Friedrich Ludwig Schröder (1744–1816).
7. From his own play *The Robbers*.
8. Lessing's *Miss Sara Sampson*.
9. Titular hero in drama by Heinrich Wilhelm v. Gerstenberg (1737–1823).
10. In *Verbrechen aus Ehrsucht*, play by August Wilhelm Iffland (1759–1814).
11. Titular heroine in drama by Friedrich Wilhelm Gotter (1746–1797).
12. From Lessing's *Nathan the Wise*.
13. In the Patent of Tolerance of 1781 the Austrian emperor Joseph II guaranteed freedom of religion to Protestants and Greek Orthodox.

FRIEDRICH (VON) SCHILLER, 1759–1805, along with Johann Wolfgang von Goethe dominant figure of Storm and Stress and the ensuing era of German classicism. Some of his best known plays are *The Robbers* (1781), *Intrigue and Love* (1784), *Don Carlos* (1787), the *Wallenstein* trilogy (1798–1799), *Mary Stuart* (1800), and *William Tell* (1804).

Johann Wolfgang von Goethe

From *Wilhelm Meister's Apprenticeship*

One evening a dispute arose among our friends about the novel and the drama, and which of them deserved the preference. Serlo said it was a fruitless and misunderstood debate; both might be superior in their kinds, only each must keep within the limits proper to it.

"About their limits and their kinds," said Wilhelm, "I confess myself not altogether clear."

"Who *is* so?" said the other; "and yet perhaps it were worth while to come a little closer to the business."

They conversed together long upon the matter; and in fine, the following was nearly the result of their discussion:

"In the novel as well as in the drama, it is human nature and human action that we see. The difference between these sorts of fiction lies not merely in the circumstance that the personages of the one are made to speak, while those of the other have commonly their history narrated. Unfortunately many dramas are but novels, which proceed by dialogue; and it would not be impossible to write a drama in the shape of letters.

"But in the novel it is chiefly *sentiments* and *events* that are exhibited: in the drama it is *characters* and *deeds*. The novel must go slowly forward; and the sentiments of the hero, by some means or another, must restrain the tendency of the whole to unfold itself and to conclude. The drama, on the other hand, must hasten, and the character of the hero must press forward to the end; it does not restrain, but is restrained. The novel hero must be suffering, at least he must not in a high degree be active; in the dramatic one

34

we look for activity and deeds. Grandison, Clarissa, Pamela, the Vicar of Wakefield, Tom Jones himself, are, if not suffering, at least retarding personages; and the incidents are all in some sort modeled by their sentiments. In the drama the hero models nothing by himself; all things withstand him, and he clears and casts away the hindrances from off his path, or else sinks under them.''

Our friends were also of opinion that in the novel some degree of scope may be allowed to Chance; but that it must always be led and guided by the sentiments of the personages; on the other hand, that Fate, which, by means of outward unconnected circumstances, carries forward men, without their own concurrence, to an unforeseen catastrophe, can have place only in the drama; that Chance may produce pathetic situations, but never tragic ones; Fate, on the other hand, ought always to be terrible; and is in the highest sense tragic, when it brings into a ruinous concatenation the guilty man, and the guiltless that was unconcerned with him.

These considerations led them back to the play of Hamlet, and the pecularities of its composition. The hero in this case, it was observed, is endowed more properly with sentiments than with a character; it is events alone that push him on; and accordingly the piece has in some measure the expansion of a novel. But as it is Fate that draws the plan; as the story issues from a deed of terror, and the hero is continually driven forward to a deed of terror, the work is tragic in the highest sense, and admits of no other than a tragic end.

1794–96   *Translated by Thomas Carlyle*

From Eckermann's *Conversations with Goethe*

March 30, 1824

This evening I was with Goethe. I was alone with him; we talked on various subjects, and drank a bottle of wine. We spoke of the French drama, as contrasted with the German.

"It will be very difficult," said Goethe, "for the German public to come to a kind of right judgment, as they do in Italy and France. We have a special obstacle in the circumstance, that on our stage a medley of all sorts of things is represented. On the same boards where we saw Hamlet yesterday, we see Staberle[1] today; and if tomorrow we are delighted with *Zauberflöte*,[2] the day after we shall be charmed with the oddities of the next lucky wight. Hence the public becomes confused in its judgment, mingling together various species, which it never learns rightly to appreciate and to understand. Furthermore, every one has his own individual demands and personal wishes, and returns to the spot where he finds them realized. On the tree where he has plucked figs today, he would pluck them again tomorrow, and would make a long face if sloes had grown in their stead during the night. If anyone is a friend to sloes, he goes to the thorns.

"Schiller had the happy thought of building a house for tragedy alone, and of giving a piece every week for the male sex exclusively. But this notion presupposed a very large city, and could not be realized with our humble means."

We talked about the plays of Iffland[3] and Kotzebue,[4] which, in their way, Goethe highly commended. "From this very fault," said he, "that people do not perfectly distinguish between *kinds* in art, the pieces of these men are often unjustly censured. We may wait a long time before a couple of such popular talents come again."

I praised Iffland's *Hagestolz (Old Bachelor),* with which I had been highly pleased on the stage. "It is unquestionably Iffland's best piece," said Goethe; "it is the only one in which he goes from prose into the ideal."

He then told me of a piece, which he and Schiller had made as a continuation to the *Hagestolz;* that is to say, in conversation, without writing it down. Goethe told me the progress of the action, scene by scene; it was very pleasant and cheerful, and gave me great delight.

Goethe then spoke of some new plays by Platen.[5] "In these pieces," said he, "we may see the influence of Calderon.[6] They are very clever, and, in a certain sense, complete; but they want specific gravity, a certain weight of import. They are not of a kind to excite in the mind of the reader a deep and abiding interest; on the contrary, the strings of the soul are touched but lightly and transiently. They are like cork, which, when it swims on the water, makes no impression, but is easily sustained by the surface.

"The German requires a certain earnestness, a certain grandeur of thought, and a certain fulness of sentiment. It is on this account that Schiller is so highly esteemed by them all. I do not in the least doubt the abilities of Platen; but those, probably from mistaken views of art, are not manifested here. He shows distinguished culture, intellect, pungent wit, and artistical completeness; but these, especially in Germany, are not enough."

January 31, 1827

". . . No poet has ever known the historical characters which he has painted; if he had, he could scarcely have made use of them. The poet must know what effects he wishes to produce, and regulate the nature of his characters accordingly. If I had tried to make Egmont as history represents him, the father of a dozen children, his light-minded proceedings would have appeared very absurd. I needed an Egmont more in harmony with his own actions and my poetic views; and this is, as Clara says, *my* Egmont.

"What would be the use of poets, if they only repeated the record of the historian? The poet must go further, and give us, if possible, something higher and better. All the characters of Sophocles bear something of that great poet's lofty soul; and it is the same with the characters of Shakespeare. This is as it ought to be. Nay, Shakespeare goes farther, and makes his Romans Englishmen; and there, too, he is right; for otherwise his nation would not have understood him.

"Here, again," continued Goethe, "the Greeks were so great, that they regarded fidelity to historic facts less than the treatment of them by the poet."

March 28, 1827 [Soret][7]

". . . But, to speak frankly, I am sorry that a man of undoubted innate power from the northern coast of Germany, like Hinrichs,[8] should be so spoilt by the philosophy of Hegel as to lose all unbiased and natural observation and thought, and gradually to get into an artificial and heavy style, both of thought and expression; so that we find passages in his book where our understanding comes to a standstill, and we no longer know what we are reading. . . .

"I think we have had enough of this. What must the English and French think of the language of our philosophers, when we Germans do not understand them ourselves." "And in spite of all this," said I, "we both agree that a noble purpose lies at the foundation of the book, and that it possesses the quality of awakening thoughts."

"His idea of the relation between family and state," said Goethe, "and the tragical conflicts that may arise from them, is certainly good and suggestive; still I cannot allow that it is the only right one, or even the best for tragic art. We are indeed all members both of a family and of a state, and a tragical fate does not often befall us which does not wound us in both capacities. Still we might be very good tragical characters, if we were merely members of a family or merely members of a state; for, after all, the only point is to get a conflict which admits of no solution, and this may arise from an antagonistical position in any relation whatever, provided a person has a really natural foundation, and is himself really tragic. Thus Ajax falls a victim to the demon of wounded honor, and Hercules to the demon of jealousy. In neither of these cases is there the least conflict between family piety and political virtue; though this, according to Hinrichs, should be the element of Greek tragedy."

"One sees clearly," says I, "that in this theory he merely had *Antigone*[9] in his mind. He also appears to have had before his eyes merely the character and mode of action of this heroine, as he makes the assertion that family piety appears most pure in woman, and especially in a sister; and that a sister can love only a brother with perfect purity, and without sexual feeling."

"I should think," returned Goethe, "that the love of sister for sister was still more pure and unsexual. As if we did not know that numerous cases have occurred in which the most sensual inclinations have existed between brother and sister, both knowingly and unknowingly!

"You must have remarked generally," continued Goethe, that Hinrichs, in considering Greek tragedy, sets out from the *idea;* and that he looks upon Sophocles as one who, in the invention and arrangement of his pieces, likewise set out from an idea, and regulated the sex and rank of his characters accordingly. But Sophocles, when he wrote his pieces, by no means started from an *idea;* on the contrary, he seized upon some ancient ready-made popular tradition in which a good idea existed, and then only thought of adapting it in the best and most effective manner for the theatre. The Atreides will not allow Ajax to be buried; but as in *Antigone* the sister struggles for the brother, so in the *Ajax* the brother struggles for the brother. That the sister takes charge of the unburied Polynices,[10] and the brother takes charge of the fallen

Ajax, is a contingent circumstance, and does not belong to the invention of the poet, but to the tradition, which the poet followed and was obliged to follow."

"What he says about Creon's[11] conduct," replied I, "appears to be equally untenable. He tries to prove that, in prohibiting the burial of Polynices, Creon acts from pure political virtue; and since Creon is not merely a man but also a prince, he lays down the proposition, that, as a man represents the tragic power of the state, this man can be no other than he who is himself the personification of the state itself—namely, the prince; and that of all persons the man as prince must be just that person who displays the greatest political virtue."

"These are assertions which no one will believe," returned Goethe with a smile. "Besides, Creon by no means acts out of political virtue, but from hatred towards the dead. When Polynices endeavored to reconquer his paternal inheritance, from which he had been forcibly expelled, he did not commit such a monstrous crime against the state that his death was insufficient, and that the further punishment of the innocent corpse was required.

"An action should never be placed in the category of political virtue which is opposed to virtue in general. When Creon forbids the burial of Polynices, and not only taints the air with the decaying corpse, but also affords an opportunity for the dogs and birds of prey to drag about pieces torn from the dead body, and thus to defile the altars—an action so offensive both to gods and men is by no means politically virtuous, but on the contrary a political crime. Besides, he has everybody in the play against him. He has the elders of the state, who form the chorus, against him; he has the people at large against him; he has Teiresias against him; he has his own family against him; but he hears not, and obstinately persists in his impiety, until he has brought to ruin all who belong to him, and is himself at last nothing but a shadow."

"And still," said I, "when one hears him speak, one cannot help believing that he is somewhat in the right."

"That is the very thing," said Goethe, "in which Sophocles is a master; and in which consists the very life of the dramatic in general. His characters all possess this gift of eloquence, and know how to explain the motives for their action so convincingly that the hearer is almost always on the side of the last speaker.

"One can see that, in his youth, he enjoyed an excellent rhetorical education, by which he became trained to look for all the reasons and seeming reasons of things. Still, his great talent in this respect betrayed him into faults, as he sometimes went too far.

"There is a passage in *Antigone* which I always look upon as a blemish, and I would give a great deal for an apt philologist to prove that it is interpolated and spurious.

"After the heroine has, in the course of the piece, explained the noble motives for her action, and displayed the elevated purity of her soul, she at last, when she is led to death, brings forward a motive which is quite unworthy, and almost borders upon the comic.

"She says that, if she had been a mother, she would not have done, either for her dead children or for her dead husband, what she has done for her brother. 'For,' says she, 'if my husband died I could have had another, and if my children died I could have had others by my new husband. But with my brother the case is different. I cannot have another brother; for since my mother and father are dead, there is no one to beget one.'

"This is, at least, the bare sense of this passage, which in my opinion, when placed in the mouth of a heroine going to her death, disturbs the tragic tone, and appears to me very far-fetched—to savor too much of dialectical calculation. As I said, I should like a philologist to show us that the passage is spurious."

We then conversed further upon Sophocles, remarking that in his pieces he always less considered a moral tendency than an apt treatment of the subject in hand, particularly with regard to theatrical effect.

"I do not object," said Goethe, "to a dramatic poet having a moral influence in view; but when the point is to bring his subject clearly and effectively before his audience, his moral purpose proves of little use, and he needs much more a faculty for delineation and a familiarity with the stage to know what to do and what to leave undone. If there be a moral in the subject, it will appear, and the poet has nothing to consider but the effective and artistic treatment of his subject. If a poet has as high a soul as Sophocles, his influence will always be moral, let him do what he will. Besides, he knew the stage, and understood his craft thoroughly."

"How well he knew the theatre," answered I, "and how much he has in view a theatrical effect, we see in his *Philoctetes*,[12] and the great resemblance which this piece bears to *Oedipus in Colonos*,[13] both in the arrangement and the course of action.

"In both pieces we see the hero in a helpless condition; both are old and suffering from bodily infirmities. Oedipus has, at his side, his daughter as a guide and a prop; Philoctetes has his bow. The resemblance is carried still further. Both have been thrust aside in their afflictions; but when the oracle declares with respect to both of them that the victory can be obtained with their aid alone, an endeavor is made to get them back again; Ulysses comes to Philoctetes, Creon to Oedipus. Both begin their discourse with cunning and honeyed words; but when these are of no avail they use violence, and we see Philoctetes deprived of his bow, and Oedipus of his daughter."

"Such acts of violence," said Goethe, "give an opportunity for excellent altercations, and such situations of helplessness excited the emotions of the audience, on which account the poet, whose object it was to produce an effect upon the public, liked to introduce them. In order to strengthen this effect in the *Oedipus*, Sophocles brings him in as a weak old man, when he still, according to all circumstances, must have been a man in the prime of life. But at this vigorous age, the poet could not have used him for his play; he would have produced no effect, and he therefore made him a weak, helpless old man."

"The resemblance to Philoctetes," continued I, "goes still further. The hero, in both pieces, does not act, but suffers. On the other hand, each of these passive heroes has two active characters against him. Oedipus has Creon and Polynices, Philoctetes has Neoptolemus and Ulysses; two such opposing characters were necessary to discuss the subject on all sides, and to gain the necessary body and fulness for the piece."

"You might add," interposed Goethe, "that both pieces bear this further resemblance, that we see in both the extremely effective situation of a happy change, since one hero, in his disconsolate situation, has his beloved daughter restored to him, and the other, his no less beloved bow.

"The happy conclusions of these two pieces are also similar; for both heroes are delivered from their sorrows: Oedipus is blissfully snatched away, and as for Philoctetes, we are forwarned by the oracle of his cure, before Troy, by Aesculapius.

"When we," continued Goethe, "for our modern purposes, wish

to learn how to conduct ourselves upon the theatre, Molière is the man to whom we should apply.

"Do you know his *Malade Imaginaire?*[14] There is a scene in it which, as often as I read the piece, appears to me the symbol of a perfect knowledge of the boards. I mean the scene where the Malade Imaginaire asks his little daughter Louison, if there has not been a young man in the chamber of her eldest sister.

"Now, any other who did not understand his craft so well would have let the little Louison plainly tell the fact at once, and there would have been the end of the matter.

"But what various motives for delay are introduced by Molière into this examination, for the sake of life and effect. He first makes the little Louison act as if she did not understand her father; then she denies that she knows anything; then, threatened with the rod, she falls down as if dead; then, when her father bursts out in despair, she springs up from her feigned swoon with roguish hilarity, and at last, little by little, she confesses all.

"My explanation can only give you a very meager notion of the animation of the scene; but read this scene yourself till you become thoroughly impressed with its theatrical worth, and you will confess that there is more practical instruction contained in it than in all the theories in the world.

"I have know and loved Molière," continued Goethe, "from my youth, and have learned from him during my whole life. I never fail to read some of his plays every year, that I may keep up a constant intercourse with what is excellent. It is not merely the perfect artistic treatment which delights me; but particularly the amiable nature, the highly formed mind, of the poet. There is in him a grace and a feeling for the decorous, and a tone of good society, which his innate beautiful nature could only attain by daily intercourse with the most eminent men of his age. . . .

"To a man like Schlegel," returned Goethe, "a genuine nature like Molière's is a veritable eyesore; he feels that he has nothing in common with him, he cannot endure him . . . . Schlegel cannot forgive Molière for ridiculing the affection of learned ladies[15] he feels, probably as one of my friends has remarked, that he himself would have been ridiculed if he had lived with Molière.

"It is not to be denied," continued Goethe, "that Schlegel knows a great deal, and one is almost terrified at his extraordinary attainments and his extensive reading. But this is not enough. All the learning in the world is still no judgment. His criticism is completely one-sided, because in all theatrical pieces he merely regards the skeleton of the plot and arrangement, and only points out small points of resemblance to great predecessors, without troubling himself in the least as to what the author brings forward of graceful life and the culture of a high soul. But of what use are all the arts of a talent, if we do not find in a theatrical piece an amiable or great personality of the author. This alone influences the cultivation of the people."

April 2, 1829

We then came to the newest French poets, and the meaning of the terms "classic" and "romantic."

"A new expression occurs to me," said Goethe, "which does not ill define that state of the case. I call the classic *healthy,* the romantic *sickly.* . . .Most modern productions are romantic, not because they are new, but because they are weak, morbid, and sickly; and the antique is classic, not because it is old, but because it is strong, fresh, joyous, and healthy. If we distinguish 'classic' and 'romantic' by these qualities, it will be easy to see our way clearly."

March 14, 1830[Soret]

The conversation then returned to the French literature, and the modern ultraromantic tendency of some not unimportant talents. Goethe was of opinion that this poetic revolution, which was still in its infancy, would be very favorable to literature, but very prejudicial to the individual authors who effect it.

"Extremes are never to be avoided in any revolution," said he. "In a political one, nothing is generally desired in the beginning but the abolition of abuses; but before people are aware, they are deep in bloodshed and horror. Thus the French, in their present literary revolution, desired nothing at first but a freer form; however, they will not stop there, but will reject the traditional contents together with the form. They begin to declare the representation of noble sentiments and deeds as tedious, and attempt to treat of all sorts of abominations. Instead of the beautiful subjects from Grecian mythology, there are devils, witches, and vampires, and the lofty heroes of antiquity must give place to jugglers and galley slaves. This is piquant! This is effective! But after the public has once tasted this highly seasoned food, and has become accustomed to it, it will always long for more, and that stronger. A young man of talent, who would produce an effect and be acknowledged, and who is great enough to go his own way, must accommodate himself to the taste of the day—nay, must seek to outdo his predecessors in the horrible and frightful. But in this chase after outward means of effect, all profound study, and all gradual and thorough development of the talent and the man from within, is entirely neglected. And this is the greatest injury which can befall a talent, although literature in general will gain by this tendency of the moment."

"But," added I, "how can an attempt which destroys individual talents be favorable to literature in general?"

"The extremes and excrescences which I have described," returned Goethe, "will gradually disappear; but at last this great advantage will remain—besides a freer form, richer and more diversified subjects will have been attained, and no object of the broadest world and the most manifold life will be any longer excluded as unpoetical. I compare the present literary epoch to a state of violent fever, which is not in itself good and desirable, but of which improved health is the happy consequence. That abomination which now often constitutes the whole subject of a poetical work, will in future only appear as an useful expedient; aye, the pure and the noble, which is now abandoned for the moment, will soon be resought with additional ardor."

1836   *Translated by John Oxenford*

Notes

1. Staberle, a Viennese clown.
2. Mozart's *The Magic Flute* (1791).
3. August Wilhelm Iffland (1759–1814).
4. August Friedrich Ferdinand von Kotzebue (1761–1819), the most frequently produced playwright of Goethe's time.
5. August Graf von Platen (1796–1835), poet and playwright.
6. Pedro Calderon de la Barca (1600–1681).
7. Frédéric Jacob Soret (1795–1865), tutor at the court in Weimar and frequent guest of Goethe's.
8. Hermann Friedrich Wilhelm Hinrichs (1794–1861).
9. Reference to *Antigone* by Sophocles.
10. Polynices, brother of Antigone.
11. Creon, king of Thebes, father of Antigone.

12. *Philoctetes* by Sophocles.
13. *Oedipus at Colonos* by Sophocles.
14. Reference to *Le Malade Imaginaire* by Molière (1673).
15. In Molière's *Les Femmes Savantes* (1672).

JOHANN WOLFGANG VON GOETHE, 1749–1832. Johann Peter Eckermann (1791–1854) was Goethe's literary assistant during the last years of his life. His *Conversations with Goethe* appeared from 1836 to 1848.

August Wilhelm von Schlegel

From *Lectures on Dramatic Art and Literature*

... It will be necessary to examine what is meant by *dramatic, theatrical, tragic, and comic.*

What is dramatic? To many the answer will seem very easy: where various persons are introduced conversing together, and the poet does not speak in his own person. This is, however, merely the first external foundation of the form; and that is dialogue. But the characters may express thoughts and sentiments without operating any change on each other, and so leave the minds of both in exactly the same state in which they were at the commencement; in such a case, however interesting the conversation may be, it cannot be said to possess a dramatic interest. I shall make this clear by alluding to a more tranquil species of dialogue, not adapted for the stage, the philosophic. When, in Plato, Socrates asks the conceited sophist Hippias what is the meaning of the beautiful, the latter is at once ready with a superficial answer, but is afterwards compelled by the ironical objections of Socrates to give up his former definition, and to grope about him for other ideas, till, ashamed at last and irritated at the superiority of the sage who has convicted him of his ignorance, he is forced to quit the field: this dialogue is not merely philosophically instructive, but arrests the attention like a drama in miniature. And justly, therefore, has this lively movement in the thoughts, this stretch of expectation for the issue, in a word, the dramatic cast of the dialogues of Plato, been always celebrated.

From this we may conceive wherein consists the great charm of dramatic poetry. Action is the true enjoyment of life, nay, life itself.

Mere passive enjoyments may lull us into a state of listless complacency, but even then, if possessed of the least internal activity, we cannot avoid being soon wearied. The great bulk of mankind merely from their situation in life, or from their incapacity for extraordinary exertions, are confined within a narrow circle of insignificant operations. Their days flow on in succession under the sleepy rule of custom, their life advances by an insensible progress, and the bursting torrent of the first passions of youth soon settles into a stagnant marsh. From the discontent which this occasions they are compelled to have recourse to all sorts of diversions, which uniformly consist in a species of occupation that may be renounced at pleasure, and though a struggle with difficulties, yet with difficulties that are easily surmounted. But of all diversions the theatre is undoubtedly the most entertaining. Here we may see others act even when we cannot act to any great purpose ourselves. The highest object of human activity is man, and in the drama we see men, measuring their powers with each other, as intellectual and moral beings, either as friends or foes, influencing each other by their opinions, sentiments, and passions, and decisively determining their reciprocal relations and circumstances. The art of the poet accordingly consists in separating from the fable whatever does not essentially belong to it, whatever, in the daily necessities of real life, and the petty occupations to which they give rise, interrupts the progress of important actions, and concentrating within a narrow space a number of events calculated to attract the minds of the hearers and to fill them with attention and expectation. In this manner he gives us a renovated picture of life; a compendium of whatever is moving and progressive in human existence.

But this is not all. Even in a lively oral narration, it is not unusual to introduce persons in conversation with each other, and to give a corresponding variety to the tone and the expression. But the gaps, which these conversations leave in the story, the narrator fills up in his own name with a description of the accompanying circumstances, and other particulars. The dramatic poet must renounce all such expedients; but for this he is richly recompensed in the following invention. He requires each of the characters in his story to be personated by a living individual; that this individual should, in sex, age, and figure, meet as near as may be the prevalent conceptions of his fictitious original, nay, assume his entire personality; that every speech should be delivered in a suitable tone of voice, and accompanied by appropriate action and gesture; and that those external circumstances should be added which are necessary to give the hearers a clear idea of what is going forward. Moreover, these representatives of the creatures of his imagination must appear in the costume belonging to their resemblance, and partly because, even in dress, there is something characteristic. Lastly, he must see them placed in a locality, which, in some degree, resembles that where, according to his fable, the action took place, because this also contributes to the resemblance: he places them, i.e., on a scene. All this brings us to the idea of the *theatre*. It is evident that the very form of dramatic poetry, that is, the exhibition of an action by dialogue without the aid of narrative, implies the theatre as its necessary complement. We allow that there are dramatic works which were not originally designed for the stage, and not calculated to produce any great effect there, which nevertheless afford great pleasure in the perusal. I am, however, very much inclined to doubt whether they would produce the same strong impression with which they affect us upon a person who had never seen or heard a description of a theatre. In reading dramatic works, we are accustomed ourselves to supply the representation. . . .

. . . Since, as we have already shown, visible representation is essential to the very form of the drama, a dramatic work may always be regarded from a double point of view—how far it is *poetical*, and how far it is *theatrical*. The two are by no means inseparable. Let not, however, the expression *poetical* be misunderstood: I am not now speaking of the versification and the ornaments of language; these, when not animated by some higher excellence, are the least effective on the stage; but I speak of the poetry in the spirit and design of a piece; and this may exist in as high a degree when the drama is written in prose as in verse. What is it, then, that makes a drama poetical? The very same, assuredly, that makes other works so. It must in the first place be a connected whole, complete and satisfactory within itself. But this is merely the negative definition of a work of art, by which it is distinguished from the phenomena of nature, which run into each other, and do not possess in themselves a complete and independent existence.

To be poetical it is necessary that a composition should be a mirror of ideas, that is, thoughts and feelings which in their character are necessary and eternally true, and soar above this earthly life, and also that it should exhibit them embodied before us. What the ideas are, which in this view are essential to the different departments of the drama, will hereafter be the subject of our investigation. We shall also, on the other hand, show that without them a drama becomes altogether prosaic and empirical, that is to say, patched together by the understanding out of the observations it has gathered from literal reality.

But how does a dramatic work become theatrical, or fitted to appear with advantage on the stage? In single instances it is often difficult to determine whether a work possesses such a property or not. It is indeed frequently the subject of great controversy, especially when the self-love of authors and actors comes into collision; each shifts the blame of failure on the other, and those who advocate the cause of the author appeal to an imaginary perfection of the histrionic art, and complain of the insufficiency of the existing means for its realization. But in general the answer to this question is by no means so difficult. The object proposed is to produce an impression on an assembled multitude, to rivet their attention, and to excite their interest and sympathy. In this respect the poet's occupation coincides with that of the orator. How then does the latter attain his end? By perspicuity, rapidity, and energy. Whatever exceeds the ordinary measure of patience or comprehension he must diligently avoid. Moreover, when a number of men are assembled together, they mutually distract each other's attention whenever their eyes and ears are not drawn to a common object without and beyond themselves. Hence the dramatic poet, as well as the orator, must from the very commencement, by strong impressions, transport his hearers out of themselves, and, as it were, take bodily possession of their attention. There is a species of poetry which gently stirs a mind attuned to solitary comtempla-tion, as soft breezes elicit melody from the Aeolian harp. However excellent this poetry may be in itself, without some other accom-paniments its tones would be lost on the stage. The melting harmonica is not calculated to regulate the march of an army, and kindle its military enthusiasm. For this we must have piercing instruments, but above all a strongly marked rhythm, to quicken the pulsation and give a more rapid movement to the animal spirits. The grand requisite in a drama is to make this rhythm perceptible in the onward progress of the action. When this has once been effected, the poet may all the sooner halt in his rapid career, and indulge the bent of his own genius. There are points when the most elaborate and polished style, the most enthusiastic lyrics, the most profound thoughts and remote allusions, the smartest coruscations of wit, and the most dazzling flights of a sportive or ethereal fancy, are all in their place, and when the willing audience, even those who cannot entirely comprehend them, follow the whole with a greedy ear, like music in unison with their feelings. Here the poet's great art lies in availing himself of the effect of contrasts, which enable him at one time to produce calm repose, profound contemplation, and even the self-abandoned indifference of exhaustion, or at another, the most tumultuous emotions, the most violent storm of the passions. With respect to theatrical fitness, however, it must not be forgotten that much must always depend on the capacities and humors of the audience, and, consequently, on the national character in general, and the particular degree of mental culture. Of all kinds of poetry the dramatic is, in a certain sense, the most secular; for, issuing from the stillness of an inspired mind, it yet fears not to exhibit itself in the midst of the noise and tumult of social life. The dramatic poet is, more than any other, obliged to court external favor and loud applause. But of course it is only in appearance that he thus lowers himself to his hearers; while, in reality, he is elevating them to himself.

The dramatic poet, as well as the epic, represents external events, but he represents them as real and present. In common with the lyric poet he also claims our mental participation, but not in the same calm composedness; the feeling of joy and sorrow which the dramatist excites is more immediate and vehement. He calls forth all the emotions which the sight of similar deeds and fortunes of living men would elicit, and it is only by the total sum of the impression which he produces that he ultimately resolves these conflicting emotions into a harmonious tone of feeling. As he stands in such close proximity to real life, and endeavors to endue his own imaginary creations with vitality, the equanimity of the epic poet would in him be indifference; he must decidedly take part with one or other of the leading views of human life, and constrain his audience also to participate in the same feeling.

To employ simpler and more intelligible language: the *tragic* and *comic* bear the same relation to one another as *earnest* and *sport*. Every man, from his own experience, is acquainted with both these states of mind; but to determine their essence and their source would demand deep philosophical investigation. Both, indeed, bear the stamp of our common nature; but earnestness belongs more to its moral, and mirth to its animal part. The creatures destitute of reason are incapable either of earnest or of sport. Animals seem indeed at times to labor as if they were earnestly intent upon some aim, and as if they made the present moment subordinate to the future; at other times they seem to sport, that is, they give themselves up without object or purpose to the pleasure of existence: but they do not possess consciousness, which alone can entitle these two conditions to the names of earnest and sport. Man alone, of all the animals with which we are acquainted, is capable of looking back toward the past, and forward into futurity; and he has to purchase the enjoyment of this noble privilege at a dear rate. Earnestness, in the most extensive signification, is the direction of our mental powers to some aim. But as soon as we begin to call ourselves to account for our actions, reason compels us to fix this aim higher and higher, till we come at last to the highest end of our existence: and here that longing for the infinite which is inherent in our being is baffled by the limits of our finite existence. All that we do, all that we effect, is vain and perishable; death stands everywhere in the background, and to it every well or ill-spent moment brings us nearer and closer; and even when a man has been so singularly fortunate as to reach the utmost term of life without any grievous calamity, the inevitable doom still awaits him to leave or to be left by all that is most dear to him on earth. There is no bond of love without a separation, no enjoyment without the grief of losing it. When, however, we contemplate the relations of our existence to the extreme limit of possibilities: when we reflect on its entire dependence on a chain of causes and effects, stretching beyond our ken: when we consider how weak and helpless, and doomed to struggle against the enormous powers of nature, and conflicting appetites, we are cast on the shores of an unknown world, as it were, shipwrecked at our very birth; how we are subject to all kinds of errors and deceptions, any one of which may be our ruin; that in our passions we cherish an enemy in our bosoms; how every moment demands from us, in the name of the most sacred duties, the sacrifice of our dearest inclinations, and how at one blow we may be robbed of all that we have acquired with much toil and difficulty; that with every accession to our stores, the risk of loss is proportionately increased, and we are only the more exposed to the malice of hostile fortune: when we think upon all this, every heart which is not dead to feeling must be overpowered by an inexpressible melancholy, for which there is no other counterpoise than the consciousness of a vocation transcending the limits of this earthly life. This is the tragic tone of mind; and when the thought of the possible issues out of the mind as a living reality, when this tone pervades and animates a visible representation of the most striking instances of violent revolutions in a man's fortunes, either prostrating his mental energies or calling forth the most heroic endurance—then the result is *Tragic Poetry*. We thus see how this kind of poetry has its foundation in our nature, while to a certain extent we have also answered the question why we are fond of such mournful representations, and even find something consoling and elevating in them. This tone of mind we have described is inseparable from strong feeling; and although poetry cannot remove these internal dissonances, she must at least endeavor to effect an ideal reconciliation of them.

As earnestness, in the highest degree, is the essence of tragic representation; so is sport of the comic. The disposition to mirth is a forgetfulness of all gloomy considerations in the pleasant feeling of present happiness. We are then inclined to view everything in a sportive light, and to allow nothing to disturb or ruffle our minds. The imperfections and the irregularities of men are no longer an object of dislike and compassion, but serve, by their strange inconsistencies, to entertain the understanding and to amuse the fancy. The comic poet must therefore carefully abstain from whatever is calculated to excite moral indignation at the conduct, or sympathy with the situations of his personages, because this would inevitably bring us back again into earnestness. He must paint their irregularities as springing out of the predominance of the animal part of their nature, and the incidents which befall them as merely ludicruous distresses, which will be attended with no fatal consequences. This is uniformly what takes place in what we call Comedy, in which, however, there is still a mixture of seriousness. . . . The oldest comedy of the Greeks was, however, entirely sportive, and in that respect formed the most complete contrast to their tragedy. Not only were the characters and situations of individuals worked up into a comic picture of real life, but the whole frame of society, the constitution, nature, and the gods, were all fantastically painted in the most ridiculous and laughable colors.

1809–1811   *Translated by John Black,*
                                                        revised by A. J. W. Morrison

AUGUST WILHELM VON SCHLEGEL, 1767–1845, professor of literature at the University of Bonn, one of the major critics and translators of the Romantic era.

Franz Grillparzer

On the Nature of the Drama

The essence of the drama, since it is supposed to present something imagined as if it were actually happening, is strict causality. In the course of real life we gladly accept the possibility of there being any number of events that cannot be accounted for by the perpetual chain of cause and effect, since we are constrained to suppose an incomprehensible maker of the whole and can always hope that what to our limited view appears to be unconnected is really, though incomprehensibly, connected in him: but in a poem, we know the maker of the events and of their interconnections, and we know that his mind is similar to ours; therefore, it would seem that we are justified in considering any element in his creation that does not, to our and to the general human understanding, connect with its other elements, as having no meaningful context at all and therefore as belonging to the class of empty fantasies, which reason, whose formal direction cannot be disavowed by the creative imagination or by any other inner faculty, repudiates unconditionally, or which at the very least completely fail to achieve the drama's intended effect of verisimilitude.

Now the causal chain, if we presuppose the concept of freedom, can be envisaged in two ways: according to the law of necessity, that is nature, and according to the law of freedom. What is here meant by necessity is everything that happens to man independently of his volition, in nature or at the hands of other men, and everything that, by its effect on the lower, involuntary mainsprings of his action, exerts an at least stimulating, if not compelling, influence on the manifestations of his activity.

The influence of these external mainsprings is known to be so powerful that in people of forceful tendencies nourished by wrong education and an unfortunate temperament it seems to annul the entire activity of freedom, and even the best among us are aware of how frequently they are torn by it from the good toward the worse, and how these mainsprings can sometimes reach such a degree of extensive and intensive magnitude that it seems half a miracle were needed to help one escape. Now that which occurs outside the circle of our volition, independently of us, that is by necessity, exerting a conditioning (but not compelling) effect upon us without our being able to reciprocally affect it by deliberate action—this, if we conceive it as an interrelationship subject to the law of causality that obtains throughout nature, is what we call *calamity;* and insofar as we posit a human mind that, without being able to influence its calamitous circumstances, perceives the calamity itself and comprehends it outside the limitations of space and time, of before and after, we speak of it as *fate.* Fate is nothing other than a foreseeing without foresight, a *passive* predestination I should like to call it, in contradistinction to the active kind which is conceived as modifying the laws of nature in favor of the law of freedom.

Now in tragedy, either freedom is granted a victory over necessity, or vice versa. To us, nowadays, the former seems the only permissible course, but I am of exactly the opposite opinion. The uplifting of the spirit that is supposed to result from the victory of freedom has absolutely nothing in common with the nature of *tragedy,* and besides, it sharply concludes the drama without encouraging that continued enactment and playing out of the story in the viewer's mind which is the characteristic effect of real tragedy. The tragic element, which Aristotle rather stiffly denotes as merely a matter of awakened fear and pity, consists rather in this: that man realize the nullity of all earthly things; that he see the dangers to which the best are exposed and often succumb; that, while firmly preserving the Just and the True for himself, he commiserate with his stumbling fellow man, that he not cease loving him who has fallen, even though he punish him, since any disturbance of eternal justice must be destroyed. Such a tragedy will engender kindness, tolerance, self-knowledge, *purification of the passions by pity and fear.* The play will continue in the mind and heart of its viewer well after the curtain has fallen, and the glorification of justice, which Schlegel wants to see sturdily and vividly depicted on the boards and in the rags of the stage, will radiantly sink down upon the quietly shivering circles of the stirred emotional nature.

There *is* a fate that casts down the just and lets the unjust triumph here below, that strikes "unavenged" injuries, unavenged *here*. Let history teach you that there is a moral world order that compensates in the generation for what is disruptive in the individual; let philosophy and religion tell you that there is a *beyond* where the individual's right action finds its fulfillment and apotheosis. With such foreknowledge and such emotions, come before our stage, and you will understand our intention. *True artistic expression is without didactic purpose,* said Goethe somewhere, and whoever is an artist will concur with him. The theater is not a house of correction for rogues, nor a finishing school for adolescents. When you come before our stage with the eternal concepts of Justice and Virtue, the shattering force of fate will elevate you just as it elevated the Greeks, for man remains man whether "in felt hat or 'Jamerlonk'," and what was once true must remain so forever.

[Journal 639, 1820]

But if someone asks me whether a play can and should have an idea as its basis, I reply: why not?—presuming the author is conscious of possessing a great animating force, as Calderón certainly did. But the other great poets only rarely practiced it, and went about producing their works as does their great teacher, nature: prompting ideas in others, but themselves proceeding from living fact. In the beginning was the *deed.*

[Journal 2175, 1834]

Dramatic action differs from an event as follows: What concerns us most in an event are the *consequences* of a given situation, while in dramatic action, the *causes* of the situation are what matter most—though the situation itself, of course, figures as one of the several causes and concludes the play as its final consequence.

[Journal 3193, 1836/37]

There has been much discussion about the meaning of the word *action* in a poetic context and the difference between action and event. They differ precisely in the ways in which they differ historically and ethically. Action is an event with an *intention* as its basis. This intention can either be that of the subject of the activity, or it can oppose that activity from outside; and again it can come either from another person or from circumstances that take on the form of an intention. The latter is what we call fate.

[Journal 3504, 1839/40]

A Letter Concerning Fate

Since so much has been recently said and written about *fate* and whether it can or cannot be used in a modern tragedy, and since my own tragedy, *Die Ahnfrau* [1817], has rekindled this quarrel, I regard it as my duty to present to the public my views on this much discussed matter.

To go straight to the point: Above all: What did the ancients (i.e., the Greeks) understand by the word *fatum*, and how did they apply it in their tragic theater? We immediately come up against various opinions. The first one interprets *fatum* as nothing more than physical necessity; a second, as a punishment by cosmic justice; a third one, as the enmity of an alien power. Our surprise at such variety of opinion will diminish if we examine the works of the ancient poets, especially the tragedians, and find fate represented in just as many shapes and guises. Sometimes we encounter it as a kind of compensating force to which even the gods are subject, as in the story of Prometheus; elsewhere it appears as absolute, ineluctable predetermination, as in the tale of the fall of the tribe of Labdakos; or as the avenging nemesis descending upon the children of Tantalos. In one instance, fate opposes the gods, in another (as with the offspring of Tantalos) it coincides with their will. Indeed, in Euripides the gods usually take the place of fate. All of this must lead us to suspect that the Greeks themselves did not have a definite, precisely defined concept in mind when they used the word *fatum*; that they employed it much as we do words like "chance" and "coincidence" to denote certain phenomena that exist without our being able to explain them—words that everyone understands without anyone's knowing their meaning. And that is indeed the case: the Greeks called fate the unknown factor— × — that underlies the phenomena of the moral world and whose cause remains hidden to our understanding, though we are cognizant of its effects. The whole concept was merely an outflow of the innately human striving to find a cause for that which exists, to create a causal connection among the phenomena of the moral world.

This striving is an essential quality in human nature, and it is as present today as it was among the heathen. It might seem that Christianity would have completely altered the state of things in this respect, but it seems that way only. Christianity has given us an almighty God who holds in his hands the causes of all existence and who is the source of all changes. That is enough to pacify the vague surmisings of the heart, but can it tame the brooding intellect and the expansive imagination? The experience of 1800 years has proven the contrary. We know God as the final ring in the chain of things, but the intermediate links are missing, and what the mind seeks is above all an unbroken sequence, a *row*. Instead of beginning, as sentiment does, with the highest, and then linking the things of the earth to it, reason, by its nature, is impelled to begin with what it can grasp, which is to say with the lowest link, from which it seeks to climb unto the topmost one, on a ladder without rungs. Its efforts exhausted after a while, the reason will let the imagination break loose from the reins with which it has been held in check, so that it can bind together the rings that are visible here and there and—*nihil novi in mundo!* thousand things which we do not understand, 1000 destinies whose compensatory reason we cannot perceive, so that we are always cast back into the irksome bounds of human nature, bewildered, and additionally bewildered by the habit of attributing a cause and effect relationship to any phenomena that appear in a series. Proof of this state of affairs is the widespread belief in, for example: luck; coincidence; precognition; ill-portending days, words, and deeds; astrology, chiromantics, etc. The belief in a kind and just God is not negated by these—devout persons may cling to such superstitions as much as anyone; rather, religious faith is briefly moved out of sight. The imagination is content with having constructed its edifice to a height whose distance prohibits a continued clarity of vision, and takes pleasure in the dissolving outlines. That is the way it is and thus it will remain until the emotional nature with its intuition and faith becomes as precise as the concepts of the intellect and as clear as the images of the imagination—which is to say, until the end of time.

This proviso will illuminate why the idea of fate, objectionable though it is from a philosophical point of view, is so highly effective in imaginative literature. For the latter does not require that its materials be theoretically proven, merely that they be practically existent, and what could be more desirable for the imagery of a poetic work than a background painted by the imagination itself, immeasurable and hence allowing the greatest possible freedom of movement. The question as to the applicability of *fatum* in poetry thus coincides with the question as to the suitablity of depicting ghosts, precognitive dreams, etc., which latter phenomena play such important roles in the *tragédies* of the French, who tend to shy away from ghosts.

Should the idea of fate be as predominant in modern tragedy as it was in ancient Greece? Certainly not. To the ancients, whose tragedies by their very origin were bound up with the religious tendencies of their time, fate was as indispensable a requirement as was their system of gods; but to the playwrights of our time, fate becomes—a machine, difficult to operate, requiring considerable caution, and useful only for tragedies, not for any other kind of poetry, such as epic poetry, for instance. The reason for this difference also determines the way in which fate must be used.

For the concept of *fate*, for us, is not a fruit of conviction but of dark intuition. In all other forms of literature, the poet himself is speaking, what he says is *his* opinion, and therefore a modern epic work founded on the idea of *fatum* would be a monstrosity. But the voices in a drama are those of the characters, and it lies in the power of the poet to present their natures in such a way, and direct the storm of their passions in such a way, that the idea of fate arises in them by necessity. As soon as that word is pronounced or as soon as the notion of fate has been introduced, a bolt of lightning strikes the viewer's soul. Everything he has ever pondered or heard or sensed or dreamed on this subject in times of pain is now set in motion, the dark forces awaken, and he is playing his part in the tragedy. But never must the poet step forward and declare the belief of his characters to be his own. The same darkness that prevails over the nature of fate must prevail in its mention; his characters may clearly express their belief in it, but let the viewer always remain uncertain as to whether he should ascribe these awful misfortunes to the changeful caprice of life or to a hidden design, let him darkly sense that it's the latter, but do not spell it out for him, for an error expressed cannot but repel. . . .

. . . This explanation will perhaps be least satisfactory to the most zealous defenders of *fatum,* who thought they were rendering it a great service by trying to bring it into connection with the tenets of the Christian church, ascribing to tragedy some impossibly lofty moral purpose. But they should take heed. This is precisely the misfortune of the Germans, that they are constantly bringing all their wisdom to market and think they haven't made a real tragedy if it can't in a pinch serve as a compendium of philosophy, religion, history, statistics, and physics, so that in their dramatic works you find everything except drama. There is nothing I can do to please them, and all genuinely *productive* minds will, I hope, agree with me. Human action and passions are the subject of the art of tragedy, and everything else, and be it the highest, though it is not excluded, is just—*a machine.* Preach religion on the pulpit, teach philosophy *ex cathedra,* and let man with his ways and doings, his joys and sorrows, mistakes and crimes, be portrayed on the stage.

That will suffice.

1817   *Translated by Joel Agee*

FRANZ GRILLPARZER, 1791–1872, the most eminent Austrian playwright of the nineteenth century. Some of his plays are *Sappho* (1818), *Der Traum, ein Leben* (1834) after Calderón, *Weh dem, der lügt* (1838), and *Bruderzwist in Habsburg* (1872).

Georg Wilhelm Friedrich Hegel

From *The Philosophy of Fine Art*

The reason that dramatic poetry must be regarded as the highest phase of the art of poetry, and, indeed, of every kind of art, is due to the fact that it is elaborated, both in form and substance, in a whole that is the most complete. For in contrast to every other sort of sensuous *matèria*, whether it be stone, wood, color, or tone, that of human speech is the only medium fully adequate to the presentation of spiritual life; and further, among the particular types of the art of articulate speech, dramatic poetry is the one in which we find the objective character of the Epos essentially united to the subjective principle of the Lyric. In other words it presents directly before our vision an essentially independent action as a definite fact, which does not merely originate from the personal life of character under the process of self-realization, but receives its determinate form as the result of the substantive interaction in concrete life of ideal intention, many individuals, and collisions. This mediated form of epic art by means of the intimate personal life of an individual viewed in the very presence of his activity does not, however, permit the drama to describe the external aspects of local condition and environment, nor yet the action and event itself in the way that they are so described in the epic. Consequently, in order that the entire art product may receive the full animation of life, we require its complete scenic representation. . . .

. . . Dramatic action, however, is not confined to the simple and undisturbed execution of a definite purpose, but depends throughout on conditions of collision, human passion, and characters, and leads therefore to actions and reactions, which in their turn call

61

for some further resolution of conflict and disruption. What we have consequently before us are definite ends individualized in living personalities and situations pregnant with conflict; we see these as they are asserted and maintained, as they work in cooperation or opposition—all in a momentary and kaleidoscope interchange of expression—and along with this, too, the final result presupposed and issuing from the entirety of this interthreading and conflicting skein of human life, movement, and accomplishment, which has nonetheless to work out its tranquil resolution. . . .

The more obvious laws of dramatic composition may be summarized in the time-honored prescription of the so-called unities of place, time, and action.

The inalterability of one exclusive *locale* of the action proposed belongs to the type of those rigid rules which the French in particular have deduced from classic tragedy and the critique of Aristotle thereupon. As a matter of fact, Aristotle merely says that the duration of the tragic action should not exceed at the most the length of a day.[1] He does not mention the unity of place at all; moreover, the ancient tragedians have not followed such a principle in the strict sense adopted by the French. As examples of such a deviation, we have a change of scene both in the *Eumenides* of Aeschylus and the *Ajax* of Sophocles. To a still less extent can our more modern dramatic writing, in its effort to portray a more extensive field of collision, dramatis personae of whatever kind and incidental event, and, in a word, an action the ideal explication of which requires, too, an external environment of greater breadth, subject itself to the yoke of a rigid identity of scene. Modern poetry, insofar, that is, as its creations are in harmony with the romantic type, which as a rule displays more variety and caprice in its attitude to external condition, has consequently freed itself from any such demand. If, however, the action is in truth concentrated in a few great motives, so that it can avoid complexity of external exposition, there will be no necessity for considerable alternation of scene. Indeed, the reverse will be a real advantage. . . .

The unity of *time* is a precisely similar case. In the pure realm of imaginative idea we may no doubt, with no difficulty, combine vast periods of time; in the direct vision of perception we cannot so readily pass over a few years. If the action is, therefore, of a simple character, viewed in its entire content and conflict, we shall do best to concentrate the time of such a conflict, from its origin to its resolution, in a restricted period. If, on the contrary, it demands character richly diversified, whose development necessitates many situations which, in the matter of time, lie widely apart from one another, then the formal unity of a purely relative and entirely conventional duration of time will be essentially impossible. To attempt to remove such a representation from the domain of dramatic poetry, on the *prima facie* ground that it is inconsistent with the strict rule of time-unity would simply amount to making the prose of ordinary facts the final court of appeal, as against the truth of poetic creation. Least of all need we waste time in discussing the purely empirical probability that as audience we could, in the course of a few hours, witness also, directly through our sense, merely the passage of a short space of time. For it is precisely in the case where the poet is most at pains to illustrate this conclusion that, from other points of view, he well-nigh invariably perpetrates the most glaring improbabilities.

In contrast to the above examples of unity, that of *action* is the one truly and inviolable rule. The true nature, however, of this unity may be a matter of considerable dispute. I will therefore develop my own views of its significance at greater length.

Every action must without exception have a *distinct* object which it seeks to achieve. It is through his action that man enters actively into the concrete actual world, in which also the most universal subject matter is in its turn accepted in the poetic work and defined under more specific manifestation. From this point of view, therefore, the unity will have to be sought for in the realization of an end itself essentially definite, and carried under the particular conditions and relations of concrete life to its consummation. The circumstances adapted to dramatic action are, however, as we have seen, of a kind that the individual end meets with obstructions at the hands of other personal agents, and this for the reason that a contradictory end stands in its path, which in its turn equally strives after fulfillment, so that it is invariably attached to the reciprocal relation of conflicts and their devolution. Dramatic action in consequence rests essentially upon an action that is involved with *resistance*; and the genuine unity can only find its *rationale* in the entire movement which consists in the assertion of this collision relatively to the definition of the particular circumstances, characters, and ends proposed, not merely under a mode consonant to such ends and characters, but in such a way as to resolve the opposition implied. Such a resolution has, precisely as the action itself has, an external and an inside point of view. In other words, on the one side, the conflict of the opposed *ends* is finally composed; and on the other the particular *characters*, to a greater or less extent, have committed their entire volitional energy and being to the undertaking they strive to accomplish. . . .

The genuine content of tragic action subject to the *aims* which arrest tragic characters is supplied by the world of those forces which carry in themselves their own justification, and are realized substantively in the volitional activity of mankind. Such are the love of husband and wife, of parents, children, and kinsfolk. Such are, further, the life of communities, the patriotism of citizens, the will of those in supreme power. Such are the life of churches, not, however, if regarded as a piety which submits to act with resignation, or as a divine judicial declaration in the heart of mankind over what is good or the reverse in action; but, on the contrary, conceived as the active engagement with and demand for veritable interests and relations. It is of a soundness and thoroughness consonant with these that the really tragical *characters* consist. They are throughout that which the essential notion of their character enables them and compels them to be. They are not merely a varied totality laid out in the series of views of it proper to the epic manner; they are, while no doubt remaining also essentially vital and individual, still only the one power of the particular character in question, the force in which such a character, in virtue of its essential personality, has made itself inseparably coalesce with some particular aspect of the capital and substantive life-content we have indicated above, and deliberately commits himself to that. It is at some such elevation, where the mere accident of unmediated[2] individuality vanish altogether, that we find the tragic heroes of dramatic art, whether they be the living representatives of such spheres of concrete life or in any other way already so derive their greatness and stability from their own free self-reliance that they stand forth as works of sculpture, and as such interpret, too, under this aspect the essentially more abstract statues and figures of gods, as also the lofty tragic characters of the Greeks more completely than is possible for any other kind of elucidation or commentary. . . .

These ethical forces, as also the characters of the action, are *distinctively defined* in respect to their content and their individual personality, in virtue of the principle of differentation to which everything is subject, which forms part of the objective world of things. If, then, these particular forces, in the way presupposed by dramatic poetry, are attached to the external expression of human activity, and are realized as the determinate aim of a human pathos which passes into action, their concordancy is cancelled, and they are asserted *in contrast* to each other in interchangeable succession. Individual action will then, under given conditions, realize an object or character, which, under such a presupposed state, inevitably stimulate the presence of a pathos[3] opposed to itself, because it occupies a position of unique isolation in virtue of its independently fixed definition, and, by doing so, brings in its train unavoidable conflicts. Primitive tragedy, then, consists in this, that within a collision of this kind both sides of the contradiction, if taken by themselves, are *justified*; yet, from a further point of view, they tend to carry into effect the true and positive content of their end and specific characterization merely as the negation and *violation* of the other equally legitimate power, and consequently in their ethical purport and relatively to this so far fall under *condemnation*. . . .

As a result of this, however, an unmediated contradiction is posited, which no doubt may assert itself in the Real, but, for all that, is unable to maintain itself as that which is wholly substantive and verily real therein; which rather discovers, and only discovers, its essential justification in the fact that it is able to *annul* itself as such contradiction. In other words, whatever may be the claim of the tragic final purpose and personality, whatever may be the necessity of the tragic collision, it is, as a consequence of our present view, no less a claim that is asserted—this is our *third* and last point—by the tragic resolution of this division. It is through *this* latter result that Eternal Justice is operative in such aims and individuals under a mode whereby it restores the ethical substance and unity in and along with the downfall of the individuality which disturbs its repose. For, despite the fact that individual characters propose that which is itself essentially valid, yet they are only able to carry it out under the tragic demand in a manner that implies contradiction and with a onesidedness which is injurious. What, however, is substantive in truth, and the function of which is to secure realization, is not the battle of particular unities, however much such a conflict is essentially involved in the notion of a real world and human action; rather it is the reconciliation in which definite ends and individuals unite in harmonious action without mutual violation and contradiction. That which is abrogated in the tragic issue is merely the *one-sided* particularity which was unable to accommodate itself to this harmony, and consequently in the tragic course of its action, through inability to disengage itself from itself and its designs, either is committed in its entire totality to destruction or at least finds itself compelled to fall back upon a state of resignation in the execution of its aim in so far as it can carry this out. . . .

. . . That which preeminently is of valid force in ancient drama, therefore, whether it be tragedy or comedy, is the universal and essential content of the end, which individuals seek to achieve. In tragedy this is the ethical claim of human consciousness in view of the particular action in question, the vindication of the act on its own account. And in the old comedy, too, it is in the same way at least the general public interests which are emphasized, whether it be in statesmen and the mode in which they direct the State, questions of peace or war, the general public and its moral conditions, or the condition of philosophy and its decline. . . .

In *modern* romantic poetry, on the contrary, it is the individual passion, the satisfaction of which can only be relative to a wholly personal end, generally speaking the destiny of some particular person or character placed under the exceptional circumstances, which forms the subject-matter of all importance. . . .

. . . What we require therefore above all in such cases is at least the formal[4] greatness of character and power of the personal life which is able to ride out everything that negates it, and which, without denial of its acts or, indeed, without being materially discomposed by them, is capable of accepting their consequences. And on the other side we find that those substantive ends, such as patriotism, family devotion, loyalty, and the rest, are by no means to be excluded, although for the individual persons concerned the main question of importance is not so much the substantive force as their own individuality. But in such cases as a rule they rather form the particular ground upon which such persons, viewed in the light of their private character, take their stand and engage in conflict, rather than have supplied what we may regard as the real and ultimate content of their volition and action.

And further, in conjuction with a personal self-assertion of this type we may have presented the full extension of individual idiosyncrasy, not merely in respect to the soul-life simply, but also in relation to external circumstances and condition within which the action proceeds. And it is owing to this that in distinctive form the simple conflicts which characterize more classical dramatic composition, we now meet with the variety and exuberance of the character dramatized, the unforeseen surprises of the ever new and complicated developments of plot, the maze of intrigue, the contingency of events, and, in a word, all those aspects of the modern drama which claim our attention, and the unfettered appearance of which, as opposed to the overwhelming emphasis attached to what is essentially most fundamental in the content, accentuates the type of romantic art in its distinction from the classic type. . . .

. . . In Greek tragedy it is not all the bad will, crime, worthlessness, or mere misfortune, stupidity, and the like, which act as an incentive to such collisions, but rather, as I have frequently urged, the ethical right to a definite course of action.[5] Abstract evil neither possesses truth in itself, nor does it arouse interest. At the same time, when we attribute ethical traits of characterization to the individual of the action, this ought not to appear merely as a matter of opinion. It is rather implied in their right or claim that they are actually there as essential on their own account. The hazards of crime, such as are present in modern drama—the useless, or quite as much the so-called noble criminal, with his empty talk about fate, we meet with in the tragedy of ancient literature, rarely, if at all, and for the good reason that the decision and deed depends on the wholly personal aspect of interest and character, upon lust for power, love, honor, or other similar passion, whose justification has its roots exclusively in the particular inclination and individuality. A resolve of this character, whose claim is based upon the content of its object, which it carries into execution in one restricted direction of particularization, violates, under certain circumstances, which are already essentially implied in the actual possibility of conflicts, a further and equally ethical sphere of human volition, which the character thus confronted adheres to, and, by his thus stimulated action, enforces, so that in this way the collision of powers and individuals equally entitled to the ethical claim is completely set up in its movement.

The sphere of this content,[6] although capable of great variety of detail, is not in its essential features very extensive. The principal source of opposition, which Sophocles in particular, in this respect following the lead of Aeschylus, has accepted and worked out in the finest way, is that of the *body politic,* the opposition, that is, between ethical life in this social universality and the family as the natural ground of moral relations. These are the purest forces of tragic representation. It is, in short, the harmony of these spheres and the concordant action within the bounds of their realized content, which constitute the perfected reality of the moral life. In this respect I need only recall to recollection the *Seven before Thebes* of Aeschylus and, as a yet stronger illustration, the *Antigone* of Sophocles. Antigone reverences the ties of blood-relationship, the gods of the nether world. Creon alone recognizes Zeus, the paramount Power of public life and the commonwealth. We come across a similar conflict in the *Iphigeneia in Aulis,* as also in the *Agamemnon,* the *Choephorae,* and *Eumenides* of Aeschylus, and in the *Electra* of Sophocles. Agamemnon, as king and leader of his army, sacrifices his daughter in the interest of the Greek folk and the Trojan expedition. He shatters thereby the bond of love as between himself and his daughter and wife, which Clytemnestra retains in the depth of a mother's heart, and in revenge prepares an ignominious death for her husband on his return. Orestes, their son, respects his mother, but is bound to represent the right of his father, the king, and strikes dead the mother who bore him.

A content of this type retains its force through all times, and its presentation, despite all difference of nationality, vitally arrests our human and artistic sympathies.

Of a more formal type is that second kind of essential collision, an illustration of which in the tragic story of Oedipus the Greek tragedians especially favored. Of this Sophocles has left us the most complete example in his *Oedipus Rex,* and *Oedipus in Colonos.* The problem here is concerned with the claim of alertness in our intelligence, with the nature of the obligation[7] implied in that which a man carries out with a volition fully aware of its acts as contrasted with that which he has done in fact, but unconscious of and with no intention of doing what he has done under the directing providence of the gods. Oedipus slays his father, marries his mother, begets children in this incestuous alliance, and nevertheless is involved in these most terrible of crimes without active participation either in will or knowledge. The point of view of our profounder modern consciousness of right and wrong would be to recognize that crimes of this description, inasmuch as they were neither referable to a personal knowledge or volition, were not deeds for which the true personality of the perpetrator was responsible. The plastic nature of the Greek on the contrary adheres to the bare fact which an individual has achieved, and refuses to face the division implied by the purely ideal attitude of the soul in the self-conscious life on the one hand and the objective significance of the fact accomplished on the other.

For ourselves, to conclude this survey, other collisions, which either in general are related to the universally accepted association of personal action to the Greek conception of Destiny, or in some measure to more exceptional conditions, are comparatively speaking less important.

In all these tragic conflicts, however, we must above all place on one side the false notion of *guilt* or *innocence*. The heroes of tragedy are quite as much under one category as the other. If we accept the idea as valid that a man is guilty only in the case that a choice lay open to him, and he deliberately decided on the course of action which he carried out, then these plastic figures of ancient drama are guiltless. They act in accordance with a specific character, a specific pathos, for the simple reason that they are this character, this pathos. In such a case there is no lack of decision and no choice. The strength of great characters consists precisely in this that they do not choose, but are entirely and absolutely just that which they will and achieve. They are simply themselves, and never anything else, and their greatness consists in that fact. Weakness in action, in other words, wholly consists in the division of the personal self as such from its content, so that character, volition, and final purpose do not appear as absolutely one unified growth; and inasmuch as no assured end lives in the soul as the very substance of the particular personality, as the pathos and might of the individual's entire will, he is still able to turn with indecision from this course to that, and his final decision is that of caprice. A wavering attitude of this description is alien to these plastic creations. The bond between the psychological state of mind and the content of the will is for them indissoluble. That which stirs them to action is just in this very pathos which implies an ethical justification and which, even in the pathetic aspects of the dialogue, is not enforced in and through the merely personal rhetoric of the heart and the sophistry of passion, but in the equally masculine and cultivated objective presence, in the profound possibilities, the harmony and vitally plastic beauty of which Sophocles was to a superlative degree master. At the same time, however, such a pathos, with its potential resources of collision, brings in its train deeds that are both injurious and wrongful. They have no desire to avoid the blame that results therefrom. On the contrary, it is their fame to have done what they have done. One can in fact urge nothing more intolerable against a hero of this type than by saying that he has acted innocently. It is a point of honor with such great characters that they are guilty. They have no desire to excite pity or our sensibilities. For it is not the substantive, but rather the wholly personal deepening[8] of the individual character, which stirs our individual pain. These securely strong characters, however, coalesce entirely with their essential pathos, and this indivisible accord inspires wonder, but does not excite heart emotions. The drama of Euripides marks the transition to that.

The final result, then, of the development of tragedy conducts us to this issue and only this, namely, that the twofold vindication of the mutually conflicting aspects are no doubt retained, but the *one-sided* mode under which they were maintained is canceled, and the undisturbed ideal harmony brings back again that condition of the chorus, which attributes without reserve equal honor to all the gods. The true course of dramatic development consists in the annulment of *contradictions* viewed as such, in the reconciliation of the forces of human action, which alternately strive to negate each other in their conflict. Only so far is misfortune and suffering not the final issue, but rather the satisfaction of spirit, as for the first time, the virtue of such a conclusion, the necessity of all that particular individuals experience, is able to appear in complete accord with reason, and our emotional attitude is tranquillized on a true ethical basis, rudely shaken by the calamitous result to the heroes, but reconciled in the substantial facts. And it is only in so far as we retain such a view securely that we shall be in a position to understand ancient tragedy. . . .

First, we have particularly to emphasize the fact, that if it is the one-sidedness of the pathos which constitutes the real basis of collisions this merely amounts to the statement that it is asserted in the action of life, and therewith has become the unique pathos of a particular individual. If this one-sidedness is to be abrogated then it is this individual which, to the extent that his action is exclusively identified with this isolated pathos, must perforce be stripped and sacrificed. For the individual here is merely this single life, and, if this unity is not secured in its stability on its own account, the individual is shattered.

The most complete form of this development is possible when the individuals engaged in conflict relatively to their concrete or objective life appear in each case essentially involved in one whole, so that they stand fundamentally under the power of that against which they battle, and consequently infringe that, which, conformably to their own essential life, they ought to respect. Antigone, for example, lives under the political authority of Creon; she is herself the daughter of a king and the affianced of Haemon, so that her obedience to the royal prerogative is an obligation. But Creon also, who is on his part father and husband, is under obligation to respect the sacred ties of relationship, and only by breach of this can give an order that is in conflict with such a sense. In consequence of this we find immanent in the life of both that which each respectively combats, and they are seized and broken by that very bond which is rooted in the compass of their own social existence. Antigone is put to death before she can enjoy what she looks forward to as bride, and Creon too is punished in the fatal end of his son and wife, who commit suicide, the former on account of Antigone's death, and the latter owing to Haemon's. Among all the fine creations of the ancient and the modern world—and I am acquainted with pretty nearly everything in such a class, and one ought to know it, and it is quite possible—the *Antigone* of Sophocles is from this point of view in my judgment the most excellent and satisfying work of art.

The tragic issue does not, however, require in every case as a means of removing both overemphasized aspects and the equal honor which they respectively claim the downfall of the contestant parties. The *Eumenides* does not end, as we all know, with the death of Orestes, or the destruction of the Eumenides, these avenging spirits of matricide and filial affection, these opponents of Apollo, who seek to protect unimpaired the worth of and reverence for the family chief and king, the god who had prompted Orestes to slay Clytemnestra, but will have Orestes released from the punishment and honor bestowed on both himself and the Furies. At the same time we cannot fail to see in this adjusted conclusion the nature of the authority which the Greeks attached to their gods when they presented them as mere individuals contending with each other. They appear, in short, to the Athenian of everyday life merely as definite aspects of ethical experience which the principles of morality viewed in their complete and harmonious coherence bind together. The votes of the Areopagus are equal on either side. It is Athena, the goddess, the life of Athens, that is, imagined in its essential unity, who adds the white pebble, who frees Orestes, and at the same time promises altars and a cult to the Eumenides no less than Apollo. . . .

But as a *further* and final class, and one more beautiful than the above rather external mode of resolution we have the reconciliation more properly of the soul itself, in which respect there is, in virtue of the personal significance, a real approach to our modern point of view. The most perfect example of this in ancient drama is to be found in the ever admirable *Oedipus in Colonos* of Sophocles. . . .

Modern tragedy accepts in its own province from the first the principle of subjectivity or self-assertion. It makes, therefore, the personal intimacy of character—the character, that is, which is no purely individual and vital embodiment of ethical forces in the classic sense—its peculiar object and content. It, moreover, makes, in a type of concurrence that is adapted to this end, human actions come into collision through the instrumentality of the external accident of circumstances in the way that a contingency of a similar character is also decisive in its effect on the consequence, or appears to be so decisive. . . .

To start with, we may observe that, however much in romantic tragedy the personal aspect of suffering and passions, in the true meaning of such an attitude, is the focal center, yet, for all that, it is impossible in human activity that the ground basis of definite ends borrowed from the concrete worlds of the family, the State, the Church, and others should be dispensed with. Insofar, however, as in the drama under discussion, it is not the substantive content as such in these spheres of life which constitutes the main interest of individuals. Such ends are from a certain point of view partic-ularized in a breadth of extension and variety, as also in exceptional modes of presentment, in which it often happens that what is truly essential is only able to force itself on our attention with attenuated strength. . . .

And, from a further point of view in this drama, it is the right of subjectivity, as above defined, absolutely unqualified, which is retained as the dominating content; and for this reason personal love, honor, and the rest make such an exclusive appeal as ends of human action that, while in one direction other relations cannot fail to appear as the purely external background on which these interests of our modern life are set in motion, in another such relations on their own account actively conflict with the require-ments of the more individual state of emotion. Of more profound significance still is wrong and crime, even assuming that a particular character does not deliberately and to start with place himself in either, yet does not avoid in order to attain his original purpose. . . .

Generally speaking, however, in modern tragedy it is not the substantive content of its object in the interest of which men act, and which is maintained as the stimulus of their passion; rather it is the inner experience of their heart and individual emotion, or the particular qualities of their personality, which insist on satis-faction. . . .

In order to emphasize still more distinctly the difference which in this respect obtains between ancient and modern tragedy, I will merely refer the reader to Shakespeare's *Hamlet*. Here we find fundamentally a collision similar to that which is introduced by Aeschylus into his *Choephorae* and that by Sophocles into his *Electra*. For Hamlet's father, too, and the King, as in these Greek plays, has been murdered, and his mother has wedded the murderer. That which, however, is the conception of the Greek dramatists possesses a certain ethical justification—I mean the death of Agamemnon—relatively to his sacrifice of Iphigenia in the contrasted case of Shakespeare's play, can only be viewed as an atrocious crime, of which Hamlet's mother is innocent; so that the son is merely concerned in his vengeance to direct his attention to the fratricidal king, and there is nothing in the latter's character that possesses any real claim to his respect. The real collision, therefore, does not turn on the fact that the son, in giving effect to a rightful sense of vengeance, is himself forced to violate morality, but rather on the particular personality, the inner life of Hamlet, whose noble soul is not steeled to this kind of energetic activity, but, while full of contempt for the world and life, what between making up his mind and attempting to carry into effect or preparing to carry into effect its resolves, is bandied from pillar to post, and finally through his own procrastination and the external course of events meets his own doom.

If we now turn, in close connection with the above conclusions, to our *second* point of fundamental importance in modern tragedy—that is to say, the nature of the characters and their collisions—we may summarily take a point of departure from the following general observations.

The heroes of ancient classic tragedy discover circumstances under which they, so long as they irrefragably adhere to the *one* ethical state of pathos which alone corresponds to their own already formed personality, must infallibly come into conflict with an ethical Power which opposes them and possesses an equal ethical claim to recognition. Romantic characters, on the contrary, are from the first placed within a wide expanse of contingent relations and conditions, within which every sort of action is possible; so that the conflict, to which no doubt the external conditions presupposed supply the occasion, essentially abides within the *character* itself, to which the individuals concerned in their passion give effect, not, however, in the interests of the ethical vindication of the truly substantive claims, but for the simple reason that they are the kind of men they are. Greek heroes also no doubt act in accordance with their particular individuality; but this individuality, as before noted, if we take for our examples the supreme results of ancient tragedy, is itself necessarily identical with an ethical pathos which is substantive. In modern tragedy the peculiar character in its real significance, and to which it as a matter of accident remains constant, whether it happens to grasp after that which on its own account is on moral grounds justifiable, or is carried into wrong and crime, forms its resolves under the dictate of personal wishes and necessities, or among other things purely external considerations. In such a case, therefore, though we may have a coalescence between the moral aspect of the object and the character, yet, for all that, such a concurrence does not constitute, and cannot constitute—owing to the divided character of ends, passions, and the life wholly personal to the individual, the *essential* basis and objective condition of the depth and beauty of the tragic drama. . . .

. . . For even in the cases where a purely formal passion, as for instance ambition in Macbeth, or jealousy in Othello, claims at its field the entire pathos of his tragic hero, such an abstraction impairs by no fraction the full breadth of the personality. . . .

The last of the subjects which we have still to discuss as proposed is the nature of the *tragic issue* which characters in our present drama have to confront, as also the type of tragic *reconciliation* compatible with such a standpoint. In ancient tragedy it is the eternal justice which, as the absolute might of destiny, delivers and restores the harmony of substantive being in its ethical character by its opposition to the particular forces which, in their strain to assert an independent subsistence, come into collision, and which, in virtue of the rational ideality implied in its operations, satisfies us even where we see the downfall of particular men. Insofar as a justice of the same kind is present in modern tragedy, it is necessarily, in part, more abstract on account of the closer differentiation of ends and characters, and, in part, of a colder nature and one that is more akin to that of a criminal court, in virtue of the fact that the wrong and crime into which individuals are necessarily carried, insofar as they are intent upon executing their designs, are of a profounder significance. Macbeth, for instance, the elder daughters of Lear and their husbands, the president in *Kabale und Liebe,*[9] Richard III, and many similar examples, on account of their atrocious conduct, only deserve the fate they get. This type of dénouement usually is presented under the guise that individuals are crushed by an actual force which they have defied in order to carry out their personal aims. . . .

From another point of view, however, we may see the tragic issue also merely in the light of the effect of unhappy circumstances and external accidents, which might have brought about, quite as readily, a different result and a happy conclusion. From such a point of view we have merely left us the conception that the modern idea of individuality, with its searching definition of character, circumstances, and developments, is handed over essentially to the contingency of the earthly state, and must carry the fateful issues of such finitude. Pure commiseration of this sort is, however, destitute of meaning; and it is nothing less than a frightful kind of external necessity in the particular case where we see the downfall of essentially noble natures in their conflict thus assumed with the mischance of purely external accidents. Such a course of events can insistently arrest our attention; but in the result it can only be horrible, and the demand is direct and irresistible that the external accidents ought to accord with that which is identical with the spiritual nature of such noble characters. Only as thus regarded can we feel ourselves reconciled with the grievous end of Hamlet and Juliet. From a purely external point of view, the death of Hamlet appears as an accident occasioned by his duel with Laertes and the interchange of the daggers. But in the background of Hamlet's soul, death is already present from the first.

1818–1829   *Translated by F. P. B Osmaston*

Translator's Notes

1. *Poetics,* chapter 5.
2. *Unmittelbaren Individualität.* Hegel means the individuality that is abstract, not soldered into the substance of concrete human life.
3. Hegel appears to understand by pathos here little more than a psychological state.
4. Formal is contrasted with really ethical content.
5. *Die sittliche Berechtigung zu einer bestimmten Tat.* The context shows that Hegel does not merely mean the justification in the individual conscience, which is demanded by and perfected in such activity, but the actual ethical claim which is vindicated in such action.
6. That is, the content of the dramatic action in Greek drama.
7. By *Rechtfertigung* Hegel here seems to mean not so much the vindicated right as the degree of responsibility which a certain attitude of mind involves. It is the nature of the subjection to the vindicated right, or its absence.
8. By *die subjektive Vertiefung der Persönlichkeit* Hegel would seem to mean the psychological analysis of character of its own account.
9. *Love and Intrigue* (1783) by Schiller.

GEORG WILHELM FRIEDRICH HEGEL, 1770–1831, philosopher, main representative of German Idealism, professor at Jena, Heidelberg, and Berlin. Of special interest to students of drama are his writings on aesthetics, collected in *The Philosophy of Fine Arts* (4 vols., London, 1916–1920).

Georg Büchner

Letter to His Family

July 28, 1835
Strasbourg

. . . The dramatic poet is in my eyes nothing but a writer of history. He is superior to the latter, however, in that he re-creates history a second time for us. Instead of telling us a dry story, he places us directly in to the life of earlier times, giving us characters instead of characteristics and figures instead of descriptions. His greatest task is to come as close as possible to history as it actually happened. His book must be neither more nor less than history itself. God did not create history as suitable entertainment for young ladies, and for that reason I cannot be blamed if my drama is equally unsuitable. I cannot make a Danton and the bandits of the Revolution into virtuous heroes! To show their decadence I had to let them be decadent, to show their godlessness I had to let them speak like atheists. Should you discover any improprieties, then think of the notoriously obscene language of that time. Whatever my characters say is only a weak approximation of it. One might reproach me for choosing such material. But such a reproach has long been refuted. If we were to let it stand, then the greatest masterpieces of literature would have to be rejected. The poet is not a teacher of morality: he creates figures, he brings past times to life, and the public ought to lear from that, as well as from the study and observation of history, what is going on around them. If you wished otherwise, you shouldn't be permitted to study history at all, for it tells of many immoral acts. You would have to walk blindfolded down the street, for you might see indecencies. You would have to cry out against a God who created a world in which so much dissoluteness occurs. If someone were to tell me that the poet should not depict the world as it is but as it should be, then I answer that I do not want to make it better than God, who certainly made the world as it should be. As far as the so-called idealistic poets are concerned, I find that they have produced hardly anything besides marionettes with sky-blue noses and affected pathos, not men of flesh and blood, with whose sorrow and happiness I sympathize and whose actions repel or attract me. In a word, I think much of Goethe or Shakespeare, but very little of Schiller. . . .

Translated by Henry J. Schmidt

GEORG BÜCHNER, 1813–1837, essayist, dramatist, scientist, and activist on behalf of civil liberties. His plays are *Danton's Death* (1835), *Leonce and Lena* (1836), and *Woyzeck* (1836).

Friedrich Hebbel

A Word about the Theater

Art deals with life, the inner and the outer life, and one might well say that it depicts both simultaneously—its purest form and its highest content. The principal art forms and their laws are the immediate expression of the different elements each of them draws from life and then elaborates in its way. But life has the two-fold appearance of being and becoming, and art accomplishes its purpose most perfectly when it succeeds in maintaining a measured balance between the two. Only in this way does it assure itself of the present as well as the future, both of which must be regarded as equally important if art is to become what it is supposed to become: life within life; for whatever is closed up in stasis throttles the creative breath without which it would remain ineffectual, while purely embryonic stirring and starting ends up by excluding all form.

Drama represents the process of life itself—not just in that it presents us with life in its whole expanse, which is something epic poetry also permits itself to do, but in that it makes us conscious of the precarious condition in which the individual finds himself when, released from his original nexus, he finds himself face to face with the Whole of which he is nevertheless still a part, despite his incomprehensible freedom. Drama, therefore, as is fitting for the highest art form, is equally concerned with being and becoming; with being, in that the theater must never tire of repeating the eternal truth that an immoderately self-centered existence does not just accidentally produce guilt but necessarily and essentially entails it; with becoming, in that is employs the ever new materials presented by the changing times and their sediment, history, to show that man's nature and destiny remain the same, no matter how things may change around him. What must not be overlooked in this context is that dramatic guilt, unlike Christian original sin, does not arise from the direction taken by the human will but immediately from that will itself, from the rigid, self-asserting expansion of the ego, so that from a dramatic point of view it is completely unimportant whether the hero fails due to a laudable or a wicked aspiration.

The dramatic material is furnished by the plot and the characters. We shall ignore the former here, for it has become a subordinate element, at least among the newer playwrights, as can be ascertained by any doubting person if he will read a play by Shakespeare and ask himself what it was that enflamed the poet—the story or the people he puts on the stage? The treatment of the characters, on the other hand, is of the utmost significance. Under no circumstances must these appear to be finished, capable of gaining and losing in external fortune or misfortune but not in their inmost essence. That is the death of drama, death before birth. Only by showing us how the individual attains his form and his center of balance in the struggle between his personal will and the general will of the world—which always modifies and transforms the deed, the expression of freedom, through the event, the expression of necessity—and by thus revealing the nature of all human activity, which constantly, as soon as it seeks to manifest an inner motive, releases at the same time an external, resistant force designed to establish equilibrium: only in this way does drama come alive. And although this fundamental idea, upon which depend both the dignity and the value we are here attributing to the drama, circumscribes the orbit within which everything must stir and move, it is also true that the task of the poet in the proper sense of the word is to multiply the interests, or rather to evoke the totality, of life and the world—and this without detriment to the true unity of the play—and to beware of placing all his characters equally near the center, as is so frequently the case in so-called lyrical plays. The most perfect image of life results when the central character becomes for the secondary characters and protagonists what the fate he is wrestling with is for him, and when in this way everything, down to the lowest gradations, is developed, conditioned, and mirrored in concert and contrast and interaction with everything else.

Now the following question arises: what is the relationship between drama and history, and to what extent must drama be historical? To the extent, it seems to me, that it is by its nature historical already, and that art may be regarded as the highest form of historiography, since it is incapable of describing the grandest and most significant life processes without casting a light on the decisive historical crises that cause and bring them about, or without, as leader and principal administrator of public education, elucidating the gradual dissolution or consolidation of the world's religious and political forms—without, in short, revealing at the same time the very atmosphere of the ages. Material history, which Napoleon already called "the fable of the social contract," this multifarious monstrous mess of dubious facts, of one- or totally un-dimensional character portraits, will sooner or later exceed the capacity of the human mind, and the new drama, especially Shakespearean drama, and not just the part singled out as "histor-ical," but all of it, may thus acquire the same significance for our distant posterity as the ancient theater holds for us. Then, and surely not before then, people will put an end to their small-minded search for a vulgar identity between art and history and to the anxious comparison between the given situations and characters and their artistically transformed counterparts, for one will have realized that this amounts only to a comparison between the first and the second portrait, not between image and reality, and it will have become apparent that dramatic art is symbolic and must be seen as symbolic, not just in its totality, which is self-evidence, but in every one of its elements, just as the painter does not give his figures red cheeks and blue eyes with colors distilled from real human blood but quietly and inoffensively makes use of indigo and vermilion.

But the content of life is inexhaustible, and the medium of art is limited. Life knows no conclusion, the thread with which it spins its phenomena extends into infinity; but art must come to a conclusion, it must tie the thread into a circle as well as it can, and this is the only point Goethe could have had in mind when he said that all art forms entailed some measure of falsehood. It is true, of course, that this falsehood can be pointed out in life itself—for life, too, cannot furnish a single form in which all its elements are equally distributed; it cannot, for example, produce the perfect man without depriving him of those excellent aspects that make up the perfect woman, and the image of the two pails in the well, only one of which can be full at one time, is the aptest symbol for the whole of creation. But the fundamental fault of art is of a much worse and more critical kind than that of life, where the whole always supports and compensates for the individual; for here, the *breach* on the one hand must be covered by an *excess* on the other.

I shall explain this idea by applying it to the drama. The most excellent plays of all literatures show us that the poet was frequently only able to forge the invisible orbit encompassing his artistic image of life by lending one or several of his main characters a degree of world- and self-consciousness that far exceeds any realistic measure. I shall leave the ancients untouched, for their treatment of character was different from ours; I merely wish to recall Shakespeare, and in particular (passing by the perhaps too conclusive example of Hamlet) the monologues in *Macbeth* and *Richard,* and the bastard in *King John.* Let me note in passing that this evident weakness in Shakespeare has been seen as a virtue and even a mark of excellence by some (even by Hegel in his *Esthetics*), instead of their resting content with the evidence that the fault lies not with the poet but with art itself. But that which, in the work of great playwrights, appears as the dominant trait of complete characters, is also frequently encountered in the particulars, in the culminating moments, where the word walks along next to the deed or even hurries ahead of it, and it is this—to draw one very important conclusion— it is this that distinguishes *conscious* artistic depiction from its *unconscious* counterpart in life: the former, if it wants to be effective, must supply sharp and complete outlines, while the latter, which need not persuade in order to be believed, and which can ultimately remain indifferent as to whether and how it is understood, can be satisfied with half measures, with ah and oh, with a glance or a gesture. Goethe's statement, which dared to touch upon the most dangerous secret of art, is frequently cited, but usually with reference only to what is called external form. The boy gazing at the most profound Bible verse will see only his good old acquaintances, the *twenty-four* letters with which it was expressed.

German drama seems to be taking new flight. What problem must it solve now? The question might seem strange, for the immediate answer would have to be: the same problem the theater has had to solve at all times. But one can ask further: should the theater take an active part in present affairs? Should it turn back to the past? Or should it concern itself with neither, that is, should it be social, historical, or philosophical? Respectable talents have already gone in these three directions. The *social* theme was taken up by Gutzkow.[1] We have four plays by him, and they make a more satisfactory impression in their entirety than individually; they are apparently correlates that illuminate the social condition in its heights and depths with sharp and cutting lights. *Richard Savage* shows what gallantry means if it combines natural inclination and respect for decorum; the crueler the better; the author was wrong to change the original conclusion, for its tragedy lay precisely in that neither the lady nor Richard could arrive at any real clarity concerning their closer relationship. *Werner* is the least satisfactory of the plays; it seems to have sprung more from a feeling than from an idea. The strength of *Patkul* lies precisely where one might search for its weakness, in the Elector's character and situation; it shows who is the most dependent person at the court, and it is equally valid whether the picture fits August the Strong or not. *The School of the Rich* teaches that the extremes of fortune and misfortune coincide in their impact on humanity.

Others have turned to the *historical* drama. Now, I believe, as I have pointed out above, that the true historical character of the drama never resides in its subject matter, and that a pure figment of the imagination, even a painting of an amorous scene, can be very historical if only the spirit of life breathes through it, keeping it fresh for posterity, which does not want to know what mental images we had of our grandfathers, but what we ourselves were like. What I mean by this is certainly not that poets should shape their dramatic works out of thin air; on the contrary, if history or legend offers them a useful point of departure, they should not spurn it out of some silly pride of independent invention, but make grateful use of it. I merely wish to contest the widespread folly that presumes the poet capable of giving something other than himself, other than his own life process; he cannot do so and need not do so, for if he is truly alive, if he does not willfully curl up in his petty little ego but allows the invisible elements that are in motion at all times, bringing forth new forms and characters, to stream through him, he may confidently follow the pull of his spirit and rest assured that in expressing his needs he will be expressing the needs of the world, and that in giving shape to his fantasies he is producing images of the future—all of which is quite compatible with his abstaining from personal participation in the struggles currently taking place in the street. For the poet, history is a vehicle for the embodiment of his views and ideas, but the poet is not, inversely, history's angel of resurrection; and as for German history in particular, Wienbarg, in his excellent essay on Uhland,[2] has very justly cast a doubt on our history's capacity to even serve as a vehicle. Those who understand me will find that my view is confirmed rather than refuted by Shakespeare and Aeschylus.

We also have *philosophical* dramas. Here everything depends on whether the metaphysics is derived from life or whether life is supposed to arise from metaphysics. In the first case, the result will be healthy, but it won't be an original genre; in the second case, the result will be a monstrosity.

Now, there is a fourth possibility, a drama that combines the characteristics of the various directions discussed here, and which therefore does not permit any one of them to stand out. Such a drama is the goal of my own aspirations, and if I have not explained my meaning sufficiently by my own attempts, by my *Judith* and my *Genoveva*, which is to appear in the near future, it would be foolish to make up for it with abstract expositions.

1843   *Translated by Joel Agee*

Notes

1. Karl Gutzkow (1811–1878), novelist and playwright.
2. Ludolf Wienbarg (1802–1872) and Ludwig Uhland (1787–1862), German writers.

FRIEDRICH HEBBEL, 1813–1863, poet, essayist, diarist, and most well known as writer of tragedies. Some of his plays are *Judith* (1839), *Maria Magdalena* (1843—"the first modern bourgeois tragedy"), *Herodes und Mariamne* (1847–1849), *Agnes Bernauer* (1851), and *Gyges und sein Ring* (1856).

Richard Wagner

From *The Art Work of the Future*

... On the stage, prepared by architect and painter, now steps
Artistic Man, as Natural Man steps on the stage of Nature. What
the statuary and the historical painter endeavored to limn on *stone*
or *canvas,* they now limn upon *themselves,* their form, their body's
limbs, the features of their visage, and raise it to the consciousness
of full artistic life. The same sense that led the sculptor in his grasp
and rendering of the human figure, now leads the *Mime* in the
handling and demeanor of his actual body. The same eye which
taught the historical painter, in drawing and in color, in arrangement
of his drapery and composition of his groups, to find the beautiful,
the graceful and the characteristic, now orders the whole breadth
of *actual human show.* Sculptor and painter once freed the Greek
Tragedian from his cothurnus and his mask, upon and under which
the real man could only move according to a certain religious
convention. With justice, did this pair of plastic artists annihilate
the last disfigurement of pure artistic man, and thus prefigure in
their stone and canvas the tragic Actor of the Future. As they once
descried him in his undistorted truth, they now shall let him pass
into reality and bring his form, in a measure sketched by them, to
bodily portrayal with all its wealth of movement.

Thus the illusion of plastic art will turn to truth in Drama: the
plastic artist will reach out hands to the *dancer,* to the *mime,* will
lose himself in them, and thus become himself both mime and
dancer. So far as lies within his power, he will have to impart the
inner man, his feeling and his willing to the eye. The breadth and
depth of scenic space belong to him for the plastic message of his

stature and his motion, as a single unit or in union with his fellows. But where his power ends, where the fulness of his will and feeling impels him to the uttering of the inner man by means of *Speech*, there will the Word proclaim his plain and conscious purpose: he becomes a *Poet* and, to be poet, a *tone-artist*. But as dancer, tone-artist, and poet, he still is one and the same thing: nothing other than *executant, artistic Man, who, in the fullest measure of his faculties, imparts himself to the highest expression of receptive power.*

It is in him, the immediate executant, that the three sister-arts unite their forces in one collective operation, in which the highest faculty of each comes to its highest unfolding. By working in common, each one of them attains the power to be and do the very thing which, of her own and inmost essence, she longs to do and be. Hereby: that each, where her own power ends, can be absorbed within the other, whose power commences where hers ends—she maintains her own purity and freedom, her independence as *that* which she is. The *mimetic dancer* is stripped of his impotence, so soon as he can sing and speak; the creations of *Tone* win all-explaining meaning through mime, as well as through the poet's word, and that exactly in degree as Tone itself is able to transcend into the motion of mime and the word of the poet; while the *Poet* first becomes a Man through his translation to the flesh and blood of the *Performer:* for though he metes to each artistic factor the guiding purpose which binds them all into a common whole, yet this purpose is first changed from "will" to "can" *by the poet's Will descending to the actor's Can.*

Not one rich faculty of the separate arts will remain unused in the United Artwork of the Future; in *it* will each attain its first complete appraisement. Thus, especially, will the manifold developments of Tone, so peculiar to our instrumental music, unfold their utmost wealth within this Artwork; nay, Tone will incite the mimetic art of Dance to entirely new discoveries, and no less swell the breath of Poetry to unimagined fill. For Music, in her solitude, has fashioned for herself an organ which is capable of the highest reaches of expression. This organ is the *Orchestra*. The tone-speech of Beethoven, introduced into Drama by the orchestra, marks an entirely fresh departure for the dramatic artwork. While Architecture and, more especially, scenic Landscape-painting have power to set the executant dramatic Artist in the surroundings of physical Nature, and to dower him from the exhaustless stores of natural phenomena with an ample and significant background, so in the Orchestra, that pulsing body of many-colored harmony, the personating individual Man is given, for his support, a stanchless elemental spring, at once artistic, natural, and human. . . .

But the individual man, in full possession of health of body, heart, and mind, can experience no higher need than that which is common to all his kind; for, to be a *true* Need, it can only be such an one as he can satisfy in Community alone. The most imperious and strongest need of full-fledged artist-man, however, is to impart himself in highest compass of his being to the fullest expression of Community; and this he only reaches with the necessary breadth of general understanding in the *Drama*. In Drama he broadens out his own particular being, by the portrayal of an individual personality not his own, to a universally human being. He must completely step outside himself, to grasp the inner nature of an alien personality with the completeness which is needful before he can portray it. This he will only attain when he so exhaustively analyzes this individual in his contact with and penetration and completion by other individualities—and therefore also the nature of these other individualities—when he forms thereof so lively a conception, that he gains a sympathetic feeling of this complementary influence on his own interior being. The perfectly artistic Performer is, therefore, the unit Man expended to the *essence of the Human Species* by the utmost evolution of his own particular nature.

The place in which this wondrous process comes to pass, is the *Theatric stage;* the collective art-work which it brings to light of day, the *Drama*. But to force his own specific nature to the highest blossoming of its contents in this *one* and highest art-work, the separate artist, like each several art, must quell each selfish, arbitrary bent toward untimely bushing into outgrowths unfurthersome to the whole; the better then to put forth all his strength for reaching of the highest common purpose, which cannot indeed be realised without the unit, nor, on the other hand, without the unit's recurrent limitation.

This purpose of the Drama, is withal the only true artistic purpose that even can be fully *realised;* whatsoever lies aloof from that, must necessarily lose itself in the sea of things indefinite, obscure, unfree. This purpose, however, the separate art-branch will never reach *alone,* but only *all together;* and therefore the most *universal* is at like time the only real, free, the only universally *intelligible* Art-work. . . .

Let us . . . first agree as to *whom* we must consider the creator of the Art-work of the Future; so that we may argue back from him to the life-conditions which alone can permit his art-work and himself to take their rise.

Who, then, will be the *Artist of the Future?*

Without a doubt, the Poet.

But *who* will be the Poet?

Indisputably the *Performer.*

Yet *who,* again will be the Performer?

Necessarily the *Fellowship of all the Artists.*

In order to see the Performer and the Poet take natural rise, we must first imagine to ourselves the artistic Fellowship of the future; and that according to no arbitrary canon, but following the logical course which we are bound to take in drawing from the Art-work itself our conclusions as to those artistic organs which alone can call it into natural life.

The Art-work of the Future is an associate work, and only an associate demand can call it forth. This demand, which we have hitherto merely treated theoretically, as a necessary essential of the being of each separate branch of art, is practically conceivable only in the *fellowship of every artist;* and the union of every artist, according to the exigencies of time and place, and for *one definite aim,* is that which forms this fellowship. This definite aim is the *Drama,* for which they all unite in order by their participation therein to unfold their own peculiar art to the acme of its being; in this unfoldment to permeate each other's essence, and as fruit thereof to generate the living, breathing, moving drama. But the thing that makes this sharing possible to all—nay that renders it necessary, and which without their cooperation can never come to manifestment—is the very kernel of the Drama, the *dramatic Action.*

The dramatic Action, as the first postulate of Drama, is withal that moment in the entire art-work which ensures its widest *understanding.* Directly borrowed from *Life,* past or present, it forms the intelligible bond that links this work therewith; exactly in degrees as it mirrors back the face of Life, and fitly satisfies its claim for understanding. The dramatic Action is thus *the bough from the Tree of Life* which, sprung therefrom by an unconscious instinct, has blossomed and shed its fruit obediently to vital laws, and now, dissevered from the stem, is *planted in the soil of Art;* there, in new, more beautiful, eternal life, to grow into the spreading tree which resembles fully in its inner, necessary force and truth the parent tree of actual Life. But now, become its "objectivation," it upholds to Life the picture of its own existence, and lifts unconscious Life to conscious knowledge of itself.

1849   *Translated by William Ashton Ellis*

WILHELM RICHARD WAGNER, 1813–1883, composer, writer, and poet. The influence of his operas and his theoretical writings on his contemporaries can hardly be overestimated, not only in music and the theater but also on men of letters such as Nietzsche and Thomas Mann.

Karl Marx

Letter to Ferdinand Lassalle

April 19, 1859

I am now coming to *Franz von Sickingen*.[1] In the first instance, I must praise the composition and action, and that is more than can be said of any other modern German drama. In the second instance, leaving aside the purely critical attitude to this work, it greatly excited me on first reading and it will therefore produce this effect in a still higher degree on readers who are governed more completely by their feelings. And this is a second and very important aspect.

Now the other side of the medal: *First*—this is a purely formal matter—now that you have written in verse, you might have polished up your iambs with a bit more artistry. But however much *professional poets* may be shocked by such carelessness I consider it on the whole as an advantage, since our brood of epigonous poets have nothing left but formal gloss. *Second:* The intended collision is not simply tragic but is really the tragic collision that spelled the doom, and properly so, of the revolutionary party of 1848–1849. I can therefore only most heartily welcome the idea of making it the pivotal point of a modern tragedy. But then I ask myself whether the theme you took is suitable for a presentation of this collision. Balthasar[2] may really imagine that if Sickingen had set up the banner of opposition to imperial power and open war against the princes instead of concealing his revolt behind a knightly feud, he would have been victorious. But can we subscribe to this illusion? Sickingen (and with him Hutten,[3] more or less) did not go under because of his cunning. He went under because as a *knight* and a *representative* of a *moribund class* he revolted against that which existed or rather against the new form of what existed. Strip Sickingen of his idiosyncracies and his particular training, natural bents, etc., and what is left is—Götz von Berlichingen.[4] Embodied in adequate form in that last-named *pitiable* fellow is the tragic contrast between knighthood on the one side and Kaiser and princes on the other; and that is why Goethe rightly made a hero of him. Insofar as Sickingen—and even Hutten himself to a certain extent, although with him, as with all ideologists of a class, such utterances should have been considerably modified— fights against the princes (after all, he takes the field against the Kaiser only because he transformed himself from a kaiser of the knights into a kaiser of the princes), he is in actual fact only a Don Quixote, although one historically justified. Beginning the revolt under color of a knightly feud means nothing else but beginning it in *knightly* fashion. Had he begun it otherwise he would have had to appeal directly and from the very beginning to the cities and peasants, i.e., precisely to the classes whose development was tantamount to the negation of the knighthood.

Therefore, if you did not want to reduce the collision to that presented in *Götz von Berlichingen*—and that was not your plan— then Sickingen and Hutten had to succumb because they imagined they were revolutionaries (the latter cannot be said of Götz) and, just like the *educated* Polish nobility of 1830, on the one hand, made themselves exponents of modern ideas, while on the other they actually represented the interests of a reactionary class.[5] The *noble* representatives of the revolution—behind whose watch-words of unity and liberty there still lurked the dreams of the old empire and of club-law—ought not, in that case, to have absorbed all interest, as they do in your play, but the representatives of the peasants (particularly these) and of the revolutionary elements in the cities should have formed a quite important active background. You could than have had the most modern ideas voiced in their most naïve form and to a much greater extent, whereas now, besides *religious* freedom, civil *unity* actually remains the main idea. You would then have had to *Shakespearize* more of your own accord, while I chalk up against you as your gravest short-coming your *Schillering*, your transforming of individuals into mere speaking tubes of the spirit of time. Did you not yourself to a certain extent fall into the diplomatic error, like your Franz von

Sickingen, of placing the Lutheran-knightly opposition above the plebian Muncerian opposition? . . .

Translated by I. Lasker

Translator's Notes

1. A play by Lassalle. Sickingen (1481–1523) was a German knight who joined the Reformation movement and led a revolt of knights in 1522–1523.
2. A character in Lassalle's play, Sler Balthasar was a friend and adviser of Sickingen; he participated in the peasant rebellion in Germany in 1525.
3. Ulrich von Hutten (1488–1523), a supporter of the Reformation and together with Sickingen a leader of the knights during their 1522–1523 revolt.
4. A German knight, Götz von Berlichingen (1480–1562) joined the 1525 peasant rebellion but betrayed the peasants. He is the title character of a play by Goethe (1773).
5. This refers to the Polish uprising against czarist rule which began in November 1830. The leadership of the rising was mainly in the hands of the Polish nobility. Since the noblemen refused to comply with the demands of the peasants to abolish serfdom, they were unable to gain the support of the peasant masses. This led to the defeat of the rising, which was cruelly put down by the czarist government.
6. Reference to Martin Luther (1483–1546), who condemned the peasant rebellion, and to the theologian Thomas Münzer (1489–1525), who sided with the rebellious peasants and was executed.

KARL HEINRICH MARX, 1818–1883, social philosopher and chief theorist of modern socialism and communism. He published a number of writings with Friedrich Engels, including the *Communist Manifesto*. Expelled from Prussia, he settled in London in 1849. Ferdinand Lassalle (1825–1864) was a German socialist, later to be criticized by Marx and Engels. In 1863 Lassalle founded what was to become the German Socialist Party (SPD).

Friedrich Engels

Letter to Ferdinand Lassalle

May 18, 1859

... Now as far as the historical content[1] is concerned, you have depicted with great clarity and justified reference to subsequent developments the two sides of the movement of that time which were of greatest interest to you: the national movement of the nobility, represented by Sickingen, and the humanistic-theoretical movement with its further development in the theological and ecclesiastical sphere, the Reformation. What I like most here is the scene between Sickingen and the Kaiser and that between the legate and the archbishop of Treves. (Here you succeeded in producing a fine specimen of character drawing—a contrast between the esthetically and classically educated and politically and theoretically foreseeing legate, a man of the world, and the narrowminded German priest-prince—a portrayal which all the same follows directly from the *representative* nature of the two characters.) The pen picture in the Sickingen-Karl scene is also very striking. In Hutten's autobiography, whose *content* you rightly described as essential, you certainly picked a desperate means of working these facts into the drama. Of great importance is also the talk between Balthasar and Franz in Act V, in which the former expounds to his master the *really revolutionary* policy he should have followed. It is here that the really tragic manifests itself; and it seems to me that just because of the significance that attaches to this fact it should have been emphasized somewhat more strongly already in Act III, where there are several convenient places. But I am again lapsing into minor matters.

The position of the cities and the princes of that time is also set forth on several occasions with great clarity and thus the *official* elements, so to speak, of the contemporary movement are fairly well accounted for. But it seems to me that you have not laid due stress upon the nonofficial, the plebeian and peasant, elements and their concomitant representatives in the field of theory. The peasant movement was in its way just as national and just as much opposed to the princes as was that of the nobility, and the colossal dimensions of the struggle in which it succumbed contrast very strongly with the frivolous way in which the nobility, leaving Sickingen in the lurch, resigned itself to its historical calling, that of lickspittles. It seems to me, therefore, that also in your conception of the drama which, as you will have seen, is somewhat too abstract, not realistic enough for me, the peasant movement deserved closer attention. While the peasant scene with Fritz Joss[2] is, true enough, characteristic and the individuality of this "agitator" presented very correctly, it does not depict with sufficient force the movement of the peasantry, as opposed to that of the nobility, which already at that time was a swelling torrent. In accordance with *my* view of the drama, which consists in not forgetting the realistic for the idealistic, Shakespeare for Schiller, the inclusion of the sphere of the so superbly variegated plebeian society of that day would have supplied, in addition, quite other material for enlivening the drama, a priceless background for the national movement of the nobility playing in the foreground, and would have set this movement in the proper light. What wonderfully expressive types were produced by this period of the dissolution of feudal bonds as illustrated by the roaming beggar kings, breadless *lansquenets* and adventurers of every description—a Falstaffian background which in an historical drama of *this* kind would have even greater effect than it did in Shakespeare! But apart from this, it seems to me that this relegation of the peasant movement to the rear is precisely the point that erroneously induced you, I believe, to misrepresent also the national movement of the nobility in one respect and at the same time to allow the *really* tragic element in Sickingen's fate to escape you. As I see it, the mass of the nobility directly subject at that time to the emperor had no intention of concluding an alliance with the peasantry. The dependence of their income on the oppressing of the latter did not permit this. An alliance with the cities would have been more feasible. But no such alliance was effected, or was effected only to a very limited extent. But a national revolution of the nobility could have been accomplished only by means of an alliance with the townsmen and the peasants, particularly the latter. Precisely herein lies, in my opinion, the whole tragedy of the thing, that this fundamental condition, the alliance with the peasantry, was impossible, that the policy of the nobility had therefore to be a petty one, that at the very moment when it wanted to take the lead of the national movement, the *mass* of the nation, the peasants, protested against its leadership and it thus necessarily had to collapse. I am unable to judge to what extent your assumption that Sickingen really did have some connection with the peasants has any basis in history. Anyhow, that is wholly immaterial. Moreover, as far as I remember, wherever Hutten in his writings addresses the peasants, he just lightly touches on this ticklish question concerning the nobility and seeks to focus the wrath of the peasants on the priests. But I do not in the least dispute your right to depict Sickingen and Hutten as having intended to emancipate the peasants. However, this put you at once up against the tragic contradiction that both of them were placed between the nobles, who were decidedly *against* this, and the peasants. Here, I dare say, lay the tragic collision between the historically necessary postulate and the practically impossible execution. By ignoring this aspect you reduce the tragic conflict to smaller dimensions, namely, that Sickingen, instead of at once tackling emperor and empire, tackled only a prince (although here too you tactfully bring in the peasants) and you simply let him perish from the indifference and cowardice of the nobility. Their cowardice would, however, have been motivated quite differently if you had previously brought out more emphatically the rumbling movement of the peasantry and the mood of the nobility, become decidedly more conservative on account of the former "Union Shoes" and "Poor Konrad."[3] However, all this is only *one* way in which the peasant and plebeian movement could have been included in the drama. At least ten other ways of doing this just as well or better are conceivable. . . .

Translated by I. Lasker

Translator's Notes

1. Engels refers to Lassalle's play *Franz von Sickingen*. See the notes to Marx's letter to Lassalle in the previous section.
2. Fritz Joss (?–c. 1517) organized secret peasant societies in Germany in the early sixteenth century.
3. *Bundschuh,* a kind of shoe worn by peasants in the Middle Ages, and *Armer Konrad,* Poor Konrad, names of secret peasants' confederations, whose activities prepared the ground in Germany for the Peasants' War of 1525.

FRIEDRICH ENGELS 1820–1895, philosopher and industrialist, life-long friend, supporter, and collaborator of Karl Marx.

Gustav Freytag

From *Technique of the Drama*

What Is Dramatic?

The dramatic includes those emotions of the soul which steel themselves to will, and to do, and those emotions of the soul which are aroused by a deed or course of action; also the inner processes which man experiences from the first glow of perception to passionate desire and action, as well as the influences which one's own and others' deeds exert upon the soul; also the rushing forth of will power from the depths of man's soul toward the external world, and the influx of fashioning influences from the outer world into man's inmost being; also the coming into being of a deed, and its consequences on the human soul.

An action, in itself, is not dramatic. Passionate feeling, in itself, is not dramatic. Not the presentation of a passion for itself, but of a passion which leads to action is the business of dramatic art; not the presentation of an event for itself, but for its effect on a human soul is the dramatist's mission. The exposition of passionate emotions as such, is in the province of the lyric poet; the depicting of thrilling events is the task of the epic poet.

The two ways in which the dramatic expresses itself are, of course, not fundamentally different. Even while a man is under stress, and laboring to turn his inmost soul toward the external, his surroundings exert a stimulating or repressing influence on his passionate emotions. And, again, while what has been done exerts a reflex influence upon him, he does not remain merely receptive, but gains new impulses and transformations. Yet, there is a difference in these closely connected processes. The first, the inward struggle of man toward a deed, has always the highest charm. The second stimulates to more external emotion, a more violent co-operation of different forces; almost all that satisfied curiosity belongs to this; and yet, however indispensable it is to the drama, it is principally a satisfying of excited suspense; and the impatience of the hearer, if he has creative power, easily runs in advance, seeking a new vehement agitation in the soul of the hero. What is occurring chains the attention most, not what, as a thing of the past, has excited wonder.

Since the dramatic art presents men as their inmost being exerts an influence on the external, or as they are affected by external influences, it must logically use the means by which it can make intelligible to the auditor these processes of man's nature. These means are speech, tone, gesture. It must bring forward its characters as speaking, singing, gesticulating. Poetry uses also as accessories in her representations, music and scenic art. . . .

Unity of Action

By *action* is meant, an event or occurrence, arranged according to a controlling idea, and having its meaning made apparent by the characters. It is composed of many elements, and consists in a number of dramatic efficients *(momente)*, which become effective one after the other, according to a regular arrangement. The action of the serious drama must possess the following qualities:

It must present complete unity.

This celebrated law has undergone a very different application with the Greeks and Romans, with the Spanish and French, with Shakespeare and the Germans, which has been occasioned partly by those learned in art, partly by the character of the stage. The restriction of its claims through the French classics, and the strife of the Germans with the three unities, of place, of time, and of action, have for us only a literary-historical interest. . . .

From this indispensable introduction, the beginning of the im-passioned action must arise, like the first notes of a melody from the introductory chords. This first stir of excitement, this stimulating impulse, is of great importance for the effect of the drama, and will be discussed later. The end of the action must, also, appear as the intelligible and inevitable result of the entire course of the action, the conjunction of forces; and right here, the inherent necessity must be keenly felt; the close must, however, represent the complete termination of the strife and excited conflicts.

Within these limits, the action must move forward with uniform consistency. This internal consistency is produced by representing an event which follows another, as an effect of which that other is the evident cause. Let that which occasions, be the logical cause of occurrences, and the new scenes and events will be conceived as probable, and generally understood results of previous actions. Or let that which is to produce an effect, be a generally comprehensible peculiarity of a character already made known. If it is unavoidable that, during the course of events, new incidents appear, unexpected to the auditor, or very surprising, these must be explained imperceptibly, but perfectly, through what has preceded. This laying the foundation of the drama is called, assigning the motive *(motivieren)*. Through the motives, the elements of the action are bound into an artistic, connected whole. This binding together of incidents by the free creation of a causative connection, is the distinguishing characteristic of this species of art. Through this linking together of incidents, dramatic idealization is effected. . . .

The poet's interest in the characters of his counter-players easily mounts so high that to them is accorded a rich, detailed portrayal, a sympathetic exposition of their striving and their fighting moods, and a peculiar destiny. Thereby arises a double action for the drama; or the action of the piece may be of such a nature as to require for its illumination and completion a subordinate action, which through the exposition of concurrent or opposing relations brings into greater prominence the chief persons, with what they do and what they suffer.

Various defects—especially one-sidedness—in material, may make such a completion desirable. One play is not to run through the whole wide range of affecting and thrilling moods; it is not to play from its sober ground color, through all the possible color-tones; but a variation in mood and modest contrasts in color are as necessary to the drama as it is that in a painting in which there are many figures, the swing of the lesser lines should be in contrast with the greater lines and groups, and that in contrast with the ground color, use should be made of dependent, supplementary colors.

If, for this reason, the Greeks classed their plays into those with single action, and those with double action, the modern drama has much less avoided the extension of counter-play into an accessory action. The interweaving of this with the main action has occurred sometimes at the expense of the combined effect. The Germans, especially, who are always inclined, during their labor, to grasp the significance of the accessory persons with great ardor, must guard themselves against too wide an extension of the subordinate action. Even Shakespeare has occasionally, in this way, injured the effect of the drama, most strikingly in *Lear,* in which the whole parallel action of the house of Gloucester, but loosely connected with the main action, and treated with no particular fondness, retards the movement, and needlessly renders the whole more bitter. The poet allowed the episodes in both parts of *Henry IV,* to develop into an accessory action, the immortal humor of which outshines the serious effect of the play; and this had made these dramas favorites of the reader. Every admirer of Falstaff will grant, however, that the general effect on the stage has not the corresponding power, in spite of this charm. Let it be noticed, in passing, that in Shakespeare's comedies the double action belongs to the nature of the play; he strives to take from his clowns the episodical, while he interweaves them with the serious action. The genial humor which beams from their scenes must sometimes conceal the harder elements in the material; as when the constables must help to prevent the sad fate threatening the hero. Among German poets, Schiller was most in danger of injury from the double action. The disproportion of the accessory action in *Don Carlos* and *Mary Stuart* rests upon this, that his ardor for the character set in contrast to the hero, becomes too great; in *Wallenstein,* the same principle has extended the piece to a trilogy. In *Tell,* three actions run parallel.

It is the business of the action to represent to us the inner consistency of the event, as it corresponds to the demands of the intellect and the heart. Whatever, in the crude material, does not serve this purpose, the poet is in duty bound to throw away. And it is desirable that he adhere strictly to this principle, to give only what is indispensable to unity. Yet he may not avoid a deviation from this; for there will be occasional deviations desirable which may strengthen the color of the piece, in a manner conformable to its purpose; which may intensify the meaning of the characters, and enhance the general effect by the introduction of a new color, or a contrast. These embellishing additions of the poet are called episodes. They are of various kinds. At a point where the action suffers a short pause, a characterizing moment may be enlarged into a situation; opportunity may be given a hero to exhibit some significant characteristic of his being in an attractive manner, in connection with some subordinate person; some subordinate role of the piece may, through ampler elaboration, be developed into an attractive figure. By a modest use, which must not take time from what is more important, these may become an embellishment to the drama. And the poet has to treat them as ornaments, and to compensate for them with serious work, if they ever retard the action. The episodes perform different duties, according to the parts of the drama in which they appear. While at the beginning they enter into the roles of the chief persons to delineate these in their idiosyncrasies, they are allowed in the last part as enlargements of those new roles which afford lesser aides to the movement of the action; in each place, however, they must be felt to be advantageous additions.

Movement and Rise of the Action

The dramatic action must represent all that is important to the understanding of the play, in the strong excitement of the characters, and in a continuously progressive increase of effects.

The action must, first of all, be capable of the strongest dramatic excitement; and this must be universally intelligible. There are great and important fields of human activity, which do not make the growth of a captivating emotion, a passionate desire, or a mighty volition easy; and again, there are violent struggles which force to the outside men's mental processes, while the subject of the struggle is little adapted to the stage, though importance and greatness are not lacking to it. For example, a politic prince, who negotiates with the powerful ones of his land, who wages war and concludes peace with his neighbors, will perhaps do all this without once exhibiting the least excited passion; and if this does come to light as secret desire or resentment toward others, it will be noticeable only by careful observation, and in little ripples. But even when it is allowed to represent his whole being in dramatic suspense, the subject of his volition, a political success or a victory, is capable of being shown only very imperfectly and fragmentarily in its stage setting. And the scenes in which this round of worldly purposes is specially active, state trials, addresses, battles, are for technical reasons not the part most conveniently put on the stage. From this point of view, warning must be given against putting scenes from political history on the boards. Of course the difficulties which this field of the greatest human activity offers, are not unsurmountable; but it requires not only maturity of genius but very peculiar and intimate knowledge of the stage to overcome them. But the poet will never degrade his action by reducing it to an imperfect and insufficient exposition of such political deeds and aims; he will need to make use of a single action, or a small number of actions, as a background, before which he presents—and in this he is infinitely superior to the historian—a most minute revelation of human nature, in a few personages, and in their most intimate emotional relations with each other. If he fails to do this, he will in so far falsify history without creating poetry.

An entirely unfavorable field for dramatic material is the inward struggles which the inventor, the artist, the thinker has to suffer with himself and with his time. Even if he is a reformer by nature, who knows how to impress the stamp of his own spirit on thousands of others; indeed, if his own material misfortunes may lay claim to unusual sympathy, the dramatist will not willingly conclude to bring him forward as the hero of the action. If the mental efforts, the mode of thought of such a hero, are not sufficiently known to the living audience, then the poet will have first to show his warrant for such a character by artful discourse, by a fulness of oral explanation, and by a representation of spiritual import. This may be quite as difficult as it is undramatic. If the poet presupposes in his auditors a living interest in such personages, acquaintance with the incidents of their lives, and makes use of this interest in order to avail himself of an occurrence in the life of such a hero, he falls into another danger. On the stage the good which is known beforehand of a man, and the good that is reported of him, have no value at all, as opposed to what the hero himself does on the stage. Indeed, the great expectations which the hearer brings with him in this case, may be prejudicial to the unbiased reception of the action. And if the poet succeeds, as is probable in the case of popular heroes, in promoting the scenic effects through the already awakened ardor of the audience for the hero, he must credit his success to the interest which the audience brings with it, not to the interest which the drama itself has merited. If the poet is conscientious, he will adopt only those moments from the life of the artist, poet, thinker, in which he shows himself active and suffering quite as significantly toward others as he was in his studio. It is clear that this will be the case only by accident; it is quite as clear that in such a case it will be only an accident, if the hero bears a celebrated name. Therefore, the making use of anecdotes from the life of such great men, the meaning of which does not show itself in the action but in the non-representable activity of their laboratory, is intrinsically right undramatic. The greatness in them is non-representable; and what is represented borrows the greatness of the hero from a moment of his life lying outside the piece. The personality of Shakespeare, Goethe, Schiller, is in this respect worse on the stage than in a novel or romance, and all the worse the more intimately their lives are known. . . .

The Construction of the Drama

Play and Counterplay

In an action, through characters, by means of words, tones, gestures, the drama presents those soul-processes which man experiences from the flashing up of an idea, to passionate desire and to a deed, as well as those inward emotions which are excited by his own deeds and those of others.

The structure of the drama must show these two contrasted elements of the dramatic joined in a unity, efflux and influx of will-power, the accomplishment of a deed and its reaction on the soul, movement and counter-movement, strife and counter-strife, rising and sinking, binding and loosing.

In every part of the drama, both tendencies of dramatic life appear, each incessantly challenging the other to its best in play and counter-play; but in general, also, the action of the drama and the grouping of characters is, through these tendencies, in two parts. What the drama presents is always a struggle, which, with strong perturbations of soul, the hero wages against opposing forces. And as the hero must be endowed with a strong life, with a certain one-sidedness, and be in embarrassment, the opposing power must be made visible in a human representative.

It is quite indifferent in favor of which of the contending parties the greater degree of justice lies, whether a character or his adversary is better-mannered, more favored by law, embodies more of the traditions of the time, possesses more of the ethical spirit of the poet; in both groups, good and evil, power and weakness, are variously mingled. But both must be endowed with what is universally, intelligibly human. The chief hero must always stand in strong contrast with his opponents; the advantage which he wins for himself, must be the greater, so much the greater the more perfectly the final outcome of the struggle shows him to be vanquished.

These two chief parts of the drama are firmly united by a point of the action which lies directly in the middle. This middle, the climax of the play, is the most important place of the structure; the action rises to this; the action falls away from this. It is now decisive for the character of the drama which of the two refractions of the dramatic light shall have a place in the first part of the play, which shall fall in the second part as the dominating influence; whether the efflux or influx, the play or the counter-play, maintains the first part. Either is allowed; either arrangement of the structure can cite plays of the highest merit in justification of itself. And these two ways of constructing a drama have become characteristic of individual poets and of the time in which they lived.

By one dramatic arrangement, the chief person, the hero, is so introduced that his nature and his characteristics speak out unembarrassed, even to the moments when, as a consequence of external impulse or internal association of ideas in him, the beginning of a powerful feeling or volition becomes perceptible. The inner commotion, the passionate eagerness, the desire of the hero, increases; new circumstances, stimulating or restraining, intensify his embarrassment and his struggle; the chief character strides victoriously forward to an unrestrained exhibition of his life, in which the full force of his feeling and his will are concentrated in a deed by which the spiritual tension is relaxed. From this point there is a turn in the action; the hero appeared up to this point in a desire, one-sided or full of consequence, working from within outward, changing by its own force the life relations in which he came upon the stage. From the climax on, what he has done reacts upon himself and gains power over him; the external world, which he conquered in the rise of passionate conflict, now stands in the strife above him. This adverse influence becomes continually more powerful and victorious, until at last in the final catastrophe, it compels the hero to succumb to its irresistible force. The end of the piece follows this catastrophe immediately, the situation where the restoration of peace and quite after strife becomes apparent.

With this arrangement, first the inception and progress of the action is seen, then the effects of the reaction; the character of the first part is determined by the depths of the hero's exacting claims; the second by the counter-claims which the violently disturbed surroundings put forward. This is the construction of *Antigone,* of *Ajax,*[1] of all of Shakespeare's great tragedies except *Othello* and *King Lear,* of *The Maid of Orleans,* less surely of the double tragedy, *Wallenstein.*[2]

The other dramatic arrangement, on the contrary, represents the hero at the beginning, in comparative quiet, among conditions of life which suggest the influence of some external forces upon his mind. These forces, adverse influences, work with increased activity so long in the hero's soul, that at the climax, they have brought him into ominous embarrassment, from which, under a stress of passion, desire, activity, he plunges downward to the catastrophe.

This construction makes use of opposing characters, in order to give motive to the strong excitement of the chief character; the relation of the chief figures to the idea of the drama is an entirely different one; they do not give direction in the ascending action, but are themselves directed. Examples of this construction are *King Oedipus, Othello, Lear, Emilia Galotti, Clavigo, Love and Intrigue.*[3]

It might appear that this second method of dramatic construction must be the more effective. Gradually, in a specially careful performance, one sees the conflicts through which the life of the hero is disturbed, give direction to his inward being. Just there, where the hearer demands a powerful intensifying of effects, the previously prepared domination of the chief characters enters; suspense and sympathy, which are more difficult to sustain in the last half of the play, are firmly fixed upon the chief characters; the stormy and irresistible progress downward is particularly favorable to powerful and thrilling effects. And, indeed, subjects which contain the gradual rise and growth of a portentous passion which in the end leads the hero to his destruction, are exceedingly favorable for such an action.

But this method of constructing a play is not the most correct, dramatically; and it is no accident, that the greatest dramas of such a character, at the tragic close, intermingle with the emotions and perturbations of the hearer, an irritating feeling which lessens the joy and recreation. For they do not specially show the hero as an active, aggressive nature, but as a receptive, suffering person, who is too much compelled by the counter-play, which strikes him from without. The greatest exercise of human power, that which carries with it the heart of the spectator most irresistibly, is, in all times, the bold individuality which sets its own inner self, without regard to consequences, over against the forces which surround it. The essential nature of the drama is conflict and suspense; the sooner these are evoked by means of the chief heroes themselves and given direction, the better.

It is true, the first kind of dramatic structure conceals a danger, which even by genius, is not always successfully avoided. In this, as a rule, the first part of the play, which raises the hero through regular degrees of commotion to the climax, is assured its success. But the second half, in which greater effects are demanded, depends mostly on the counter-play; and this counter-play must here be grounded in more violent movement and have comparatively greater authorization. This may distract attention rather than attract it more forcibly. It must be added, that after the climax of the action, the hero must seem weaker than the counteracting figures. Moreover, on this account, the interest in him may be lessened. Yet in spite of this difficulty, the poet need be in no doubt to which kind of arrangement to give the preference. His task will be greater in this arrangement; great art is required to make the last act strong. But talent and good fortune must overcome the difficulties. And the most beautiful garlands which dramatic art has to confer, fall upon the successful work. Of course the poet is dependent on his subject and material, which sometimes leaves no choice. Therefore, one of the first questions a poet must ask, when contemplating attractive material, is "does it come forward in the play or in the counterplay?"

Five Parts and Three Crises of the Drama

Through the two halves of the action which come closely together at one point, the drama possesses—if one may symbolize its arrangement by lines—a pyramidal structure. It rises from the *introduction* with the entrance of the exciting forces to the *climax*, and falls from here to the *catastrophe*. Between these three parts lie (the parts of) the *rise* and *fall*. Each of these five parts may consist of a single scene, or a succession of connected scenes, but the climax is usually composed of one chief scene.

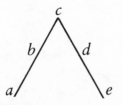

These parts of the drama, *(a)* introduction, *(b)* rise, *(c)* climax, *(d)* return or fall, *(e)* catastrophe, have each what is peculiar in purpose and in construction. Between them stand three important scenic effects, through which the parts are separated as well as bound together. Of these three dramatic moments, or crises, one, which indicates the beginning of the stirring action, stands between the introduction and the rise; the second, the beginning of the counter-action, between the climax and the return; the third, which must rise once more before the catastrophe, between the return and the catastrophe. They are called here the exciting moment or force, the tragic moment or force, and the moment or force of the last suspense. The operation of the first is necessary to every play; the second and third are good but not indispensable accessories. In the following sections, therefore, the eight component parts of the drama will be discussed in their natural order.

The Introduction. It was the custom of the ancients to communicate in a prologue, what was presupposed for the action. The prologue of Sophocles and also of Aeschylus is a thoroughly necessary and essential part of the action, having dramatic life and connection, and corresponding exactly to our opening scene; and in the old stage-management signification of the word, it comprised that part of the action which lay before the entrance song of the chorus. In Euripides, it is, by a careless return to the older custom, an epic messenger announcement, which a masked figure delivers to the audience, a figure who never once appears in the play,—like Aphrodite in *Hyppolitus* and the ghost of the slain Polydorus in *Hecuba*. In Shakespeare, the prologue is entirely severed from the action; it is only an address of the poet; it contains civility, apology, and the plea for attention. Since it is no longer necessary to plead for quiet and attention, the German stage has purposely given up the prologue, but allows it as a festive greeting which distinguishes a single representation, or as the chance caprice of a poet. In Shakespeare, as with us, the introduction has come back again into the right place; it is filled with dramatic movement, and has become an organic part of the dramatic structure. Yet, in individual cases, the newer stage has not been able to resist another temptation, to expand the introduction to a situation scene, and set it in advance as a special prelude to the drama. Well-known examples are *The Maid of Orleans* and *Kätchen of Heilbronn, Wallenstein's Camp,* and the most beautiful of all prologues, that to *Faust.* . . . [4]

Since it is the business of the introduction of the drama to explain the place and time of the action, the nationality and life relations of the hero, it must at once briefly characterize the environment. Besides, the poet will have opportunity here, as in a short overture, to indicate the peculiar mood of the piece, as well as the time, the greater vehemence or quiet with which the action moves forward. . . .

If Shakespeare and the Germans of the earlier times,—*Sara Sampson,*[5] *Clavigo*—have not avoided the changing of scenes in the introduction, their example is not to be imitated on our stage. The exposition should be kept free from anything distracting; its task, to prepare for the action, it best accomplishes if it so proceeds that the first short introductory chord is followed by a well-executed scene which by a quick transition is connected with the following scene containing the exciting force. *Julius Caesar, Mary Stuart,*[6] *Wallenstein,* are excellent examples in this direction.

The difficulty of giving also to the representative of the counter-play a place in the introduction, is not insurmountable. In the arrangement of scenes, at least, the poet must feel the full mastery of his material; and it is generally an embarrassment of his power of imagination when this seems impossible to him. However, should the fitting of the counter-party into the exposition be impracticable, there is always still time enough to bring them forward in the first scenes of the involution.

Without forcing all possible cases into the same uniform mould, therefore, the poet may hold firmly to this: the construction of a regular introduction is as follows: a clearly defining keynote, a finished scene, a short transition into the first moment of the excited action.

The Exciting Force. The beginning of the excited action (complication) occurs at a point where, in the soul of the hero, there arises a feeling or volition which becomes the occasion of what follows; or where the counter-play resolves to use its lever to set the hero in motion. Manifestly, this impelling force will come forward more significantly in those plays in which the chief actor governs the first half by his force of will; but in any arrangement, it remains an important motive force for the action. In *Julius Caesar,* this impelling force is the thought of killing Caesar, which, by the conversation with Cassius, gradually becomes fixed in the soul of Brutus. In *Othello,* it comes into play after the stormy night-scene of the exposition, by means of the second conference between Iago and Roderigo, with the agreement to separate the Moor and Desdemona. In *Richard III.,* on the contrary, it rises in the very beginning of the piece along with the exposition, and as a matured plan in the soul of the hero. In both cases, its position helps to fix the character of the piece; in *Othello,* where the counter-play leads at the conclusion of a long introduction; in *Richard III.,* where the villain alone rules in the first scene. In *Romeo and Juliet,* this occasioning motive comes to the soul of the hero in the interview with Benvolio, as the determination to be present at the masked ball; and immediately before this scene, there runs as parallel scene, the conversation between Paris and Capulet, which determines the fate of Juliet; both scenic moments, in such significant juxtaposition, form together the compelling force of this drama, which has two heroes, the two lovers. In *Emilia Galotti,* it sinks into the soul of the prince, as he receives the announcement of the impending marriage of the heroine; in *Clavigo,* it is the arrival of Beaumarchais at his sister's; in *Mary Stuart,* it is the confession which Mortimer makes to the queen. . . .

From the examples cited, it is evident that this force of the action treads the stage under very diverse forms. It may fill a complete scene; it may be comprised in a few words. It must not always press from without into the soul of the hero or his adversary; it may be, also, a thought, a wish, a resolution, which by a succession of representations may be allured from the soul of the hero himself. But it always forms the transition from the introduction to the ascending action, either entering suddenly, like Mortimer's declaration in *Mary Stuart,* and the rescue of Baumgarten in *William Tell,*[7] or gradually developing through the speeches and mental processes of the characters, like Brutus's resolve to do the murder, where in no place in the dialogue the fearful words are pronounced, but the significance of the scene is emphasized by the suspicion which Caesar, entering meantime, expresses.

Yet is is for the worker to notice, that this force seldom admits of great elaboration. Its place is at the beginning of the piece, where powerful pressure upon the hearer is neither necessary nor advisable. It has the character of a motive which gives direction and preparation, and does not offer a single resting-place. It must not be insignificant; but it must not be so strong that, according to the feeling of the audience, it takes too much from what follows, or that the suspense which it causes, may modify, or perhaps determine, the fate of the hero. Hamlet's suspicion can not be raised to unconditional certainty by the revelation of the ghost, or the course of the piece must be entirely different. The resolution of Cassius and Brutus must not come out in distinct words, in order that Brutus's following consideration of the matter, and the administration of the oath, may seem a progress. The poet will, probably, sometimes have to moderate the importance attached to this force, which has made it too conspicuous. But he must always bring it into operation as soon as possible; for only from its introduction forward does earnest dramatic work begin.

A convenient arrangement for our stage is to give the exciting force in a temperate scene after the introduction, and closely join to this the first following rising movement, in greater elaboration. *Mary Stuart,* for example, is of this regular structure.

The Rising Movement. The action has been started; the chief persons have shown what they are; the interest has been awakened. Mood, passion, involution have received an impulse in a given direction. In the modern drama of three hours, they are not insignificant parts, which belong to this ascent. Its arrangement has comparatively little significance. The following are the general rules:

If it has not been possible to accord a place in what has gone before, to the most important persons in the counter-play, or to the chief groups, a place must be made for them now, and opportunity must be given for an activity full of meaning. Such persons, too, as are of importance in the last half, must eagerly desire now to make themselves known to the audience. Whether the ascent is made by one or several stages to the climax, depends on material and treatment. In any case, a resting place in the action, and even in the structure of a scene, is to be so expressed that the dramatic moments, acts, scenes, which belong to the same division of the action, are joined together so as to produce a unified chief scene, subordinate scene, connecting scene. In *Julius Caesar,* for instance, the ascent, from the moment of excitation to the climax, consists of only one stage, the conspiracy. This makes, with the preparatory scene, and the scene of the contrast belonging to it, an attractive scene-group very beautifully constructed, even according to the demands of our stage; and with this group, those scenes are closely joined which are grouped about the murder-scene, the climax of the play. On the other hand, the rising movement in *Romeo and Juliet,* runs through four stages to the climax. The structure of this ascending group is as follows. First stage: masked ball; three parts, two preparatory scenes (Juliet with her mother, and nurse) (Romeo and his companions); and one chief scene (the ball itself, consisting of one suggestion—conversation of the servants—and four forces—Capulet stirring up matters; Tybalt's rage and setting things to rights; conversation of the lovers; Juliet and the nurse as conclusion). Second stage: The garden scene; short preparatory scene (Benvolio and Mercutio seeking Romeo) and the great chief scene (the lovers determining upon marriage). Third stage: The marriage; four parts; first scene, Lorenzo and Romeo; second scene, Romeo and companions, and nurse as messenger; third scene, Juliet, and nurse as messenger; fourth scene, Lorenzo and the lovers, and the marriage. Fourth stage: Tybalt's death, fighting scene.

Then follows the group of scenes forming the climax, beginning with Juliet's words, "Gallop apace you fiery footed steeds," and extending to Romeo's farewell, "It were a grief, so brief to part with thee; farewell." In the four stages of the rise, one must notice the different structure of individual scenes. In the masked ball, little scenes are connected in quick succession to the close; the garden scene is the elaborate great scene of the lovers; in beautiful contrast with this, in the marriage scene-group, the accomplice, Lorenzo, and the nurse are kept in the foreground, the lovers are concealed. Tybalt's death is the strong break which separates the aggregate rise from the climax; the scenes of this part have a loftier swing, a more passionate movement. The arrangement of the piece is very careful; the progress of both heroes and their motives are specially laid for each in every two adjoining scenes with parallel course.

This same kind of rise, slower, with less frequently changing scenes, is common with the Germans. In *Love and Intrigue,* for example, the exciting force of the play is the announcement of Wurm to his father that Ferdinand loves the daughter of the musician. From here the piece rises in counterplay through four stages. First stage: (the father demands the marriage with Milford) in two scenes; preparatory scene (he has the betrothal announced through Kalb); chief scene (he compels the son to visit Milford). Second stage: (Ferdinand and Milford) two preparatory scenes; great chief scene (the lady insists on marrying him). Third stage: Two preparatory scenes; great chief scene (the president will put Louise under arrest, Ferdinand resists). Fourth stage: Two scenes (plan of the president with the letter, and the plot of the villains). The climax follows this: Chief scene, the composition of the letter. This piece also has the peculiarity of having two heroes—the two lovers.

The import of the play is, it must be owned, painful; but the construction is, with some awkwardness in the order of scenes, still, on the whole, regular, and worthy of special consideration, because it is produced far more through the correct feeling of the young poet, than through a sure technique.

As to the scenes of this rising movement, it may be said, they have to produce a progressive intensity of interest; they must, therefore, not only evince progress in their import, but they must show an enlargement in form and treatment, and, indeed, with variation and shading in execution; if several steps are necessary, the next to the last, or the last, must preserve the character of a chief scene.

The Climax. The climax of the drama is the place in the piece where the results of the rising movement come out strong and decisively; it is almost always the crowning point of a great, amplified scene, enclosed by the smaller connecting scenes of the rising, and of the falling action. The poet needs to use all the splendor of poetry, all the dramatic skill of his art, in order to make vividly conspicuous this middle point of his artistic creation. It has the highest significance only in those pieces in which the hero, through his own mental processes, impels the ascending action; in those dramas which rise by means of the counter-play, it does not indicate an important place, where this play has attained the mastery of the chief hero, and misleads him in the direction of the fall. Splendid examples are to be found in almost every one of Shakespeare's plays and in the plays of the Germans. The hovel scene in *King Lear,* with the play of the three deranged persons, and the judgment scene with the stool, is perhaps one of the most effective that was ever put on the stage; and the rising action in *Lear,* up to the scene of this irrepressible madness, is of terrible magnificence. The scene is also remarkable because the great poet has here used humor to intensify the horrible effect, and because this is one of the very rare places, where the audience, in spite of the awful commotion, perceives with a certain surprise that Shakespeare uses artifices to bring out the effect. Edgar is no fortunate addition to the scene. In another way, the banquet scene in Macbeth is instructive. In this tragedy, a previous scene, the night of the murder, had been so powerfully worked out, and so richly endowed with the highest dramatic poetry, that there might easily be despair as to the possibility of any further rise in the action. And yet it is effected; the murderer's struggle with the ghost, and the fearful struggles with his conscience, in the restless scene to which the social festivity and royal splendor give the most effective contrasts, are pictured with a truth, and in a wild kind of poetic frenzy, which make the hearer's heart throb and shudder. In *Othello,* on the other hand, the climax lies in the great scene in which Iago arouses Othello's jealousy. It is slowly prepared, and is the beginning of the convulsing soul-conflict in which the hero perishes. In *Clavigo,* the reconciliation of Clavigo with Marie, and in *Emilia Galotti,* the prostration of Emilia, form the climax, concealed in both cases by the predominating counter-play. Again, in Schiller, it is powerfully developed in all plays.

This outburst of deed from the soul of the hero, or the influx of portentous impressions into the soul; the first great result of a sublime struggle, or the beginning of a moral inward conflict,— must appear inseparably connected with what goes before as well as with what follows; it will be brought into relief through broad treatment or strong effect; but it will, as a rule, be represented in its development from the rising movement and its effect on the environment; therefore, the climax naturally forms the middle point of a group of forces, which, darting in either direction, course upward and downward.

In the case where the climax is connected with the downward movement by a tragic force, the structure of the drama presents something peculiar, through the juxtaposition of two important passages which stand in sharp contrast with each other. This tragic force must first receive attention. This beginning of the downward movement is best connected with the climax, and separated from the following forces of the counter-play to which it belongs by a division—our close of an act; and this is best brought about not immediately after the beginning of the tragic force, but by a gradual modulation of its sharp note. It is a matter of indifference whether this connection of the two great contrasted scenes is effected by uniting them into one scene, or by means of a connecting scene. A splendid example of the former is in *Coriolanus*.

In this piece, the action rises from the exciting force (the news that war with the Volscians is inevitable) through the first ascent (fight between Coriolanus and Aufidius) to the climax, the nomination of Coriolanus as consul. The tragic force, the banishment, begins here; what seems about to become the highest elevation of the hero, becomes by his untamable pride just the opposite; he is overthrown. This overthrow does not occur suddenly; it is seen to perfect itself gradually on the stage—as Shakespeare loves to have it—and what is overwhelming in the result is first perceived at the close of the scene. The two points, bound together here by the rapid action, form together a powerful group of scenes of violent commotion, the whole of far-reaching and splendid effect. But, also, after the close of this double scene, the action is not at once cut into; for there is immediately joined to this, as contrast, the beautiful, dignified pathos scene of the farewell, which forms a transition to what follows; and yet after the hero has departed, this helps to exhibit the moods of those remaining behind, as a trembling echo of the fierce excitement, before the point of repose is reached.

The climax and the tragic force are still more closely united in *Mary Stuart*. Here, also, the beginning of the climax is sharply denoted by the monologue and the elevated lyric mood of Mary, after the style of an ancient pathos scene; and this mood scene is bound by a little connecting song to the great dialogue scene between Mary and Elizabeth; but the dramatic climax reaches even into this great scene, and in this lies the transition to the ominous strife, which again in its development is set forth in minute detail.

Somewhat more sharply are the climax and tragic force in *Julius Caesar* separated from each other by a complete connecting scene. The group of murder scenes is followed by the elaborate scene of the conspirators' conversation with Antony—this interpolated passage of beautiful workmanship—and after this the oration scenes of Brutus and Antony; and after this follow little transitions to the parts of the return.

This close connection of the two important parts gives to the drama with tragic force a magnitude and expanse of the middle part, which—if the playful comparison of the lines may be carried out,—changes the pyramidal form into one with a double apex.

The most difficult part of the drama is the sequence of scenes in the downward movement, or, as it may well be called, the return; specially in powerful plays in which the heroes are the directing force, do these dangers enter most. Up to the climax, the interest has been firmly fixed in the direction in which the chief characters are moving. After the deed is consummated, a pause ensues. Suspense must now be excited in what is new. For this, new forces, perhaps new roles, must be introduced, in which the hearer is to acquire interest. On account of this, there is already danger in distraction and in the breaking up of scenic effects. And yet, it must be added, the hostility of the counter-party toward the hero cannot always be easily concentrated in one person nor in one situation; sometimes it is necessary to show how frequently, now and again, it beats upon the soul of the hero; and in this way, in contrast with the unity and firm advance of the first half of the play, the second may be ruptured, in many parts, restless; this is particularly the case with historical subjects, where it is most difficult to compose the counter-party of a few characters only.

And yet the return demands a strong bringing out and intensifying of the scenic effects, on account of the satisfaction already accorded the hearer, and on account of the greater significance of the struggle. Therefore, the first law for the construction of this part is that the number of persons be limited as much as possible, and that the effects be comprised in great scenes. All the art of technique, all the power of invention, are necessary to insure here an advance in interest.

One thing more. This part of the drama specially lays claims upon the character of the poet. Fate wins control over the hero; his battles move toward a momentous close, which affects his whole life. There is no longer time to secure effects by means of little artifices, careful elaboration, beautiful details, neat motives. The essence of the whole, idea and conduct of the action, comes forward powerfully; the audience understands the connection of events, sees the ultimate purpose of the poet; he must now exert himself for the highest effects; he begins, testing every step in the midst of his interest, to contribute to this work from the mass of his knowledge, of his spiritual affinities, and of what meets the wants of his own nature. Every error in construction, every lack in characterization, will now be keenly felt. Therefore the second rule is valuable for this part; only great strokes, great effects. Even the episodes which are now ventured, must have a certain significance, a certain energy. How numerous the stages must be through which the hero's fall passes, cannot be fixed by rule, farther than that the return makes a less number desirable than, in general, the rising movement allows. For the gradual increase of these effects, it will be useful to insert, just before the catastrophe, a finished scene which either shows the contending forces in the strife with the hero, in the most violent activity, or affords a clear insight into the life of the hero. The great scene, Coriolanus and his mother, is an example of the one case; the monologue of Juliet, before taking the sleep potion, and the sleep-walking scene of Lady Macbeth, of the other case.

The Force of the Final Suspense. It is well understood that the catastrophe must not come entirely as a surprise to the audience. The more powerful the climax, the more violent the downfall of the hero, so much the more vividly must the end be felt in advance; the less the dramatic power of the poet in the middle of the piece, the more pains will he take toward the end, and the more will he seek to make use of striking effects. Shakespeare never does this, in his regularly constructed pieces. Easily, quickly, almost carelessly, he projects the catastrophe, without surprising, with new effects; it is for him such a necessary consequence of the whole previous portion of the piece, and the master is so certain to bear forward the audience with him, that he almost hastens over the necessities of the close. This talented man very correctly perceived, that it is necessary, in good time to prepare the mind of the audience for the catastrophe; for this reason, Caesar's ghost appears to Brutus; for this reason, Edmund tells the soldier he must in certain circumstances slay Lear and Cordelia; for this reason, Romeo must, still before Juliet's tomb, slay Paris, in order that the audience, which at this moment, no longer thinks of Tybalt's death, may not after all, cherish the hope that the piece will close happily; for this reason, must the mortal envy of Aufidius toward Coriolanus be repeatedly expressed before the great scene of the return of the action; and Coriolanus must utter these great words, "Thou hast lost thy son;" for this reason the king must previously discuss with Laertes the murdering of Hamlet by means of a poisoned rapier. Notwithstanding all this, it is sometimes hazardous to hasten to the end without interruption. Just at the time when the weight of an evil destiny has already long burdened the hero, for whom the active sympathy of the audience is hoping relief, although rational consideration makes the inherent necessity of his destruction very evident,—in such a case, it is an old, unpretentious poetic device, to give the audience for a few moments a prospect of relief. This is done by means of a new, slight suspense; a slight hindrance, a distant possibility of a happy release, is thrown in the way of the already indicated direction of the end. Brutus must explain that he considers it cowardly to kill one's self; the dying Edmund must revoke the command to kill Lear; Father Lorenzo may still enter before the moment when Romeo kills himself; Coriolanus may yet be acquitted by the judges; Macbeth is still invulnerable from any man born of woman, even when Burnam Wood is approaching his castle; even Richard III receives the news that Richmond's fleet is shattered and dispersed by the storm. The use of this artifice is old; Sophocles used it to good purpose in *Antigone;* Creon is softened, and revokes the death sentence of Antigone; if it has gone so far with her as he commanded, yet she may be saved. . . .

Yet it requires a fine sensibility to make good use of this force. It must not be insignificant or it will not have the desired effect; it must be made to grow out of the action and out of the character of the persons; it must not come out so prominent that it essentially changes the relative position of the parties. Above the rising possibility, the spectator must always perceive the downward compelling force of what has preceded.

The Catastrophe. The catastrophe of the drama is the closing action; it is what the ancient stage called the *exodus*. In it the embarrassment of the chief characters is relieved through a great deed. The more profound the strife which has gone forward in the hero's soul, the more noble its purpose has been, so much more logical will the destruction of the succumbing hero be.

And the warning must be given here, that the poet should not allow himself to be misled by modern tender-heartedness, to spare the life of his hero on the stage. The drama must present an action, including within itself all its parts, excluding all else, perfectly complete; if the struggle of a hero has in fact, taken hold of his entire life, it is not old tradition, but inherent necessity, that the poet shall make the complete ruin of that impressive. . . .

For the construction of the catastrophe, the following rules are of value: First, avoid every unnecessary word, and leave no word unspoken which the idea of the piece can, without restraint, make clear from the nature of the characters. Further, the poet must deny himself broad elaboration of scenes; must keep what he presents dramatically, brief, simple, free from ornament; must give in diction and action, the best and most impressive; must confine the scenes with their indispensable connections within a small body, with quick, pulsating life; must avoid, so long as the action is in progress, new or difficult stage-effects, especially the effects of masses. . . .

. . . It is instructive to set forth distinctly in a scheme, the artistic combination of the drama[8] from the constituent parts already discussed. What is according to plan, what is designed for a certain purpose, has not been found by the poet entirely through the same consideration which is necessary to the reader when instituting his review. Much is evidently without careful weighing; it has come into being as if by natural necessity, through creative power; in other places, the poet is thoughtful, considerate, has doubted, then decided. But the laws of his creation, whether they directed his invention secretly and unconsciously to himself; or whether, as rules known to him, they stimulated the creative power for certain effects, they are for us readers of his completed works, everywhere, distinctly recognizable. This self-developing organization of the drama, according to a law, will here be briefly analyzed, without regard to the customary division into acts.

Introduction. 1. The key-note; the ghost appears on the platform; the guards and Horatio. 2. The exposition itself; Hamlet in a room of state, before the beginning of the exciting force. 3. Connecting scene with what follows; Horatio and the guards inform Hamlet of the appearance of the ghost. Interpolated exposition scene of the accessory action. The family of Polonius, at the departure of Laertes.

The Exciting Force. 1. Introductory key-note; expectation of the ghost. 2. The ghost appears to Hamlet. 3. Chief part, it reveals the murder to him. 4. Transition to what follows. Hamlet and his confidants.

Through the two ghost scenes, between which the introduction of the chief persons occurs, the scenes of the introduction and of the first excitement are enclosed in a group, the climax of which lies near the end.

Ascending action in four stages. First stage: the counter-players. Polonius propounds that Hamlet has become deranged through love for Ophelia. Two little scenes: Polonius in his house, and before the king; transition to what follows. Second stage: Hamlet determines to put the king to a test by means of a play. A great scene with episodical performances, Hamlet against Polonius, the courtiers, the actors. Hamlet's soliloquy forms the transition. Third stage: Hamlet's examination by the counter-players. 1. The king and the intriguers. 2. Hamlet's celebrated monologue. 3. Hamlet warns Ophelia. 4. The king becomes suspicious. These three stages of the rising action are worked out with reference to the effect of the two others; the first becomes an introduction, the broad and agreeable elaboration of the second forms the chief part of the ascent; the third, through the continuation of the monologue, beautifully connected with the second, forms the climax of the group, with sudden descent. Fourth stage, which leads up to the climax: the play, confirmation of Hamlet's suspicion. 1. Introduction. Hamlet, the players and courtiers. 2. The rendering of the play, the king. 3. Transition, Hamlet, Horatio, and the courtiers.

Climax. A scene with a prelude, the king praying. Hamlet hesitating. Closely joined to this, the

Tragic Force or Incident. Hamlet, during an interview with his mother, stabs Polonius. Two little scenes, as transition to what follows; the king determines to send Hamlet away. These three scene-groups are also bound into a whole, in the midst of which the climax stands. At either side in splendid working-out, are the last stage of the rising action and the tragic force.

The Return. Introductory side-scene. Fortinbras and Hamlet on the way. First stage: Ophelias's madness, and Laertes demanding revenge. Side scene: Hamlet's letter to Horatio. Second stage: A scene; Laertes and the king discuss Hamlet's death. The announcement of the queen that Ophelia is dead, forms the conclusion, and the transition to what follows. Third stage: Burial of Ophelia. Introduction scene, with great episodical elaboration. Hamlet and the grave-diggers. The short, restrained chief scene; the apparent reconciliation of Hamlet and Laertes.

Catastrophe. Introductory scene: Hamlet and Horatio, hatred of the king. As transition, the announcement of Osric; the scene, the killing. Arrival of Fortinbras.

The three stages of the falling action are constructed less regularly than those of the first half. The little side scenes without action, through which Hamlet's journey and return are announced, as well as the episode with the grave-diggers, interrupt the connection of scenes. The work of the dramatic close is of ancient brevity and vigor.

1863   *Translated by Elias J. MacEwan*

Notes

1. *Antigone* and *Ajax* by Sophocles.
2. *The Maid of Orleans* and *Wallenstein* by Schiller.
3. *Emilia Galotti* by Lessing, *Clavigo* by Goethe, and *Love and Intrigue* by Schiller.
4. *Käthchen of Heilbronn* by Kleist, *Wallenstein's Camp* by Schiller, and *Faust* by Goethe.

5. *Miss Sara Sampson* by Lessing.
6. *Mary Stuart* by Schiller.
7. *William Tell* by Schiller.
8. Reference to Shakespeare's *Hamlet*.

GUSTAV FREYTAG, 1816–1895, German novelist, playwright, and essayist. *The Journalists* (1853) became his most popular comedy.

Friedrich Nietzsche

From *The Birth of Tragedy*

Much will have been gained for esthetics once we have succeeded in apprehending directly—rather than merely *ascertaining*—that art owes its continuous evolution to the Apollonian-Dionysiac duality, even as the propagation of the species depends on the duality of the sexes, their constant conflicts and periodic acts of reconciliation. I have borrowed my adjectives from the Greeks, who developed their mystical doctrines of art through plausible *embodiments,* not through purely conceptual means. It is by those two art-sponsoring deities, Apollo and Dionysos, that we are made to recognize the tremendous split, as regards both origins and objectives, between the plastic, Apollonian arts and the nonvisual art of music inspired by Dionysos. The two creative tendencies developed alongside one another, usually in fierce opposition, each by its taunts forcing the other to more energetic production, both perpetuating in a discordant concord that agon which the term *art* but feebly denominates: until at last, by the thaumaturgy of an Hellenic act of will, the pair accepted the yoke of marriage and, in this condition, begot Attic tragedy, which exhibits the salient features of both parents.

To reach a closer understanding of both these tendencies, let us begin by viewing them as the separate art realms of *dream* and *intoxication,* two physiological phenomena standing toward one another in much the same relationship as the Apollonian and Dionysiac. . . .

. . . This deep and happy sense of the necessity of dream experiences was expressed by the Greeks in the image of Apollo.

Apollo is at once the god of all plastic powers and the soothsaying god. He who is etymologically the "lucent" one, the god of light, reigns also over the fair illusion of our inner world of fantasy. The perfection of these conditions in contrast to our imperfectly understood waking reality, as well as our profound awareness of nature's healing powers during the interval of sleep and dream, furnishes a symbolic analogue to the soothsaying faculty and quite generally to the arts, which make life possible and worth living. But the image of Apollo must incorporate that thin line which the dream image may not cross, under penalty of becoming pathological, of imposing itself on us as crass reality: a discreet limitation, a freedom from all extravagant urges, the sapient tranquility of the plastic god. His eye must be sunlike, in keeping with his origin. Even at those moments when he is angry and ill-tempered there lies upon him the consecration of fair illusion. In an eccentric way one might say of Apollo what Schopenhauer[1] says, in the first part of *The World as Will and Idea,* of man caught in the veil of Maya: "Even as on an immense, raging sea, assailed by huge wave crests, a man sits in a little rowboat trusting his frail craft, so, amidst the furious torments of this world, the individual sits tranquilly, supported by the *principium individuationis*[2] and relying on it." One might say that the unshakable confidence in that principle has received its most magnificent expression in Apollo, and that Apollo himself may be regarded as the marvelous divine image of the *principium individuationis,* whose looks and gestures radiate the full delight, wisdom, and beauty of "illusion."

In the same context Schopenhauer has described for us the tremendous awe which seizes man when he suddenly begins to doubt the cognitive modes of experience, in other words, when in a given instance the law of causation seems to suspend itself. If we add to this awe the glorious transport which arises in man, even from the very depths of nature, at the shattering of the *principium individuationis,* then we are in a position to apprehend the essence of Dionysiac rapture, whose closest analogy is furnished by physical intoxication. Dionysiac stirrings arise either through the influence of those narcotic potions of which all primitive races speak in their hymns, or through the powerful approach of spring, which penetrates with joy the whole frame of nature. So stirred, the individual forgets himself completely. It is the same Dionysiac power which in medieval Germany drove ever increasing crowds of people singing and dancing from place to place; we recognize in these St. John's and St. Vitus's dancers the bacchic choruses of the Greeks, who had their precursors in Asia Minor and as far back as Babylon and the orgiastic Sacaea. . . .[3]

If this apotheosis of individuation is to be read in normative terms, we may infer that there is one norm only: the individual— or, more precisely, the observance of the limits of the individual: *sophrosyne.* As a moral deity Apollo demands self-control from his people and, in order to observe such self-control, a knowledge of self. And so we find that the esthetic necessity of beauty is accompanied by the imperatives, "Know thyself," and "Nothing too much." Conversely, excess and *hubris* come to be regarded as the hostile spirits of the non-Apollonian sphere, hence as properties of the pre-Apollonian era—the age of Titans—and the extra-Apollonian world, that is to say the world of the barbarians. It was because of his Titanic love of man that Prometheus had to be devoured by vultures; it was because of his extravagant wisdom which succeeded in solving the riddle of the Sphinx that Oedipus had to be cast into a whirlpool of crime: in this fashion does the Delphic god interpret the Greek past.

The effects of the Dionysiac spirit struck the Apollonian Greeks as titanic and barbaric; yet they could not disguise from themselves the fact that they were essentially akin to those deposed Titans and heroes. They felt more than that: their whole existence, with its temperate beauty, rested upon a base of suffering and *knowledge* which had been hidden from them until the reinstatement of Dionysos uncovered it once more. And lo and behold! Apollo found it impossible to live without Dionysos. The elements of titanism and barbarism turned out to be quite as fundamental as the Apollonian element. And now let us imagine how the ecstatic sounds of the Dionysiac rites penetrated ever more enticingly into that artificially restrained and discreet world of illusion, how this clamor expressed the whole outrageous gamut of nature—delight, grief, knowledge—even to the most piercing cry; and then let us imagine how the Apollonian artist with his thin, monotonous harp music must have sounded beside the demoniac chant of the multitude! The muses presiding over the illusory arts paled before an art which enthusiastically told the truth, and the wisdom of

Silenus cried "Woe!" against the serene Olympians. The individual, with his limits and moderations, forgot himself in the Dionysiac vortex and became oblivious to the laws of Apollo. Indiscreet extravagance revealed itself as truth, and contradiction, a delight born of pain, spoke out of the bosom of nature. Wherever the Dionysiac voice was heard, the Apollonian norm seemed suspended or destroyed. Yet it is equally true that, in those places where the first assault was withstood, the prestige and majesty of the Delphic god appeared more rigid and threatening than before. . . .

. . . If the earlier phase of Greek history may justly be broken down into four major artistic epochs dramatizing the battle between the two hostile principles, then we must inquire further . . . what was the true end toward which that evolution moved. And our eyes will come to rest on the sublime and much lauded achievement of the dramatic dithyramb and Attic tragedy, as the common goal of both urges; whose mysterious marriage, after long discord, ennobled itself with such a child, at once Antigone and Cassandra. . . .

Thus we have come to interpret Greek tragedy as a Dionysiac chorus which again and again discharges itself in Apollonian images. Those choric portions with which the tragedy is interlaced constitute, as it were, the matrix of the *dialogue*, that is to say, of the entire stage-world of the actual drama. This substratum of tragedy irradiates, in several consecutive discharges, the vision of the drama—a vision on the one hand completely of the nature of Apollonian dream-illusion and therefore epic, but on the other hand, as the objectification of a Dionysiac condition, tending toward the shattering of the individual and his fusion with the original Oneness. Tragedy is an Apollonian embodiment of Dionysiac insights and powers, and for that reason separated by a tremendous gulf from the epic.

On this view the chorus of Greek tragedy, symbol of an entire multitude agitated by Dionysos, can be fully explained. Whereas we who are accustomed to the role of the chorus in modern theatre, especially opera, find it hard to conceive how the chorus of the Greeks should have been older, more central than the dramatic action proper (although we have clear testimony to this effect); and whereas we have never been quite able to reconcile with this position of importance the fact that the chorus was composed of such lowly beings as—originally—goatlike satyrs; and whereas, further, the orchestra in front of the stage has always seemed a riddle to us—we now realize that the stage with its action was originally conceived as pure vision and that the only reality was the chorus, who created that vision out of itself and proclaimed it through the medium of dance, music, and spoken word. Since, in this vision, the chorus beholds its lord and master Dionysos, it remains forever an *attending* chorus; it sees how the god suffers and transforms himself, and it has, for that reason, no need to act. But, notwithstanding its subordination to the god, the chorus remains the highest expression of nature, and, like nature, utters in its enthusiasm oracular words of wisdom. Being compassionate as well as wise, it proclaims a truth that issues from the heart of the world. Thus we see how that fantastic and at first sight embarrassing figure arises, the wise and enthusiastic satyr who is at the same time the "simpleton" as opposed to the god. The satyr is a replica of nature in its strongest tendencies and at the same time a herald of its wisdom and art. He combines in his person the roles of musician, poet, dancer and visionary.

It is in keeping both with this insight and with general tradition that in the earliest tragedy Dionysos was not actually present but merely imagined. Original tragedy is only chorus and not drama at all. Later an attempt was made to demonstrate the god as real and to bring the visionary figure, together with the transfiguring frame, vividly before the eyes of every spectator. This marks the beginning of drama in the strict sense of the word. It then became the task of the dithyrambic chorus so to excite the mood of the listeners that when the tragic hero appeared they would behold not the awkwardly masked man but a figure born of their own rapt vision. If we imagine Admetus[4] brooding on the memory of his recently departed wife, consuming himself in a spiritual contemplation of her form, and how a figure of similar shape and gait is led toward him in deep disguise; if we then imagine his tremor of excitement, his impetuous comparisons, his instinctive conviction—then we have an analogue for the excitement of the spectator beholding the god, with whose sufferings he has already identified himself, stride onto the stage. Instinctively he would project the shape of the god that was magically present to his mind onto that masked figure of a man, dissolving the latter's reality into a ghostly unreality. This is the Apollonian dream state, in which the daylight world is veiled and a new world—clearer, more comprehensible, more affecting than the first, and at the same time more shadowy—falls upon the eye in ever-changing shapes. Thus we may recognize a drastic stylistic opposition: language, color, pace, dynamics of speech are polarized into the Dionysiac poetry of the chorus, on the one hand, and the Apollonian dream world of the scene on the other. The result is two completely separate spheres of expression. The Apollonian embodiments in which Dionysos assumes objective shape are very different from the continual interplay of shifting forces in the music of the chorus, from those powers deeply felt by the enthusiast, but which he is incapable of condensing into a clear image. The adept no longer obscurely senses the approach of the god: the god now speaks to him from the proscenium with the clarity and firmness of epic, as an epic hero, almost in the language of Homer. . . .

It is an unimpeachable tradition that in its earliest form Greek tragedy records only the sufferings of Dionysos, and that he was the only actor. But it may be claimed with equal justice that, up to Euripides, Dionysos *remains* the sole dramatic protagonist and that all the famous characters of the Greek stage, Prometheus, Oedipus, etc., are only masks of that original hero. The fact that a god hides behind all these masks accounts for the much-admired "ideal" character of those celebrated figures. Someone, I can't recall who, has claimed that all individuals, as individuals, are comic, and therefore untragic; which seems to suggest that the Greeks did not tolerate individuals at all on the tragic stage. And in fact they must have felt this way. The Platonic distinction between the idea and the *eidolon*[5] is deeply rooted in the Greek temperament. If we wished to use Plato's terminology we might speak of the tragic characters of the Greek stage somewhat as follows: the one true Dionysos appears in a multiplicity of characters, in the mask of warrior hero, and enmeshed in the web of individual will. The god ascends the stage in the likeness of a striving and suffering individual. That he can *appear* at all with this clarity and precision is due to dream interpreter Apollo, who projects before the chorus its Dionysiac condition in this analogical figure. Yet in truth that hero is the suffering Dionysos of the mysteries. . . .

What were you thinking of, overweening Euripides, when you

hoped to press myth, then in its last agony, into your service? It died under your violent hands; but you could easily put in its place an imitation that, like Heracles' monkey, would trick itself out in the master's robes. And even as myth, music too died under your hands; though you plundered greedily all the gardens of music, you could achieve no more than a counterfeit. And because you had deserted Dionysos, you were in turn deserted by Apollo. Though you hunted all the passions up from their couch and conjured them into your circle, though you pointed and burnished a sophistic dialectic for the speeches of your heroes, they have only counterfeit passions and speak counterfeit speeches. . . .

. . . Let us recollect how strangely we were affected by the chorus and by the tragic hero of a kind of tragedy which refused to conform to either our habits or our tradition—until, that is, we discovered that the discrepancy was closely bound up with the very origin and essence of Greek tragedy, as the expression of two interacting artistic impulses, the Apollonian and the Dionysiac. Euripides' basic intention now becomes as clear as day to us: it is to eliminate from tragedy the primitive and pervasive Dionysiac element, and to rebuild the drama on a foundation of non-Dionysiac art, custom and philosophy.

Euripides himself, towards the end of his life, propounded the question of the value and significance of this tendency to his contemporaries in a myth. Has the Dionysiac spirit any right at all to exist? Should it not, rather, be brutally uprooted from the Hellenic soil? Yes, it should, the poet tells us, if only it were possible, but the god Dionysos is too powerful: even the most intelligent opponent, like Pentheus in the *Bacchae,* is unexpectedly enchanted by him, and in his enchantment runs headlong to destruction. The opinion of the two old men in the play—Cadmus and Tiresias—seems to echo the opinion of the aged poet himself: that the cleverest individual cannot by his reasoning overturn an ancient popular tradition like the worship of Dionysos, and that it is the proper part of diplomacy in the face of miraculous powers to make at least a prudent show of sympathy; that it is even possible that the god may still take exception to such tepid interest and—as happened in the case of Cadmus—turn the diplomat into a dragon. We are told this by a poet who all his life had resisted Dionysos heroically, only to end his career with a glorification of his opponent and with suicide—like a man who throws himself from a tower in order to put an end to the unbearable sensation of vertigo. The *Bacchae* acknowledges the failure of Euripides' dramatic intentions when, in fact, these had already succeeded: Dionysos had already been driven from the tragic stage by a daemonic power speaking through Euripides. For in a certain sense Euripides was but a mask, while the divinity which spoke through him was neither Dionysos nor Apollo but a brand-new daemon called Socrates. Thenceforward the real antagonism was to be between the Dionysiac spirit and the Socratic, and tragedy was to perish in the conflict. . . .

. . . The anti-Dionysiac spirit won a mighty victory when it estranged music from itself and made it a slave to appearances. . . .

We see a different aspect of this anti-Dionysiac, antimythic trend in the increased emphasis on character portrayal and psychological subtlety from Sophocles onward. Character must no longer be broadened so as to become a permanent type, but on the contrary must be so finely individualized, by means of shading and nuances and the strict delineation of every trait, that the spectator ceases to be aware of myth at all and comes to focus on the amazing lifelikeness of the characters and the artist's power of imitation. Here, once again, we see the victory of the particular over the general and the pleasure taken in, as it were, anotomical drawing. We breathe the air of a world of theory, in which scientific knowledge is more revered than the artistic reflection of a universal norm. The cult of the characteristic trait develops apace: Sophocles still paints whole characters and lays myth under contribution in order to render them more fully; Euripides concentrates on large single character traits, projected into violent passions; the new Attic comedy gives us masks, each with a single expression: frivolous old men, hoodwinked panders, roguish slaves, in endless repetition. Where is now the mythopoeic spirit? All that remains to music is to excite jaded nerves or call up memory images, as in tone painting.

1871   *Translated by Francis Golffing*

Notes

1. Arthur Schopenhauer (1788–1860), German philosopher.
2. Reference to Thomas Aquinas (1225–1274), theologian and philosopher, with regard to the principle of individuation.

3. Festival of the ancient nomadic tribes of the Scythians celebrating freedom and equality.

4. Character in *Alcestis* by Euripides.

5. *Eidolon*: appearance.

FRIEDRICH NIETZSCHE, 1844–1900. His *The Birth of Tragedy* is one of the most influential essays in the history of dramatic theory.

Arno Holz

From *Evolution of the Drama*

Not long ago, the manner of the latest great Norwegians was considered the embodiment of the whole modern anti-classical and anti-romantic movement. Nevertheless, there is no essential difference between the diction of, say, Ibsen and the rhetoric of, for instance, Schiller, and I could of course illustrate my case with any number of other examples. Despite the century and the many worlds that separate these two artists, they meet in a single conviction: that the language of the theater is not the language of life. Just as Shakespeare did not present the language of life; nor did anyone after him or before him in any country.

Whenever this language ventured to show itself in public—and it did so repeatedly, though always tentatively and never in a thoroughly developed manner—it would appear next to the properly literary language as a more or less tolerated presence, a cinderella outshone by the princess; no one, least of all the so-called science of aesthetics, suspected that she, the disregarded one, might turn out to be secretly artistic, and that her celebrated sister would be seen as the one who was obviously crude.

But our younger playwrights take the opposite position: the language of the theater is the language of life. Only of life! And obviously, to anyone who knows how immediately to recognize such a fundamental (and, for understandable reasons, rare) revolution in an art form, this will be an advance, not just a possible but, what is much more significant, a necessary phase in that art's development, and one more broadly based than any similar breakthrough in the past. Its goal is clearly defined: to reduce as much as possible the unavoidable limitations imposed by the reproductive materials at hand, and thus to supplant with more and more virtually real life those posed versions of life that have been traditionally in use until recently—in short, gradually to push "theater" out of the theater.

May I be permitted to repeat the prognosis I gave this new technique from the very beginning:

". . . as fundamentally important an innovation for the whole field of literature as the substitution of natural outdoor light for artificial studio light was for painting. And in the long run no one will be able to escape it, whether he welcomes it or not. It is no exaggeration to say that by the time its effects have taken their course, not a single stone of the old conventions will have been left unturned. What the old art accomplished with its primitive means, which we no longer believe in and which no longer provide us with an illusion, will be accomplished once again by this new art with its more sophisticated means, behind which, again, we can't for the time being quite see the puppeteer's strings: this art will give us the whole human being anew! And no gift of prophecy is needed to see that in view of the enormous amount of work that awaits this more complex technique—a labor whose gradual accomplishment, by means of this technique, will produce a drama that will represent life with an immediacy and accuracy of which we perhaps don't have even the remotest conception today—a whole series of generations will pass before a similarly incisive moment in the history of the theater will even be possible."

It must be evident that I am not construing my argument by hindsight. I have never had any doubt as to the all-transforming significance of this revolutionary new language. At the very least, I did not underestimate it. Indeed, I would even assert that compared to its final achievement, to the bare fact that one lovely day the language of life was really on the stage, every particular achievement since then could be no more than secondary, however skillful one or the other work may have been—and I would be the last one to deny their excellence. For it is self-evident that between the creation of a work of art in an already established style and the creation of this style itself there exists a difference not in degree but in kind. . . . Also, and more conclusively: if the law hypostatized by the old aesthetics were really true—that action is the ultimate purpose of the theater—then the language of life which we are putting in place of the traditional paper language would have had no significance at all. For a plot remains the same whether it is accompanied by primitive or sophisticated language. But if the opposite holds true, if, as I claim, man himself and his maximally intense depiction are the essential law of the theater, then, obviously, our revolutionizing of the most central means of this art provided a more profound basis for a possible new development than could even be conceived at the time. And now, honorable Mr. Harden,[1] seven years later, I open the *Zukunft* and read: "Eternally valid rules and laws that have their foundation in the idea of the theater and which can only be mastered by obediently adapting to them? What meaningless academic drivel! . . . Rules, laws, ideas: good riddance, thank God we've scrapped the lot of them—such might have been the gist of their jeering!" Oh no. We were never such brainless scarecrows, such pathetic, lamentable characters. On the contrary, our entire crime—and I am proud that I was the first, just as in your opinion, which I do not share, I am also supposed to be the last—our entire crime consisted simply of not blindly accepting from our fathers these supposedly eternal laws and rules which were so visibly stranded on the most dismal sandbanks, but considered it our duty instead to seek out these laws in the things themselves and then to adapt ourselves to them all the more obediently in that we would truly and reverently believe in them! . . .

Already in the late summer of 1891, in the foreword to *Neue Gleise,* which I published together with my friend Johannes Schlaf[2] and in which our works were collected, we were able to write: "It was no homunculus that had escaped from our alembic, no consumptive lamentable something whose life didn't have to be snuffed out because it would expire by itself; rather, we had conquered a new art form, a new technique, for the German theater, which, in despite of our opponents, is sinking its roots in the life around us with a more instinctual surety and depth than the drama that existed before us, and wherever we look in the youngest literature of our time, we encounter its traces everywhere." We had drawn all this from ourselves and the things themselves, and even the most richly endowed foreign cultures around us had nothing to offer us. So, if we are really supposed to have been such fools—very well, at least this much you would have to grant us:

that at least we were fools of our own volition and with our own method!

And now, if you please, the folly itself. It consisted, you claim, in our wanting to attack the vital principle of the theater itself, the iron law that was the foundation of dramatic art for the last two thousand years. "That this law," you argued, "was not the product of a despot's whim, not a resolution passed at some aesthetic parliament, that it is firmly rooted in the soil from which the theater first emerged in the infancy of nations, this was something the young gentlemen weren't considering when they cried: Away with the intrigues, the colorful adventures, away with concentration, away with plot!" Most highly esteemed Mr. Harden: You underestimate those erstwhile young gentlemen! Not just that these young gentlemen were most definitely thinking of that law—and incidentally, they never disavowed concentration and plot—but their whole striving (whose selfless ardor you may perhaps not fully and justly appreciate in its, I'm almost tempted to say: historical significance) found its most glad fulfillment precisely in enabling this ancient law to attain its victory at last, after such long neglect by previous generations, who had considered various other problems to be more important. Except that the question presented itself—and here's the nub—: what is this law? You cite a sentence by Brunetière[3]: "*Ce qui n'appartient qu'aut théâtre, ce qui fait à travers les âges l'unité permanente de l'espèce dramatique, si j'ose ainsi parler, ce que l'histoire, ce que la vie même ne nous montrent pas toujours, c'est le déploiement de la volonté,—et voilà pourquoi l'action demeurera la loi du théâtre, parce qu'elle est enveloppée dans son idée même.*[4] You could just as well have invoked any author since Aristotle to expatiate on this subject. Their oracular pronouncements evince the most touching unanimity. But I trust in the multiplication table and appeal to your sense of logic: " . . . *c'est le déploiement de la volonté,—et voilà pourquoi l'action demeurera la loi du théâtre.*" Where, I ask, is the granite bridge of necessity that leads from that principal clause to this subsidiary clause? I'm sorry. All I see is a dash and behind it an assertion kicking its legs in the air. I myself would not venture to cast any doubt on the first part of Brunetière's sentence, and it seems to me that it allows for only one corollary: the people on the stage are not there for the sake of the plot, but rather it is the plot that is there for the sake of the people on the stage. The plot is not the end but the means, not the primary but the secondary thing. In other words: the law of the theater is not action but the depiction of characters. And to have been the first to sense in the nature of things this fundamental law of all dramatic art, after all the academicians of two millennia had been turning in circles like a cow in the pasture—this, I'll admit, was our misfortune! But that the baby was quickly poured out with the bath, and that we were accused of violently rejecting any plot whatsoever—as if a plotless play were even conceivable, and of demanding plays that had no beginning, middle, or end—all this was not really to our detriment, since we had never perpetrated such rubbish, but was merely the handiwork of those many great minds, so superior to our own, who found it so easy, from the vantage of their editorial chairs, to understand us more thoroughly and more profoundly than we understood ourselves. This is a well-known process. It takes place in all fields almost every day. No art form should dare to want to achieve what can be accomplished more effectively in another medium. Certainly. I admit it without reservation. But precisely because this sentence is so irrefutably valid, precisely for this reason, I repeat, action is not the law of the theater. It is technically possible to stuff more action into a three-page novella than can be accommodated in a ten-act drama. And vice versa: even the most mediocre playwright, given the support of a Duse or a Reicher, is technically in a position to provide more immediately effective characterization than the most extravagantly gifted novelist could in a whole chapter. The means that are a hindrance to one, are a support to the other. That is the difference.

1897(?)   *Translated by Joel Agee*

Notes

1. Maximilian Harden (1861–1927), writer and critic.
2. Johannes Schlaf (1862–1941).
3. Ferdinand Brunetière (1849–1906), French critic.
4. "What belongs only to the theatre, what through the ages has held up the continuing unity of the dramatic form, if I may say so, which neither history nor

life itself is always able to show us, is the application of the will. That's why action will remain the law of the theatre, because it is contained in the idea itself."

ARNO HOLZ, 1863–1929, representative of German Naturalism, best known for his plays *Familie Selicke* (1890) and *Papa Hamlet* (1899). The excerpt is taken from an open letter to Maximilian Harden, who had attacked Holz in an article entitled "Das hölzerne Berlin" (1897).

Gerhart Hauptmann

Thoughts on Drama

Drama is surely the greatest literary form. Aren't all thoughts dramatically conceived, is not all life lived dramatically?

The origin of drama is the ego split up into two, three, four, five and more parts.

The earliest theatrical stage is the human brain. Plays were performed there long before the first stage-play was produced.

The most primitive drama to be given external expression was the first dialogue a man held with himself, addressing and answering himself out loud.

There is no human brain, however constituted, that does not carry around within itself its own drama. Over and over again, contemporary consciousness fashions episodes from the great epic drama of one's own life. For this reason, dramatic form, the drama itself, is perfectly contemporaneous. The mind in its synthesizing activity operates with a residue of clear and lively perception in which one's situation relative to father, mother, siblings, friends, to one's social superiors and inferiors and especially to one's enemies, is both vocally and actively contained.

Genius makes use of this primordial inner form of dramatic consciousness, as one might call it, so as to let the dramatic art-form grow out of its basic elements.

When the dramatic consciousness becomes creative, it proves the presence of a dramatist; and he in turn, thanks to the dramatic consciousness, which encompasses new areas every day, will be exceptionally fruitful.

137

Harmony is the product of struggles: its ethical value must be judged accordingly. This applies to the value and the nature of drama as well.

Drama is struggle. The greatest epic is rooted in the drama of adultery: Helen, Menelaus, Paris and the battle for Troy. Eventually it dissolved into individual plays.

A play that is not *exposition* from the first to last word does not possess the ultimate degree of vitality.

The epic walks its road, the drama cannot move from its place of battle. The epic develops in time, the dramatic primarily in space.

Epic art lives on historical fiction. It presupposes a narrator.

Dramatic art simulates presence. It has an invisible creator, an invisibly present one, to be sure, who documents himself in his creatures.

To be truly productive, one must look at the dramatic material, that is, at human beings and their inner and outer relationships and struggles, independently of their being human or of their being men, women, aristocrats, burghers, workers or potentates, old, young, poor, or rich. One must look at them as if one didn't know how they breathe, what they eat and drink, how they have to live in order to live, nor that they speak, sing, write, wake and sleep and relieve themselves—as if one were ignorant of what they do and what they have achieved in the arts and sciences. One must see them as if one didn't know anything about them and were experiencing everything for the first time. The tiniest part of this utter strangeness must express to the viewer all the marvelousness and incomprehensibility of mystery.

A play must move of its own accord, it should not be moved by the poet. The origin of its movement must be concealed, just as the origin of life is hidden to all.

Whoever wants to study the nature of the dramatic should not forget to look at Rembrandt's free-hand drawings.

The true syntheses of true drama are much more intricate—though they aren't apparent except insofar as they are fully translated into life—than all the mechanically calculated intricacies.

The language of the moment is unarticulated—only in the course of time does it develop into a language proper. The moment, which would otherwise live and die, survives by means of language. Always and everywhere, dramatic language is rooted in the living moment.

Strong destinies are strong life: that is why people are drawn to tragedy and to the Passion of Jesus.

One has to distinguish: thought in its becoming and thought as a finished matter. There is the notion that finished thoughts should rarely or never be formulated in a drama. It is thought in gestation that should be voiced. At the very most, thought at the moment of birth or scarcely born, unbathed, with its umbilical cord still unsevered. Or perhaps a thought that was born blind and brightly opens its eyes for the first time. There are many thoughts like this in my plays, but they are not always recognized as such, perhaps because they are so unusual, and they can't be added to one's treasury of citations.

To conceive more and more "undramatic" material in dramatic form: that is progress.

The theater will not achieve its ultimate and profoundest power until we have given it the sanction of religious service, as the Greeks did. Our theater is strong within itself, but it is merely tolerated, not cultivated. It stands under the pressure of a hostile judgment, not under the protection of religious sanction.

Only the Athenians erected a monument to pity. Pity has a voice in us. The Greek fashioned a human form for this voice, its exclusive habitation, as it were. Voices, like statues, are links in the great drama we are all creating.

Every drama is historical, there is no other kind.

The realm of what is called healthy and normal is abandoned in the affect. A drama without affect is unthinkable, and that is why it must always extend somewhat into the pathological.

Fanatics can only be used episodically in a play: their intransigent delusional system is quickly demonstrated, and so is the fortitude with which they assert it: beyond that, there is nothing that could further the life of the play.

Stillness in drama does not even take place among the fish in the sea.

Ibsen usually sees the tragic element only in the so-called failed life. Tragedy in the fullness of life is greater.

Every single tragedy has always been weakened, indeed essentially rejected. There isn't a tragedy that hasn't been muted, tamed and spoiled. Medusa's head was not even endurable on the scholar's desk, let alone in the salon or the boudoir.

The satyr's mask grinning behind the final conflagration of the tragedy in a divine triumph of life. Irony is the fundamental trait of triumphant life.

Translated by Joel Agee

GERHART HAUPTMANN, 1862–1946, received the Nobel Prize in Literature for 1912. His play *Before Dawn* (1889) ushered in the new style of Naturalism in Germany, followed by its most important example: *The Weavers* (1892). Other important plays are *The Beaver Coat* (1893), *Fuhrmann Henschel* (1898), *Rose Bernd* (1903), *The Rats* (1910), and *The Atreus Tetralogy* (1941–47).

Georg Lukács

The Sociology of Modern Drama

Modern drama is the drama of the bourgeoisie; modern drama is bourgeois drama. By the end of our discussion, we believe, a real and specific content will have filled out this abstract formulation. . . .

The drama has now taken on new social dimensions.[1] This development became necessary, and necessary at this particular time, because of the specific social situation of the bourgeoisie. For bourgeois drama is the first to grow out of conscious class confrontation; the first with the set intention of expressing the patterns of thought and emotion, as well as the relations with other classes, of a class struggling for power and freedom. . . . Although in Elizabethan drama the representatives of several classes appear, the true human beings, the dramatic characters, are derived on the whole from a single class. Infrequently, we find a figure that represents the petty nobility, as in *Arden of Feversham*.[2] The lower classes merely take part in comic episodes, or they are on hand simply so their inferiority will highlight the refinements of the heroes. For this reason, class is not decisive in structuring the character and action of these plays. . . .

A new determinant is joined to the new drama: value judgement. In the new drama not merely passions are in conflict, but ideologies, *Weltanschauungen*, as well. Because men collide who come from differing situations, value judgements must necessarily function as importantly, at least, as purely individual characteristics. . . . The moral outlooks of Hamlet and Claudius, and even of Richard and Richmond, are at bottom identical. Each man is resolute, and feels contemptible if he acts contrary to this moral view. Claudius knows the murder of his brother to be a sin; he is even incapable of seeking motives that might justify his action, and it is inconceivable that he would attempt a relativist justification (as Hebbel's Herodes[3] will, following the murder of Aristobolus). Also the 'sceptical' and 'philosophical' Hamlet never for a moment doubts that he is impelled as though by categorical imperative to seek blood revenge. So long as he remains incapable of acting as he knows he must, he feels sinful and blameworthy. Hegel is therefore correct when he says the deeds of Shakespeare's heroes are not 'morally justified'. For the ethical value judgement of that epoch rested upon such solid metaphysical foundations, showed such little tolerance for any kind of relativity, and gained universality from such mystic, non-analyzable emotions, that no person violating it—for whatever reasons and motive—could justify his act even subjectively. His deed could be explained by his soul's condition, but no amount of reasoning could provide absolution. . . .

The conflict of generations as a theme is but the most striking and extreme instance of a phenomenon new to drama, but born of general emotion. For the stage has turned into the point of intersection for pairs of worlds distinct in time; the realm of drama is one where 'past' and 'future', 'no longer' and 'not yet', come together in a single moment. What we usually call 'the present' in drama is the occasion of self-appraisal; from the past is born the future, which struggles free of the old and of all that stands in opposition. The end of each tragedy sees the collapse of an entire world. The new drama brings what in fact is new, and what follows the collapse differs qualitatively from the old; whereas in Shakespeare the difference was merely quantitative. Looked at from an ethical perspective; the bad is replaced by the good, or by something better than the old, and at any rate decidedly different in kind. In *Götz von Berlichingen* Goethe depicts the collapse of a world; a tragedy is possible in this case only because Götz was born at that particular time. A century or perhaps even a generation earlier, and he would have become a hero of legend, perhaps rather like a tragi-comic Don Quixote; and a scant generation later as well, this might have been the result. . . .

What we are discussing here is the increased complexity which determines dramatic character. We find it can be viewed from different sides, in numerous perspectives; characters in the new drama are more complicated than in the old, threads that are more intricate run together and knot with one another and with the external world, to express the interrelationship. In turn the concept of the external world grows more relative than ever. We have said of the drama that, in general, destiny is what confronts man from without. In Greek and even in Shakespearean drama we can still easily distinguish between man and his environment, or, speaking from the viewpoint of drama, between the hero and his destiny. But now these lines of division have blurred. So much of the vital centre streams out of the peripheries, and so much streams from there into the vital centre of man, that the concepts which distinguish man from his environment, flesh from spirit, free will from circumstance, hero from destiny, character from situation, are nearly deprived of meaning in the face of the complexity of constant interactions. Destiny is what comes to the hero from without. If we are to continue composing dramas, we must hold to this definition regardless of whether it is true in life; otherwise we would find it impossible to maintain the contending parties in equilibrium (supposing a two-dimension composition), nor would there be foreground or background. . . . Most simply, what must be located is the equilibrium between man and the external world; the relation of a man to his action is really still his.

The more that circumstances define man, the more difficult this problem seems, and the more the very atmosphere appears to absorb all into itself. Man, distinct contours, no longer exist; only air, only the atmosphere. All that modern life has introduced by way of enriching the perceptions and emotions seems to vanish into the atmosphere, and the composition is what suffers. . . .

To what extent is modern man the enactor of his actions? In his actions man elaborates his entire being, he arrives at himself in them: how much are they really his? How much is the vital centre of man really deep within him? This relation will be the prime determinant of style in every drama. All stylization, all structure bases itself on where the one and the other diverge and coincide, how the one determines the other. . . . All reflection on the drama comes to this: how does man achieve a tragic action? Is it indeed he who achieves it? By what means? The question truly at the bottom of the theory of tragic guilt is this: did the tragic personage really do his tragic deed, and if he did not, can it be tragic? And the real meaning of 'constructing the guilt' exists in building bridges between the deed and the doer, in finding a point from which one will see that all proceeds from within despite every opposition, a perspective which rescues the autonomy of tragic man. . . .

We have to ask whether there can still be a drama. The threat to it is indisputably great, and in naturalism, for instance, we see that it virtually ceases to be dramatic. And yet only the origin of the mutually-opposing forces has been altered; the forces themselves must not be allowed in turn to grow so out of balance that a drama is not possible. In other words, we are faced in the final analysis with a problem of expression, and need not necessarily concern ourselves with the problem of the drama's existence. It matters little whether the will which is set against destiny originates entirely from within; it matters as little whether it is free or constrained, or determined by circumstances of whatever sort. These matters count for little, because a drama remains possible so long as the dynamic force of the will is strong enough to nourish a struggle of life and death dimensions, where the entire being is rendered meaningful.

Hebbel was the first to recognize that the difference between action and suffering is not quite so profound as the words suggest; that every suffering is really an action directed within, and every action which is directed against destiny assumes the form of suffering. Man grows dramatic by virtue of the intensity of his will, by the outpouring of his essence in his deeds, by becoming wholly identical with them. So long as this capacity retains sufficient force to symbolize the entirety of man and his destiny, the displacement earlier noted results merely in a new form of the same relation. The heroes of the new drama—in comparison to the old—are more passive than active; they are acted upon more than they act for themselves; they defend rather than attack; their heroism is mostly a heroism of anguish, of despair, not one of bold aggressiveness. Since so much of the inner man has fallen prey to destiny, the last battle is to be enacted within. We can best summarize by saying that the more the vital motivating centre is displaced outward (*i.e.*, the greater the determining force of external factors), the more the centre of tragic conflict is drawn inward; it becomes internalized, more exclusively a conflict in the spirit. For up to a certain limit, the inner powers of resistance upon which the spirit can depend become greater and more intense in direct proportion to the greatness and intensity of the outwardly opposing forces. And since the hero now is confronted not only with many more external factors than formerly, but also by actions which have become not his own and turn against him, the struggle in which he engages will be heightened into anguish. He must engage in the struggle: something drives him into it which he cannot resist; it is not his to decide whether he even wishes to resist.

This is the dramatic conflict: man as merely the intersection point of great forces, and his deeds not even his own. Instead something independent of him mixes in, a hostile system which he senses as forever indifferent to him, thus shattering his will. And the why of his acts is likewise never wholly his own, and what he senses as his inner motivating energy also partakes of an aspect of the great complex which directs him toward his fall. The dialectical force comes to reside more exclusively in the idea, in the abstract. Men are but pawns, their will is but their possible moves, and it is what remains forever alien to them (the *abstractum*) which moves them. Man's significance consists only of this, that the game cannot be played without him, that men are the only possible hieroglyphs with which the mysterious inscription may be composed. . . .

The new drama is nevertheless the drama of individualism, and that with a force, an intensity and an exclusiveness no other drama ever had. Indeed, one can well conceive an historical perspective on the drama which would see in this the most profound distinction between the old and new drama; such an outlook would place the beginnings of new drama at the point where individualism commences to become dramatic. . . . We said previously that new drama is bourgeois and historicist; we add now that it is a drama of individualism. And in fact these three formulas express a single point of demarcation; they merely view the parting of ways from distinct vantage-points. The first perspective is the question of sociological basis, the foundation on which the other two are based and from which they grow. It states simply that the social and economic forms which the bourgeoisie opposed to remaining vestiges of the feudal order became, from the eighteenth century onward, the prevailing forms. Also, that life proceeds within this framework, and in the tempo and rhythm it dictates, and thus the problems this fact provokes are precisely the problems of life; in a word, that culture today is bourgeois culture. . . . Both historicism and individualism have their roots in the soil of this one culture, and though it may seem from several points of view that they would be sharply conflicting, mutually exclusive opposites, we must nevertheless ask how much this opposition really amounts to an antagonism. . . .

In the course of German Romanticism the historicist sense grew to consciousness together with and parallel to Romantic Individualism, and the two were never felt to exclude one another. We must regard as no accident the way both of these sensibilities rose to consciousness coincidentally and closely associated with the first great event of bourgeois culture, and perhaps its most decisive, the French Revolution, and all that happened around and because of it. . . .

If we examine even the superficial externals of modern life, we are struck by the degree to which it has grown uniform, though it theoretically has engendered a most extreme individualism. Our clothing has grown uniform, as has the communications system; the various forms of employment, from the employee's viewpoint, have grown ever more similar (bureaucracy, mechanized industrial labour); education and the experiences of childhood are more and more alike (the effect and increasing influence of big-city life); and so on. Parallel to this is the ongoing *rationalizing* of our life. Perhaps the essence of the modern division of labour, as seen by the individual, is that ways are sought to make work independent of the worker's capacities, which, always irrational, are but qualitatively determinable; to this end, work is organized according to production outlooks which are objective, super-personal and independent of the employee's character. This is the characteristic tendency of the economics of capitalism. Production is rendered more objective, and freed from the personality of the productive agent. An objective abstraction, capital, becomes the true productive agent in capitalist economy, and it scarcely has an organic relation with the personality of its accidental owner; indeed, personality may often become superfluous, as in corporations.

Also, scientific methodologies gradually cease to be bound up with personality. In medieval science a single individual personally would command an entire sphere of knowledge (*e.g.*, chemistry, astrology), and masters passed on their knowledge or 'secret' to the pupils. The same situation was true in the medieval trades and commerce. But the modern specialized methodologies become continually more objective and impersonal. The relation between work and its performers grows more loose; less and less does the work engage the employee's personality, and conversely, the work is related ever less to the worker's personal qualities. Thus work assumes an oddly objective existence, detached from the particularities of individual men, and they must seek means of self-expression outside their work. The relations between men grow more impersonal as well. Possibly the chief characteristic of the feudal order was the way men's dependencies and relations were brought into unity; by contrast, the bourgeois order rationalizes them. The same tendency to depersonalize, with the substitution of quantitative for qualitative categories, is manifested in the overall state organization (electoral system, bureaucracy, military organization, etc.). Together with all this, man too develops a view of life and the world which is inclined toward wholly objective standards, free of any dependency upon human factors.

The style of the new individualism, especially the aspect of importance to us, is defined by this displacement in the relations of liberty and constraint. The transformation can be briefly formulated: previously, life itself was individualistic, now men, or rather their convictions and their outlooks on life, are. Earlier ideology emphasized constraint, because man felt his place within a binding order to be natural and consistent with the world system; and yet, all occasions of concrete living offered him the opportunity to inject his personality into the order of things by means of his deeds. Hence a spontaneous and continuous individualism of this sort was feasible, whereas today it has grown conscious and problematic as a result of the transformation we have sketched. Previously it was—in Schiller's sense—naïve, and today sentimental. The formulation is this, applied to drama: the old drama, by which we mean here primarily that of the Renaissance, was drama of great individuals, today's is that of individualism. In other words, the realization of personality, its *per se* expression in life, could in no wise become a theme of earlier drama, since personality was not yet problematic. It is, in the drama of today, the chief and most central problem. Though it is true that in most tragedies the action consisted of the clash at some point of someone's maximum attainment with what lay outside him, and the existing order of things refused to let a figure rise to the peak of his possibilities without destroying him, yet this was never associated, consciously at least, with the blunt concept of maximized attainment. The arrangement of the situation was never such that the tragedy had necessarily to result, as it were, from the bare fact of willing, the mere realization of personality. In summary: where the tragedy was previously brought on by the particular *direction* taken by the will, the mere *act* of willing suffices to induce it in the new tragedy. Once again Hebbel offers the most precise definition. He stated that it did not matter for the purposes of drama whether the hero's fall was caused by good or bad actions.

The realization and maintenance of personality has become on the one hand a conscious problem of living; the longing to make the personality prevail grows increasingly pressing and urgent. On the other hand, external circumstances, which rule out this possibility from the first, gain ever greater weight. It is in this way that survival as an individual, the integrity of individuality, becomes the vital centre of drama. Indeed the bare fact of Being begins to turn tragic. In view of the augmented force of external circumstance, the least disturbance or incapacity to adjust is enough to induce dissonances which cannot be resolved. Just so, the aesthetic of Romanticism regarded tragedy—with a metaphysical rationale and explanation, to be sure—as a consequence of mere being, and the necessary inevitable consequence and natural correlate of individuation. Thus, the contention of these mutually opposed forces is emphasized with increasing sharpness. The sense of being constrained grows, as does its dramatic expression; likewise the longing grows for a man to shatter the bonds which bind men, even though the price he pays is his downfall.

Both these tendencies already had become conscious by the time of *Sturm und Drang* drama, but—in theory at least—they were considered as complementary elements serving to differentiate the genres of art. Lenz[4] saw here the distinction between comedy and tragedy. For him, comedy portrayed society, the men rooted in it, and relationships against which they were incapable of successful struggle; whereas tragedy presented great personalities, who challenged relationships and struggled though it might mean ruin. As early as Goethe's tragedy *Götz* and the first dramas of Schiller, however, relationships are nearly as emphasized as in Lenz's comedies; moreover, what prevents Lenz's comedies from qualifying as real tragedies is not to be found in his idea of what distinguishes the genres (here he was influenced by Diderot and Mercier).[5]

Thus we can say that the drama of individualism (and historicism) is as well the drama of milieu. For only this much-heightened sense of the significance of milieu enables it to function as a dramatic element; only this could render individualism truly problematic, and so engender the drama of individualism. This drama signals the collapse of eighteenth century doctrinaire individualism. What then was treated as a formal contention between ideologies and life, now becomes a portion of content, an integral part of the historicist drama. Modern life liberates man from many old constraints and it causes him to feel each bond between men (since these are no longer organic) as a bondage. But in turn, man comes to be enclasped by an entire chain of abstract bondages, which are yet more complicated. He feels, whether or not he is conscious of it, that every bond whatsoever is bad and so every bond between men must be resisted as an imposition upon human dignity. In every case, however, the bondage will prove stronger than the resistance. In this perspective Schiller's first play is one typical commencement of the new drama, just as Goethe's play was in another perspective.

Artistically this all implies, in the first place, a paradox in the dramatic representation of character. For in the new drama, compared to the old, character becomes much more important and at the same time much less important. Our perspective alone determines whether we count its formal significance as everything or as nothing. Even as the philosophies of Stirner and Marx are basically drawn from the same source, Fichte, so every modern drama embodies this duality of origin, this dialectic out of the life that gives it birth. (We perhaps see this conflict most clearly in the historical dramas of Grabbe.)[6] Character becomes everything, since the conflict is entirely for the sake of character's vital centre; for it alone and for nothing peripheral, because the force disposed of by this vital centre alone determines the dialectic, that is, the dramatic, quality of drama. Conversely, character becomes nothing, since the conflict is merely *around* and *about* the vital centre, solely for the *principle* of individuality. Since the great question becomes one of to what degree the individual will finds community possible, the direction of the will, its strength, and other specifics which might render it individual in fact, must remain unconsidered. Thus—and the essence of the stylistic problem is here—character is led back to more rational causes than ever before, and becomes at the same time ever more hopelessly irrational. The old drama was founded in a universal sensibility, unifying and meta-rational, which circumscribed as well as permeated its composition and psychology. The old drama's religious origins thus afforded man what was virtually an unconscious and naïve mode of expression. Indeed, to the extent that this drama grew conscious of its tendency, efforts were made to eliminate it. (Euripides is perhaps the best example here.) By contrast, the foundations of the new drama are rational: from its origins it lacks the quality of mystical religious emotion. Only when this emotion once again appears in life does a real drama again appear; to be sure, it re-emerges at first as an exclusively artistic demand, but later it seeks to serve as the unifying foundation of life and art. And yet this meta-rational, indissoluble sensibility could never again escape the mark of consciousness, of being *a posteriori*; never could it be once more the unifying, enveloping atmosphere of all things. Both character and destiny had acquired a paradoxical duality, had become at once mystically irrational and geometrically constructed. The expression of the meta-rational becomes in this way more mysterious in psychology than it was earlier, but also, in its technique, more rational and conceptual. The drama comes to be built upon mathematics, a complicated web of abstractions, and in this perspective character achieves significance merely as an intersection; it becomes, as Hofmannsthal[7] once remarked, equivalent to a contrapuntal necessity. And yet, no such systemization can contain the real sum of what humanity makes out of a human being (and drama without human beings is inconceivable). Therefore the dramatic and the characteristic aspects of modern man do not coincide. That which is truly human in the human being must remain to a degree outside the drama. Seen in the perspective of a single life, the personality turns inward, becomes spiritualized, whereas the outward data in turn become abstract and uniform, until a true connexion between the two is impossible. The data, actions manifested in the external world, fail to account for the whole man, who in turn is not able to arrive at an action revelatory of his entire self. (Here lies the most profound stylistic contradiction of the intimate drama: as drama increasingly becomes an affair of the spirit, it increasingly misses the vital centre of personality.) This—in context with that indissoluble irrationality whereby man is represented—explains the heavy burden of theory encumbering much of the new drama. Since the vital centre of character and the intersecting point of man and his destiny do not necessarily coincide, supplemental theory is brought in to contrive a dramatic linkage of the two. One could indeed say that the maintenance of personality is threatened by the totality of external data. The data perhaps cannot drain the personality dry—but personality can, by a process of internalization, seek to flee the individual data, avoiding them, keeping out of contact with them.

In sum, life as the subject of poetry has grown more epic, or to be precise, more novelistic than ever (we refer, of course, to the psychological rather than the primitive form of the novel). The transposition of life into the drama is achieved only by the symptomatic rendering of the life data. For the significance of life's external particulars has declined, if we regard them with the task in mind of rendering man dramatic. Thus, the threat to personality becomes almost of necessity the subject of theoretical discussion. Only if the problem is presented abstractly, dialectically, can we succeed in turning the particular event, which is the basic stuff of drama, into an event touching upon, and expressive of, dramatic man's inner essence. The personage must be consciously aware that in the given case directly involving him, the perpetuation of his personality is at stake. The new drama is on this account the drama of individualism: a drama of demands upon personality made conscious. For this reason men's convictions, their ideologies, are of the highest artistic importance, for they alone can lend a symptomatic significance to the naked data. Only they can bring the vital centres of drama and of character into adjustment. However, this adjustment will always remain problematic; it will never be more than a 'solution', an almost miraculous coherence of mutually antagonistic forces, for the ideology threatens in turn to reduce character to a 'contrapuntal necessity'.

Thus heroism in the new drama is quite different from what it was in the old; and the French *tragédie classique* relates most intimately to the old in this regard. Heroism is now more passive, requires less of outward splendour, success, and victory (here again we refer to Hebbel's theory of suffering and action); but on the other hand it is more conscious, judicious and, in expression, more pathetic and rhetorical than was the old. Perhaps we will be somewhat dubious about this last assertion, in view of the sparse simplicity of language in many modern dramas; even so, the essence of the question here concerns not so much rhetoric or its absence in direct expression, but rather the underlying tone in the pathetic scenes, and how much or relatively little this approaches expression. When Hebbel's Clara, Ibsen's Hedda, or even Hauptmann's Henschel dies (to name but the least obtrusively pathetic dénouements)[8] the death partakes of the very same tone as did the emotions of heroes in Corneille and Racine. In the face of death, the heroes of Greek and Shakespearean drama were composed; their pathos consists of bravely looking death in the eye, of proudly bearing what is not to be averted. The heroes of the new drama always partake of the ecstatic; they seem to have become conscious of a sense that death can vouchsafe them the transcendence, greatness, and illumination which life withheld (e.g., the Antigone of Sophocles compared with that of Alfieri),[9] and together with this a sense that death will fulfill and perfect their personalities. This sense arose only among the spectators in the old drama. That is why Schopenhauer[10] valued the modern tragedy more highly than the ancient; he called the tone resignation, and regarded it as the essence of tragedy. With this the outer event becomes wholly inward—that is, at the moment when the two vital centres coincide most exactly—and form has in a sense become content. We might well say that the ancients regarded tragedy naïvely. The tragedy is a posteriori to the viewpoint of the acting personages and the stylistic means. Thus it is not so important that the problem be thought through to its end. By contrast, in the new tragedies the tragedy is asserted as primary; the various particular phenomena of man, life, and the events of drama are all regarded as tragic; here the tragedy is a priori to life.

A dramatic problem exists in this antimony of an individualism which relates to the external world within a reduced scope of expressive significations. It is not the only problem. As we have seen, one of the important new forms of our life results from the slackening and loosening of constraints in the realm of the particular and the immediate, while the abstract constraints correspondingly grow and assume augmented force. The individual's sense of autonomy in his relations with others is ever-increasing, he tolerates less and less any purely personal bond between men, which by its nature will demand more of personality than do those bonds which are purely abstract. Simmel provides an interesting case of this transformation in sensibility. At the beginning of the modern epoch, he states, should an impoverished Spanish nobleman enter the personal service of a rich man (*i.e.*, work as a servant or lackey), he would not lose his title of nobility, whereas he would should he turn to a trade. In contrast, a young American woman today is not ashamed to work in a factory, but she does feel shame if she takes up housework in another's employ. Thus the relations among men have grown much more complex. For if the realization of personality is not to become a hollow ideology, somebody must achieve it. But since this someone will feel his personal autonomy to be sacred, he will tolerate intrusion upon it no more than will those who aspire to be his master. In this way new conflicts result from the new patterning of sensibility, and this at precisely the juncture where, in the old order of society, the relation of higher to lower rank (master to servant, husband to wife, parents to children, etc.) found stability, the point where a tradition which dated back countless centuries had the energy to confirm and perpetuate tendencies through which the lives of men mingled in the most intimate manner. And so again, and in yet another perspective, the new drama emerges as the drama of individualism. For one of individualism's greatest antimonies becomes its foremost theme: the fact that realization of personality will be achieved only at the price of suppressing the personalities of others (which, in turn, require for their realization the ruin of the personalities of others).

As a formal relationship, this adds a new development to human relations in drama. Behind a belief that man's full personality is realized in his relationships with others, lies an emotion, a sensibility that suffuses all of life. When the emotion vanishes or diminishes, characters whose spirit functions chiefly on the basis of that emotion (the servant, confidante, etc.) will vanish from the drama. As the emotion ceases to be universal they become no more than hollow, illusion-disrupting technical properties. This is an evident fact of the French and Spanish drama, and we might better mention that Kent's whole personality is fulfilled in the relationship to Lear, as is Horatio's in his relationship to Hamlet. By contrast, in Goethe's first play, and in Schiller's,[11] we find the theme of a servant at the crucial moment turning against his master (Weislingen—Franz; Franz Moor—Herman), thus ceasing to exist merely in relationship to the master. Here the means elude the one who proposes to use them, they take on new life, become an end. As in many other realms we see here, too, how purely decorative relationships are shattered by the new life; relations become more complex, and where once only gestures made contact, psychological bonds and complex reciprocal effects that are barely expressible are now produced.

The stylistic problem is defined under these conditions, that is, by displacements in the relations among men as caused by the new life (the dramatic material) and by the new ways men have of regarding and evaluating their relationships (the dramatic *principium stilisationis*). Limitations set by these possibilities become the limits of the new drama's expressive potential; and both types of limitation produce the questions which can set the stylistic problem. Perhaps we may briefly formulate these questions: what kind of man does this life produce, and how can he be depicted dramatically? What is his destiny, what typical events will reveal it, how can these events be given adequate dramatic expression?

How does man in the new life relate to the men in the world about him? We must phrase the question thus, if we wish to arrive at a man suitable for drama. Man in isolation is not suited to the drama; no literary art can result from an isolation of human existence which would correspond to the art of portraiture. Literature shows man only in the succession of his feelings and thoughts, which means it cannot entirely exclude the causes of the feelings and thoughts; at most it will somewhat conceal a portion of these causes, that is, the external world, which is their immediate origin. Every other literary form can if it wishes, however, present causes as though sprung straight from the soul of man, as though impressions were drawn but from the soul. They can, in other words, depict arbitrarily the relation of man to his external world, showing it as something other than a web of complex interactions.

The dramatic form forbids such an approach, and it moreover focuses relations to the external world in relations to other men. Thus investigation of a man suited for drama coincides with an investigation of the problem of man's relation to other men. (Elsewhere we have discussed, and will discuss again, this relation in its totality, *e.g.,* so-called destiny, the unity that symbolizes this totality.) How do men make contact with one another? Or better, what is their maximum potential for approaching one another, and what is the maximum distance they can place between themselves? Better yet, to what extent is man isolated in modern drama, to what degree is he alone?

Doubtless the old drama offers numerous examples of incomprehension between men. They can be of social origin, resulting because men of low origins and temperament must always see an eternal riddle in all refinement. However, this kind of incomprehension is not an aspect of the problem, for it depends merely upon social distinctions. Other instances are of a moral origin, inasmuch as a refined spirit (Claudius says of Hamlet), 'being remiss, most generous, and free from all contriving', just cannot imagine that other men are otherwise. This is the blindness of noble soul, confronted by a calculating evil which sees quite through it. Incomprehension such as this always has a rational basis, either in the qualities of particular men, or in the consequences of certain specific circumstances. It is part of the dramatic groundplan, built in from the first as a 'given'. As some men will understand one another, other will not, and the one relationship is as absolute and constant as the other. Yet the continued viability of the confidante should be a sign that the potential of absolute understanding among men was never in doubt. Confidantes are almost eliminated in the modern drama, and where they remain, they are felt to function as a disruptive technical device. Now gone out of life is that universal emotion for which alone they could function as symbol, which lifted them above their merely technical function so they might appear as the stylization of a palpable something in reality, rather than a mere convention. The emotion for which they stood could only have been one of the absolute possibility of understanding. If we consider the most complex of these relationships, the one closest to our own emotion, we will see the functioning of Horatio vis-à-vis Hamlet only confirms that no discord of spirits did or could exist between them; all Hamlet's actions and all his motives are rightly regarded and valued by Horatio, in their original sense. What one says to the other is understood and felt as the other understood and felt. Hamlet—remarkable as this may sound— is thus not alone. When he dies he does so with sure knowledge that a man lives in whom his own spirit is mirrored, pure, without the distortion of incomprehension. The new drama has no confidantes, and this is a symptom that life has robbed man of his faith that he can understand another man; 'nous mourrons tous inconnus', Balzac says somewhere. . . . I do not allude here to Fausts's *Alleinsein,* nor to that of Tasso,[12] nor to the loneliness of Grillparzer's Kaiser Rudolf nor to that of Hebbel's Herodes, next to whom an understanding friend never stood nor ever could stand. Rather I will direct attention to the first great friendship of the new drama, that between Carlos and Posa (and, to a lesser degree to be sure, that between Clavigo and Carlos);[13] and to that of Kandaules and Gyges Gregers Werle and Ekdal, Borkmann and Foldal, etc.[14] This is no result of spiritual greatness, either, for neither Hebbel's Clara, nor Hauptmann's Henschel, nor Rose Bernd ever finds a person so near to them as Horatio is to Hamlet. Men become simply incapable of expressing the truly essential in them and what truly directs their actions; even should they in rare moments find words to fit the inexpressible, these words will at any rate go unheard past the spirits of others, or reach them with meaning transformed.

A new element is correspondingly introduced into the dialogue— or rather, a new style problem confronts dialogue. . . . What is said becomes ever more peripheral to what in not expressible. The melody in dialogue is ever more submerged in the accompaniment, the openly spoken in the allusion, in silence, in effects achieved by pauses, change of tempo, etc. For the process which proceeds exclusively within, which will not even seek for words, which *can* not, is better expressed by word groupings than by their sense, and better by their associative power than by their real meaning, by their painterly or musical rather than compressive energy. The more lonely men in drama become (and the development is ever more in this direction, or at least toward awareness of it), the more the dialogue will become fragmented, allusive, impressionistic in form rather than specific and forthright. As a form, monologue is not capable of fulfilling this task. . . . A monologue is in fact the compression of a situation, or else a commentary in programmatic form upon what will come later. In a monologue the loneliness of a specific situation is compressed and expressed together with all that must remain unsaid because of the situation; and certain matters at most remain concealed: shame, for instance. But because the monologue always comes either at the start of the end of a dialogue, it cannot express the ever-shifting nuances of understand-ing and incomprehension which evade formulation and which we speak of here. The new dramatic man is not isolated because he must conceal certain matters for specific reasons, but because he strongly feels he wants, and is aware of wanting, to come together— and knows he is incapable of it. . . .

The only ideology which men will not feel to be an ideology is one which prevails absolutely and tolerates no opposition or doubt; only such a one ceases to be abstract and intellectual and is entirely transformed into feeling, so that it is received emotionally just as though no problem of value-judgement were ever involved (*e.g.,* the medieval ideology of Revenge as still found in Shakespeare, or the dictates of Honour among the Spanish). Until the ideologies motivating men became relativized, a man was right or he was wrong. If right, he recognized no relative justification of his opponents whatsoever; nothing might justify them since they were wrong. Were one to suppose that demonic passions drove them to transgress norms which otherwise were absolutely binding, then the nature of the motivating forces was itself enough to forbid sympathy for the others' state of mind, especially with opponents. The final implication of a struggle between persons was such that one could scarcely see in the opponent anyone less than a mortal enemy, and this is precisely because the struggle was irrational. How different are conflicts where the individual is taken for the mere proxy of something external to him, something objective, conflicts where the pairing of particular opponents is virtually accidental, the result of intersected necessities. This is why the man of Shakespeare's time, ripping and tearing his opponent in the wild grip of unbridled passions, could hardly be thought to conceive a sense of community with those whom he destroyed and who destroyed him. . . .

In the main, this explains why intrigue has become superfluous and even disruptive. When every action can be 'understood', man's wickedness (though its forms remain unchanged) can no longer be regarded as the ultimate cause of events (as, *e.g.*, Shakespeare's Iago still was). The Count in Lessing's *Emilia Galotti* represents the first stage of this development; and, after the wild excesses of his initial dramas, Schiller comes to this point almost against his will, in the opinion of Philipp.[15] Again it is Hebbel who grasps the situation in its theoretical purity, when he declares that a dramatist's worth is in inverse ratio to the number of scoundrels he requires. . . . In this way the tragic experience is elevated entirely into the realm of absolute necessity. Everything which is merely personal, merely empirical, disappears from it, even from its form as a phenomenon. Nothing remains but the bare tragic content, a perspective upon life in the form of inevitably tragic conflicts. . . . In this way the dramatic conflicts grow not merely more profound, but at either side of certain limits they vanish entirely. All becomes a matter of viewpoint. The subjective extreme descends from the minds of acting personages, as it were, and into the very foundations of the play. Whether or not a matter is tragic becomes strictly a matter of viewpoint. The tragi-comedy appears, a genre of art whose essence is that an event played out before us is, at one and the same time, inseparably comic and tragic. The genre has little positive significance and it is simply impracticable in performance, since the simultaneous duality of vision cannot become spontaneous experience, and the tragic aspect in a comic situation, or the comic in a tragic situation, will only be felt subsequently and then for the most part intellectually. Thus, though this sort of effort may deepen comedy from the perspective of a *Weltanschauung,* it nevertheless disrupts the purity of style and keeps tragedy to the level of the banal and trivial, if indeed it is not distorted into grotesquery. . . .

The conflicts become ever more decisively and exclusively inward, they become so much an affair of man's spirit that they can scarcely by communicated to others; and no data, no actions may be conceived which might express the conflicts, leaving nothing in reserve. Thus does action become not merely superfluous (for the release of tragic emotions does not inherently require it), but it may be felt as positively disruptive. Often enough action is no more than an accidental instigation of the real event, which occurs somewhere beyond its reach and independent of it. 'Our life has become too inward,' Hebbel laments, 'and, barring a miracle, it will never again become external.' Goethe too was aware of the immense advantages which Shakespeare had over him; for in his time the decisive conflicts might still occur in a form which worked strongly upon the senses. . . .

The new life lacks a mythology; what this means is that the thematic material of tragedies must be distanced from life artificially. For the aesthetic significance of mythology is twofold. In the first place it projects, in the concrete symbols of concrete fables, man's vital emotions concerning the most profound problems of his life. These fables are not so rigid that they cannot incorporate displacements of the general sensibility, should these occur. Should it happen, however, the retained elements will always outweigh the added elements; the perceptible event will amount to more than the new way of valuing it. The second aspect, and possibly the more important, is that the tragic situation so expressed is held at a constant natural distance from the public—a constant distance, since the event is projected into vast dark distances of time. A natural distance, since subject and content, and indeed form, have been moulded in the public's midst as something their own life partakes of, something passed along from their ancestors and without which life itself could scarcely be imagined. Whatever can be made into myth is by its nature poetic. This means, in the always paradoxical fashion of every poetic work, that it is both distant and near to life, and bears in itself, without conscious stylization, the real and irreal, the naïve and all-signifying, the spontaneous and symbolic, adornment and simple pathos. At its origins, or in the process of turning the past into myth (as for instance, Shakespeare with the War of the Roses), everything that is accidental or superfluous or derives from the individual will, or depends for its effect upon the wilfulness of individual taste—everything which, despite its 'interestingness', renders the profound trivial—is torn from the subjects of poetry. . . .

The bourgeois drama is by nature problematic, as theory and practice both agree, and countless circumstantial and formal signs indicate. Apart from the general stylistic problems of any new drama, drama becomes problematic at its base as soon as its subject is a bourgeois destiny enacted among bourgeois personages. The thematic material of bourgeois drama is trivial, because it is all too near to us; the natural pathos of its living men is nondramatic and its most subtle values are lost when heightened into drama; the fable is wilfully invented and so cannot retain the natural and poetic resonance of an ancient tradition. In consequence, most modern dramas are historical, whether they are set in a definite epoch or the timeless past, and, in view of the foregoing, their historicity gains new meaning. History is meant as a substitute for mythology, creating artificial distances, producing monumentality, clearing away trivia and injecting a new pathos. However, the distance to be gained by projecting back in history is more conscious than formerly, and it is for this reason less spirited and forced to appeal more to the facts, forced, because more timid, to cling more strongly to empirical data. The essence of historical distancing is that it substitutes what happened long ago for what happens today. But always, one event takes the place of another; never does a symbol replace a reality. (Naturally I am not concerned here with trivial 'historical truth'. A modern fantasy drama is historical; it is less free of the facts than are Shakespeare's historical dramas.) . . .

Tragedy itself has become problematic. There are, that is, no longer any absolute, overriding, external, easily discerned criteria by which one judges whether a given man and a given destiny are tragic. The tragic becomes strictly a matter of viewpoint, and— important as a problem of expression—strictly an inward, spiritual problem. Something becomes tragic only by the suggestive force of expression, and only spiritual intensities can lend the pathos of tragedy to it. . . . This is why the heroism of the new drama has grown more stylized, more rhetorical, than in the old: the heroism of the hero must be asserted consciously. On the one hand, this serves to hold his tragic experience at the distance of tragedy, as compared to the corresponding events of his life which will refuse to assume a tragic figuration. On the other hand, this affords the possibility of lending a certain force of pathos, of nay-saying significance, to this destiny within the drama, which otherwise lacks the means to render itself objectively conspicuous. What is essential in the hero, what involves him in tragedy, is in this fashion overtly stylized on the plan of a conscious heroism. Dramatic character depiction becomes artificed, hard, places distance between itself and life, whenever it endeavours to rise to tragedy. And the more it aspires to the true tragic peaks of life, or attains them, the more will it be gripped by an obstinate and cold majesty, which will in turn exclude more and more of life's richness and subtleties. . . .

The stylization, however, can no longer be simply the pathos of abstract and conscious heroism. It can be only the stylization of a single quality, exaggerated to a degree beyond any found in life, so that this single quality will be seen to rule the entire man and his destiny as well. To use the language of life, a pathology will be needed. For what does such extremism signify, if not a kind of illness, a pathological overgrowth of a certain specific into the whole life of a man? . . .

Pathology is a technical necessity and as such is related to the problems we have sketched—as even Schiller could sense, when he wrote of Goethe's *Iphigenie*: 'On the whole, Orestes is the most self-aware among them; without the Furies he would not be Orestes, and yet, since the cause of his condition is not perceptible to the eye, but remains wholly in his spirit, his condition becomes an overly long and unrelieved torment without an object.'

When a mythology is absent—which explains why this case is perhaps more striking than others—the basis on which everything must be justified is character. When the motivations are wholly based upon character, however, the wholly inward origin of this destiny will drive the character relentlessly to the limits of pathology. The non-pathological Orestes of Aeschylus was driven from without by what drives Goethe's from within; what once was destiny, becomes character for the modern poets. When we find a pathological trait in one or another personage of the ancient poets (Heracles, Ajax, Lear, Ophelia, etc.),[16] then it is the destiny of that personage to so become and his tragedy is that this is what becomes of him; but his tragedy does not originate in his being so. Even where the tragedy is built upon a pathological situation, as in *Phaedra*,[17] it is still projected entirely from without: the gods have inflicted it. Perhaps this seems only a technical problem; it may appear to matter little whether Orestes is pursued by the Furies or his own heated imagination, whether it is the witches' enticing words which bring Macbeth's stormy hunger for power to ripeness, or whether Holophernes seeks his own ruin.[18] In practice, however, we will see that what comes from without, what is sent upon man by the gods, is universal; it is destiny. In the same way, to the same degree, it might happen to anyone, and in the final analysis it becomes a destiny without reference to the composition of the particular character—or at any rate, not solely with reference to it. But when all has become an inner event and can follow only from the character—if, indeed, all is not so infinitely far from the nature of the concerned that they become incapable of dramatic action (as Oswald, Rank)—its intensity must be heightened into an illness if it is to be seen and heard. In pathology and in it alone lies the possibility of rendering undramatic men dramatic. Nothing else is capable of lending them that concentration of action, that intensity of the senses, which will make the act and the situation symbolic and raise the figures above the ordinary, above the everyday. Says Kerr,[19] 'in disease we find the permitted poetry of naturalism. . . . The figure is lent infinitely more dimensions and yet can be justified in reality.' . . .

We must therefore ask whether today pathology is to be avoided, if the content and form of life are to be expressed in dramatic form. It is a tendency destructive of the true dramatic essence, since it relegates causation to the Universal and becomes lost in a maze of psychological subtleties and imponderables. But can we see another possibility that remains open to the drama? . . .

As we see, it is a question transcending the realm of purely artistic or technical problems. To solve this technical task becomes a problem of life itself: it becomes a search for the vital centre of life. For the ancients and their drama, this question offered no problem; the vital centre was their point of departure and everything else grouped itself around it. . . . Now the vital centre is invented by the poet himself; no longer is it to be discovered, except as an inspiration or vision, as a profound philosophy or the intuition of genius; and even then, on an individual basis, as a particular, thus wholly accidental, insight. . . .

This is the crux of the paradox: the material of drama consists of the interrelatedness of ethical systems, and the dramatic structure which arises from this relationship is aesthetic-formal. From a different viewpoint, what is involved is an equilibrium of forces, of aesthetic interrelations, and this equilibrium can be achieved only in the medium of ethics. More simply, so long as tragedy did not become ethically problematic, either inwardly or outwardly, the pure aesthetics of structure functioned quite naturally: from a given beginning only a single given result can follow, since the ethical structure is a given precondition known to the poet and public alike. But when ethics cease to be a given, the ethical knotting within the drama—thus, its aesthetics—has to be created; whereupon ethics, as the cornerstone of the artistic composition, move necessarily into the vital centre of motivation. In this way the great and spontaneous unity of ethics and aesthetics, within the tragic experience, commences to be the problem.

1914   *Translated by Lee Baxandall*

Notes

1. Discussed in detail in a portion of the essay here omitted, which dealt chiefly with development of the stage as an institution. Lukács argues that truly bourgeois plays were first written by the Germans Lenz, Grabbe, Goethe, Schiller, and others who were the first dramatists to develop historicist ideas. Emphasis upon reasoned argument, together with environmental determinism, is seen to distinguish bourgeois playwrights from their predecessors, who had enjoyed spontaneous communication with their audiences by virtue of shared religious sensibility. According to Lukács, this unity was shattered by a new rationalism, introduced to society by the bourgeoisie's organization of economy and social relations along the most productive lines. The playwright found himself isolated from the broad public; he produced intellectualist compositions for minority audiences, while the public, cut off alike from the rationalist stage and from religious drama, sought theatre offering amusement for its own sake. The Little Theatre movement which emerged after 1885 sought to provide bourgeois drama with a stage, but with poor results. (E. Bentley)

2. Anonymous Elizabethan tragedy ascribed to Thomas Kyd (1558–1594).

3. *Herod and Mariamne* by Friedrich Hebbel (1813–1863).

4. Jakob Michael Reinhold Lenz (1751–1792).

5. Denis Diderot (1713–1784); Sebastian Mercier (1740–1814).

6. Christian Dietrich Grabbe (1801–1836), German playwright.

7. Hugo von Hofmannsthal (1874–1929), Austrian poet, playwright, and essayist.

8. Characters in *Maria Magdalena, Hedda Gabler,* and *Fuhrmann Henschel.*

9. Vittorio Alfieri (1749–1803), Italian writer and playwright.

10. Arthur Schopenhauer (1788–1860), German philosopher.

11. *Götz von Berlichingen* by Goethe; *The Robbers* by Schiller.

12. *Tasso* by Goethe.

13. Reference to *Don Carlos* by Schiller and *Clavigo* by Goethe, respectively.

14. Kandaules and Gyges: characters in Hebbel's *Gyges and His Ring;* Gregers Werle and Ekdal: in Ibsen's *The Wild Duck;* Borkmann and Foldal: in Ibsen's *John Gabriel Borkman.*

15. Reference to *Don Carlos* by Schiller.

16. The first two plays by Euripides and Sophocles, respectively; the last two referring to *King Lear* and *Hamlet.*

17. By Jean Racine (1639–1699).

18. *Judith* by Hebbel.
19. Alfred Kerr (1867–1948), German critic.

GEORG (VON) LUKÁCS, 1885–1971, Hungarian by birth, one of the most influential Marxist literary critics. The excerpt is taken from *The Dramatic Form,* which appeared in Hungarian in 1909 and in German in 1914.

Carl Sternheim

Thoughts Concerning the Nature of Drama

Inscribed above the work of the poet, and especially the work of the dramatist, who is conscious of having the most forceful impact, is the word "responsibility." His judgment, so visibly manifest on the stage, has an immediate and far-reaching influence; weighed in a hundred consciences, it must have all the qualities of a divine fiat intended for the benefit of mankind.

The poet follows no inclination. Should the hero or the most charming heroine of his play seek to persuade him to take some step, he turns his ear from their enticements to the calling of that voice which, though it is not always easy to hear, imparts to him the counsels of heaven. As soon as the creative spirit perceives some visibly gaping damage somewhere in the order of earthly values, there begins, in outraged and zealous love, the work of summoning the general attention to the disorder and administering the balm of new understanding derived from the revelations of poetry.

The dramatic poet is the doctor tending to the body of his times. His undeniable duty is to preserve all the qualities of ideal humanity in their immaculate radiance.

To attain his high purpose, he makes use, as a doctor does, of the allopathic or homoeopathic method. He can place a finger on the diseased part of humanity and have his hero oppose that ill with eager and militant defiance at the risk of his life (this is the nature of tragedy), or he can inject the moribund quality into the hero and have him be fanatically possessed by it (this is the essence of comedy). In tragedy, the world surrounding the hero will, by failing to recognize the evil, appear tragic, while in comedy it is the hero himself who seems tragic for the same reason. The effect on the viewer is in both cases the same: gazing down into the abyss, he sees the desperate struggle between the divine and a humanity that closes its eyes to knowledge, and remains profoundly stirred and illumined.

1914   *Translated by Joel Agee*

CARL STERNHEIM, 1878–1942, wrote prose, essays, and dramas. His satirical comedies *Die Hose* (1911), *Bürger Schippel* (1913), and *Der Snob* (1914) are still regularly performed.

Georg Kaiser

The Dramatic Poet and the Man in the Audience

Platform for the loudest call to action—the theater! A call to action!—for here no decisions are reached—no vote is being taken—what's being said is neither yes nor no.

Only that agitation takes hold which incites to creation.

The work that's being performed up there, what is it?

An inducement. Not a command. Not a decree. Complete freedom is left to the one who watches-listens below.

Freedom for what?

For his own creatively transformative power which does not distort the work up there (sole measure of the value of the work—but I am not speaking of works beneath this standard!)—but makes it flow from all the apertures that are shut up by a hundred accidents.

No one is exalted above another person—in each, the image of the all is made perfect and fulfilled—and the image of the all is a million times perfect in infinity.

Thus each of us upholds *his* cosmic image—dark behind curtains and more weakly visible and clear—: and the work that's being performed up there is a call to the great labor of uncovering—: for here is one who made arduous effort to interpret and make visible his image of the all—in effort an example to the other and to each below, to make the same effort of that creation that pulses in each.

No work of art is valid in itself. That work is dangerous that is accepted with yes and no, for it mutilates the receiver, who is a visionary in his own right—just as each of us can only give from himself in his own right, so as not to take from anyone and to give to all what is their own already.

[1918; 1923]   *Translated by Joel Agee*

Man in the Tunnel, or: The Poet and the Play

To write a play is to think a thought through to the end. (One who has exhausted his thinking turns back to his past plays and assists in their theatrical executions: genesis of the exalted master.) An idea without a character remains nonsense: Plato writes the most exciting scenes and in doing so develops his philosophical work. Other philosophical tomes depart further and further from their title with each page (and even the title is nebulous).

One should subject himself—presuming he wants to reflect at all—to the enormous labor of formulating his drama. Whatever can't be presented to my neighbor with a sparse dialogue will float off into stupidity. Man speaks in order to think—thinks in order to speak. Since ancient times the best mouths have preached their way into the *genus humanum*—just listen! You can't keep caning bottoms if what you want is to bring in some light at the top. The human race has undertaken tremendous things in its dramatic thinkers; if they make life hard for you today—the result will triumph in your grandchildren: the individual gives form to his thoughts and takes thought in the making of forms.

Of what value is the play to the poet in the end? He is done with it. The long preoccupation with an idea is already an excessive torment. Ten new ones have shot up since then. But the playwright heroically keeps a grip on the rope until he has groped his way through to the end. That brings his thought to a conclusion. Immediately he sets forth into another area—one must make use of the brief span given hereabouts to brain and blood. (And this gives rise to the image of the dramatist's back-side: the playwright who fondly returns to his works, talking about them, pointing at them with lantern-poles, visualizing himself in a highly visible loge before the performance, stuffing his mattress with old laurels that rustle with fame at night under his snoring broadside.)

Once we have seen the multiplicity of unconceived thoughts, there is very little time left for love. (That sounds gloomy—but in a moment I'll pull the loveliest summer sun into my sky.) But no head has an unendurable quantum of thoughtfulness implanted in it. The totality of man is excellently balanced. However, this supreme understanding is required: To stop when you come to the end. Whoever hangs on will lose his life. To live—that's what it's about. That is the meaning of existence. Its exhausting experience. All roads lead there—but all the roads must be trodden. *One* path leads through the head. To travel it, the most severe training is needed: knowing how to think. The shaping of a play is the means— never the goal. (Whoever mistakes the two—see above: exalted master. I am not naming negative examples here; I don't want to fill the following pages with an index of the history of literature— instead, the positive one of Rimbaud, who as a merchant in Egypt laughed at his Parisian poet's fame.) It is villainous to define an excellent human being by *one* of his abilities—and he who accepts this mutilation is ridiculous. It is almost a moral question: remaining a poet.

The goal of existence is: the record. Setting a record in all areas. Man at the peak of his achievements typifies the time that begins tomorrow and never ends. The Hindu model of universal activity through inactivity is being surpassed in our climes: here the universally active man vibrates at a rate that makes his movement visible.

Drama is a passageway—but the springboard directly into completion. After this schooling, a person is excellently equipped to find his place in the world. He hates stupidity—but he no longer exploits it. (Only the idiot wants a bargaining advantage—in commerce and in the life of the mind. He ends up being frequently cheated—viz.: literary history.)

A creator's duty is: to turn away from each of his works and go into the desert; if he reappears, he must bring a great deal with him—but building a villa with garage in the shadow of his sycamores: that won't do. That's pushing shamelessness a bit too far, and entering into infamous competition with the underpaid prostitutes.

Everything is a passageway: but to rest and remain in passageways (tunnels)—good luck to the one who's hardnosed enough to do it——and woe to him!

1923   *Translated by Joel Agee*

GEORG KAISER, 1878–1945, successful playwright in the Berlin of the Weimar Republic (*Die Bürger von Calais*, 1914) and one of the main representatives of German expressionist drama (*Die Koralle*, 1917; *Gas I*, 1918; *Gas II*, 1920).

Hugo von Hofmannsthal

The Theater of the New

THIMIG: . . . So what we have to do now is decide on the opening work.

HOMOLKA: The opening work is here. (*He points to a stage manuscript protruding from his breast pocket.*)

THIMIG: So you have already made your choice? I thought though it was jointly—well, may I see it?

HOMOLKA: This play is the work for opening the "Theater of the New" if we are what we want to be.

THIMIG: Oh please can't I see it? . . . Understandably enough, I am interested.

HOMOLKA: *Baal* by Brecht. I believe that says enough. The name is a programme. It means the latest thing, the breakthrough into the unconditional, the new, the elementary.

THIMIG: Oh, sure! But wouldn't you let me take a look at the work? A look provides some idea. I really am interested.

HOMOLKA: A look would tell you nothing. A work like this is the ultimate unity, not thought-out words glued onto a thought-out scenario. Gesture and word are one. Inner force is unleashed and creates the new living space by fulfilling itself with it.

THIMIG: But it is historical?

HOMOLKA: Historical? How do you arrive at that spooky concept?

THIMIG: *Baal* . . . I assume!

HOMOLKA: It is the myth of our existence, the elementary understanding of our existence. The contemporary person goes through everything, absorbs everything vital for the purpose of ultimately returning to the soil.

171

THIMIG: And you assume this will be readily understood? Here? After all, this is not Berlin.

HOMOLKA: But today is still today, perhaps even here.

THIMIG: Certainly.

HOMOLKA: And people of today are people of today? Even here maybe?

THIMIG: Without any doubt.

HOMOLKA: And you believe it is possible to exclude oneself from one's own era without shrinking into a shadow? What do you think, Dr. Friedell?

FRIEDELL: I am convinced that the moment I wanted to exclude myself from my era I would shrink into a shadow, regardless of however difficult that would be for me personally.

WANIEK: I, in any case, would immediately hang myself if I were to assume that in the era in which I am breathing, despite radio, trusts, and spotlights, that myth-creating force were extinguished.

THIMIG: The issue is not only us, the issue is those who sit in the audience. After all, the theater is a social institution. If we want a new poet to speak in a new language through us to them, we must also want them to understand it.

HOMOLKA: The poet we espouse does not speak.

THIMIG: Oh!

HOMOLKA: The new poet of a chaotic era is a prophet of goals.

FRIEDELL (*pouring himself a glass of schnaps*): The issue is that contemporary material finally be grasped. (*He finishes his drink.*)

WANIEK: You could just as well say: solved. But go ahead and formulate as you please and meanwhile let me prepare.

(*Getting up from his work*)

It does have something new and soulful!

HOMOLKA: We feel it.

WANIEK: It touches us.

HOMOLKA: It strives to assume form through our body.

THIMIG: Excellent, I wouldn't wish anything better for myself. But that is possible only through the medium of language.

HOMOLKA: Precisely, through this language. (*He beats his breast.*) It needs our body. Our scream. Our muteness.

THIMIG: But this is mainly what it needs (*pointing to his mouth*). Without language, no content. Without spirit, no world.

HOMOLKA: We don't have to dish up a lot of spirit. What we have to do is integrate the universe with the soul.

WANIEK: Our task is to create magical space in which material and social limitations dissolve and the human being himself becomes the symbol.

HOMOLKA: People today hate the word. They hate the machinations of the spirit. They want the thing, blood, essence.

FRIEDELL: You hear it!

THIMIG: Yes, yes, yes, yes. I know the text. I also know the melody. But why we should borrow the recipes from precisely those people who appear to themselves gigantic because they can't deal with life, I don't know. We here, can. For us form is not a nightmare. We deal with forms without sacrificing the secret of life to them. We use, if you will, an articulated language, regardless of whether the words come from Shakespeare or Nestroy! After all, traditional language is the bridge, standing on which we survive the crash of generations. If it be antiquated on the surface, it is nonetheless our pride that we, penetrating it, make tangible that life eternally entrusted to it, and our reward is the fact that we are understood by those sitting in front of us regardless of whether they are not the elderly whose origins are of yesterday or whether they are boys heading toward tomorrow.

HOMOLKA (*getting up*): Mr. Thimig, as long as you think vertically to this degree, we will not be able to understand each other.

THIMIG (*somewhat startled*): I think vertically?

FRIEDELL (*comfortably*): Yes, I too have had this impression. It is an infection that is in the Vienna air.

HOMOLKA: You think in terms of ancestors, with yourself as their culmination. The new man thinks horizontally, in the cross-section of the present. We have no predecessors.

THIMIG: Are you sure of that?

HOMOLKA: Language as the vehicle of what is called spirit is for the time being done for.

THIMIG: I don't know about that.

HOMOLKA: It has become weary of life.

THIMIG: I am not convinced of that.

FRIEDELL: Very understandable. It had enough of being on every tongue. In the long run that is no existence for a spiritual being.

THIMIG: A man of true spirit will renew it today or tomorrow.

HOMOLKA: Time has no time to wait, it wants to be redeemed.

THIMIG: A rough, unarticulated language will not redeem it, but will only undermine our existence.

HOMOLKA (*vigorously*): Chaos does not primp, Mr. Thimig! (*Thimig falls silent. A short pause. The telephone rings loudly. Waniek grabs the telephone.*)

WANIEK: The connection with Berlin. Yes, I am coming. What should I do? What should I say? (*Hangs up.*) Can I justify on the phone a spiritual world that was developed in the course of reflection for months? (*Hurries away, comes into view again at the window on the right.*)

HOMOLKA: What you must say is fifteen words. The "Theater of the New" is taking place, and the opening is *Baal* by Brecht.

(*Waniek leaves. A pause.*)

FRIEDELL (*to Homolka*): You just said something very interesting. Unintentionally, I assume.

HOMOLKA: How so?

FRIEDELL: I always assume that the most interesting things slip out unintentionally—except with me, of course.

HOMOLKA: Really!

FRIEDELL: Namely, the time is unredeemed. And do you also know what it would like to be redeemed by?

THIMIG: I am eager.

FRIEDELL: By the individual.

THIMIG: How?

FRIEDELL: Time pulls too hard on this sixteenth-century offspring that was raised by the nineteenth.

THIMIG: But that is quite a far-reaching paradox.

HOMOLKA: Not at all. We are anonymous forces. Spiritual possibilities. Individuality is one of the arabesques we have gotten rid of. You will see how I perform *Baal*.

THIMIG: Oh, you are going to play the role of Baal? (*paces back and forth*) You call the individual a construct of the imagination? I can't go along with that. You too? Maybe the fact that, after I have seen *Baal*. . .

FRIEDELL: Yes indeed, Mr. Thimig, and I would go so far as to assert that all the ominous events we have been experiencing in Europe for the last twelve years are nothing but a very roundabout way of putting the worn out idea of the European individual into the grave he dug himself.

THIMIG (*at the end of his patience*): I can't go along with that!

WALDAU (*entering*): Am I disturbing? I see you are in the middle of your discussion. I don't want to disturb you, for God's sake. (*starts to leave*)

THIMIG: On the contrary, you arrive at the right moment to hear about a somewhat surprising but interesting piece of news.

WALDAU (*politely*): Is there anything new?

THIMIG: Yes indeed, the individual no longer exists.

WALDAU: What?

THIMIG: Modern thinking has done away with it. It is an arabesque of the past. (*Waldau smiles in embarrassment.*)

THIMIG: These two gentlemen put me, so to speak, in contact with the era.

WALDAU: Which individual? I don't quite understand. What's the issue?

THIMIG: You, me. The concept of the individual in general.

WALDAU: Whenever I don't understand a joke and try to behave as if I did, I never succeed.

THIMIG: It is no joke, Mr. Waldau. We are conducting a very serious conversation.

HOMOLKA: Certainly.

WALDAU: Well, you look so serious. Are you having a quarrel? That would be terrible between close colleagues.

THIMIG: Not at all. I am just dreadfully backward. Until now I believed I was an individual and, on the basis on my individuality, able to portray individuals.

WALDAU: Extremely sympathetic individuals, dear Hermann.

THIMIG: That is not the issue, dear Waldau. The issue is that, for horizontal-thinking people of today, the restricted ego of the individual no longer exists. You will understand that after having seen him play the role of Baal.

WALDAU: Oh, Baal?

THIMIG: *Baal* by Brecht, with which we are opening the "Theater of the New."

1926   *Translated by Martha Humphreys*

HUGO VON HOFMANNSTHAL, 1874–1929, eminent Austrian man of letters, wrote poetry, prose fiction, essays, and plays. Together with Max Reinhardt and Richard Strauss he founded the Salzburg Festival in 1917, which to this day traditionally opens with a performance of his *Jedermann* (1911) or *Das Salzburger Grosse Welttheater* (1921–1922). His collaboration with Strauss resulted in five operas: *Der Rosenkavalier* (1911), *Die Frau ohne Schatten* (1911–1919), *Ariadne auf Naxos* (1912–1916), *Die Ägyptische Helena* (1927), and *Arabella* (1933). For an example of Hofmannsthal's fiction, see *German Literary Fairy Tales*, Volume 30 in The German Library, for his "Tale of the 672nd Night."

The excerpt here is taken from a one-act play, *The New Theater: An Announcement*. The characters are actors at the Josefstadt-Theater and "are, as it were, playing themselves." *Baal* was Brecht's first play, written in 1918, and first performed in 1923.

Ernst Toller

Remarks Concerning German Post-War Drama

We employ the concept "post-war drama" without asking ourselves whether there really is a special type of post-war drama that is completely different from the pre-war drama in its problematics and its plot, in genre and in form. Has the war brought about such a decisive turnabout in the German theater? Not at all. It is a curious thing to take note today, ten years later, of how the essential tendencies of post-war theater began to develop years earlier, the only difference being that after the war they erupted into sudden visibility. The young writers who counted for something felt separated from the older generation by an abyss. The struggle of the generations, the father-son problem, the struggle between compromise and independence, between the bourgeois and the anti-bourgeois spirit, all these things agitated young minds before the war proved the validity of their premonitions. No doubt, the war made a shambles of many moral and social, spiritual and artistic values. But what was struck down was already falling, the foundation of these values had been rotting. The idea was despised. "*Realpolitik*" was the motto of the day. It led to the destruction of reality.

The first plays of the "*Junges Deutschland*"[1] were animated by hatred for the generation of the fathers. And it was these fathers who failed to prevent the war, who made a romantic lie of it, fathers without mercy, who sent battalion after battalion of young people to their deaths.

During the war, very little managed to slip past the strict censorship into public view. After the country's defeat, every day

177

brought new works informed by a libertarian spirit. The form of that art was called Expressionism. Expressionism was as much reaction as synthetic, creative action. It opposed that direction in art that thought it sufficient to line up impressions without asking for the essential, for responsibility, for the idea. The expressionists were not content with photographing images, they knew that the environment sinks into the depth of the artist and is refracted in the mirror of his soul, that it is necessary to depict this environment anew, not in its appearances but in its essence. For the Expressionists wanted to affect this environment, change it, give it a more just and luminous face. Reality was to attain new definition by the ray of the idea, was to be reborn.

Every happening disintegrated into an outer and inner event, both of them equally important, equally strong as moving forces. In its style, expressionism was trenchant, almost telegram-like, avoiding peripheral matters, always pushing through to the center of things. Man in the expressionist theater was not an accidental private person. He was a type, representative of a multitude, stripped of their superficial traits. The expressionists skinned the human being and believed they had found his soul beneath the skin.

During the expressionist epoch, a momentous event announced its coming: a new type of man stepped onto the stage, proletarian man. To be sure, there had been plays set in a proletarian milieu before. But there is a fundamental difference between the expressionist proletarian drama and a play like Hauptmann's *Weavers*[2] or Büchner's *Woyzeck*[3]: In the old dramas, proletarian man was a dull and gloomy creature who rebelled against his fate out of a strong but vague emotion. The artist portraying him wanted to awaken compassion in the viewer. In the new drama, the proletarian man is active, conscious, and he is rebelling against his fate for the sake of a new reality, fighting for a new social order. He is impelled by feeling *and* insight.

It is a complete mistake to speak of a fiasco of expressionism. Those who scold expressionism where it was truly capable are blind. They do not see that at that time the fullness of the concrete was so powerful that the artist could only master it by means of abstraction. Today a thousand details have been forgotten, a thousand others have split up into more or less irrelevant distinctions. Since experience and distance bind one another, great realistic works are once again being produced.

Whether expressionism created lasting works won't be known until at least fifty years have passed. But one must not forget that expressionism, born of its times, wanted to affect history. Not since Schiller's *Robbers,* not since *Love and Intrigue* had the theater become this kind of tribunal of public events or been so embattled by the attacks and counter-attacks of public opinion. Passionate participation on one side, violent reproaches for its one-sided tendentiousness on the other.

Let us examine for a moment the reproach that expressionist drama profaned artistic values by its political tendency. A certain totality of feelings, insights, intellectual attitudes, and reactions to various phenomena of life are called untendentious by the bourgeois because they have become traditional and because they correspond to his world view, his philosophy, his power interests. He overlooks that this totality has a tendency too, namely his own. Now if in a play he encounters new points of view that conflict with the ones he is used to, he calls it "tendentious." Insofar as the atmosphere of a work is determined by social milieu, we may confidently call it tendentious.

There is only one kind of tendentiousness which must be rejected by the artist, and that is the tendency to black-and-white characterization, painting the people on one side as devils and those on the other as angels. The interpenetration of good and bad qualities cannot overpower the strength of the idea. But despite the law of strict objectification, which develops characters out of their own innate compulsions and conditionings, the artist is conscious of the fact that it is precisely he who arrives at a collectively applicable subjectivism. He does not equate values and ideas. A hierarchy is established in him which strictly separates higher values from inferior ones.

Political literature must not be confused with propaganda that uses literary means. Propaganda serves the immediate goals of the day, it is both more and less than literature. More, because it contains the possibility, at least in the strongest, in the best hypothetical case, to impel the viewer to immediate action. Less, because it never plumbs the depths that poetry can reach: to convey to the viewer a sense of the tragic-cosmic foundation. In other words: when propaganda points out ten "problems," it does so on the psychological presumption that all of them can be solved, and the propagandist has the right to demand the solution of every one of them. Literature (this can only be described with a vague example) will depict the ways in which nine of these problems can be solved and point out the tragically unsolvable nature of the tenth. Whether this is done with pathos or resignation, pessimistically or with a defiant "despite all this" is a question of one's intellectual attitude and artistic temperament, but it doesn't touch the essence.

Since the works of the mind did not transform the face of the times, since the old reality raised its head again, showing the same atrociousness, greed and savagery and the same danger zones, since the peace everyone had yearned for had turned into a grimacing mask behind which lurked the menace of a new war, since the spirit had again been turned into a facade and an object of derision, young dramatists appeared who believed that ideas did not belong in a work of art at all. They wanted to depict "life," nothing but "pure life." They overlooked the fact that the conflict of ideas is one of the elements of life. For them, "life" was the unrestrained attraction and repulsion of sexual drives. Chaotic sexuality became the central issue of the new theater. Language became naturalistic again, but what distinguished these plays from the old naturalism was a dynamism that added a peculiar rhythm.

Without a doubt, the youngest German playwrights are influenced by America, but German Americanism does not take its bearings from the few leading great minds in America. What is being adopted is: speed, banal optimism, unrelatedness, in short, that *"Neue Sachlichkeit"* [New Objectivity] which has very little to do with being close to people and to things. *"Neue Sachlichkeit"* is often equated with reportage. Reportage has its importance. Drama, like all art, must achieve more than that, namely concentration, gradation, and form. Only then does reportage arrive at artistic truth.

Like all art today, the theater lives between two worlds. The bourgeois world is spiritually and ethically shaken, and the world of the productive workers is as yet only reflected in small or tiny art forms. The generation of people in their thirties, the war generation, seems to be living in a hiatus as far as the theater is concerned. Let us hope that it is a creative hiatus. Those who experienced the war as children are hardly moving. What we can see of their work is with few exceptions not very original, is classicistic, strangely lacking in vigor, almost senile. The last few years have brought us several important novels (the culture of the novel seems to be just beginning to develop in Germany), but they have brought us few plays that can be considered artistic documents of our time.

1929   *Translated by Joel Agee*

Notes

1. Anti-romantic movement of the eighteen thirties.
2. 1892.
3. 1836, but not published until 1879.

ERNST TOLLER, 1893–1939, socialist, then communist, was a reluctant leader of the short-lived Munich putsch of 1919. He continued anti-fascist activities until his suicide in exile in New York. His plays, mounted in collaboration with Erwin Piscator, were widely discussed not only because of their literary merit but for their political impact and as examples of early documentary drama: *Die Wandlung* (1919), *Masse Mensch* (1920), *Die Maschinenstürmer* (1922—on the English Luddite movement), *Hinkemann* (1923), and *Hoppla, wir leben* (1927).

Erwin Piscator

The Berlin Production of Paquet's *Flags*[1]

I was now able to develop a type of direction which, years later, was proclaimed by others to be "epic theater."[2] What was it all about? Briefly, it was about the extension of the action and the clarification of the background to the action, that is to say it involved a continuation of the play beyond the dramatic framework. A didactic play was developed from the spectacle-play. This automatically led to the use of stage techniques from areas which had never been seen in the theater before. It had started, as has been mentioned, in the Proletarisches Theater. At the Volksbühne[3] I could see what tremendous possibilities the theater offered if you had the courage to extend your forms of expression. I had broad projection screens erected on either side of the stage. During the prologue at the beginning, in which the play was introduced with character sketches of the figures who were to appear, photographs of the persons in question were projected on the screen. Throughout the play I used the screens to connect the separate scenes by projecting linking texts. To my knowledge, it was the first time that projections had been used in this way in the theater. Apart from this I restricted myself to staging the play, which had a cast of fifty-six, as clearly and objectively as possible. . . .

As the performance went on the audience's approval became more and more noisy. And after three large flags of mourning had been lowered from the flies over the final scene, a thunder of applause broke loose which was almost revolutionary in character. For Paquet, for me, and for everybody involved the evening was a major success. In the review I have already mentioned—and it was

182

typical of many—Lania[4] wrote: "At the Berlin Volksbühne a drama is now being performed which, in spite of the heat of summer, has full houses every night, while all the other theaters are empty and abandoned. . . . *Flags,* which was written in 1918, is a direct response to the Revolution, a loosely connected series of scenes that radiate the heat and the stirring rhythms of those days. . . . The effect was profound and prolonged."

Much as I enjoyed my personal success—whatever people might say against me, this was something like a breakthrough for me at one of Berlin's major theaters—it was the success of the new venture which really pleased me. Once again the way ahead seemed clearer, a way which would lead to political drama and to the hotly disputed technical revolution in the theater. But we were not there yet. The first thing I turned my hand to was more political agitation by theatrical means.

From *Outline of a Sociological Dramaturgy*

For us, man portrayed on the stage is significant as a social function. It is not his relationship to himself, nor his relationship to God, but his relationship to society which is central. Whenever he appears, his class or social stratum appears with him. His moral, spiritual or sexual conflicts are conflicts with society. The Ancients may have focused on his relationship to the Fates, the Middle Ages on his relationship to God, Rationalism on his relationship to nature, Romanticism on his relationship to the power of the emotions—: a time in which the relationship of individuals in the community to one another, the revision of human values, the realignment of social relationships is the order of the day cannot fail to see mankind in terms of society and the social problems of the times, i.e., as a political being.

The excessive stress on the political angle—and it is not our work, but the disharmony in current social conditions which makes every sign of life political—may in a sense lead to a distorted view of human ideals, but the distorted view at least has the advantage of corresponding to reality.

We, as revolutionary Marxists, cannot consider our task complete if we produce an uncritical copy of reality, conceiving the theater as a mirror of the times. We can no more consider this our task than we can overcome this state of affairs by theatrical means alone, nor can we conceal the disharmony with a discreet veil, nor can we present man as a creature of sublime greatness in times which in fact socially distort him—in a word, it is not our business to produce an idealistic effect. The business of revolutionary theater is to take reality as its point of departure and to magnify the social discrepancy, making it an element of our indictment, our revolt, our new order.

Drama and History

History? For us? What meaning can history have for times like these, which are themselves bursting with enormous problems, with remarkable events and destinies! The present day has no need to reawaken dead heroes; it has pitilessly desecrated its living heroes and can see itself only as the reflex of conflicting social trends and forces while are themselves more gigantic and embittered than all the wars and conflicts of times past. If we stand still in the midst of the raging turmoil of today and look back, we do so only because we see the past in terms as exclusively political as the present. Historical drama is not the tragedy of the fate of some hero or other, it is the political document of an epoch.

If we dispensed with these political documents it would mean casting to the wind experiences and discoveries which cost generations before us untold blood and sacrifice. But neither can we content ourselves with viewing history purely historically. Historical drama is not just a matter of education: only if it has a life of its own can it bridge the gap between then and now and release the forces which are destined to shape the appearance of the present and of the immediate future.

Where does history end and politics begin? This frontier does not exist in our historical drama. The Peasants' War, the French Revolution, the Commune,[5] 1848, 1813, the October Revolt—only in relation to the year 1927 can we experience these things. *Danton's Death* and *Florian Geyer* tell us just as much about the time when they were written as about their historical subjects.[6]

But we wish documents from the past to be seen in the light of the present moment, not episodes from times past but those times themselves, not fragments but a unified whole, history not as background but as political reality.

This basic attitude toward historical drama means a complete revision of traditional dramatic form; not the inner arc of dramatic events is important, but the most accurate and comprehensive epic account of the epoch from its roots to its ultimate ramifications. Drama is important for us only where it can be supported by documentary evidence. Film, the constant interruption of external events by projections and film clips, are a means of achieving this documentary breadth and depth; they are inserted between the acts and after decisive turns of events and provide areas of illumination as the searchlight of history penetrates the uttermost darkness of the times.

1929   *Translated by Hugh Rorrison*

Notes

1. Alfons Paquet (1881–1944), editor of the *Frankfurter Zeitung* and writer. His "dramatic novel" *Fahnen* was first produced by Edwin Piscator in Berlin in 1924.
2. Reference to Bertolt Brecht.
3. Volksbühne: theater in Berlin.
4. Leo Lania, in *Wiener Arbeiterzeitung,* 2 June 1924.
5. The Peasants' War of 1524–1525; the Commune: short-lived socialist uprising in Paris in 1870, subject of a play by Brecht, *Die Tage der Kommune* (1948).
6. In *Danton's Death* (1835) Georg Büchner depicts events in Paris during the Reign of Terror of 1794; in *Florian Geyer* (1896) Gerhart Hauptmann deals with events during the Peasants' War.

ERWIN PISCATOR, 1893–1966, important Berlin director and stage innovator, director from 1940 to 1949 of the Dramatic Workshop of the New School for Social Research in New York. His directing style anticipated Brecht's epic theater and paved the way for the documentary theater of Rolf Hochhuth's *The Deputy* (1963), Heinar Kipphardt's *In the Matter of J. Robert Oppenheimer* (1964), and Peter Weiss's *The Investigation* (1965), all of which Piscator first produced.

Ödön von Horvath

User's Instructions

The basic dramatic theme of all my plays
is the eternal struggle between the conscious
and the subconscious.

Until today I've always intensely resisted making any sort of comment about my plays—I was simply naive enough to imagine that people (the exception unfortunately proves the rule) would understand my plays without the need for user's instructions. Today I admit straight out that this was a crude mistake and that I'm forced to write a set of user's instructions.

First of all, it's my own fault: for I thought that many parts that surely allow only one interpretation would be easily understood, but this is not the case—I often did not completely succeed in achieving the synthesis between irony and realism I was aiming at.

Second: So far it's the fault of the productions:—all my plays have not been performed in the right style, and this necessarily led to countless misunderstandings. It's not the fault of anyone in the theater, I can't blame any of the directors and actors, I want this very clearly understood—no, it's entirely my fault. For I completely entrusted my plays to the appropriate authorities—but now I see clearly, I know exactly how my plays should be performed.

Third, it's the fault of the audience; for it is unfortunately no longer used to paying attention to the words in a play; frequently all it sees is the plot—it sees the dramatic action but no longer hears the dramatic dialogue. Anyone, if you please, can look up my plays and read them: there is not a single scene there that isn't

186

dramatic—what I mean by "dramatic" is the collision of two temperaments, the transformations, etc. In the course of every dialogue, a person is changing. Please look it up! The fact that this hasn't come out yet is the fault of the productions. But it's also the audience's fault.

For ultimately, the essence of this synthesis of seriousness and irony is the unmasking of consciousness. Perhaps you remember a statement in my *Italian Night*,[1] which goes like this: "You all look so blandly the same and you all enjoy being so smugly self-confident."

That is my dialogue.

It should be obvious from all of this that parody can't be my intent—I'm often reproached for being a parodist, but this is not at all true. I hate parody! Satire and caricature yes, once in a while. But you can count the satirical and caricaturistic moments in my plays on the fingers of one hand—I am not a satirist, gentlemen, I have no other goal than this one: the unmasking of consciousness. Not the unmasking of a person, of a city—that would be awfully cheap! Nor an unmasking of southern Germans, needless to say—the only reason why I write like a southern German is because I can't write in any other way.

I pursue this unmasking for two reasons: first of all, because it gives me pleasure—second, because one of my insights into the nature of the theater, into its purpose, and ultimately into the purpose of every art, is the following (and word of this must have gotten around by now): people go to the theater to be entertained, to elevate themselves, to be able perhaps to weep, to experience something. So there are entertainment theaters, aesthetic theaters and pedagogic theaters. They all have one thing in common: they supply fantasies and perform this function for more masses of people than does any other art.—So the theater fantasizes for the audience and at the same time it lets the audience experience the products of this fantasy. As we all know, fantasy is an outlet for wishes—and if we look closer we find that they're usually anti-social drives—and highly primitive ones at that. Therefore, in the theater the audience finds at one and the same time the outlet and the experiential satisfaction of its anti-social drives.

A communist is murdered on the stage, in a cowardly manner, by an overwhelming number of beast-like men. The communist audience is filled with resentment and hate against the White soldiers—but actually they're living the enemies' deeds, committing the murder themselves, and the resentment and the hatred increase because they are directed against one's own anti-social desires. Proof: isn't it peculiar that people go to the theater to witness the murder of a (decent) man whose values they share—and pay the price of admission and later leave the theater in a solemn and elevated mood? What is going on here if not a participation in murder by vicarious experience? People leave the theater with fewer anti-social impulses than they brought in with them. (What I mean by "anti-social" are drives that have a criminal foundation—I don't mean movements that are directed against a society—I want to make this especially clear, that's how anxious I've gotten as a result of all those misunderstandings.)

This is a noble pedagogical purpose for the theater. And the theater will not die, for people will always want to learn about these kinds of things—in fact, the stronger collectivism gets, the bigger the imagination gets. Of course not as long as you're fighting for collectivism, not yet, but then—sometimes I already think of the time that will be referred to as proletarian romanticism. (I am convinced that it will come.) With my unmasking of consciousness, I naturally bring about a disturbance of those murderous feelings—that's why people often find my plays disgusting and repulsive, because this way they can't vicariously participate in atrocities. They are pushed into confrontation of these atrocities—they are aware of them, but they don't experience them vicariously. For me there is one law, and that law is the truth.

I understand it when someone asks—Dear sir, why do you call your plays folk plays? This too is something I would like to answer today, so that I'll have some peace and quiet with regard to such things for a while. So: this is why.

Six years ago I wrote my first play, *The Mountain Train*,[2] and gave it the subtitle and genre specification: "A folk play." This term had been pretty much forgotten in the most recent theater work. Naturally I wasn't using this term arbitrarily; that is, I didn't just call my play a folk play because it's written in Bavarian dialect and the characters are railroad workers, but because what I had in mind was something like a continuation, a renewal of the old folk play—in short, a play in which problems are treated and dealt with in as popular a form as possible, questions that concern the so-called common people, their simple concerns, as seen through the eyes of the people. A grass-roots play in the best sense of the word, and one that will perhaps stimulate others to work along with me in this direction—in order to create a real folk theater that appeals to the instincts of the people and not to their intellect.

But one indispensable element in a folk play as in any other kind of play is that there has to be a human being on the stage. And furthermore: this human being doesn't come alive except through language.

But ninety percent of Germany, as of the rest of the European states, consists of petty-bourgeois of both the fulfilled and the would-be variety, in any case petty-bourgeois. So if I want to describe the people at large, I mustn't just depict the ten percent; as faithful chronicler of my time, my subject must be the vast masses of people—all of Germany!

Now the petty-bourgeoisie's liking for Educatese, the jargon of the well taught, has brought about a deterioration of the original dialects. In order realistically to characterize a person of today, I mush have him speak Educatese. But Educatese (and its causes) provoke us to take a stand—and this produces the dialogue of the new folk play, and with it the people who speak it, and, finally, the dramatic action—a synthesis of seriousness and irony.

I am fully conscious, then, of destroying the old folk play, formally and ethically—and I am trying to find the new form of the folk play. In doing this, I am closer to the tradition of the folk singers and folk comedians than to the authors of the classical folk plays. And this already brings us to the subject of how to direct my plays. I will attempt to give mainly practical instructions, as far as possible: (these apply to all my plays except for *Mountain Train*). If just one of these points is rejected by a director, I shall withdraw the play, for it will have been falsified.

Among the deadly sins of a theatrical director I would list the following:

1. Dialect. Not a single word of dialect must be spoken! Every word must be spoken in high German, but in a way that is characteristic of people who usually speak in dialect and are now forcing themselves to speak in high German. Very important! For this will already give to every word the synthesis between realism

and irony. The comedy of the subconscious. Classical speakers. Don't forget that the plays stand and fall with the dialogue!

2. In all my plays there is not a single moment of parody! In life you can often see people running around like their own parodies—in that sense yes, but in no other!

3. I also find very little satire in my plays. Nobody must be played as a caricature, except for a few extras who are more or less part of the stage set. And please do not make the stage set into a caricature either—as simple as possible, please, in front of a backdrop, with a really primitive landscape, but please use beautiful colors.

4. Of course the plays must be performed in a stylized manner—naturalism and realism will kill them, it would turn them into the sort of scenes that depict a *millyoo* and not into scenes that show the fight between the conscious and the subconscious—it'll just get lost. Please pay careful attention to the pauses in the dialogue which I have indicated with the word "silence"—this is where the conscious and the subconscious fight with one another, and that must become visible.

5. There are a few exceptions to this stylized delivery of the dialogue—certain sentences, sometimes just one sentence, which must suddenly be spoken in a completely realistic, completely naturalistic manner.

6. All my plays are tragedies—they only become funny because they're uncanny. This element of the uncanny has to be there.

7. Every dialogue must be made to stand out—any mute playing or mugging on the part of the others is strictly forbidden. Take a look at the folksong groups. For instance in the first picture in *Zeppelin:*[3] no extras—single people with pasted-on beards, fat ones, skinny ones, children, Elli and Maria, etc., have to watch—without moving, except for the speakers themselves. From the moment when the zeppelin disappears, everyone except for Kasimir and Karoline has to leave the stage—the ice-cream man only comes when you need him, he'll step up to the box—when Kasimir bangs the sledgehammer down, the people come in, watch silently while the marker runs up the pole, and leave the stage again.

The acting has to be stylized so that the essential universality of these people is emphasized—it can't be emphasized enough, otherwise no one will notice. The parts of the dialogue and monologue that must be delivered realistically are those where a person suddenly becomes visible—where he just stands there without any sort of life, but this necessarily only happens once in a rare while.

. . . This style is the result of practical work and experience, not a theoretical postulate. And it does not make any claim to universality, it applies mainly to my plays.

1935   *Translated by Joel Agee*

Notes

1. *Italienische Nacht* (1935).
2. *Bergbahn* (1929).
3. Reference to his play *Kasimir und Karoline* (1932).

ÖDÖN VON HORVATH, 1901–1938, Austro-Hungarian dramatist, lived in Munich, Berlin, and Vienna. His best-known play is *Geschichten aus dem Wiener Wald* (1931). He had a marked influence on the younger post–World War II generation of playwrights like Martin Sperr, Franz Xaver Kroetz, Rainer Werner Fassbinder, Peter Handke, and Wolfgang Bauer.

Bertolt Brecht

Shouldn't We Abolish Aesthetics?

Dear Mr. X,[1]

When I invited you to look at the drama from a sociological point of view I did so because I was hoping that sociology would be the death of our existing drama. As you immediately saw, there was a simple and radical task for sociology: to prove that there was no justification for this drama's continued existence and no future for anything based (now or in the future) on the assumptions which once made drama possible. To quote a sociologist whose vocabulary I hope we both accept, there is no sociological space for it. Yours is the only branch of knowledge that enjoys sufficient freedom of thought; all the rest are too closely involved in perpetuating our period's general level of civilization.

You were immune to the usual superstition which holds that a play has undertaken to satisfy *eternal* human urges when the only eternal urge that it sets out to satisfy is the urge to see a play. You know other urges change, and you know why. As you don't feel that the disappearance of an urge means the collapse of humanity, you, the sociologist, are alone in being prepared to admit that Shakespeare's great plays, the basis of our drama, are no longer effective. These works were followed by three centuries in which the individual developed into a capitalist, and what killed them was not capitalism's consequences but capitalism itself. There is little point in mentioning post-Shakespearean drama, as it is invariably much feebler, and in Germany has been debauched by Latin influences. It continues to be supported just out of local patriotism.

Once we adopt the sociological point of view we realize that so far as literature is concerned we are in a bog. We may possibly be able to persuade the aesthete to admit what the sociologist believes— namely that present-day drama is no good—but we shall never deprive him of his conviction that it can be improved. (The aesthete won't hesitate to admit that he can only conceive of such an 'improvement' of the drama by using the hoary old tricks of the trade: 'better' construction in the old sense, 'better' motivation for those spectators who are used to the good old motivation, and so on.) Apparently the sociologist will only support us if we say that this kind of drama is beyond repair and beg for it to be done away with. The sociologist knows that there are circumstances where improvement no longer does any good. His scale of judgment runs not from 'good' to 'bad' but from 'correct' to 'false'. If a play is 'false' then he won't praise it on the grounds that it is 'good' (or 'beautiful'); and he alone will remain deaf to the aesthetic appeal of a 'false' production. Only he knows what is false; he does not deal in relativity; he bases himself on vital interests; he gets no fun from being able to prove everything but just wants to find out the one thing worth proving; he doesn't by any means take responsibility for everything, but only for one thing. The sociologist is the man for us.

The aesthetic point of view is ill-suited to the plays being written at present, even where it leads to favourable judgments. You can see this by looking at any move in favour of the new playwrights. Even where the critics' instincts guided them right their aesthetic vocabulary gave them very few convincing arguments for their favourable attitude, and no proper means of informing the public. What is more, the theatre, while encouraging the production of new plays, gave absolutely no practical guide. Thus in the end the new plays only served the old theatre and helped to postpone the collapse on which their own future depended. It is impossible to understand what is being written today if one ignores the present generation's active hostility towards all that preceded it, and shares the general belief that it too is merely clamouring to be let in and taken notice of. This generation doesn't want to capture the theatre, audience and all, and perform good or merely contemporary plays in the same theatre and to the same audience; nor has it any chance of doing so; it has a duty and a chance to capture the theatre for a *different* audience. The works now being written are coming more and more to lead towards the great epic theatre which corresponds to the sociological situation; neither their content nor their form can be understood except by the minority that understands this. They are not going to satisfy the old aesthetics; they are going to destroy it.

With you in this hope,
Brecht

1927   *Translated by John Willett*

Notes

1. "Mr. X" was Professor Fritz Sternberg, who was also the sociologist referred to in this paragraph.

Theatre for Pleasure or Theatre for Instruction

A few years back, anybody talking about the modern theatre meant the theatre in Moscow, New York and Berlin. He might have thrown in a mention of one of Jouvet's productions in Paris or Cochran's in London, or *The Dybbuk* as given by the Habima (which is to all intents and purposes part of the Russian theatre, since Vakhtangov was its director). But broadly speaking there were only three capitals so far as modern theatre was concerned.

Russian, American and German theatres differed widely from one another, but were alike in being modern, that is to say in introducing technical and artistic innovations. In a sense they even achieved a certain stylistic resemblance, probably because technology is international (not just that part which is directly applied to the stage but also that which influences it, the film for instance), and because large progressive cities in large industrial countries are involved. Among the other capitalist countries it is the Berlin theatre that seemed of late to be in the lead. For a period all that is common to the modern theatre received its strongest and (so far) maturest expression there.

The Berlin theatre's last phase was the so-called epic theatre, and it showed the modern theatre's trend of development in its purest form. Whatever was labelled '*Zeitstück*' or '*Piscatorbühne*' or '*Lehrstück*' belongs to the epic theatre.

The Epic Theatre

Many people imagine that the term 'epic theatre' is self-contradictory, as the epic and dramatic ways of narrating a story are held, following Aristotle, to be basically distinct. The difference between the two forms was never thought simply to lie in the fact that the one is performed by living beings while the other operates via the written word; epic works such as those of Homer and the medieval singers were at the same time theatrical performances, while dramas like Goethe's *Faust* and Byron's *Manfred* are agreed to have been more effective as books. Thus even by Aristotle's definition the difference between the dramatic and epic forms was attributed to their different methods of construction, whose laws were dealt with by two different branches of aesthetics. The method of construction depended on the different way of presenting the work to the public, sometimes via the stage, sometimes through a book; and independently of that there was the 'dramatic element' in epic works and the 'epic element' in dramatic. The bourgeois novel in the last century developed much that was 'dramatic', by which was meant the strong centralization of the story, a momentum that drew the separate parts into a common relationship. A particular passion of utterance, a certain emphasis on the clash of forces are hallmarks of the 'dramatic'. The epic writer Döblin provided an excellent criterion when he said that with an epic work, as opposed to a dramatic, one can as it were take a pair of scissors and cut it into individual pieces, which remain fully capable of life.

This is no place to explain how the opposition of epic and dramatic lost its rigidity after having long been held to be irreconcilable. Let us just point out that the technical advances alone were enough to permit the stage to incorporate an element of narrative in its dramatic productions. The possibility of projections, the greater adaptability of the stage due to mechanization, the film, all completed the theatre's equipment, and did so at a point where the most important transactions between people could no longer be shown simply be personifying the motive forces or subjecting the characters to invisible metaphysical powers.

To make these transactions intelligible the environment in which the people lived had to be brought to bear in a big and 'significant' way.

This environment had of course been shown in the existing drama, but only as seen from the central figure's point of view, and not as an independent element. It was defined by the hero's reactions to it. It was seen as a storm can be seen when one sees the ships on a sheet of water unfolding their sails, and the sails filling out. In the epic theatre it was to appear standing on its own.

The stage began to tell a story. The narrator was no longer missing, along with the fourth wall. Not only did the background adopt an attitude to the events on the stage—by big screens recalling other simultaneous events elsewhere, by projecting documents which confirmed or contradicted what the characters said, by concrete and intelligible figures to accompany abstract conversations, by figures and sentences to support mimed transactions whose sense was unclear—but the actors too refrained from going over wholly into their role, remaining detached from the character they were playing and clearly inviting criticism of him.

The spectator was no longer in any way allowed to submit to an experience uncritically (and without practical consequences) by means of simple empathy with the characters in the play. The production took the subject-matter and the incidents shown and put them through a process of alienation: the alienation that is necessary to all understanding. When something seems 'the most obvious thing in the world' it means that any attempt to understand the world has been given up.

What is 'natural' must have the force of what is startling. This is the only way to expose the laws of cause and effect. People's activity must simultaneously be so and be capable of being different.

It was all a great change.

The dramatic theatre's spectator says: Yes, I have felt like that too—Just like me—It's only natural—It'll never change—The sufferings of this man appal me, because they are inescapable—That's great art; it all seems the most obvious thing in the world—I weep when they weep, I laugh when they laugh.

The epic theatre's spectator says: I'd never have thought it—

That's not the way—That's extraordinary, hardly believable—It's got to stop—The sufferings of this man appal me, because they are unnecessary—That's great art; nothing obvious in it—I laugh when they weep, I weep when they laugh.

The Instructive Theatre

The stage began to be instructive.

Oil, inflation, war, social struggles, the family, religion, wheat, the meat market, all became subjects for theatrical representation. Choruses enlightened the spectator about facts unknown to him. Films showed a montage of events from all over the world. Projections added statistical material. And as the 'background' came to the front of the stage so people's activity was subjected to criticism. Right and wrong courses of action were shown. People were shown who knew what they were doing, and others who did not. The theatre became an affair for philosophers, but only for such philosophers as wished not just to explain the world but also to change it. So we had philosophy, and we had instruction. And where was the amusement in all that? Were they sending us back to school, teaching us to read and write? Were we supposed to pass exams, work for diplomas?

Generally there is felt to be a very sharp distinction between learning and amusing oneself. The first may be useful, but only the second is pleasant. So we have to defend the epic theatre against the suspicion that it is a highly disagreeable, humourless, indeed strenuous affair.

Well: all that can be said is that the contrast between learning and amusing oneself in not laid down by divine rule; it is not one that has always been and must continue to be.

Undoubtedly there is much that is tedious about the kind of learning familiar to us from school, from our professional training, etc. But it must be remembered under what conditions and to what end that takes place.

It is really a commercial transaction. Knowledge is just a commodity. It is acquired in order to be resold. All those who have grown out of going to school have to do their learning virtually in secret, for anyone who admits that he still has something to learn devalues himself as a man whose knowledge is inadequate. Moreover the usefulness of learning is very much limited by factors outside the learner's control. There is unemployment, for instance, against which no knowledge can protect one. There is the division of labour, which makes generalized knowledge unnecessary and impossible. Learning is often among the concerns of those whom no amount of concern will get any forwarder. There is not much knowledge that leads to power, but plenty of knowledge to which only power can lead.

Learning has a very different function for different social strata. There are strata who cannot imagine any improvement in conditions: they find the conditions good enough for them. Whatever happens to oil they will benefit from it. And: they feel the years beginning to tell. There can't be all that many years more. What is the point of learning a lot now? They have said the final word: a grunt. But there are also strata 'waiting their turn' who are discontented with conditions, have a vast interest in the practical side of learning, want at all costs to find out where they stand, and know that they are lost without learning; these are the best and keenest learners. Similar differences apply to countries and peoples. Thus the pleasure of learning depends on all sorts of things; but none the less there is such a thing as pleasurable learning, cheerful and militant learning.

If there were no such amusement to be had from learning the theatre's whole structure would unfit it for teaching.

Theatre remains theatre even when it is instructive theatre, and in so far as it is good theatre it will amuse.

Theatre and Knowledge

But what has knowledge got to do with art? We know that knowledge can be amusing, but not everything that is amusing belongs to the theatre.

I have often been told, when pointing out the invaluable services that modern knowledge and science, if properly applied, can perform for art and specially for the theatre, that art and knowledge are two estimable but wholly distinct fields of human activity. This is a fearful truism, of course, and it is as well to agree quickly that, like most truisms, it is perfectly true. Art and science work in quite different ways: agreed. But, bad as it may sound, I have to admit that I cannot get along as an artist without the use of one or two sciences. This may well arouse serious doubts as to my artistic capacities. People are used to seeing poets as unique and slightly unnatural beings who reveal with a truly godlike assurance things that other people can only recognize after much sweat and toil. It is naturally distasteful to have to admit that one does not belong to this select band. All the same, it must be admitted. It must at the same time be made clear that the scientific occupations just confessed to are not pardonable side interests, pursued on days off after a good week's work. We all know how Goethe was interested in natural history, Schiller in history: as a kind of hobby, it is charitable to assume. I have no wish promptly to accuse these two of having needed these sciences for their poetic activity; I am not trying to shelter behind them; but I must say that I do need the sciences. I have to admit, however, that I look askance at all sorts of people who I know do not operate on the level of scientific understanding: that is to say, who sing as the birds sing, or as people imagine the birds to sing. I don't mean by that that I would reject a charming poem about the taste of fried fish or the delights of a boating party just because the writer had not studied gastronomy or navigation. But in my view the great and complicated things that go on in the world cannot be adequately recognized by people who do not use every possible aid to understanding.

Let us suppose that great passions or great events have to be shown which influence the fate of nations. The lust for power is nowadays held to be such a passion. Given that a poet 'feels' this lust and wants to have someone strive for power, how is he to show the exceedingly complicated machinery within which the struggle for power nowadays takes place? If his hero is a politician, how do politics work? If he is a business man, how does business work? And yet there are writers who find business and politics nothing like so passionately interesting as the individual's lust for power. How are they to acquire the necessary knowledge? They are scarcely likely to learn enough by going round and keeping their eyes open, though even then it is more than they would get by just rolling their eyes in an exalted frenzy. The foundation of a paper like the *Völkischer Beobachter* or a business like Standard

Oil is a pretty complicated affair, and such things cannot be conveyed just like that. One important field for the playwright is psychology. It is taken for granted that a poet, if not an ordinary man, must be able without further instruction to discover the motives that lead a man to commit murder; he must be able to give a picture of a murderer's mental state 'from within himself'. It is taken for granted that one only has to look inside oneself in such a case; and then there's always one's imagination. . . . There are various reasons why I can no longer surrender to this agreeable hope of getting a result quite so simply. I can no longer find in myself all those motives which the press or scientific reports show to have been observed in people. Like the average judge when pronouncing sentence, I cannot without further ado conjure up an adequate picture of a murderer's mental state. Modern psychology, from psychoanalysis to behaviourism, acquaints me with facts that lead me to judge the case quite differently, especially if I bear in mind the findings of sociology and do not overlook economics and history. You will say: but that's getting complicated. I have to answer that it *is* complicated. Even if you let yourself be convinced, and agree with me that a slice of literature is exceedingly primitive, you may still ask with profound concern: won't an evening in such a theatre be a most alarming affair? The answer to that is: no.

Whatever knowledge is embodied in a piece of poetic writing has to be wholly transmuted into poetry. Its utilization fulfils the very pleasure that the poetic element provokes. If it does not at the same time fulfil that which is fulfilled by the scientific element, none the less in an age of great discoveries and inventions one must have a certain inclination to penetrate deeper into things—a desire to make the world controllable—if one is to be sure of enjoying its poetry.

Is the Epic Theatre Some Kind of 'Moral Institution'?

According to Friedrich Schiller the theatre is supposed to be a moral institution. In making this demand it hardly occurred to Schiller that by moralizing from the stage he might drive the audience out of the theatre. Audiences had no objection to moralizing in his day. It was only later that Friedrich Nietzsche attacked him for blowing a moral trumpet. To Nietzsche any concern with morality was a depressing affair; to Schiller it seemed thoroughly enjoyable. He knew of nothing that could give greater amusement and satisfaction than the propagation of ideas. The bourgeoisie was setting about forming the ideas of the nation.

Putting one's house in order, patting oneself on the back, submitting one's account, is something highly agreeable. But describing the collapse of one's house, having pains in the back, paying one's account, is indeed a depressing affair, and that was how Friedrich Nietzsche saw things a century later. He was poorly disposed towards morality, and thus towards the previous Friedrich too.

The epic theatre was likewise often objected to as moralizing too much. Yet in the epic theatre moral arguments only took second place. Its aim was less to moralize than to observe. That is to say it observed, and then the thick end of the wedge followed: the story's moral. Of course we cannot pretend that we started our observations out of a pure passion for observing and without any more practical motive, only to be completely staggered by their results. Undoubtedly there were some painful discrepancies in our environment, circumstances that were barely tolerable, and this not merely on account of moral considerations. It is not only moral considerations that make hunger, cold and oppression hard to bear. Similarly the object of our inquiries was not just to arouse moral objections to such circumstances (even though they could easily be felt—though not by all the audience alike; such objections were seldom for instance felt by those who profited by the circumstances in question) but to discover means for their elimination. We were not in fact speaking in the name of morality but in that of the victims. These truly are two distinct matters, for the victims are often told that they ought to be contented with their lot, for moral reasons. Moralists of this sort see man as existing for morality, not morality for man. At least it should be possible to gather from the above to what degree and in what sense the epic theatre is a moral institution.

Can Epic Theatre Be Played Anywhere?

Stylistically speaking, there is nothing all that new about the epic theatre. Its expository character and its emphasis on virtuosity bring it close to the old Asiatic theatre. Didactic tendencies are to be found in the medieval mystery plays and the classical Spanish theatre, and also in the theatre of the Jesuits.

These theatrical forms corresponded to particular trends of their time, and vanished with them. Similarly the modern epic theatre is linked with certain trends. It cannot by any means be practised universally. Most of the great nations today are not disposed to use the theatre for ventilating their problems. London, Paris, Tokyo, and Rome maintain their theatres for quite different purposes. Up to now favourable circumstances for an epic and didactic theatre have only been found in a few places and for a short period of time. In Berlin Fascism put a very definite stop to the development of such a theatre.

It demands not only a certain technological level but a powerful movement in society which is interested to see vital questions freely aired with a view to their solution, and can defend this interest against every contrary trend.

The epic theatre is the broadest and most far-reaching attempt at large-scale modern theatre, and it has all those immense difficulties to overcome that always confront the vital forces in the sphere of politics, philosophy, science and art.

1936   *Translated by John Willett*

The Street Scene
A Basic Model for an Epic Theatre

In the decade and a half that followed the World War a comparatively new way of acting was tried out in a number of German theatres. Its qualities of clear description and reporting and its use of choruses and projections as a means of commentary earned it the name of 'epic'. The actor used a somewhat complex technique to detach himself from the character portrayed; he forced the spectator to look at the play's situations from such an angle that they necessarily became subject to his criticism. Supporters of this epic theatre argued that the new subject-matter, the highly involved incidents of the class war in its acutest and most terrible stage, would be mastered more easily by such a method, since it would thereby become possible to portray social processes as seen in their causal relationships. But the result of these experiments was that aesthetics found itself up against a whole series of substantial difficulties.

It is comparatively easy to set up a basic model for epic theatre. For practical experiments I usually picked as my example of completely simple, 'natural' epic theatre an incident such as can be seen at any street corner: an eyewitness demonstrating to a collection of people how a traffic accident took place. The bystanders may not have observed what happened, or they may simply not agree with him, may 'see things a different way'; the point is that the demonstrator acts the behaviour of driver or victim or both in such a way that the bystanders are able to form an opinion about the accident.

Such an example of the most primitive type of epic theatre seems easy to understand. Yet experience has shown that it presents astounding difficulties to the reader or listener as soon as he is asked to see the implications of treating this kind of street corner demonstration as a basic form of major theatre, theatre for a scientific age. What this means of course is that the epic theatre may appear richer, more intricate and complex in every particular, yet to be major theatre it need at bottom only contain the same elements as a street-corner demonstration of this sort; nor could it any longer be termed epic theatre if any of the main elements of the street-corner demonstration were lacking. Until this is understood it is impossible really to understand what follows. Until one understands the novelty, unfamiliarity and direct challenge to the critical faculties of the suggestion that street-corner demonstration of this sort can serve as a satisfactory basic model of major theatre one cannot really understand what follows.

Consider: the incident is clearly very far from what we mean by an artistic one. The demonstrator need not be an artist. The capacities he needs to achieve his aim are in effect universal. Suppose he cannot carry out some particular movement as quickly as the victim he is imitating; all he need do is to explain that *he* moves three times as fast, and the demonstration neither suffers in essentials nor loses its point. On the contrary it is important that he should not be too perfect. His demonstration would be spoilt if the bystanders' attention were drawn to his powers of transformation. He has to avoid presenting himself in such a way that someone calls out 'What a lifelike portrayal of a chauffeur!' He must not 'cast a spell' over anyone. He should not transport people from normality to 'higher realms'. He need not dispose of any special powers of suggestion.

It is most important that one of the main features of the ordinary theatre should be excluded from our street scene: the engendering of illusion. The street demonstrator's performance is essentially repetitive. The event has taken place; what you are seeing now is a repeat. If the scene in the theatre follows the street scene in this respect then the theatre will stop pretending not to be theatre, just as the street-corner demonstration admits it is a demonstration (and does not pretend to be the actual event). The element of rehearsal in the acting and of learning by heart in the text, the whole machinery and the whole process of preparation: it all becomes plainly apparent. What room is left for experience? Is the reality portrayed still experienced in any sense?

The street scene determines what kind of experience is to be prepared for the spectator. There is no question but that the street-corner demonstrator has been through an 'experience', but he is not out to make his demonstration serve as an 'experience' for the audience. Even the experience of the driver and the victim is only partially communicated by him, and he by no means tries to turn it into an enjoyable experience for the spectator, however lifelike he may make his demonstration. The demonstration would become no less valid if he did not reproduce the fear caused by the accident; on the contrary it would lose validity if he did. He is not interested in creating pure emotions. It is important to understand that a theatre which follows his lead in this respect undergoes a positive change of function.

One essential element of the street scene must also be present in the theatrical scene if this is to qualify as epic, namely that the demonstration should have a socially practical significance. Whether our street demonstrator is out to show that one attitude on the part of driver or pedestrian makes an accident inevitable where another would not, or whether he is demonstrating with a view to fixing the responsibility, his demonstration has a practical purpose, intervenes socially.

The demonstrator's purpose determines how thoroughly he has to imitate. Our demonstrator need not imitate every aspect of his characters' behaviour, but only so much as gives a picture. Generally the theatre scene will give much fuller pictures, corresponding to its more extensive range of interest. How do street scene and theatre scene link up here? To take a point of detail, the victim's voice may have played no immediate part in the accident. Eye-witnesses may disagree as to whether a cry they heard ('Look out!') came from the victim or from someone else, and this may give our demonstrator a motive for imitating the voice. The question can be settled by demonstrating whether the voice was an old man's or a woman's or merely whether it was high or low. Again, the answer may depend on whether it was that of an educated person or not. Loud or soft may play a great part, as the driver could be correspondingly more or less guilty. A whole series of characteristics of the victim ask to be portrayed. Was he absent-minded? Was his attention distracted? If so, by what? What, on the evidence of his behaviour, could have made him liable to be distracted by just that circumstance and no other? Etc. etc. It can be seen that our street-corner demonstration provides opportunities for a pretty rich and varied portrayal of human types. Yet a theatre which tries to restrict its essential elements to those provided by our street scene will have to acknowledge certain limits to imitation. It must be able to justify any outlay in terms of its purpose.

The demonstration may for instance be dominated by the question of compensation for the victim, etc. The driver risks being sacked from his job, losing his licence, going to prison; the victim risks a heavy hospital bill, loss of job, permanent disfigurement, possibly unfitness for work. This is the area within which the demonstrator builds up his characters. The victim may have had a companion; the driver may have had his girl sitting alongside him. That would bring out the social element better and allow the characters to be more fully drawn.

Another essential element in the street scene is that the demonstrator should derive his characters entirely from their actions. He imitates their actions and so allows conclusions to be drawn about them. A theatre that follows him in this will be largely breaking with the orthodox theatre's habit of basing the actions on the characters and having the former exempted from criticism by presenting them as an unavoidable consequence deriving by natural law from the characters who perform them. To the street demonstrator the character of the man being demonstrated remains a quantity that need not be completely defined. Within certain limits he may be like this or like that; it doesn't matter. What the demonstrator is concerned with are his accident-prone and accident-proof qualities. The theatrical scene may show more fully-defined individuals. But it must then be in a position to treat their individuality as a special case and outline the field within which, once more, its most socially relevant effects are produced. Our street demonstrator's possibilities of demonstration are narrowly restricted (indeed, we chose this model so that the limits should be as narrow as possible). If the essential elements of the theatrical scene are limited to those of the street scene then its greater richness must be an enrichment only. The question of border-line cases becomes acute.

Let us take a specific detail. Can our street demonstrator, say, ever become entitled to use an excited tone of voice in repeating the driver's statement that he has been exhausted by too long a spell of work? (In theory this is no more possible than for a returning messenger to start telling his fellow-countrymen of his talk with the king with the words 'I saw the bearded king'.) It can only be possible, let alone unavoidable, if one imagines a street-corner situation where such excitement, specifically about this aspect of the affair, plays a particular part. (In the instance above this would be so if the king had sworn never to cut his beard off until . . . etc.) We have to find a point of view for our demonstrator that allows him to submit this excitement to criticism. Only if he adopts a quite different point of voice can he be entitled to imitate the driver's excited voice; e.g. if he blames drivers as such for doing too little to reduce their hours of work. ('Look at him. Doesn't even belong to a union, but gets worked up soon enough when an accident happens. "Ten hours I've been at the wheel." ')

Before it can get as far as this, i.e. be able to suggest a point of view to the actor, the theatre needs to take a number of steps. By widening its field of vision and showing the driver in other situations besides that of the accident the theatre in no way exceeds its model; it merely creates a further situation on the same pattern. One can imagine a scene of the same kind as the street scene which provides a well-argued demonstration showing how such emotions as the driver's develop, or another which involves making comparisons between tones of voice. In order not to exceed the model scene the theatre only has to develop a technique for submitting emotions to the spectator's criticism. Of course this does not mean that the spectator must be barred on principle from sharing certain emotions that are put before him; none the less to communicate emotions is only one particular form (phase, consequence) of criticism. The theatre's demonstrator, the actor, must apply a technique which will let him reproduce the tone of the subject demonstrated with a certain reserve, with detachment (so that the spectator can say: 'He's getting excited—in vain, too late, at last. . . . ' etc.). In short, the actor must remain a demonstrator; he must present the person demonstrated as a stranger, he must not suppress the '*he* did that, *he* said that' element in his performance. He must not go so far as to be wholly transformed into the person demonstrated.

One essential element of the street scene lies in the natural attitude adopted by the demonstrator, which is two-fold; he is always taking two situations into account. He behaves naturally as a demonstrator, and he lets the subject of the demonstration behave naturally too. He never forgets, nor does he allow it to be forgotten, that he is not the subject but the demonstrator. That is to say, what the audience sees is not a fusion between demonstrator and subject, not some third, independent, uncontradictory entity with isolated features of (a) demonstrator and (b) subject, such as the orthodox theatre puts before us in its productions. The feelings and opinions of demonstrator and demonstrated are not merged into one.

We now come to one of those elements that are peculiar to the epic theatre, the so-called A-effect (alienation effect). What is involved here is, briefly, a technique of taking the human social incidents to be portrayed and labelling them as something striking, something that calls for explanation, is not to be taken for granted, not just natural. The object of this 'effect' is to allow the spectator to criticize constructively from a social point of view. Can we show that this A-effect is significant for our street demonstrator?

We can picture what happens if he fails to make use of it. The following situation could occur. One of the spectators might say: 'But if the victim stepped off the kerb with his right foot, as you showed him doing. . . .' The demonstrator might interrupt saying: 'I showed him stepping off with his left foot'. By arguing which foot he really stepped off with in his demonstration, and, even more, how the victim himself acted, the demonstration can be so transformed that the A-effect occurs. The demonstrator achieves it by paying exact attention this time to his movements, executing them carefully, probably in slow motion; in this way he alienates the little sub-incident, emphasizes its importance, makes it worthy of notice. And so the epic theatre's alienation effect proves to have its uses for our street demonstrator too; in other words it is also to be found in this small everyday scene of natural street-corner theatre, which has little to do with art. The direct changeover from representation to commentary that is so characteristic of the epic theatre is still more easily recognized as one element of any street demonstration. Wherever he feels he can the demonstrator breaks off his imitation in order to give the explanations. The epic theatre's choruses and documentary projections, the direct addressing of the audience by its actors, are at bottom just this.

It will have been observed, not without astonishment I hope, that I have not named any strictly artistic elements as characterizing our street scene and, with it, that of the epic theatre. The street demonstrator can carry out a successful demonstration with no greater abilities than, in effect, anybody has. What about the epic theatre's value as art?

The epic theatre wants to establish its basic model at the street corner, i.e. to return to the very simplest 'natural' theatre, a social enterprise whose origins, means and ends are practical and earthly. The model works without any need or programmatic theatrical phrases like 'the urge to self-expression', 'making a part one's own', 'spiritual experience', 'the play instinct', 'the story-teller's art', etc. Does that mean that the epic theatre isn't concerned with art?

It might be as well to begin by putting the question differently, thus: can we make use of artistic abilities for the purposes of our street scene? Obviously yes. Even the street-corner demonstration includes artistic elements. Artistic abilities in some small degree are to be found in any man. It does no harm to remember this when one is confronted with great art. Undoubtedly what we call artistic abilities can be exercised at any time within the limits imposed by our street scene model. They will function as artistic abilities even though they do not exceed these limits (for instance, when there is meant to be no complete transformation of demonstrator into subject). And true enough, the epic theatre is an extremely artistic affair, hardly thinkable without artists and virtuosity, imagination, humour and fellow-feeling; it cannot be practised without all these and much else too. It has got to be entertaining, it has got to be instructive. How then can art be developed out of the elements of the street scene, without adding any or leaving any out? How does it evolve into the theatrical scene with its fabricated story, its trained actors, its lofty style of speaking, its make-up, its team performance by a number of players? Do we need to add to our elements in order to move on from the 'natural' demonstration to the 'artificial'?

Is it not true that the additions which we must make to our model in order to arrive at epic theatre are of a fundamental kind? A brief examination will show that they are not. Take the *story*. There was nothing fabricated about our street accident. Nor does the orthodox theatre deal only in fabrications; think for instance of the historical play. None the less a story can be performed at the street corner too. Our demonstrator may at any time be in a position to say: 'The driver was guilty, because it all happened the way I showed you. He wouldn't be guilty if it had happened the way I'm going to show you now.' And he can fabricate an incident and demonstrate it. Or take the fact that the text is learnt by heart. As a witness in a court case the demonstrator may have written down the subject's exact words, learnt them by heart and rehearsed them; in that case he too is performing a text he has learned. Or take a rehearsed programme by several players: it doesn't always have to be artistic purposes that bring about a demonstration of this sort; one need only think of the French police technique of making the chief figures in any criminal case re-enact certain crucial situations before a police audience. Or take make-up. Minor changes in appearance—ruffling one's hair, for instance—can occur at any time within the framework of the non-artistic type of demonstration. Nor is make-up itself used solely for theatrical purposes. In the street scene the driver's moustache may be particularly significant. It may have influenced the testimony of the possible girl companion suggested earlier. This can be represented by our demonstrator making the driver stroke an imaginary moustache when prompting his companion's evidence. In this way the demonstrator can do a good deal to discredit her as a witness. Moving on to the use of a real moustache in the theatre, however, is not an entirely easy transition, and the same difficulty occurs with respect to *costume*. Our demonstrator may under given circumstances put on the driver's cap—for instance if he wants to show that he was drunk: (he had it on crooked)—but he can only do so conditionally, under these circumstances; (see what was said about borderline cases earlier). However, where there is a demonstration by several demonstrators of the kind referred to above we can have costume so that the various characters can be distinguished. This again is only a limited use of costume. There must be no question of creating an illusion that the demonstrators really are these characters. (The epic theatre can counteract this illusion by especially exaggerated costume or by garments that are somehow marked out as objects for display.) Moreover we can suggest another model as a substitute for ours on this point: the kind of street demonstration given by hawkers. To sell their neckties these people will portray a badly-dressed and a well-dressed man; with a few props and technical tricks they can perform significant little scenes where they submit essentially to the same restrictions as apply to the demonstrator in our street scene: (they will pick up tie, hat, stick, gloves and give certain significant imitations of a man of the world, and the whole time they will refer to him as '*he*'!) With hawkers we also find *verse* being used within the same framework as that of our basic model. They use firm irregular rhythms to sell braces and newspapers alike.

Reflecting along these lines we see that our basic model will work. The elements of natural and of artificial epic theatre are the same. Our street-corner theatre is primitive; origins, aims and methods of its performance are close to home. But there is no doubt that it is a meaningful phenomenon with a clear social function that dominates all its elements. The performance's origins lie in an incident that can be judged one way or another, that may repeat itself in different forms and is not finished but is bound to have consequences, so that this judgment has some significance. The object of the performance is to make it easier to given an opinion on the incident. Its means correspond to that. The epic theatre is a highly skilled theatre with complex contents and far-reaching social objectives. In setting up the street scene as a basic model for it we pass on the clear social function and give the epic theatre criteria by which to decide whether an incident is meaningful or not. The basic model has a practical significance. As producer and actors work to build up a performance involving many difficult questions—technical problems, social ones—it allows them to check whether the social function of the whole apparatus is still clearly intact.

1950   *Translated by John Willett*

On Experimental Theatre

For at least two generations the serious European drama has been passing through a period of experiment. So far the various experiments conducted have not led to any definite and clearly established result, nor is the period itself over. In my view these experiments were pursued along two lines which occasionally intersected but can none the less be followed separately. They are defined by the two functions of *entertainment* and *instruction;* that is to say that the theatre organized experiments to increase its ability to amuse, and others which were intended to raise its value as education.

[Brecht then lists various experiments from Antoine on, designed to increase the theatre's capacity to entertain, and singles out Vakhtanghov and the constructivist Meyerhold—who 'took over from the asiatic theatre certain dance-like forms and created a whole choreography for the drama'—Reinhardt, with his open-air productions of *Faust, Jedermann* and *Midsummer Night's Dream,* and his seating of actors among the audience in Büchner's *Danton's Death;* Okhlopkov, and the elaboration of crowd scenes by Stanislavsky, Reinhardt, and Jessner. But 'on the whole the theatre has not been brought up to modern technological standards'.

The second line he sees as pursued primarily by the playwrights, instancing Ibsen, Tolstoy, Strindberg, Gorki, Tchekov, Hauptmann, Shaw, Georg Kaiser and Eugene O'Neill, and mentioning his own *Threepenny Opera* as 'a parable type plus ideology-busting'. Piscator's theatre was 'the most radical' of all such attempts. 'I took part in all his experiments, and every single one was aimed to increase the theatre's value as education.']

These discoveries [he goes on] have not yet been taken up by the international theatre; this electrification of the stage has been virtually forgotten; the whole ingenious machinery is rusting up, and grass is growing over it. Why is that?

The breakdown of this eminently political theatre must be attributed to political causes. The increase in the theatre's value as political education clashed with the growth of political reaction. But for the moment we shall restrict ourselves to seeing how its crisis developed in aesthetic terms.

Piscator's experiments began by causing complete theatrical chaos. While they turned the stage into a machine-room, the auditorium became a public meeting. Piscator saw the theatre as a parliament, the audience as a legislative body. To this parliament were submitted in plastic form all the great public questions that needed an answer. Instead of a Deputy speaking about certain intolerable social conditions there was an artistic copy of these conditions. It was the stage's ambition to supply images, statistics, slogans which would enable its parliament, the audience, to reach political decisions. Piscator's stage was not indifferent to applause, but it preferred a discussion. It didn't want only to provide its spectator with an experience but also to squeeze from him a practical decision to intervene actively in life. Every means was justified which helped to secure this. The technical side of the stage became extremely complicated. Piscator's stage manager had before him a book that was as different from that of Reinhardt's stage manager as the score of a Stravinsky opera is from a lute-player's part. The mechanism on the stage weighed so much that the stage of the Nollendorftheater had to be reinforced with steel and concrete supports; so much machinery was hung from the dome that it began to give way. Aesthetic considerations were entirely subject to political. Away with painted scenery if a film could be shown that had been taken on the spot and had the stamp of documentary realism. Up with painted cartoons, if the artist (e.g., George Grosz) had something to say to the parliamentary audience. Piscator was even ready to do wholly without actors. When the former German Emperor had his lawyers protest at Piscator's plan to let an actor portray him on his stage, Piscator just asked if the Emperor wouldn't be willing to appear in person; he even offered him a contract. In short, the end was such a vast and important one that all means seemed justified. And the plays themselves were prepared in much the same way as the performance. A whole staff of playwrights worked together on a single play, and their work was supported and checked by a staff of experts, historians, economists, statisticians.

Piscator's experiments broke nearly all the conventions. They intervened to transform the playwright's creative methods, the actor's style of representation, and the work of the stage designer. *They were striving towards an entirely new social function for the theatre.*

Bourgeois revolutionary aesthetics, founded by such great figures of the Enlightenment as *Diderot* and *Lessing,* defines the theatre as a place of entertainment and instruction. During the Enlightenment, a period which saw the start of a tremendous upsurge of the European theatre, there was no conflict between these two things. Pure amusement, provoked even by objects of tragedy, struck men like Diderot as utterly hollow and unworthy unless it added something to the spectators' knowledge, while elements of instruction, in artistic form of course, seemed in no wise to detract from the amusement; in these men's view they gave depth to it.

If we now look at the theatre of our day we shall find an increasingly marked conflict between the two elements which go to make it up, together with its plays—entertainment and instruction. Today there is an opposition here. That 'assimilation of art to science' which gave naturalism its social influence undoubtedly hamstrung some major artistic capacities, notably the imagination, the sense of play and the element of pure poetry. Its artistic aspects were clearly harmed by its instructive side.

The expressionism of the postwar period showed the World as Will and Idea and led to a special kind of solipsism. It was the theatre's answer to the great crisis of society, just as the doctrines of Mach were philosophy's. It represented art's revolt against life: here the world existed purely as a vision, strangely distorted, a monster conjured up by perturbed souls. Expressionism vastly enriched the theatre's means of expression and brought aesthetic gains that still have to be fully exploited, but it proved quite incapable of shedding light on the world as an object of human activity. The theatre's educative value collapsed.

In Piscator's productions or in *The Threepenny Opera* the

educative elements were so to speak *built in:* they were not an organic consequence of the whole, but stood in contradiction to it, they broke up the flow of the play and its incidents, they prevented empathy, they acted as a cold douche for those whose sympathies were becoming involved. I hope that the moralizing parts of *The Threepenny Opera* and the educative songs are reasonably entertaining, but it is certain that the entertainment in question is different from what one gets from the more orthodox scenes. The play has a double nature. Instruction and entertainment conflict openly. With Piscator it was the actor and the machinery that openly conflicted.

This is quite apart from the fact that such productions split the audience into at least two mutually hostile social groups, and thus put a stop to any common experience of art. The fact is a political one. Enjoyment of learning depends on the class situation. Artistic appreciation depends on one's political attitude, which can accordingly be stimulated and adopted. But even if we restrict ourselves to the section of the audience which agreed politically we see the sharpening of the conflict between ability to entertain and educative value. Here is a new and quite specific old kind of learning, and it can no longer be reconciled with a specific old kind of entertainment. At one (later) stage of the experiments the result of any fresh increase in educative value was an immediate decrease in ability to entertain. ('This isn't theatre, it's secondary-school stuff'.) Conversely, emotional acting's effect on the nerves was a continual menace to the production's educative value. (It often helped the educational effect to have bad actors instead of good ones.) In other words, the greater the grip on the audience's nerves, the less chance there was of its learning. The more we induced the audience to identify its own experiences and feelings with the production, the less it learned; and the more there was to learn, the less the artistic enjoyment.

Here was a crisis: half a century's experiments, conducted in nearly every civilized country, had won the theatre brand-new fields of subject-matter and types of problem, and made it a factor of marked social importance. At the same time they had brought the theatre to a point where any further development of the intellectual, social (political) experience must wreck the artistic experience. And yet, without further development of the former, the latter occurred less and less often. A technical apparatus and a style of acting had been evolved which could do more to stimulate illusions than to give experiences, more to intoxicate than to elevate, more to deceive than to illumine.

What was the good of a constructivist stage if it was socially unconstructive; of the finest lighting equipment if it lit nothing but childish and twisted representations of the world; of a suggestive style of acting if it only served to tell us that A was B? What use was the whole box of tricks if all it could do was to offer artificial surrogates for real experience? Why this eternal ventilating of problems that were always left unsolved? This titillation not only of the nerves but of the brain? We couldn't leave it at that.

The development tended towards a fusion of the two functions, instruction and entertainment. If such preoccupations were to have any social meaning, then they must eventually enable the theatre to project a picture of the world by artistic means: models of men's life together such as could help the spectator to understand his social environment and both rationally and emotionally master it.

[Brecht goes on, in terms that anticipate the Short Organum and perhaps reflect his work on the first version of *Galileo,* to lament man's failure to understand the laws governing his life in society. His knowledge of these has not kept pace with his scientific knowledge, so that 'nowadays nearly every new discovery is greeted with a shout of triumph which transforms itself into a shout of fear'. (Cf. the long speech in Scene 14 of *Galileo.*) But art ought to be able to give 'a workable picture of the world'.

As it is, he argues, art gets its effects more by empathy than by accuracy. He attacks empathy on the same grounds as before, and describes the attempt to stave it off by methods of 'alienation'.[1] This technique was developed at the Theater am Schiffbauerdamm in Berlin with 'the most talented of the younger generation of actors ... Weigel, Peter Lorre, Oskar Homolka, (Carola) Neher and Busch', and also with amateur groups, workers' choruses, etc.]

This all represented a continuation of previous experiments, in particular of Piscator's theatre. Already in his last experiments the logical development of the technical apparatus had at last allowed the machinery to be mastered and led to a beautiful simplicity of performance. The so-called *epic* style of production which we developed at the Schiffbauerdamm Theater proved its artistic merits relatively soon, and the *non-aristotelian school of playwriting* tackled the large-scale treatment of large-scale social objects. There was some prospect of changing the choreographic and grouping aspects of Meyerhold's school from artifice into art, of transforming the Stanislavsky school's naturalistic elements into realism. Speech was related to gestics; both everyday language and verse speaking were shaped according to the so-called *gestic principle*. A complete revolution took place in stage design. By a free manipulation of Piscator's principles it became possible to design a setting that was both instructive and beautiful. Symbolism and illusion could be more or less dispensed with, and the *Neher principle* of building the set according to the requirements established at the actors' rehearsals allowed the designer to profit by the actors' performance and influence it in turn. The playwright could work out his experiments in uninterrupted collaboration with actor and stage designer; he could influence and be influenced. At the same time the painter and the composer regained their independence, and were able to express their view of the theme by their own artistic means. The integrated work of art (or 'Gesamtkunstwerk') appeared before the spectator as a bundle of separate elements.

From the start the *classical repertoire* supplied the basis of many of these experiments. The artistic means of alienation made possible a broad approach to the living works of dramatists of other periods. Thanks to them such valuable old plays could be performed without either jarring modernization or museum-like methods, and in an entertaining and instructive way.

It plainly has a particularly good effect on the contemporary amateur theatre (worker, student and child actors) when it is no longer forced to work by hypnosis. It seems conceivable that a line may be drawn between the playing of amateur actors and professionals without one of the theatre's basic functions having to be sacrificed.

Such very different ways of acting as those of, say, the Vakhtangov or Okhlopkov companies and the workers' groups can be reconciled on this new foundation. The variegated experiments of half a century seem to have acquired a basis that allows them to be exploited.

None the less these experiments are not so easy to describe, and I am forced here simply to state our belief that we can indeed encourage artistic understanding on the basis of alienation. This is not very surprising, as the theatre of past periods also, technically speaking, achieved results with alienation effects—for instance the Chinese theatre, the Spanish classical theatre, the popular theatre of Brueghel's day and the Elizabethan theatre.

So is this new style of production *the* new style; is it a complete and comprehensible technique, the final result of every experiment? Answer: no. It is *a* way, the one that *we* have followed. The effort must be continued. The problem holds for all art, and it is a vast one. The solution here aimed at is only *one* of the conceivable solutions to the problem, which can be expressed so: How can the theatre be both instructive and entertaining? How can it be divorced from spiritual dope traffic and turned from a home of illusions to a home of experiences? How can the unfree, ignorant man of our century, with his thirst for freedom and his hunger for knowledge; how can the tortured and heroic, abused and ingenious, changeable and world-changing man of this great and ghastly century obtain his own theatre which will help him to master the world and himself?

1939; 1959   *Translated by John Willett*

Translator's Notes

1. The term here translated as 'alienation' is *Entfremdung* as used by Hegel and Marx, and not the *Verfremdung* which Brecht himself was soon to coin and make famous. The former also occurs in a short note called 'Episches Theater, Entfremdung', which refers to the need for any situation to be 'alienated' if it is to be seen socially. Alfred Döblin, the friend of Brecht's referred to early in the essay, wrote *Die drei Sprünge des Wang-lun, Berlin Alexanderplatz* and other novels which critics of the time likened to Joyce and Dos Passos. He too was interested in the theory of epic form. The *Völkischer Beobachter* was the chief Nazi daily paper.

Can the Present-day World Be Reproduced by Means of Theatre?

I was interested to hear that in a discussion about the theatre Friedrich Dürrenmatt raised the question whether it is still at all possible to reproduce the present-day world by means of theatre. In my view this question, once posed, has to be admitted. The time has passed when a reproduction of the world by means of theatre need only be capable of being experienced. To be an experience it needs to be accurate.

Many people have noticed that the theatrical experience is becoming weaker. There are not so many who realize the increasing difficulty of reproducing the present-day world. It was this realization that set some of us playwrights and theatre directors looking for new artistic methods.

As you know, being in the business yourselves, I have made a number of attempts to bring the present-day world, present-day men's life together, within the theatre's range of vision.

As I write, I am sitting only a few hundred yards from a large theatre,[1] equipped with good actors and all the necessary machinery, where I can try out various ideas with a number of mainly youthful collaborators, while around me on the tables lie 'model' books with thousands of photographs of our productions, together with more or less precise descriptions of the most variegated problems and their provisional solutions. So I have every possibility; but I cannot say that the dramatic writing which I call 'non-aristotelian', and the epic style of acting that goes with it, represent the only solution. However, one thing has become quite plain: the present-day world can only be described to present-day people if it is described as capable of transformation.

People of the present-day value questions on account of their answers. They are interested in events and situations in face of which they can do something.

Some years ago in a paper I saw an advertisement showing the destruction of Tokyo by an earthquake. Most of the houses had collapsed, but a few modern buildings had been spared. The caption ran 'Steel stood.' Compare this description with the classic account of the eruption of Etna by Pliny the Elder, and you will find that his is a kind of description that the twentieth-century playwright must outgrow.

In an age whose science is in a position to change nature to such an extent as to make the world seem almost habitable, man can no longer describe man as a victim, the object of a fixed but unknown environment. It is scarcely possible to conceive of the laws of motion if one looks at them from a tennis ball's point of view.

For it is because we are kept in the dark about the nature of human society—as opposed to nature in general—that we are now faced (so the scientists concerned assure me), by the complete destructibility of this planet that has barely been made fit to live in.

It will hardly surprise you to hear me say that the question of describing the world is a social one. I have maintained this for many years, and now I live in a state where a vast effort is being made to transform society. You may not approve of the means used—I hope, by the way, that you are really acquainted with them, and not just from the papers; you may not accept this particular ideal of a new world—I hope you are acquainted with this too; but you can hardly doubt that in the state where I live the transformation of the world, of men's life together, is being worked at. And you may perhaps agree with me that the present-day world can do with transforming.

For this short essay, which I beg you to treat as a friendly contribution to your discussion, it may be enough if I anyway report my opinion that the present-day world can be reproduced even in the theatre, but only if it is understood as being capable of transformation.

1955   *Translated by John Willett*

Translator's Notes

1. The 'larger theatre' is the Theater am Schiffbauerdamm in East Berlin, which the Berliner Ensemble took over in March 1954. Previously the company had been a guest of the Deutsches Theater when playing in Berlin. This Theater am Schiffbauerdamm, home of the original *Threepenny Opera,* has since been rechristened 'Theatre am Bertolt Brecht-Platz'. It seats around 700.

BERTOLT BRECHT, 1898–1956, the most influential German dramatist and theoretician of the theater of the first half of the twentieth century. Volumes 75, 76, and 77 of the German Library will be devoted to his major plays and other writings.

Arnold Hauser

The Origins of Domestic Drama

The middle-class novel of manners and family life represented a complete innovation compared with the various forms of heroic, pastoral and picaresque novel, which had dominated the whole field of light fiction until the middle of the eighteenth century, but it was by no means so deliberately and methodically opposed to the older literature as the middle-class drama, which arose in conscious antithesis to classical tragedy and became the mouthpiece of the revolutionary bourgeoisie. The mere existence of an elevated drama, the protagonists of which were all members of the middle class, was in itself an expression of the claim of this class to be taken just as seriously as the nobility from which the heroes of tragedy had sprung. The middle-class drama implied from the very outset the relativizing and belittling of the heroic and aristocratic virtues and was in itself an advertisement for bourgeois morality and the middle-class claim to equality of rights. Its whole history was determined by its origins in bourgeois class-consciousness. To be sure, it was by no means the first and only form of the drama to have its source in a social conflict, but it was the first example of a drama which made this conflict its very theme and which placed itself openly in the service of a class struggle. The theatre had always propagated the ideology of the classes by which it had been financed, but class differences had never before formed more than the latent, never the manifest and explicit content of its productions. Such speeches as, shall we say, the following had never been heard before: 'Ye Athenian aristocrats, the injunctions of your kinship morality are inconsistent with the principles of our democratic state: your heroes are not only fratricides and matricides, they are also guilty of high treason'. Or: 'Ye English barons, your reckless manners threaten the peace of our industrious cities; your crown-pretenders and rebels are no more than imposing criminals.' Or: 'You Paris shopkeepers, money-lenders and lawyers, know that if we, the French nobility, go under, a whole world will go under which is too good to compromise with you.' But now such things were stated quite frankly: 'We, the respectable middle class, will not and cannot live in a world dominated by you parasites, and even if we ourselves must perish, our children will win the day and live.'

Because of its polemical and programmatical character, the new drama was burdened from the very outset with problems unknown to the older forms of the drama. For, although these also were 'tendentious', they did not result in plays with a thesis to propound. It is one of the peculiarities of dramatic form that its dialectical nature makes it a ready vehicle for polemics, but the dramatist himself is prevented from taking sides in public by its 'objectivity'. The admissibility of propaganda has been disputed in this form of art more than in any other. The problem first arose, however, after the enlightenment had turned the stage into a lay-pulpit and a platform and had in practice completely renounced the Kantian 'disinterestedness' of art. Only an age which believed as firmly as this one in the educable and improvable nature of man could commit itself to purely tendentious art; every other age would have doubted the effectiveness of such clumsy moral teaching. The real difference, however, between the bourgeois and the pre-bourgeois drama did not consist exactly in the fact that the political and social purpose which was formerly latent was now given direct expression, but in the fact that the dramatic conflict no longer took place between single individuals but between the hero and institutions, that the hero was now fighting against anonymous forces and had to formulate his point of view as an abstract idea, as a denunciation of the prevailing social order. The long speeches and indictments now usually begin with a plural 'Ye' instead of the singular 'You'. 'What are your laws, of which you make your boast,' declaims Lillo, 'but the fool's wisdom, and the coward's valour, the instrument and screen of all your villainies? By them you punish in others what you act yourselves, or would have acted, had you been in their circumstances. The judge who condemns the poor man for being a thief, had been a thief himself, had he been poor.'[1] Speeches like that had never been heard before in any serious play. But Mercier goes even further: 'I am poor, because there are too many rich'—says one of his characters. That is already almost the voice of Gerhart Hauptmann. But, in spite of this new tone, the middle-class drama of the eighteenth century no more implies the criteria of a people's theatre than does the proletarian drama of the nineteenth; both are the result of a development in which all connexion with the common people has long been lost, and both are based on theatrical conventions which have their source in classicism.

In France the popular theatre, which had masterpieces like *Maître Pathelin* to its credit, was completely forced out of literature by the court theatre; the biblical-historical play and the farce were supplanted by high tragedy and the stylized, intellectualized comedy. We do not precisely know what had survived of the old medieval tradition on the popular stage in the provinces in the age of classical drama, but in the literary theatre of the capital and the court hardly any more of it had been preserved than was contained in the plays of Molière. The drama developed into the literary genre in which the ideals of court society in the service of absolute monarchy found the most direct and imposing expression. It became the representative genre, if only for the reason that it was suitable for presentation with an impressive social framework and theatrical performances offered a special opportunity for displaying the grandeur and splendour of the monarchy. Its motifs became the symbol of a feudalistic-heroic life, based on the idea of authority, service and loyalty, and its heroes the idealization of a social class which, thanks to its exemption from the trivial cares of everyday life, was able to see in this service and loyalty the highest ethical ideals. All those who were not in a position to devote themselves to the worship of these ideals were regarded as a species of humanity beyond the pale of dramatic dignity. The tendency to absolutism, and the attempt to make court culture more exclusive and more like the French model, led in England, too, to the displacement of the popular theatre that, at the turn of the sixteenth century, had been still completely fused with the literature of the upper classes. Since the reign of Charles I, dramatists had limited themselves more and more to producing for the theatre of the court and the higher ranks of society, so that the popular tradition of the Elizabethan age had soon been lost. When the Puritans proceeded to close down the theatres, the English drama was already on the decline.[2]

The peripeteia had always been regarded as one of the essentials of tragedy and until the eighteenth century every dramatic critic had felt that the sudden turn of destiny makes the deeper impression, the higher the position from which the hero falls. In an age like that of absolutism this feeling must have been particularly strong, and in the poetic theory of the baroque, tragedy is simply defined as the genre whose heroes are princes, generals and suchlike notabilities. However pedantic this definition may appear to us today, it does lay hold of a basic characteristic of tragedy and even points perhaps to the ultimate source of the tragic experience. It was, therefore, really a decisive turning point when the eighteenth century made ordinary middle-class citizens the protagonists of serious and significant dramatic action and showed them as the victims of tragic fates and the representatives of high moral ideas. In earlier times this kind of thing would never have occurred to anyone, even though the assertion that middle-class persons had always been portrayed on the older stage merely as comic figures is by no means in accordance with the facts. Mercier is slandering Molière when he reproaches him for having tried to 'ridicule and humiliate' the middle class.[3] Molière generally characterizes the bourgeois as honest, frank, intelligent and even witty. He usually combines such descriptions, moreover, with a sarcastic thrust at the upper classes.[4] In the older drama, however, a person from the middle class had never been made to bear a lofty and soul-stirring destiny and to accomplish a noble and exemplary deed. The representatives of the bourgeois drama now emancipate themselves so completely from this limitation and from the prejudice of considering the promotion of the bourgeois to the protagonist of a tragedy as the trivialization of the genre, that they can no longer understand a dramaturgical sense in raising the hero above the social level of the average man. They judge the whole problem from the humanitarian angle, and think that the high rank of the hero only lessens the spectator's interest in his fate, since it is possible to take a genuinely sympathetic interest only in persons of the same social standing as oneself.[5] This democratic point of view is already hinted at in the dedication of Lillo's *London*

Merchant, and the middle-class dramatists abide by it on the whole. They have to compensate for the loss of the high social position held by the hero in classical tragedy by deepening and enriching his character, and this leads to the psychological overloading of the drama and creates further series of problems unknown to earlier playwrights.

Since the human ideals followed by the pioneers of the new middle-class literature were incompatible with the traditional conception of tragedy and the tragic hero, they emphasized the fact that the age of classical tragedy was past and described its masters, Corneille and Racine, as mere word-spinners.[6] Diderot demanded the abolition of the tirades, which he considered both insincere and unnatural and in his fight against the affected style of the *tragédie classique,* Lessing also attacked its mendacious class character. It was now discovered for the first time that artistic truth is valuable as a weapon in the social struggle, that the faithful reproduction of facts leads automatically to the dissolution of social prejudices and the abolition of injustice, and that those who fought for justice need not fear the truth in any of its forms, that there is, in a word, a certain correspondence between the idea of artistic truth and that of social justice. There now arose that alliance, so familiar in the nineteenth century, between radicalism and naturalism, that solidarity which the progressive elements felt existed between themselves and the naturalists even when the latter, as in the case of Balzac, thought differently from them in political matters.

Diderot already formulated the most important principles of naturalistic dramatic theory. He requires not merely the natural, psychologically accurate motivation of spiritual processes but also exactness in the description of the milieu and fidelity to nature in the scenery; he also desires, as he imagines, still in accordance with the spirit of naturalism, that the action should lead not to big scenic climaxes but to a series of optically impressive tableaux, and here he seems to have in mind 'tableaux vivants' in the style of Greuze. He obviously feels the sensual attractiveness of the visual more strongly than the intellectual effects of dramatic dialectics. Even in the linguistic and acoustic field he favours purely sensual effects. He would prefer to restrict the action to pantomime, gestures and dumb-show and the speaking to interjections and exclamations. But, above all, he wants to replace the stiff, stilted Alexandrine by the unrhetorical, unemotional language of every day. He attempts everywhere to tone down the loudness of classical tragedy and to curb its sensational stage effects, guided as he is by the bourgeois fondness for the intimate, the direct and the homely. The middle-class view of art, which sees in the representation of the immanent, self-sufficient present the real aim, strives to give the character of a self-contained microcosm. This approach also explains the idea of the fictitious 'fourth wall', which is first hinted at by Diderot. The presence of spectators on the stage had been felt to be a disturbing influence in earlier times, it is true, but Diderot goes so far as to desire that plays should be performed as if no audience were present at all. This marks the beginning of the reign of total illusion in the theatre—the displacement of the play-element and the concealment of the fictitious nature of the representation.

Classical tragedy sees man isolated and describes him as an independent, autonomous intellectual entity, in merely external contact with the material world and never influenced by it in his innermost self. The bourgeois drama, on the other hand, thinks of him as a part and function of his environment and depicts him as a being who, instead of controlling concrete reality, as in classical tragedy, is himself controlled and absorbed by it. The milieu ceases to be simply the background and external framework and now takes an active part in the shaping of human destiny. The frontiers between the inner and the outer world, between spirit and matter, become fluid and gradually disappear, so that in the end all actions, decisions and feelings contain an element of the extraneous, the external and the material, something that does not originate in the subject and which makes man seem the product of a mindless and soulless reality. Only a society that had lost its faith in both the necessity and the divine ordinance of social distinctions and in their connexion with personal virtue and merit, that experiences the daily growing power of money and sees men becoming merely what external conditions make them, but which, nevertheless, affirms the dynamism of human society, since it either owes its own ascendancy to it or promises itself that it will lead to its ascendancy, only that kind of society could reduce the drama to the categories of real space and time and develop the characters out of their material environment. How strongly this materialism and naturalism was conditioned by social factors is shown most strikingly by Diderot's doctrine of the characters in the drama— namely, the theory that the social standing of the characters possesses a higher degree of reality and relevance than their personal, spiritual habitus and that the question whether a man is a judge, an official or a merchant by profession is more important than the sum total of his individual qualities. The origin of the whole doctrine is to be found in the assumption that the spectator is able to escape from the influence of a play much less easily, when he sees his own class portrayed on the stage, which he must acknowledge to be his class if he is logical, than when he merely sees his own personal character portrayed, which he is free to disown if he wants to.[7] The psychology of the naturalistic drama, in which the characters are interpreted as social phenomena, has its origin in this urge which the spectator feels to identify himself with his social compeers. Now, however much objective truth there may be in such an interpretation of the characters in a play, it leads, when raised to the status of an exclusive principle, to a falsification of the facts. The assumption that men and women are merely social beings results in just as arbitrary a picture of experience as the view according to which every person is a unique and incomparable individual. Both conceptions lead to a stylization and romanticizing of reality. On the other hand, however, there is no doubt that the conception of man held in any particular epoch is socially conditioned and that the choice as to whether man is portrayed in the main as an autonomous personality or as the representative of a class depends in every age on the social approach and political aims of those who happen to be the upholders of culture. When a public wishes to see social origins and class characteristics emphasized in the human portraiture, that is always a sign that society has become class-conscious, no matter whether the public in question is aristocratic or middle-class. In this context the question whether the aristocrat is only an aristocrat and the bourgeois only a bourgeois is absolutely unimportant.

The sociological and materialistic conception of man, which makes him appear to be the mere function of his environment, implies new form of drama, completely different from classical tragedy. It means not only the degradation of the hero, it makes the very possibility of the drama in the old sense of the term questionable, since it deprives man of all autonomy and, therefore, to some extent of responsibility for his actions. For, if his soul is nothing but the battle-ground for contending anonymous forces, for what can he himself still be called to account? The moral evaluation of actions must apparently lose all significance or at least become highly problematical, and the ethics of the drama become dissolved into mere psychology and casuistry. For, in a drama in which the law of nature and nothing but the law of nature predominates, there can be no question of anything beyond an analysis of the motives and a tracking down of the psychological road at the end of which the hero attains his deed. The whole problem of tragic guilt is in question. The founders of the bourgeois drama renounced tragedy, in order to introduce into the drama the man whose guilt is the opposite of tragic, being conditioned by everyday reality; their successors deny the very existence of guilt, in order to save tragedy from destruction. The romantics eliminate the problem of guilt even from their interpretation of earlier tragedy and, instead of accusing the hero of wrong, make him a kind of superman whose greatness is revealed in the acceptance of his fate. The hero of romantic tragedy is still victorious in defeat and overcomes his inimical destiny by making it the pregnant and inevitable solution of the problem with which his life confronts him. Thus Kleist's Prince of Homburg overcomes his fear of death, and thereby abolishes the apparent meaninglessness and inadequacy of his fate, as soon as the decisive power over his life is put into his own hands. He condemns himself to death, since he recognizes therein the only way to resolve the situation in which he finds himself. The acceptance of the inevitability of fate, the readiness, indeed the joyfulness, with which he sacrifices himself, is his victory in defeat, the victory of freedom of necessity. The fact that in the end he does not have to die, after all, is in accordance with the sublimation and spiritualization which tragedy undergoes. The acknowledgement of guilt, or of what remains over of guilt, that is, the successful struggle to escape from the throes of delusion into the clear light of reason, is already equivalent to expiation and the restoration of the balance. The romantic movement reduces tragic guilt to the wilfulness of the hero, to his mere personal will and individual existence, in revolt against the primal unity of all being. According to Hebbel's interpretation of this idea, it is absolutely indifferent whether the hero falls as a result of a good or evil action. The romantic conception of tragedy, culminating in the apotheosis of the hero, is infinitely remote from the melodramas of Lillo and Diderot, but it would have been inconceivable without the revision to which the first bourgeois dramatists submitted the problem of guilt.

Hebbel was fully aware of the danger by which the form of the drama was threatened by the middle-class ideology, but, in contrast to the neo-classicists, he in no way failed to recognize the new dramatic possibilities inherent in middle-class life. The formal disadvantages of the psychological transformation of the drama were obvious. The tragic deed was an uncanny, inexplicable, irrational phenomenon in Greek drama, in Shakespeare and still, to some extent, in French classical drama; its shattering effect was due, above all, to its incommensurability. The new psychological motivation gave it a human measure and, as the representatives of the domestic drama intended, it was made easier for the audience to sympathize with the characters on the stage. The opponents of the domestic drama forget, however, when they deplore the loss of the terrors, the incalculability and inevitability of tragedy, that the irrational effect of tragedy was not lost as a consequence of the invention of psychological motivation and that the irrational content of tragedy had already lost its influence, when the need for that kind of motivation was first felt. The greater danger with which the drama, as a form, was threatened by psychological and rational motivation was the loss of its simplicity, of its overwhelmingly direct, brutally realistic character, without which 'good theatre' in the old sense was impossible. The dramatic treatment became more and more intimate, more and more intellectualized and withdrawn from mass effects. Not merely the action and stage procedure but also the characters themselves lost their former sharpness of definition; they became richer but less clear, more true to life but less easy to grasp, less immediate to the audience and more difficult to be reduced to a directly evident formula. But it was precisely in this element of difficulty that the main attraction of the new drama resided, though it thereby became increasingly remote from the popular theatre.

The ill-defined characters were involved in obscure conflicts, situations in which neither the opposing figures nor the problems with which they were concerned were fully brought to light. This indefiniteness was conditioned, above all, by the comprehensive and conciliatory bourgeois morality which attempted to discover explanatory and extenuating circumstances and stood for the view that 'to understand everything is to forgive everything'. In the older drama a uniform standard of moral values had prevailed, accepted even by the villains and scoundrels;[8] but now that an ethical relativism had emerged from the social revolution, the dramatist often wavered between two ideologies and left the real problem unsolved, just as Goethe, for example, left the conflict between Tasso and Antonio undecided. The fact that motives and pretexts were now open to discussion weakened the element of inevitability in the dramatic conflict, but this was compensated for by the liveliness of the dramatic dialectic, so that it is by no means possible to maintain that the ethical relativism of the domestic drama merely had a destructive influence on dramatic form. The new bourgeois morality was all in all dramatically no less fertile than the feudal-aristocratic morality of the old tragedy. The latter knew of no other duties than those owed to the feudal lord and to honour, and it offered the impressive spectacle of conflicts in which powerful and violent personalities raged against themselves and each other. The domestic drama, on the other hand, discovers the duties which are owed to society,[9] and describes the fight for freedom and justice waged by men who are materially more narrowly tied, but are, nonetheless, spiritually free and brave—a fight which is perhaps less theatrical but in itself no less dramatic than the bloody conflicts of heroic tragedy. The outcome of the struggle is not, however, inevitable to the same degree as hitherto, when the simple morality of feudal loyalty and knightly heroism allowed of no escape, no compromise, no 'having it both ways'. Nothing describes the new moral outlook better than Lessing's words in *Nathan der Weise:* 'Kein Mensch muss müssen'—words which do not, of course, imply that man has no duties at all, but that he is inwardly free, that is to say, free to choose his means, and that he is accountable for his actions to none but himself. In the older drama inward, in the new drama outward ties are stressed; but oppressive as the latter are in themselves, they allow absolutely free play to the dramatically relevant action. 'The old tragedy rests on an unavoidable moral duty'—Goethe says in his essay *Shakespeare and No End:* '. . . All duty is despotic . . . the will, on the other hand, is free . . . It is the god of the age . . . Moral duty makes tragedy great and strong, the will makes it weak and slight'. Goethe here takes a conservative standpoint and evaluates the drama according to the pattern of the old, quasi-religious immolation, instead of according to the principles of the conflict of will and conscience into which the drama has developed. He reproaches the modern drama for granting too much freedom to the hero; later critics usually fall into the opposite error and think that the determinism of the naturalistic drama makes any question of freedom, and therefore of dramatic conflict, impossible. They do not understand that it is dramaturgically completely irrelevant where the will originates, by what motives it is guided, what is 'intellectual' and what 'material' in it, provided that a dramatic conflict takes place one way or another.[10]

These critics put quite a different interpretation on the principle which they oppose to the hero's will from that of Goethe; it is a matter of two entirely different kinds of necessity. Goethe is thinking of the antinomies of the older drama, the conflict of duty and passion, loyalty and love, moderation and presumption, and deplores that the power of the objective principles of order has diminished in the modern drama, in comparison with that of the subjectivity. Later, necessity is usually taken as meaning the laws of empirical reality, especially those of the physical and social environment, the inescapability of which was discovered by the eighteenth century. In reality, therefore, three different things are in question here: a wish, a duty and a compulsion. In the modern drama individual inclinations are confronted by two different objective orders of reality: an ethical-normative and a physical-factual order. Philosophical idealism described the conformity of law of experience as accidental, in contrast to the universal validity of ethical norms, and in accordance with this idealism, modern classicistic theory regards the predominance of the material conditions of life in the drama as depraving. But it is no more than a prejudice of romantic idealism to assert that the hero's dependence on his material environment thwarts all dramatic conflict, all tragic effects and makes the very possibility of true drama problematical. It is true, however, that, as a consequence of the conciliatory morality and non-tragic outlook of the middle class, the modern world offers tragedy less material than former ages. The modern bourgeois public likes to see plays with a 'happy ending' more than great, harrowing tragedies, and feels, as Hebbel remarks in his preface to *Maria Magdalene,* no real difference between tragedy and sadness. It simply does not understand that the sad is not tragic and the tragic not sad.

The eighteenth century loved the theatre and was an extraordinarily fertile period in the history of the drama, but it was not a tragic age, not an epoch which saw the problems of human existence in the form of uncompromising alternatives. The great ages of tragedy are those in which subversive social displacements take place, and a ruling class suddenly loses its power and influence. Tragic conflicts usually revolve around the values which form the moral basis of the power of this class and the ruinous end of the hero symbolizes and transfigures the ruinous end which threatens the class as a whole. Both Greek tragedy and the English, Spanish and French drama of the sixteenth and seventeenth centuries were produced in such periods of crisis and symbolize the tragic fate of their aristocracies. The drama heroizes and idealizes their downfall in accordance with the outlook of a public that still consists for the most part of members of the declining class itself. Even in the case of the Shakespearian drama, the public of which is not dominated by this class, and where the poet does not stand on the side of the social stratum threatened with destruction, tragedy draws its inspiration, its conception of heroism and its idea of necessity from the sight afforded by the fate of the former ruling class. In contrast to these ages, the periods in which the fashion is set by a social class which believes in its ultimate triumph are not favourable for tragic drama. Their optimism, their faith in the capacity of reason and right to achieve victory, prevents the tragic outcome of dramatic entanglements, or seeks to make a tragic accident out of tragic necessity and a tragic error out of tragic guilt. The difference between the tragedies of Shakespeare and Corneille, on the one hand, and those of Lessing and Schiller, on the other, is that in the one case the destruction of the hero represents a higher and in the other case a mere historical necessity. There is no conceivable order of society in which a Hamlet or Anthony would not inevitably come to ruin, whereas the heroes of Lessing and Schiller, Sara Sampson and Emilia Galotti, Ferdinand and Luise, Carlos and Posa, could be happy and contented in any other society and any other time except their own, that is to say, except that of their creator. But an epoch which sees human unhappiness as historically conditioned, and does not consider it an inevitable and inescapable fate, can certainly produce tragedies, even important ones; it will, however, in no way utter its final and deepest word in this form. It may, therefore, be right that 'every age produces its own necessity and thus its own tragedy',[11] yet the representative genre of the age of the enlightenment was not tragedy but the novel. In the ages of tragedy the representatives of the old institutions combat the world-view and aspirations of a new generation; in times in which the non-tragic drama prevails, a younger generation combats the old institutions. Naturally, a single individual can be wrecked by old institutions just as much as he can be destroyed by the representatives of a new world. A class, however, that believes in its ultimate victory, will regard its sacrifices as the price of victory, whereas the other class, that feels the approach of its own inevitable ruin, sees in the tragic destiny of its heroes a sign of the coming end of the world and a twilight of the gods. The destructive blows of blind fate offer no satisfaction to the optimistic middle class which believes in the victory of its cause; only the dying classes of tragic ages find comfort in the thought that in this world all great and noble things are doomed to destruction and wish to place this destruction in a transfiguring light. Perhaps the romantic philosophy of tragedy, with its apotheosis of the self-sacrificing hero, is already a sign of the decadence of the bourgeoisie. The middle class will, at any rate, not produce a tragic drama in which fate is resignedly accepted until it feels threatened with the loss of its very life; then, for the first time, it will see, as happens in Ibsen's play, fate knocking at the door in the menacing shape of triumphant youth.

The most important difference between the tragic experience of the nineteenth century and that of earlier ages was that, in contrast to the old aristocracies, the modern middle class felt itself threatened not merely from outside. It was a class made up of such multifarious and contrary elements that it seems menaced by the danger of dissolution from the very outset. It embraced not only elements siding with reactionary groups and others who felt a sense of solidarity with the lower ranks of society, but, above all, the socially rootless intelligentsia that flirted now with the upper now with the lower classes, and, accordingly, stood partly for the ideas of the anti-revolutionary and anti-rationalist romantics, partly agitated for a state of permanent revolution. In both cases it aroused in the mind of the middle class doubts about its right to exist at all and about the lasting quality of its own social order. It bred a 'super-bourgeois' attitude to life—a consciousness that the middle class had betrayed its original ideals and that it now had to conquer itself and struggle to attain a universally valid humanism. On the whole, these 'super-bourgeois' tendencies had an anti-bourgeois origin. The development through which Goethe, Schiller and many other writers passed, especially in Germany, from their revolutionary beginnings to their later, conservative and often anti-revolutionary attitude, was in accordance with the reactionary movement in the middle class itself and with its betrayal of the enlightenment. The writers were merely the spokesmen of their public. But it often happened that they sublimated the reactionary convictions of their readers and, with their less robust conscience and their greater readiness to sham, simulated higher, super bourgeois ideals, when they had really sunk back to a pre- and anti-bourgeois level. This psychology of repression and sublimation created such a complicated structure that it is often difficult to differentiate the various tendencies. It has been possible to establish that in Schiller's *Kabale und Liebe,* for example, three different generations, and therefore, three ideologies intersect each other: the pre-bourgeois of the court circles, the bourgeois of Luise's family and the 'super-bourgeois' of Ferdinand.[12] But the super-bourgeois world here differs from the bourgeois merely by reason of its greater breadth and lack of bias. The relation between the three attitudes is really much more complicated in a work like *Don Carlos,* in which the super-bourgeois philosophy of Posa enables him to understand Philip and even to sympathize to a certain degree with the 'unhappy' king. In a word, it becomes increasingly difficult to ascertain whether the dramatist's 'super-bourgeois' ideology corresponds to a progressive or a reactionary disposition, and whether it is a question of the middle class achieving victory over itself or simply one of desertion. However that may be, the attacks on the middle class become a basic characteristic of the bourgeois drama, and the rebel against the bourgeois morality and way of life, the scoffer at bourgeois conventions and philistine narrow-mindedness, becomes one of its stock figures. It would shed an extraordinarily revealing light on the gradual alienation of modern literature from the middle classes, to examine the metamorphoses this figure underwent from the 'Storm and Stress' right up to Ibsen and Shaw.

For he does not represent simply the stereotyped insurgent against the prevailing social order, who is one of the basic types of the drama of all times, nor is he merely a variant of rebellion against the particular rule of the moment, which is one of the fundamental dramatic situations, but he represents a concrete and consistent attack on the bourgeoisie, on the basis of its spiritual existence and on its claim to stand for a universally valid moral norm. To sum up, what we are here confronted with is a literary form which from being one of the most effective weapons of the middle class developed into the most dangerous instrument of its self-estrangement and demoralization.

1952   *Translated in collaboration with the author*
by Stanley Godman

Notes

1. George Lillo, *The London Merchant or the History of George Barnwell* (1731), iv 2.
2. L. Stephen, *English Literature and Society in the Eighteenth Century* (1960), p. 66.
3. Mercier, *Du Théâtre, ou Nouvel essai sur l'art dramatique* (1773).
4. Clara Stockmeyer, *Soziale Probleme im Drama des Sturmes und Dranges* (1922), p. 68.
5. Beaumarchais, *Essai sur le genre dramatique sérieux* (1767).
6. Rousseau, *La Nouvelle Héloïse,* II, Lettre 17.
7. Diderot, 'Entretiens sur le Fils naturel', *Oeuvres* (1875–77), VII, p. 150.
8. George Lukács, 'Zur Soziologie des Dramas', *Archiv f. Sozialwiss. u. Sozialpolit.* 38 (1914), pp. 330f.
9. A. Eloesser, *Das bürgerliche Drama* (1898), p. 13. Paul Ernst, *Ein Credo* (1912) I, p. 102.
10. G. Lukács, loc. cit., p. 343.
11. A. Eloesser, op. cit., p. 215.
12. Fritz Brueggermann, 'Der Kampf um die büegerliche Welt- und Lebensanschauung i. d. deutschen Lit. d. 18. Jahrh', *Deutsche Vierteljahrsschr. f. Literaturwiss. u. Geistesgsch.,* III 1 (1925).

Arnold Hauser, 1892–1978, art historian. Born in Austria-Hungary, he taught in England and the United States and died in Budapest. The excerpt constitutes one chapter in his monumental *Social History of Art* (1952).

Friedrich Dürrenmatt

Friedrich Schiller

Ladies and gentlemen:
As you have just heard, the city of Mannheim has awarded me this year's Schiller prize, so I can't very well avoid including Schiller in the celebration; this task is incumbent upon me despite the fact that I am not at all certain who it is that I ought to thank: Schiller or the Chief Mayor of Mannheim. But if many might be inclined to deny me the right to speak here—for reasons that are understandable not only to yourselves but to me as well—there is a certain justification that I at least am able to grant myself: not only that my German is as Swiss as Schiller's is said to have been Swabian, but also because Schiller, after all, wrote the national drama of the Swiss and not the Germans. Of course he knew the Germans far better than he knew us; had he been Swiss, say a subject of their lordships in Bern, he probably wouldn't have gone through with it either.

However, I find giving this talk difficult despite the high honor. Other misgivings arise. I am neither a literary scholar nor a Schiller connoisseur. My literary profession prohibits a more than occasional and recreational preoccupation with literature. For purely technical reasons, I am not in a position to take the exact measurements, from a southerly angle, of Schiller as a crag in the panorama of great men at the end of the eighteenth century. I also lack the desire to study that species of literature that has literature as its subject. I can only express suppositions, catch the scent of a possible truth without there being any chance of my ferreting it out and confirming it with scientific rigor; nor do I want to, perhaps because I sense that very little can actually be proven in the field of literature and because I suspect that such proof would be meaningless, since proofs are established on a different plane, namely on the chessboard of speculation, where no attention can or ought to be given to the many incongruities that crowd in upon the phenomena of real life so stubbornly and with such a disruptive effect. Besides, a celebration requires a solemn address, an evocation of the person being celebrated, an unrolling of his life, an investigation of his works, and all this must be profound and lofty, but there must also be a certain amount of lying, a little exaggeration, a little too much praise.

Please forgive me, but I shall have to disappoint you in this regard. It is not lack of respect that prevents me from exalting Schiller into the realm of absolute, final, and exemplary things, or from behaving as if the classics were the most sacred national assets (not that I don't consider the classics an asset, but I don't trust nations in this matter). The reason is that for a practicing writer only a human relationship with the classic authors can be of any use. He does not want to idolize them or regard them as unattainable examples, he wants them as friends, as stimulating partners in conversation; or, with equal justification, as enemies, as the authors of frequently boring novels and pathetical plays. He wants to come close to them and then move away from them; indeed, when he writes, he wants to be allowed to forget them, because—and this is legitimate as well—it actually bothers him, in the state of writing, planning, and carrying out his plans, that others have written before him, *and how*!, for very artistic production entails a certain momentary megalomania.

So I don't want to talk about the effect some of Schiller's works still deservedly exert on the theater, but about the dialogue I conduct with Schiller, the image I have of him—completely unscientifically, as I've already admitted; I shall talk about the image I have formed of him for my personal use in my work, for the management of my own writing. Occasionally we writers should also know what we are doing, and the best way to find out is to examine what others have done. Now, though this method has the advantage of allowing me to restrict myself to talking about what concerns and interests me in Schiller, it has the disadvantage of suppressing significant aspects of his work, for example Schiller's relationship to classical Greece, his poetry, his importance as a historian, etc. Furthermore, it is not so much his plays that interest me—I usually politely step out of their way, with a certain caution that is prompted, in part, by self-protection and also by the fact that I have a hard time with them—why not admit it; it is rather the dramaturgical and philosophical thought concealed behind the plays that is my concern. This, I suppose, requires some explanation. While it is true that Schiller is still regarded as an exceptionally clear-headed individual who gave exceptionally lucid testimony concerning the special difficulties of his work as a writer, it is also true that a clear-headed individual was not as rare a thing in the literature of that time as it is in today's literature. Just consider a few names pulled out of the hat: Lessing, Herder, Wieland, Lichtenberg, Humboldt, Goethe, etc. It seems idle, therefore, in view of this general, powerful, and totally usual brightening-up in the German-speaking countries, to make special mention of Schiller's lucidity. And it seems needless to mention, too, that in his philosophical and aesthetic works, in particular, Schiller impresses one with his greatness and lucidity. However, these are undeniably not counted among his popular works.

His philosophizing strikes many as antiquated, speculative, schematic. His essays—on the nature of tragedy, on grace and dignity, on naive and sentimental poetry, on the nature of the sublime, etc.—are admired as great prose, but they seem petrified in conceptual structure, overloaded with significance, simultaneously aesthetic and ethical, moralizing, virtually irrefutable, but isolated, irrelevant for our time, sublime but sterile.

So it is difficult to gain access to Schiller's thought, despite the fact that he displays it openly everywhere, especially in his letters. He is incessantly commenting on himself. We are granted an inside view of his work as a writer, a miserably unprofitable profession at the time. Our initial admiration goes to the organizer. This is Schiller's most uncanny side. Newspapers are founded, fees are negotiated, contributors are solicited, publicity is organized (often in a rather dubious manner smelling of literary cliquishness), the public itself is considered a factor that wants to be deceived and with which one entertains warlike relations, a factor you have to reckon with frequently and can rarely count on for a living. But, in addition, and more importantly, he reveals the inner driveshafts and cogwheels of his workshop. We see mechanisms being set into motion. Plans are executed, begun, conceived; materials are examined, the pros and cons of a project are tabulated—does this enterprise demand a great deal of work? does that one require just a small effort? what kinds of studies would this one require? what sorts of investigations? where is the dramatic difficulty? how to proceed? where should the action stagnate, slow down, accelerate? There are no professional secrets here; everything's explainable, aimed at effect, designed for the stage. He practices dramaturgy the way Lessing practiced it: as an art of playwriting, as a reflection on what the theater can do and what it wants to do, as something that can be learned, as, in effect, a science. Schiller masters the rules of dramaturgy by allowing them to govern his stage. His dramatic art is founded on a thoroughly secure and solid dramaturgy; it's no accident that he has become the schoolmasters' dramatist par excellence.

His dramaturgy aims at rhetorical effect. Human beings are put on the stage for the sake of rhetorical outbursts. Operatic dramaturgy. But this procedure has its definite consequences in the theatrical world that is being staged. We don't voluntarily accept rhetorical displays unless they result from the dramatic functions of the characters sustaining the action. For example, at a trial. The *dramatis personae* are given, their roles have been assigned: the judge, the prosecutor, the accused, the defense lawyer. Each of them has his definite function within the action. Argument and counterargument, accusation and defense and judgment arise naturally and in rhetorical form, aim at something definite, reveal something definite. Now, the characters of the historical dramas are set up very much in the manner of this basic model: their functions are sanctioned by the social stratification of their world: king, soldier, burgher, etc.

The rhetorical drama assumes a closed and socially stratified world, a hierarchy that is presupposed on the stage but that can also be portrayed, condensed into a kind of playing field with rules by which the various moves of the players can be tested for their correctness. This presupposition of the old drama is also Schiller's presupposition. The conception of his plays is thought through to its ultimate possibilities—often too precisely, for a perfect conception really makes the execution superfluous and when carried out, can often lead to mistakes, to peculiar poetic failures. They occur for the sake of the conception and are less likely to happen to someone whose initial conception is vague, who starts out from poetry *and* experience, from the stage, and who necessarily make all sorts of blunders from a dramaturgical point of view, Shakespeare, for instance. And yet Schiller, who preconceives everything, has the most precise knowledge of all the rules, tricks, possibilities; it's simply astonishing, they way he knows how to map out his story, divide the action, intensify it, retard it, set up the entrances and exits, deliver the pointed last word: "the man can be helped," "Cardinal, I have done my part, now you do yours," "to *Prince* Piccolomini," "his Lordship begs your pardon, he's left by boat for France," and "I declare my bondsmen to be free." [1] What ultimate poetic condensations these are, but how he goes for the stage effect, unscrupulously sometimes. Hollywood couldn't lay it on better or thicker. Admittedly.

And yet, concealed behind all this astonishing technical capacity, behind all his instinct for the show, for the theatrical and the dramatic, behind all the rhetorical arias and disputes that are made possible by his dramaturgy, there is another kind of knowledge, a knowledge of laws not of the drama. This is apparently achieved by mere classification. He divides poetry into a naive and a sentimental variety. Actually, though, this permits him to start out not from the rules or a concept of style but from the poet, and to define poetry by the poet's relationship of his times. If the rules used to be made by dramaturgy, now they are dictated by the times. Poets everywhere, he writes, are, purely by definition, the custodians of nature. Where they are no longer fully capable of being that and are already experiencing in themselves the destructive influence of arbitrary and artificial forms—or have at least struggled against that influence—they become the witnesses and avengers of nature. Either they *are* nature or they seek the nature that has been lost. This, according to Schiller, gives rise to two completely different kinds of poetry by which the entire field of poetic expression can be measured and fully covered. All poets who really deserve the name are, in Schiller's view, either naive or sentimental, depending on the nature of the time when their art comes to fruition, or on the influence of accidental circumstances on their general education or transitory mood. The claim being put forward here is of no small order. The entire field of poetry is supposed to be fully measured and covered by the distinction between naive and sentimental poets. This includes the art of the drama, whose fundamental problem centers upon the question of whether the world can be reproduced on the stage at all.

Now, if there are two modes of making poetry, the naive and the sentimental, there must also be two different ways of portraying the world on the stage. But we must make one necessary qualification. In a certain sense, the theater is always naive. For if we are speaking of the rules of dramatic art, we must keep in mind that the purpose of these rules is not just to produce a self-enclosed work of art, but—if the stage is to have any meaning—to achieve an immediacy of theatrical effectiveness. But this immediate impact is only possible if we assume, from the outset, a certain naiveté in the audience. A play is taking place on the stage, unfolding before the eyes of the audience—an immediate happening, in short; so, at the moment of watching a play, the audience is necessarily naive, willing to be led, to play along. A reflective audience cancels itself as such, and the theater *turns into* a theater. The playwright's art consists in making the audience reflect *after* the play. However, the natural naiveté of the audience presupposes an agreement between the audience and the author, if the intended immediacy is to come about. The naive poet of the theater will share his audience's naiveté, the sentimental one will calculate upon it. That is why actor-playwrights have the easiest time of it, and thinkers the hardest.

Shakespeare, Molière, but also Nestroy[2] are the most legitimate kings of the stage, and Schiller is one of their greatest usurpers. For the former, theatrical immediacy presents no problem. Shakespeare in fact can get away with nearly incomprehensible monologues; the stage always supports him; he is rhetorical for the sheer joy of rhetoric, while Schiller is rhetorical out of a will to be clear, to be lucid. His language transforms the most abstract matter into something immediate and instantly understandable. Hence the stage-effectiveness of this language which has nothing intimate about it, which in its great moments seems to embody the law itself; hence also its popularity, its leaning to the proverbial and the easily accessible; but hence, too, its tendency to seem all too moral, too much like a treatise.

But the difference between the naive and the sentimental play-wright goes beyond the varying degree of difficulty presented to them by the stage. For if the naive poet *is* nature, as Schiller puts it, he must also see nature in the real world and hence accept reality, imitate it in the theater, turn it into a play. He induces pity and terror, or else he makes the audience laugh. In the naive theater, reality is not something you get to the bottom of: it is experienced as divine order, as creation, as natural law, as the effect of environment and origin—a possibility for the drama which Schiller could not foresee, an option that presupposes the scientific framework of the nineteenth century but which actually produced a new kind of naive theater. The naive poet is not a rebel. The fate of Oedipus reveals the gods, it does not lead them *ad absurdum;* the crimes of Claudius put *his* kingship into question, not kingship as such; but for the sentimental poet, that is what these themes would have to express. He is not conceivable except as a rebel. For him reality is not nature but an abnormity, an un-nature which he must judge in the name of nature. The theater is the podium of his indictment. *In Tyrannos.*[3] The show becomes a tribunal. The sentimental poet enlightens the members of his audience. They should not merely experience the injustice of the world, should not just feel pity and fear, they should also recognize an effect of some very particular causes, they should not merely experience the raging of a Karl Moor, of a Ferdinand,[4] with pity and terror, they should approve it, their own wrath should be inflamed. Man is defeated by the unnatural conditions of the world. The son rises up against the father, and brother against brother. Man is innocently destroyed. His sacrifice is meaningful only in an inner way. It reveals the tragedy of freedom or a false social order; but in an external sense the sacrifice is in vain, because it does not bring about the right social order.

At this point the following question seems justified: is this attitude really sufficient, doesn't the realization that the world is in bad shape presuppose an insight into the way the world ought to be, and doesn't it also morally require some indication as to the way in which the world can be set aright again, and doesn't such an indication necessarily involve the demand that one take these steps? Now, if this question is answered in the affirmative, it is not sufficient to describe the world as unjust. It must be described as a world that can be changed, that can be set aright again and in which man need no longer be a victim. But if this is the case, the writer turns from a rebel into a revolutionary.

Having said this, my lecture will unfortunately become a little less comfortable. It will have to depart from the purely dramaturgical domain where one can talk shop without risk. Schiller is an all too uncomfortable subject, a highly political case, unfortunately. It must be fairly evident that in my exposition of the naive and sentimental theater I passed Schiller by and ran into Brecht, who on closer examination has many things in common with Schiller, including some friendly traits, for instance the tendency to be inadvertently funny. With both of them, you sometimes have the feeling that Friederike Kempner[5] was helping them along: "Honor the women, they braid and they weave!" "Forth went the tribe of the agronomers." This great writer represents the most extreme form of the sentimental poet. He moved from the level of rebellion to become a revolutionary, to change society with his theater. He became a communist, as we know.

But here I must insert something that is quite obvious. Brecht's ideology may be painful for many people, annoying to many others, but it must not be treated as a mere mistake, a side-issue. It is an essential part of Brecht, and it's no less essential to his works and their effectiveness on the stage, their poetic precision, their dramaturgic boldness, and, last but not least, their humanity. This legitimate achievement forces us to take a sober look at Brecht's communism. We must not make excuses; admit what has to be admitted.

Brecht's poetry is an answer to our world, to our guilt, one of the few honest answers to our empty phrases, a depiction of our sins of omission, even though it is a communist answer. We have to deal with him. As the ghost of our fears, communism has paralyzed us for a long time; we are frozen in terror, and in the same way we, the ghost of its fears, have for a long time paralyzed communism. We are both petrified. But what is natural on communism's part, since it represents an ideology which by its nature is incapable of dialogue, is unnatural for us. We can carry on a genuine dialogue with communism, but communism can't do so with us. We can overcome communism by looking at it without fear, thinking it through again and again, separating its truth from its error, but communism cannot look upon itself or us without fear. We must do what communism fails to do, otherwise we too will freeze in an ideology. For this reason, if we are annoyed by the fact that the greatest German playwright of our time became a militant revolutionary because he believed that his humanity demanded it, we are faced with this question: what is *our* answer to the time we live in? Do we actually have an answer, or are we just pretending to have one? Aren't we just frightened? Afraid of an unavoidable operation? Are we just drifting? Isn't our constant talk about freedom just a pretext that allows us to neglect what is necessary, so that we can stay with the old values, because we can live off their dividends, values which we adopted without reexamining them?

So when we ask Schiller why he didn't become a revolutionary, we are actually addressing ourselves. For in his time, too, there was a great revolution which not only elected him as its honorary citizen but gave us many of those things which we now claim to be defending against communism. And something more. In Schiller's time, too, there was a German defeat, and a German empire collapsed as it did in Brecht's time, but also a German revolution failed to occur, though for completely different reasons: Napoleon's invasion led to the wars of liberation, while the invasion of the Allies led to the Economic Miracle, and in a much shorter time.

Now how did Schiller act? What conclusions did he draw? Can we claim him, deploy him in the cause of our freedom? Having inquired into his dramaturgy, we must now in our own interest question him as to his ethics and his politics. Did he provide an answer to his time? Did he even depict his time? Is the opinion justified that in the plays of his youth he dared boldly to seize hold of the times, scourge the despotism of the nobility, their intrigues, the abjection of their lackeys, the impotence of the laws and the defenselessness of the middle class; but that he later abandoned his times to pursue things classical, timeless, symbolic, with the result that in his later works we can no longer recognize either his times or ours?

It's a little dubious, though, to compare our times and his without further ado. Where in our time, a homogenous, centralistic, dictatorial empire collapsed, it was a heterogenous, fragmented, uncentralized empire that came to an end in his; the Third Reich could be broken, the Holy Roman Empire was as unbreakable as sand; it simply disintegrated into its constituent parts; the various regions were regrouped without losing their structure. Furthermore, German particularism had a tempering effect on absolutism; its impact varied from place to place, and in between there were the free cities, like islands, there was more room to get out of harm's way, you could sneak by, take precautions, slip from one state into another. When Schiller emigrated, he didn't have to go further than Mannheim.

It was in this inadequate but politically deactivated conglomerate of petty states, which could not be transformed into a world bomb, that Schiller lived his life. He was surrounded by half measures, lived in straitened circumstances, sick, always short of money. Dependent on his benefactors and friends, chained to the slave-post of his professorship for general history, he never got away, never saw the sea; the whirlpool into which his diver throws himself[6]—he explored it by the edge of a mill. His membership in the nation that exalted him as its national poet was something he deplored, and he detested the century he lived in. This prisoner of a world that was not tailored to his measurements took his political circumstances into sober and realistic consideration. If he thought the Germans incapable of forming a politically unified, great nation, if he regarded German greatness apart from politics as something spiritual, his judgment was not apolitical—he wasn't all that mistaken, after all—but particularistic. He can only be understood in the context of the Empire's particularism at that time; he was a citizen of the dwarf state of Weimar.

One of his fundamental emotions was a sense of political impotence, of living in a world that established itself without any regard for the nation he belonged to, while the revolutionary not only needs the sense of acting in the name of a party, but in the name of the whole world, no less. Brecht came from that dubious epoch when Germany really was a world power. Only if we take this into consideration will we be able to rediscover our time in Schiller's, not just because Germany's significance is extremely second rate and Europe itself has become a collection of rather questionable little states, but because we too are being put in our place.

We have to think it through again: what is the state's and what is the individual's, where do we have to submit, where must we resist, wherein lies our freedom? Political revolutions haven't changed the world as much as is claimed; the real impact comes from the explosion of humanity into billions, the necessary erection of the machine world, the unavoidable transformation of motherlands into states, of peoples into masses, of love of one's country into fidelity to one's company. The old maxim of the revolutionaries, that man can and must change the world, has become unrealizable for the individual, out of date, this sentence is now applicable only to the crowd, as a slogan, as political dynamite, as an incentive for the masses, as a hope for the gray armies of the hungry. The part is no longer absorbed in the whole, nor the individual in collectivity, nor man in humanity. The individual is left with a feeling of impotence, of being left out, of no longer being able to step in and influence things, of having to lie low in order not to go under, but also there is the presentiment of a great liberation, of new possibilities, of the time having come bravely, decisively to do one's part.

With this admission, an involvement with Schiller suggests itself strongly once again. As a playwright, if he's set up as a teacher, he may be bad news for the German theater. The viability of his rules and tricks may be due only to Schiller himself; already with Grillparzer and Hebbel everything starts getting more questionable, good for scholars in German studies. Evidently there is nothing more to be learned in Schiller,—he is probably the most unrepeatable of all, an exceptional case, praised to death and encumbered with prejudices about him. Let's put all that aside and not go into it any further, it isn't important: What remains is a mighty impulse, a pure strength, singular venture, not for great times, but for difficult ones. He was forced by historical circumstances to accept a world which he condemned (Brecht in East Berlin was forced to condemn what he had accepted, the fate of every genuine revolutionary). He did not attack but attempted to make human liberty unassailable. The revolution was meaningless for him because he had pondered the nature of freedom more deeply than the revolution had. He did not try to change conditions in order to liberate man, he hoped to change man for the sake of liberty. To his nation he commended the realm of the spirit, from which of course it soon emigrated. Like the gods of Greece, he divided the world. In the realm of nature, necessity is king; in the realm of reason, liberty; and life and spirit are opposed to one another. Liberty is not realized by politics, not attained by revolutions; it is always present as man's fundamental condition, even if he were born in chains. Only in art does it manifest itself purely; life knows no liberty. The greatest evil is not bondage but guilt. Revolution removes bondage only to replace it with guilt: Schiller opposed to the idea of revolution the revolt of the Swiss Confederacy, the uprising of the simple and natural nation of shepherds which we Swiss supposedly once were. The ideal of liberty, for Schiller, can only be realized in a naive world; in the world of un-nature, liberty becomes a tragic thing. It can no longer be realized except by sacrifice. Schiller's dramas reveal an absolute world, decreed from on high with iron laws, and between its huge flywheels runs the path of liberty, straight and narrow.

If we dare to envision this world, we must reject it just as we usually reject Brecht's world. In the former we sense our downfall, in the latter our oppression, and so we prefer to accept both as poetic worlds, and enjoy them. For we demand freedom in and of itself, regardless of our guilt. We justify Brecht by failing before Schiller: Both poets are our judges, but we don't care about their judgment, rather we admire the style in which they wrote it down.

So we haven't received any useful answers to our questions, but perhaps only coded answers exist. If behind Brecht lies the impulse of Marxism and, even further back, Hegel, what we see in Schiller is the continued working out of that great and strange moment in philosophy that began with Kant, when reason examined itself and searched out its own limits, but also became powerfully active by no longer explaining experience as something originating in things but by declaring it to be its own creation instead, thus leaving the world untouched, a mystery concealed behind appearances, behind what can be grasped by science. Schiller's conception of poetry seems to have a similar structure. Just as, with Kant, reason lends the world its appearances by way of the perceiving subject, so the poet, for Schiller, must create the world anew, portray it, seek to reach it, through his idea. But this course of action meets with an inexorable limit: thought always falls short of reality; all it can attain—this is how Schiller expressed it—is the realm of laws, of symbols, of types. Schiller's greatest significance may well lie in this capacity to know his limits. His way of thinking was stern and unconditional, but he made a halt where a halt was called for;

above all, he knew himself, he was his own greatest critic, understood himself more incisively than his admirers did. Only if understood in this light, in the light of a "critique of knowledge," are his compromises not shady, his idealism not starry-eyed, his thought not merely abstract. Schiller mastered the reality in which he was placed. His friendship with Goethe is like a work of practical reason; the famous definition which distinguishes Schiller's art from Goethe's and yet makes both dependent on one another, is at once philosophical and diplomatic, a compromise of thought for the sake of life, a formula that makes friendship possible. He knew exactly what he was undertaking. The phenomenon of Goethe profoundly refutes Schiller's conception; Goethe cannot be explained by the concept of the naive; philosophical and artistic options arise which Schiller had rendered inaccessible to himself; and Schiller began to tear down his own construction. Pure thought does not change its nature; the thinker who dares to abandon himself finds the form that enables him to think his way through to the end.

From then on, Schiller dared to act anew, to act differently. He dropped philosophy and wrote his classical works. He broke the law he had once imposed on himself, he moved away from his time by seeking to push forward into the poetic drama. But even as a man of action, he is left with the fate which it was his nature to embrace as a thinker: to reach out to things by way of thought, and never to reach them. Only in this way can we recognize his pathos, his rhetoric, as something unique, not as something hollow, exaggerated, as it so often seems to be, and necessarily seems to be, but as an enormous movement of thought plunging down to the world, as the passion of the power of thought itself, which wants to convince without losing clarity, which wants to embody the greatest complexity in simplicity. Although he is popular, he is nevertheless the most difficult, the most inaccessible, the most contradictory of playwrights. No one is so difficult to evaluate as he is, or so difficult to domesticate, no other playwright's faults are so obvious as his, and no one's are so irrelevant. As one involves oneself with him, he stops being remote and grows near.

One would have to be what he was to do justice to him. One would have to possess the passion of his thinking; without the passion, the results of that thinking are falsified. You can't dilute fire: you can only extinguish it. The object of his thinking was art and nature, mind and life, the ideal and the common, but he did not flee into the world of ideas. He drew the lines and endured. His concept of freedom was sterner than that of the others, but not for the sake of a system, but for the sake of life; he set up tensions in order to produce sparks, he elevated man because he loved man more than generality—more than the state. He couldn't see anything more in the state than a means to an end.

In Schiller we can sense the great sobriety which we need with regard to the state, whose tendency to become total has become immanent: man is only in part a political creature, his fate will not be fulfilled by his politics but by that which lies beyond politics, after politics. That is where he will live or fail.

A writer cannot make a covenant with politics. He belongs to the whole human being. And thus Schiller *and* Brecht are transformed from condemning judges into a conscience that never leaves us in peace.

But what Schiller discovered when he had given up his preoccupation with philosophy is something that will always remain for us as an insight, independent of whether Schiller impresses us as a dramatist or not, whether he's an example for us or not: The whole point of dramatic art, he said, is to find a poetic story. Dramatic art, then, is an effort to employ ever new models to shape a world which in its turn provokes ever new models.

1959   *Translated by Joel Agee*

Notes

1. Last lines, respectively, of *The Robbers, Don Carlos, Wallenstein, Mary Stuart,* and *William Tell.*
2. Johann Nestroy (1801–1862), author of numerous comedies, many in Viennese dialect.
3. "Against Tyranny": motto of several of Schiller's plays.
4. Characters in Schiller's *The Robbers* and *Love and Intrigue.*
5. Friederike Kempner (1836–1904) wrote poetry which was meant seriously but involuntarily sounded funny.
6. Reference to Schiller's ballad "The Diver."

FRIEDRICH DÜRRENMATT, born in 1921 near Berne, Switzerland,

exerts a powerful influence on the modern German stage, not only through his plays but through his theoretical writings. Most noteworthy are his essays "Problems of the Theater" and "A Monster Lecture on Justice and Law: A Brief Discourse on the Dramaturgy of Politics," both of which are to be found in Friedrich Dürrenmatt, *Plays and Essays,* Volume 89 in The German Library.

Wolfgang Hildesheimer

On the Theater of the Absurd

The planning commission of the Erlangen Theater Weeks has invited me to speak to you here about the theater of the absurd. I gladly accepted this invitation, but I pointed out to those who invited me that my presentation would be nonacademic and rather onesided. Nonacademic because I am neither a theoretician nor a systematizer, especially not in this field. Onesided because I myself write "absurd" plays, and this out of such profound conviction that nonabsurd theater sometimes strikes me as absurd.

Perhaps a theater historian could have given a more impartial and critical lecture on the subject than I can. Perhaps his lecture would also have been better founded, more soundly informed. Almost certainly he would have provided you with a larger overview. For many plays of the theater of the absurd are unknown to me. Nor have I ever read anything about the theater of the absurd. What you can expect from me is little more than the self-justification of one who is at home in the so-called "absurd," and an attempt to explore the motives that might prompt an author to make himself at home there and write absurd plays. Furthermore, I'm afraid these comments of mine will be strictly subjective. But this I feel is to my credit. I harbor a deep mistrust of all those who protest their objectivity in defense of their own cause.

The first question presenting itself is: what is absurd theater? Is it a theater that is felt to be absurd by the audience because it depicts seemingly unreal happenings? Or is it a theater that clothes the ontological concept of absurdity—as Camus conceives of it—in certain kinds of happenings, in order to confront the audience with it? Two possibilities. If we examine these two possibilities more closely, they melt into one. The theater of the absurd serves to confront the audience with the absurd by showing the audience its own absurdity. But since the audience is generally not readily willing to accept the philosophy of the absurd, let alone relate it to itself and regard itself as absurd, it will regard the confrontation on the stage as absurd. This gives rise to a stimulating mutual relationship. The theater and the audience appear to one another to be absurd.

But presumably I would never have thought of this if I didn't have to give a lecture. I admit, it took a certain effort of will for me to adopt the concept of the absurd as it is understood by an outside observer—by the audience, that is. I did it in the interest of these elucidations. And if I make use of it in my following remarks, I shall be doing so, for the time being, as if I were someone standing face to face with myself. And for him my right eye is on the left.

Now, the concept of "theater of the absurd" is a much less tested and defined matter for the audience than, say, the concepts of the "epic" or "poetic" theater. It has more to do with form or, if you will, content, than those concepts do. A play can be "absurd" *and* "poetic." Perhaps it could even be "absurd" and "epic"—one would have to try it out. At any rate, there seem to be as many forms as there are exponents of the theater of the absurd. The scale is very large if you feel at home within its expanse. That it doesn't appear to be very large from the outside is proven by the fact that conservative critics always name Ionesco and Beckett in a single breath, while to me the one thing they have in common seems to be that they both write differently from Schiller. It reminds me of the anecdote about the first Japanese ambassador in Berlin. After a brief probationary period he asked to be relieved for two reasons: the first was that Europeans had an unpleasant odor, and the second was that they all looked alike.

What I mean by that is that Beckett and Ionesco have little in common. Little more than their common homeland in the absurd. But since this is the place where most people live, even though they don't know it—at least according to the absurd playwrights—such joint residence hardly constitutes a common denominator. So, what they seem to have in common only looks that way from the outside.

Let's stay with this "outside," with the viewpoint of the audience which does not consider itself absurd. How does the absurd theater manifest itself to the audience?—For it would be a mistake to claim that for the audience the main characteristic of the absurd theater is that it manifests a "rebellious" or "anti-Aristotelian" character. The audience knows that revolt against a conventional art form is not a creative motive. When a theater adopts this stance—Dadaism for instance—it is usually as comical as it is short-lived. Revolt against a form is a creative motive only when the conventional form no longer suffices for what one is trying to express. But the "theater of the absurd" is a philosophical theater, and therefore it is less a revolt against a theatrical convention than against a conventional world view and its way of using the theater and manifesting on the stage.

But how do I explain to myself the things that take place in an absurd play, and what do the various plays of this genre have in common?

Let's set up a working hypothesis: Every absurd play is a parable! However, "the story of the prodigal son" is also a parable. But it is a completely different kind of parable. Let us analyze the difference: the "story of the prodigal son" is consciously conceived with a view toward its indirect message—its possible inference by analogy, that is—while the absurd play becomes a parable of life precisely by virtue of the absence of any message whatsoever. For life doesn't deliver messages either. On the contrary: it poses a permanent, unanswered question, as the playwright of the absurd would argue if he didn't prefer to clothe his argument in the parable of a play that deals with the confrontation between man and the alien world, and hence between man and that question.

This argument of the playwright of the absurd—that life doesn't "say" anything—can be emblematically expressed in all sorts of forms and on all kinds of levels. But in no form and on no level is the possibility of analogical inference more evident than in the simple direct parable. The parable of the prodigal son analogizes a certain kind of human attitude by a fictive parallel event, regarding both from the point of view of religious faith. The parallel event is supposed symbolically to represent the real event. But the absurd play cannot depict an event analogous to the meaninglessness and questionableness of life, for it is hardly possible to find an analogue for something that is absent, something that *isn't*. It is possible, however, to find an analogue for the *fact* that something is absent; but this can only be done by the demonstration of a parallel condition on the symbolic level. The absurd theater, however, does not know symbolism, or rather it despises it; absurd theater does not depict anything that could be revealed in logically sequential action; rather, it identifies with the subject—the absurd—in all its monstrous illogic by depicting certain absurd conditions, but especially by its own absurd behavior, thereby revealing sudden glimpses of the human condition. The whole picture emerges only with the sum of these various depictions. And only the sum of the absurd plays—that is, the existence of the theater of the absurd as a phenomenon—becomes an analogue of life. So I am modifying my previous thesis that every absurd play is a parable by saying that only the theater of the absurd as a whole manifests the didactic tendency of the parable. The common denominator of absurd plays therefore resides in the affinity of their authors, who, as I said, have the same homeland. But it does not reside in their having the same visual angle, nor does it reside in any sameness in what they perceive.

Accordingly, the theater of the absurd affords all sorts of views. Sometimes it's a grand panorama, as in Ionesco's *Chairs*. Or a tiny snapshot, a small diabolical disturbance, a sort of message concerning the instability of the world, as for example in Günter Grass's *Ten More Minutes to Buffalo*.

And now I have already mentioned three plays, a drama, and a burlesque which for me are prototypes and, besides, successful realizations of absurd dramatic art.

Ionesco wrote a little preface to *The Chairs* which I would like to recite to you—though I assume that most of you are acquainted with it:

> The world sometimes appears to me to be void of concepts and what is real seems unreal. This feeling of unreality, the search for an essential, forgotten, unnamed reality outside of which I believe myself not to be, is what I wanted to express—by means of my characters, who are wandering about in an incoherent world, calling nothing their own but their fear, their regret, their failure, the

emptiness of their life. Beings who have been cast out into something that is devoid of meaning can only appear grotesque, and their suffering is nothing but a tragic mockery. How could I, to whom the world is incomprehensible, understand my own play? I am waiting for someone to explain it to me.

As for the last sentence, I presume that by now Ionesco has had one of his plays explained to him by many a German critic. Whether this explanation made sense to him is a question which, thank God, I don't have to answer. At any rate, this sentence as well as the whole preface—in addition to presenting a concise explanation of absurd theater altogether—supports my thesis, insofar as we can conclude the following from it: the absurd play confronts the audience with the incomprehensibility, the questionableness of life. But the incomprehensibility of life cannot be depicted by an attempt at an answer, for that would imply that it is interpretable, that life is comprehensible after all. Incomprehensibility can only be depicted by allowing the incomprehensible to reveal itself in all its enormity and mercilessness and letting it hover in space as a quasi-rhetorical question: Whoever expects an explanation will be waiting in vain. He will not receive it until the meaning of creation is revealed to him by a competent authority, which is to say never. So the absurd play depicts a condition which, however it may end on the stage, never departs from the interrogative. And therein lies one of the essential distinctions from the Aristotelian and the epic theater, which are always giving or at least intimating an answer. Therefore, of all the receptive capacities an absurd play requires of its audience, the most elementary one is that the audience follow the author in moving from the answer to the question.

"The absurd," says Camus, "arises from the juxtaposition of man posing a question and the world maintaining its irrational silence."

Thus the theater of the absurd becomes the site for a sort of symbolic ceremonial in which the audience takes on the role of man posing his question and the play represents the world maintaining its irrational silence—i.e., in this case, giving absurd substitutionary answers, which have nothing more to convey than the painful fact that no truly compelling answer exists.

For the absurd play demands active participation of its audience—as does all art. The audience, however, is rarely willing to follow the author all the way. The events on the stage are felt to be incoherent and illogical. The fact that life itself is incoherent and illogical is something the viewer in the audience isn't aware of, since his own life may be unfolding within the limits of a logical system, so that he does not require and consequently does not seek a larger scheme of things. In the theater he expects to find excerpts of his system: topical issues, people of our time, historical events, relationships between people. Occasionally he'll enjoy smiling at a satire. He may even find pleasure in a fantastical plot as long as it is sharply and definitely distinguished from reality as he perceives it. But the absurd stands outside the conceptual world he's accustomed to. For him the absurd is absurd—and he would use the word as a synonym for "crazy" or "outrageous." He will indignantly reject any point of contact, any clue of an analogy, let alone identification.

If the whole thing strikes him as just *too* absurd—for instance when two human beings emerge from a garbage can—he feels ridiculed. But he's particularly wrong about that. The intention is just the opposite. He, the viewer, should ridicule the activities on the stage—respond to them with the "tragic mockery" of which Ionesco speaks—or rather, not to the business on the stage itself—not to the parable, but to its subject: life. And in doing so, of course, he would be mocking himself as one who asks and receives no answer. But he doesn't succeed in climbing the various levels of transposition. He's rebuffed at the outset by seemingly superficial things, for instance banalities in the form of linguistic cliches he hears uttered on the stage. He does not notice that some of these are actually artificial linguistic constructions, artful simulations which appear to be commonplaces only to those who feel at home with the commonplaces of life.

Now there are some absurd plays that have become popular, that have even reached a large audience. But in each case this seems to be due to something other than their absurdity. I saw *Waiting for Godot* in the Phoenix Theatre in London, where it was running for months. Always during the intermission, about one fifth of the audience left the house—a fact, incidentally, of which the taxi drivers were particularly aware: their cars stood in a long line in front of the theater at intermission time. But the rest of the audience stayed to the end and applauded heartily—in fact, for Londoners, almost frenetically. And why? Not because a truth had conveyed itself to them emblematically from the stage, but rather because they had witnessed a fascinating interpretation of a fascinating work of art. A performance that applied a quasi-musical organization to the stychomythical play between two Irish vagabonds, with magnificent effectiveness. Even an opponent of the theater of the absurd—assuming he isn't devoid of all receptive talent for language and rhythm—would have to confirm that Beckett is a legitimate poet. And that he is a poet even where his material seems to be leading him into monomania.

Another great success is Ionesco's *Rhinoceros*. But this success is due to the fact that this is not an absurd play. There are absurd elements in its—frequently splendid—dialogues, but otherwise its author is employing a very direct and obvious sort of parable with as clear-cut a meaning as the one about the prodigal son.

Let us take a closer look at this play! By demonstrating what an absurd play *isn't*, we shall be able to cast an additional light on the nature of absurd theater. I assume that most of you are acquainted with its content. The citizens of a provincial town turn into rhinoceroses—one after the other. An interpretation comes forcibly to mind. The provincial town is our world. We are the citizens. The metamorphosis represents the well-known process of leveling or massification or stupification—whatever we wish to call it—which we are all subject to. So the rhinoceroses are us, projected into a not-too-distant future. That's how simple it all is. So it's a social-critical play that uses symbolism. Unfortunately, the prognosis itself has by now become a commonplace, since we hear it being rattled off right and left ad nauseam. It would have been nicer if Ionesco had written a play about the cliché quality of this prognosis. But this is not what I wanted to discuss.

One of these citizens escaped the metamorphosis. We are not wrong in supposing that this citizen embodies the positive principle of the play. This positive principle, however, doesn't advocate anything in itself, it exists purely in contrast to, and only by virtue of its resistance to, the negative principle. It expresses only one thing, one categorical imperative: one should not become a rhinoceros. This in turn makes it a morally didactic play. Now, if we ask ourselves how one can avoid turning into a rhinoceros, the play will provide only one answer: by refusing to do so. But this answer is not unambiguous. For it is never completely clear whether this metamorphosis is a willful act, quiet resignation, fate or punishment. In any case it is activated by a higher authority (which however remains anonymous and about which we learn absolutely nothing in the course of five acts). So the play depicts the successful struggle of the individual against fate, and is therefore a classical drama. But it isn't that either. For it remains quite uncertain whether the hero, a second after our applause has congratulated him for his fortitude, might not also turn into a rhinoceros. The possibility exists. If we knew it to be the case, the play would be about the impotence of man against the will of higher powers, and it would be a tragedy in the classical Greek sense. But it isn't that either, otherwise the outcome of the struggle would have had to determine the course of the story retroactively. But this play has no outcome other than the prognosis. Whether the hero undergoes the metamorphosis or not is irrelevant for the didactic value of the parable. The message remains the same in both cases, namely: we are all turning into rhinoceroses. And that brings us back to the beginning.

Now the fact that a play deliberately and, it seems, schematically disregards conventional dramatic rules does not in itself mean that it's an absurd play, not even if it evinces the secondary characteristics of the absurd. Even a metamorphosis isn't an element of the absurd, it's an element of the fairy play. So we're dealing with a peculiar product of compromise: a hybrid. The play depicts a catastrophe wreathed in dialogue of a commentative and diagnostic sort, uninfluenced by human words or deeds, lethargically striding along through four acts like a well-fed rhinoceros, without granting its characters any chance of intervening. The individual may be in a position to protect himself against the metamorphosis—and one of them does so—but he can't save the others. The play is as clear as a fairy tale for children, as interpretable as an allegory, but the interpretation will reveal a logical inconsistency.

It has been said that Ionesco's strength is his ability to lead a perfectly ordinary and banal initial situation *ad absurdum* simply by exaggerating it. Now, in *Rhinoceros* he does something like that, for inside every one of the figures in the first scene there is already a small rhinoceros—but I think it is wrong to say that Ionesco's strength lies in this kind of invention. His strongest play— I myself consider it one of the masterpieces of modern drama— *The Chairs,* is in the realm of the fantastic right from the beginning. The characters, constellations, and situations are fantastical, or at least surreal. And it is precisely this play that provides a magnificent view, in emblematic form, of certain aspects of an inner world. The art of the absurd theater, after all, does not consist in smoothing the audience's path, providing it with a donkey-bridge from the real to the unreal, surreal, and grotesque by carefully and gradually deconstructing reality. Rather, it consists in transporting the audience into the realm of the absurd as soon as the curtain rises and having them settle down, making them at home, as it were, where, according to the author, they have been living all along: in the questionableness of this life that will not declare its meaning. The viewer should feel so at home there that once he has accepted the initial situation, even the most absurd element can no longer upset his equilibrium, since it's no more than a corollary of the initial situation. Only in this way and on this plan can the absurd parable unfold.

One effect of the development of our world view has been the extraordinary freedom of expression at the disposal of the artist today: but only so long as he doesn't change his mode of expression, i.e. his style—at least not within a single work! A tachist painting can be a great work of art, but it is certainly not a work of art if somewhere in the picture we can recognize an untransposed bouquet of flowers. For that would run counter to the inner and consequently essential principle of style. Similarly, trying to operate on two different planes, as Ionesco seems to do in *Rhinoceros*—on the one hand the plane of the slickly performed parable preparing for the final catharsis through four straight acts, and on the other, the parabolic content of absurd theater as such, which scorns catharsis—is to offend against all the fundamental laws of the theater. I cannot intend to produce a catharsis by a demonstration on the stage if the means I am using are the means of the absurd. For to want a catharsis implies a belief in the mission of the theater. But the theater of the absurd implies an admission of the theater's inability to ennoble mankind; and it is this impotence which provides the pretext for making theater in the first place. Impotence and doubt, the strangeness of the world, are the meaning and tendency of every absurd play, which thereby becomes a contribution toward elucidating the human condition. It scorns the depiction of reality, since only a tiny portion of reality can be depicted anyway, a portion that can never stand proxy for the entirety of life and by its nature bears no relationship to man's position in the world. Absurd theater therefore does not want to use the interplay of characters to tell a story or exemplify a thesis. It does not want to demonstrate something typical by some historical or fictitious individual example. It is not at all interested in championing some principle represented or—even worse—symbolized by a hero. The absurd playwright is of the opinion that no struggle in the world was ever carried out on the stage, that the theater has never ennobled a single human being or improved any condition whatsoever—and from this fact his theater draws the bitter or comical conclusions, depending on its author's bent. Experience has taught him that politician A will not recognize himself on the stage even if the point is driven home to him with a sledgehammer, and that A will be convinced that that other politician, B, whom he considers to be more corrupt than himself, is the one being portrayed; the absurd playwright knows, too, that both politicians will be heartily amused by an author who becomes bitter or even—as the saying goes—writes with his heart's blood.

The absurd playwright may, in my view, be prepared, in life, to commit himself to a good cause, even if it's a losing battle, as is commonly the case with good causes. But the theater is the wrong place for both the cause and his commitment to it. What he wants to do in the theater is to play out his play of absurd evidential, and in doing so he will have to rest assured that his morality, being part and parcel of his personal microcosm, will become transparent in this play, too: transparent in the absurd as well—indeed, for him, exclusively in the absurd.

While writing down this lecture I discovered that these notes were increasingly assuming the character of a manifesto. That there is even a certain pathos about them which is quite foreign to their subject, the absurd theater. This is probably due to the abnormal position one assumes in trying to analyze from outside something one is intimately identified with. The playwright of the absurd who does not have to give a lecture doesn't analyze, he writes plays, and at the most he'll wait, like Ionesco, for someone to explain what he's written. But, if I understand him correctly, he isn't holding his breath. He knows there is no explanation for any one particular play, and also that his theater needs no further explanation as soon as the audience acknowledges—that is to say, recognizes—the existence, or rather the dominion, of the absurd. The absurd is his only point of reference. He has decided upon it, perhaps not even consciously. It may have decided itself within him. For his inherent sense of the absurd is rooted more deeply than his capacity for personal decision. In any case, he came to his decision on his own. And no propaganda—not even the most subliminal kind—has brought it to his attention. For there is no absurdist propaganda other than the human condition. Granted, there was an initial stage for learning its expressive potential: Surrealism, which prepared the way for the recognition of the absurd. But it would take me too far afield to talk about that.

Only one who lives in the absurd, who experiences the absurdity of life, its situations and its props, can put them into an artistic form; which of course is not to say that the absurd view alone will provide the capacity for this kind of activity. It is as impossible to experiment with the absurd as it would be for an atheist playwright to write a religious play. And it is just as impossible for the dramatist of the absurd to switch to another form, unless some radical inner reversion has taken place.

The absurd dramatist is not interested in the "burning issues" of the theater. It doesn't matter to him whether the theater as an institution has a future or not; he knows that the theater has as much and as little of a future as man does. He's quite satisfied with the format of the stage as he finds it: a peep-show. He doesn't erect a false proscenium, doesn't have actors emerge from among the audience, all he needs is the stage, wood, glue, and dust. Contrary to general opinion, he's not interested in experimentation.

While there are no dramaturgical rules for what he wants to depict, his play does proceed in accord with a certain law. To express himself completely, he cannot rely exclusively on words. The plane of the absurd is not limited to language. The absurd character "functions," it uses gestures, mimicry, and where that's not enough, props come into play, sometimes literally as partners or protagonists. Every one of the characters appearing on the stage is in a sense a *deus ex machina* that is needed without having been expected. Therefore the play doesn't presuppose any knowledge. You don't have to have read a playbill telling you that, say, Karl Rösler is a forty-eight-year-old retired railroad employee on a pension and that he is Klara's former lover. The initial situation is immediately grasped, since the characters have had no relationships prior to those that are revealed the moment the curtain rises. For this reason, no anterior state of affairs has to be explained, no one has to be told that A is the brother-in-law of B, who's just now returning late from the war, too late to prevent the adultery which took place when the members of the audience were still unsuspectingly eating their supper. Any mention of the past in an absurd play indicates a collective absurd past, and any mention of the future takes the form of a question. And the end of the play contains the beginning.

The actor of the absurd theater sometimes has a hard time, for the author makes no allowances for his vanity. Naturally there can be roles any actor would be more than happy to play—what comedian would not be delighted to wait for Godot in so gratifying a manner—but occasionally the absurd theater produces roles that seem to demand more of an actor—given the way actors tend to be nowadays—than can be reasonably expected. Imagine a proud actor of the *Burgtheater* crawling out of one of Beckett's garbage cans. But above all, roles are developed that have no human likeness at all, no matter which way you turn them. Characters used as props, for example, or grotesque characters, or else characters that represent several types in quick succession or simultaneously. Now here the playwright of the absurd may indeed ask himself whether such a role, which you might say lacks a center from which it could be grasped, is compatible with the dignity of its potential player.

This is a serious objection. But when I consider the contemporary nonabsurd theater—and note that I am not speaking of the two great playwrights Frisch and Dürrenmatt, who incidentally also use the parable, with supreme artistry—but rather when I consider realism, so-called, I find myself confidently putting to sleep my scruples concerning the potential indignity of certain absurd roles. To illustrate this point, I shall recite to you a passage from a new play by a young Italian actor, which is being very successfully performed in Italy. I admit that this is a rather crass example, but it demonstrates clearly what I mean. The hero, Renato, is addressing his adored Elena—for the issue here, as it is so frequently in life, is love:

"Farewell! Give me a kiss, so that I'll know it's the last one. (Stage direction: he steps up to her. Their lips meet, his head slides down Elena's neck. He weeps silently. She says nothing. He continues:) Forgive me! I'll never get over this. I'll never get over the thought of what might have been. You don't know the peace of mind love can bestow. No more encounters, not with any woman. That's the decisive thing for a man, and that's peace: working at home, while life goes on outside."

And Elena, moved, says: "Renato!"

I'm not concerned with the artistic quality of such a speech or such a play. I don't believe any sort of symbolization is taking place here, but I may be mistaken. This may be a very good play, I'm not competent to judge that. But—and here's my concern—I believe that it is fundamentally more degrading for an actor to have to play such a scene than to play a character of the theater of the absurd, even if this character comes crawling out of a trash can. It is considerably more humiliating for an actor to have to utter words and perform gestures which—who knows—he may use in the intimacy of his private life to express his real feelings, than to lend stage-life to a character of the active imagination which even the most naive audience would never personally identify with. Alienation preserves the dignity of the actor. It gives him the opportunity at every moment to demonstrate his distance from his role.

The actor of the theater of the absurd is in a position to make sovereign use of the entire scale of mimic expression without turning into a parodist of life. But if you put tears in his eyes and the words "I love you" in his mouth, he'll turn into the kind of actor who performs embarrassing little genre pictures from everyday life.

The absurd theater is a parable about man's alien status in the universe. Therefore it is play in the service of alienation. It is the ultimate and radical consequence of alienation. And alienation means play in the best, truest, and—incidentally—oldest sense.

1960 *Translated by Joel Agee*

WOLFGANG HILDESHEIMER, born in 1916, has lived in England, Palestine, West Germany, and Switzerland. He is the author of surreal short stories, novels, and plays. Satirical comedies: *Die Eroberung der Prinzessin Turandot* (1961) and *Das Opfer Helena* (1969); novels: *Tynset* (1965) and *Marbot* (1981).

Rolf Hochhuth

Should the Theater Portray the Contemporary World?

Should the theater portray the contemporary world?

It should portray contemporary man, yes—and in doing so (but without misconstruing this goal as some kind of crudely obligatory commitment) it should fight against those phrases one hears repeated *ad nauseam* about "the demise of the individual, as a category of the bourgeois era, in the total organization of industrial society" (Adorno).

It would be the death of the theater if it were ever to admit that the human being in the mass ceases to be an individual—an unacceptable formula, no matter how stereotypically it's been recited for us in every other newspaper think-piece for decades. It's just as inhuman as the telegraphically ordained murders themselves, this refusal to recognize that the individual has to endure *his* suffering, *his* dying, by himself, individually—today as always—particularly when he has no choice and no weapon, and when he's dying simultaneously with eight hundred other people whom he doesn't know, in the same gas chamber, where he can no more look his murderer in the eye than the citizen can confront the bomber pilot—or than the galley slave three thousand years ago could ever meet face to face with the captain of the ship that rammed and sank his own. Naturally death comes in a different guise in the technological age than it did in the early nineteenth century. And yet every human being dies "his" death as an individual in Rilke's sense, just as he was condemned to love or not to love "his" partner, to drag his way through life, be it as a man of enterprise or of deprivation, as an administrator or the one administered to. If a snob fails to notice that a factory worker and her brothers and sisters who have never read any books are and will always be more than some nameless slum-bred litter, that they are human beings involved in very personal situations, he shouldn't complain when he himself is some day reduced to the anonymity of numbers by those who ordain terror through the microphone; for these scoundrels are only too eager to let themselves be persuaded that their victims have lost their faces, that they are mere vote-providing cattle, that they are less individual than, say, the city-dwellers of the middle ages, who didn't have television blasting in their ears all day, but the pastor's preachments instead. Even if the most paralyzing crime ever committed by human beings, even if Auschwitz—or a natural catastrophe that drowns entire countries—even if these should be at least mentioned in a dramatic play—for no play and no poet can go beyond the mere mention of such indescribable catastrophes—even this touching, in a drama, upon the most frightful *mass* fate, can only occur under the eternally valid aesthetic law formulated by Schiller:

Ehret ihr immer das Ganze, ich kann nur einzelne achten,
Immer im einzelnen nur hab ich das Ganze erblickt.[1]

The fact that at this time we cannot see the tree for the forest—that we don't respect it, because Hitler's cry: "You are nothing, your people are everything" still has the ring of truth for us—has brought about the grotesque circumstance that in common German usage, to say of someone: "He starts getting *personal* right away!" has become a reproach, an accusation. In reality a person is *fair* to the degree to which his judgments are personal and *ad personam*. Unless we agreed to capitulate as human beings, and acknowledged our defeat by the world of things. But to be human, in the true sense of the word, is *not* to separate the world of things from the personal; the drama that leads a human being into making decisions—for where there is nothing to decide, there is no drama, a group of people buried by an avalanche has no dramatic tension whatsoever, and neither does their destruction by a bomb dropped from a plane; the only dramatic question is whether that bomb should be dropped—decisions in drama, then, presuppose the personalization of conflicts: and this is true even though vulgar

Marxists reject this as a violation of their faith. Human beings do not change from the bottom up. An epoch that gives rise to such a claim overestimates its part in the course of history. And this is a claim that is being made every day.

So I cannot agree with Adorno when he says that "any supposed drama of the atomic age would be a mockery of itself, if only because its plot would consolingly falsify the historical horror of anonymity by fitting it into characters and actions and possibly gaping with fascination at those who decide whether to push the button or not."

These formulations of a famous man will keep us captivated until we're primitive enough or outrageous enough to ask whether the opposite isn't true—whether a drama of the atomic age isn't precisely possible to the extent and only to the extent that we are willing to feel, in a completely old-fashioned manner, what Kogon[2] demanded in view of the mountains of skeletons in Buchenwald: "Observer of history, imagine that these remains of flesh and bone are *your* father, *your* child, *your* wife, are the person *you* love!"— And those prominent people who press the button—we don't have to gape at them with fascination, no: but isn't this fascinating scene, Stalin and Truman in Potsdam, both of them much too preoccupied with the scrapping of Germany to devote more than a few subsidiary clauses to the question of whether, in view of Tenno's offer of surrender ten days ago, the war against Japan should be continued? And Truman's remark, delivered in as offhand a manner as possible, that he has a new weapon; Stalin pretends to be barely listening—and then the decision to try this thing out, of course not without having the chaplain bless the plane crew before they take off . . .

Surely this is the essential task of dramatic theater: to insist that human beings are responsible for their actions. Or was Truman not responsible for the destruction of Hiroshima? True, the atomic age had begun. Whether the president's name was Truman or Smith, whether he was a middle-class fellow or a born *condottiere:* it wasn't he who ushered in this era, even Roosevelt could at best have forestalled it, never prevented it, if, after receiving a letter from Szillard with Einstein's signature on October 11, 1939, he hadn't ordered the development of the bomb. Einstein himself never tired of asserting later on that he had "merely served as a mailbox"—that's the kind of formulation by which those who were put in the position of driving the wheels of history later pretend they were mere cogs. And no doubt Burckhardt's[3] phrase applies to many: "Vain and ambitious men like Peter of Amiens and his accomplices at the beginning of the first crusade; they considered themselves the initiators and were no more than pathetic phenomena or symptoms . . . The gaily colored, windblown sail considers itself the source of the ship's movement, but all it does is catch the wind, which may turn at any moment or cease altogether." And though the mathematician Whitehead, referring to the meeting of the Royal Academic Society of November 6, 1918, when the validity of the Einsteinian theory of "curved space" was experimentally confirmed for the first time, wrote: "The laws of physics are the judgments of fate"—nevertheless *this* fate, to be born in the atomic age and not in the rococo, not in India and not in Bolivia, does not constitute an emergency exit for a flight from responsibility: for Truman and his intellectual underlings from Stimson to Oppenheimer were demonstrably in possession of *the absolute freedom* to decide whether the beaten Japanese—or more precisely: their wives and children—should be "given" the two A-bombs, or whether they should be spared that experience! Just take a look at the secret documents of the Potsdam Conference, which were first examined by Julius Epstein (*Spiegel,* March 22, 1961), or the journal of the British Marshall Lord Alanbrooke. Three men or five were in possession of *complete freedom* of decision—and they decided in favor of a mass murder that was as effective militarily as the decapitation of an infant. War criminals virtually *live* off the notions of our fashionable philosophers that history isn't made by people but by "anonymous agencies," because that would acquit *them* of their crimes!

Adorno obliges them by "establishing" the supposed "impossibility of portraying fascism" in the theater with the claim that "the freedom of the thinking subject no longer exists either in fascism or in our way of seeing."

Well formulated—but is it true? I would think that from the Führer on down (or was Hitler also no longer an individual) to the last of his henchmen, the block supervisor who had the choice—he usually *had* the choice, let's not forget that—merely to warn someone who had been denounced to him for listening to illegal radio transmissions, or to drag him before the tribunal; I would think that for all of these people, the freedom of the thinking subject existed the way it always does—more or less. Whoever denies this, would have to be decent enough to protest when SS-men get sent to jail nowadays for once having given orders to murder Jews. A uniform comes to an end at the neck. Faces seem indistinguishable only to someone whose habits of observation are as superficial as those of traveling Europeans, who see Asians as looking uniform—or of those intellectuals who debate one another on the subject of "massification" in congresses attended by thousands, without ever considering whether their own congress might not be an excrescence of the phenomenon they're so indignant about. To look at "the mass" from outside instead of seeing oneself as part of it, an individual in the mass along with all the other individuals: it is this point of view that gives rise to the level of morality that provides the modern killers and their thoughtless pimps in every social stratum with their "intellectual" weaponry—and it also leads to drastically inhumane insights, such as: "There are many people in whose mouths the word 'I' amounts to an effrontery" (Adorno).

A drama that respects man as an individual does not need any further "commitment" beyond that. It's already accomplishing more than the current fashion wishes to allow.

Can today's world be portrayed in the theater at all?
Not all of its aspects. But impassable limits have always existed. Klopstock, in the second song of his *Messias,* speaks of Hell as the "Unimageable" (*das Unbildsame*): "Eternally unimageable, endlessly vast fields full of misery." The truth of this is confirmed when we think of Auschwitz—and find that on the stage we can do no more than provide intimations of its railroad platforms, of the comparatively humane limbo on the outer limits of the camp, whose personnel, as we know, consisted of good average Germans. We might say that where humane behavior is no longer required even in its more reduced forms, the theater, too, loses its right. Hence its absolutely legitimate impotence with regard to the technical world, which is totally inhuman, even in its external aspect: faceless, because it has banished man, who was once the measure of all things, from its realm. A speed record, an industrial

capacity cannot be measured against human strength and are not even comprehensible to the human mind, no more than the sea, which is limitless to the eye, or natural catastrophes, or the battlefield and its waste matter, the mutilated men in their locked barracks: inhuman deserts, and hence closed to art. (We know about Schiller's regret at not being able to show the army as the basis of the whole.)

Other art forms, especially fiction, might be able to accomplish what the theater can only dimly intimate: love, for example. Can a play be imagined that would so thoroughly plumb this subject as certain chapters in Musil's[4] *The Man Without Qualities,* or in Flake's[5] *Fortunat,* or Ludwig Marcuse's[6] *Nachruf?*

Can the world still be portrayed by realistic means?

Realism—if what we mean by this label is the most exact representation conceivable of man's inner and outer situation: then, it seems to me, the stage can no more dispense with "realistic means" today than it ever could. It all depends how narrowly we demarcate the world of the realistic. A dream, a memory, can contain much more reality for us than a conversation in the bookstore or at the tailor's. Or death, which robs me of a relative today, and tomorrow of myself: unquestionably it is an incomparably stronger reality for me than the mailman. So why not bring death onto the stage, even in the so-called realistic drama. Realism in itself was never more than a resolution: it was only by tightening, intellectualizing, spiritualizing and metaphorizing it, especially in language, that realism was eventually transfigured, hardened, or sublimated into art. Or take old age, which is constantly at our heels, much more significant and worthy of portrayal than the policeman or the journalist, insofar as they bother us only in passing; it should be possible to portray that great mystery, time. Of course these are realities.

In literature too, the only valid theories are those that haven't been generalized. I can only speak of my experiences as a beginner, and only for my own sketches. What is still *possible* in contemporary drama? This question will naturally make a more insistent claim on one who is groping insecurely than the one of what is *needed* on the stage. And now a brief digression: it is characteristic of our epochal insecurity with regard to art that for the past several decades every other person will nod when a portrait painter declares that his subject, Karl Barth,[7] say, or Jaspers,[8] "hasn't had a face for the past forty years" and that therefore he, the painter, will have to "introduce" the essential content. As if nature (a dirty word at the moment) and life had not contributed enough to the elevation and spiritualization of even such heads as these. This comical presumption frequently culminates in the claim that only the artists themselves can understand the result of their brushwork, because they alone have the x-ray vision to see what is essential in such a person; everyone else has to make a big effort. And whoever still doesn't understand (and is stupid enough to admit it) is clearly not with it. But please don't infer from this that I'm putting in a plug for photography: a photograph does no more than capture a moment; a first-rate portrait painter captures the sum of countless moments. A while ago I had an assignment to search, in private and public collections as well as in libraries, for portraits, both drawings and paintings, of the important German fiction writers of the first half of the century: I had to confront the fact that an entire genre of the visual arts, and typically the most human genre, had fallen prey to the slick gimmick. There is almost nothing presentable left. The marvelous drawing of the eighty-year-old Thomas Mann by Marini, a picture by Orlik, by Corinth, Liebermann, Konig, Kollwitz, three or four others and about as few unknown ones in private collections—and that's it: the most depressing "illustration" of Hofmannsthal's statement that it is possible to end up in a time, in a climate, that no longer permits any growth. "It's no different than vegetation, than fauna: hosts of them start to die out. The word that just yesterday held the power of enchantment drops to the ground today like a meaningless thing."

How can realistic drama survive a realization like that? I have often been advised to modernize my play, which contains elements of realism, by transposing its plot into a surrealistic or absurd world. But "the most absurd thing in the world" is—not the absurd theater, but, according to Goethe, history itself. He referred to it with disgust as "a confused tangle of nonsense" (*"verworrener Quark"*), and in his later years he refused to contemplate it altogether. And it's true: history, the reality of history, which over and over enters its infanticidal laws of Bethlehem or Nuremberg into the menu of the man of action—it can't be topped by transposition into an absurd world. The Enabling Act[9] or the selling of Alaska, the 20th of July[10] or the betrayal of Christendom to the state of Constantine—that was global theater of the absurd. Nevertheless the temptation to slip away into the surreal is almost inescapable for a beginner, if only because that way he'd be spared having to contend with those richly endowed cowards from the cultural industry who since the collapse of Hitlerism have never lifted a finger against any product of nonrepresentational or absurd art, for the simple reason that it's so perfectly innocuous. It certainly won't upset the philistine consumer—he's had a nonrepresentational print by Neckermann or Piper hanging over his "kidney table" for a long time, and a regular plague of standardized opinion salesmen has convinced him that he will look extremely foolish if he should shrug his shoulders at so-called modern art—rather like the citizen who dares to laugh at the emperor's new clothes in Andersen's fairy tale.

And one who avoids putting the pope and one of Krupp's engineers on the stage[11] and plays it safe by calling his characters "The Lord of the Oracle" and "an ephor of the helots"—such a one could not only count on the applause of the Würzburg Sunday paper and the employers' associations, the *Weltwoche* in Zürich and the Christian-Democratic Party, he could also have adopted a richly metaphorical, or, as they like to call it, *poetical* linguistic model, from the *"Turm"*[12] for example. It's no fun to spend years with reams of diplomatic double-talk, orders of the day, medical records of torture sessions, and to Mendelize a language, a rhythm, out of these things and out of the soliloquies of the hopeless, dialogues that in part are quite consciously faithful to the stupefying vocabulary of the facts, employing it economically along with the genial sound of our north coast dialect in the mouth of an expert at shooting people in the neck, or the biblical pathos in the monologue of a raped man.

Avoiding these labors would also have spared the writer the reproach of having written "mere reportage"—a criticism which the author of a historical drama will have to accept from a newspaper critic, if only because he was so pedantic as to study his sources, and because he has used slides of documents, "realities," which he—to call on Goethe's assistance once more—actually considers to have more "genius" than the greatest poet. (If "reportage" is still synonymous with "report," as my dictionary always led me to believe, I shall never understand why a reportage should no longer be what it has always been since Herodotus and Sophocles: not only a legitimate, but an indispensable basic element of all nonlyrical literature.)

Such "realities" as a British Air Force Marshall's expert analysis of the effects of large-scale conflagrations in residential areas; as Stalin's dialogue with Sikorsky about the seemingly magical disappearance of eight thousand Polish officers; as the collective orgasm of the Viennese when their Hitler marched into town in 1938—and their subsequent disenchantment: are these not nightmares, folk tales and parables, and are they not, even as raw material, just as oppressive and frightening as anything in Poe, Grimm, and Kafka? Picasso, in his "Guernica," didn't juggle away any of the terrors of his historical model, nor did he merely copy it: *this* surrealism is legitimate because it remains indebted to reality even in the act of dismantling and abstracting it. Similarly, a speech by Hitler, tightened, stylized, and rhythmically cadenced, delivered to the accompaniment of a brass band playing the "*Badenweiler*"— this will send shivers up anyone's spine, but Chaplin's infantile dictator movie, or even Brecht's *Arturo Ui*? Aren't they just making merry with horror?

Adorno himself recently wrote: "The loss of tension that has been observed in those products of painting and music that move away from representational concreteness and tangible meanings is frequently met with, as well, in that species of literature that a revolting linguistic usage has elected to call 'texts.' It approaches the edge of indifference and degenerates, unawares, into a technical hobby . . ."

"Loss of tension"—the condition Adorno is adumbrating with this phrase can probably be attributed to the banishment of Eros from art. After the thirst for water, the thirst for beauty is probably the most elemental craving—and it grows in us proportionally with the inner and outer pollution that typifies our century. If Thomas Mann as a school boy—to give just *one* example—still regularly hung prints of contemporary artists over his bed, then van Gogh and Marc were perhaps the last who aimed at this kind of impact, not only in its extent but in its depth; for what could reach deeper or take root more tenaciously than works of art that are able to nourish the dreams and the longings of adolescents.

In the most intimate portrayal of youth, in *Henri Brulard,* we find the confession that the discovery of art and the eruption of sexuality were *identical* for Stendhal—but what young person of *today* could say of himself: "Around this time the arts took possession of my imagination, and they did this . . . by way of my sensuality"?

Today's adolescents no longer derive their posters and nudes and songs and ideas and ideals (which they still have) from *art,* which elicits from them a shrug which Adorno weakly intimates when he calls it "indifference"; it is a death sentence. Why don't we ever ask whether we can afford to ignore Stendhal's most radical maxim: "For me, beauty is in every historical era the highest quality of the useful." If that is true—and if we measure against this insight our inability to satisfy the thirst for beauty: then hardly anyone among us is "useful." Then we survive, not thanks to the needs of our contemporaries, but thanks to subsidies. State and industry no longer commission a mosaic in order to decorate a wall—they do it to get rid of the legally prescribed tax contribution to the arts. To search for the reason why Eros was chased out of the arts—and Eros is the most powerful communicator of all—to seek for this reason outside of the artists themselves is cheap. Artists no longer oppose the value judgments and aesthetic laws that have been dogmatized for decades—and they wonder why they repeat themselves and why people are bored by them. Burckhardt wrote in 1852—and this has to be achieved again and again: "The whole operation requires, in addition, that you close your eyes tightly against every kind of 'aesthetics' that is being preached today." To do this takes the courage to be alone—and according to Benn[13] all art is the product of an "act of violence performed in isolation." A few hours before Goethe's death, perhaps in his last hour, he was shown the portrait of the beautiful countess Vaudreuil, which had just arrived—and his last authenticated word was a praise of Eros: "How good it is when the artist does not spoil what God has made so beautiful."

But our age, which has made a fashionable word of alienation, has moved so far away from nature in the arts that anyone still insisting on beauty, on Eros—"which started it all"—seems faintly ridiculous.

We would make more progress, too, if there weren't this tendency to canonize every new artistic direction as the one and only salvation as soon as it's been proclaimed. For example, the usual mischief of pitting realistic theater against the theater of the absurd as if they were opposites. Our world, which is so full of absurdity that there isn't a day when one isn't tempted at some point to find it absurd altogether, this world should at least be of service to a future theater in its capacity as inexhaustible prop-storage-room and ineluctable controlling agency; for with every increase in our distance from the world, the realm of the unaccountable, the aimless, grows.

A simple example: if someone wanted to portray a judge of the Hitler era who sentenced eleven people to death by decapitation and who in 1950, holding office as a senior government councillor, appraises applications for annuity by victims of fascism—an absurd and hence typical situation in our real world—such an author would surely do well to model this contemporary with all his dreams, suppressed desires, sons-in-law, pets, and Christmas tree, reproduce him with virtually photographic perfidy, and without making a caricature of him either; humor, in this as in most cases, would be a conciliatory and therefore weakening surrogate. For if the viewer, faced with this character, doesn't feel the last trace of a smile melting out of his face; if he is not so frightened that he wants to tear his eye out; if he does not recognize in this man of justice his boss, his brother, his father, or himself: then you might as well exhibit a monkey in a circus arena.

1963   *Translated by Joel Agee*

Notes

1. "While you always honor the Whole, I can only respect individuals/It is in the individual alone that I have always perceived the Whole."
2. Eugen Kogon, born 1903, Roman Catholic writer, survivor of Buchenwald, which he described in *The SS-State* (1946).
3. Jakob Burckhardt (1818–1897), Swiss historian.
4. Robert Musil (1880–1942), Austrian writer.
5. Otto Flake (1880–1963), expressionist writer.
6. Ludwig Marcuse (1894–1971), theater critic, writer.
7. Karl Barth (1886–1968), eminent Swiss-German theologian.
8. Karl Jaspers (1883–1969), philosopher.
9. Parliamentary device that brought Hitler to power.

10. Unsuccessful military putsch against Hitler in 1944.
11. Reference to his own play *The Deputy*.
12. Play by Hugo von Hofmannsthal.
13. Gottfried Benn (1886–1956).

ROLF HOCHHUTH, born in 1931, aroused considerable political controversy, mainly through his plays *The Deputy* (1963) on the role of Pope Pius XII and *The Soldiers* (1967) on the role of Winston Churchill during World War II. These plays were prototypes of the documentary drama.

Max Frisch

The Author and the Theater

Speaking of the theater—let's say: the theater you are in charge of as a producer, or advising as an artistic director, or keeping an eye on as a critic; not the theater as a concept, but concretely and locally: your theater, the familiar house on so-and-so street, precisely this one theater which you are basically talking about when in the course of this conference you speak of your fundamental experiences and demands and of theater in general, which will exist as long as our human race will exist—*your* theater has been shut down overnight. Out of commission. You just don't know it yet. Yesterday you still had a sold-out performance, I'm sure: the actors took their bows, removed their makeup in their dressing rooms, the doors and gates were closed as usual, and this morning, while you solemnly sit in St. Paul's church,[1] no one's got the key any longer. And what's even more amazing: you haven't even been informed of the fact. That's how out of commission the theater's suddenly become. And not only yours; the colleagues sitting next to you just don't know it yet . . .

Well, you simply wouldn't believe it, I knew it, and that's just what tempted me to imagine this; your theater, no matter whether it's an old house with the radiance of the twenties in its chandeliers or a brand-new one made of steel, concrete, and glass with dimensions that correspond to the boom we're experiencing in other areas—the house stands unharmed, as usable as the theater of Epidauros, and just as silent. Not even the doorman is there when you come home from this lively (we hope) conference. If you ask a passerby, he might be able to remember that this used to be a place where they put on plays, and he will walk on good-naturedly, as if the age of the theater were long past. You alone still believe in it and stand there, the producer of a monument, with pigeons cooing around your feet.

Now don't think: the state has cut our subsidies. That's not it. The state can't afford to do that as long as it needs our taxes for tanks and jet bombers; these too are sometimes steered in the wrong direction. And don't reproach yourselves for (I don't know) having spent too much time recently as guest directors in others houses. It's not that either. If a theater dies because of its producer, it just proves that this theater wasn't viable. Nor does it have anything to do with whether you play Hochhuth or don't play Hochhuth. The repertory, which you can still read on a yellowing poster, is nothing to be ashamed of: just a short while ago you could still see Brecht performed here, Shakespeare—Schiller—Kleist—Büchner—Chekhov, and in addition Walser—Albee—Dürrenmatt—Beckett, etc. A Weiss play was being announced for the future; a workshop stage was also in use, intimate and open to the world, always ready for something new and bold. What more could you *do*? And now you're sitting on the stoop in front of the theater feeding the pigeons, and that fellow coming in your direction, let's say he's myself, an author. Let our handshake be cordial, if earnest.

How are things going, I ask. There's no more theater in Germany, I know, that's why I ask: How are things going? I have to admit: I find the notion of all the theaters being closed down rather enlivening. Now's the time to find out what our theater meant, and what it didn't mean. Let's say our society changes in some way, maybe only by moving more rapidly towards the Restoration, as a result of there no longer being any theater: that would at least prove that the theater really is, was, could have been a political institution. I'm eager to find out.—Losing our royalties, yes, that's a bitter pill to swallow, and it makes me immediately think of our friends, the actors, who are making so much more money acting for the movies and TV, and yet I suspect it will be bitter for them as well no longer to be able to bring sacrifices to the stage; there was something to be said for the stage after all. And let's not forget the ladies and gentlemen who supplied our critiques: I don't know what they'll do without our mistakes. It's all very bitter, but it's no reason to open up the theater again; the fact that it's of vital importance only for us who produce it, indispensable only for our own social importance, is just not enough.

So: two socially prominent gentlemen out of commission, sitting on a stoop with pigeons cooing at their feet, and I ask ourselves whether we didn't perhaps overestimate the theater—theater as a moral institution, theater as a political institution, theater as a tribunal or whichever way we want to label it in contradistinction to the circus and the nightclub . . . Let's ask ourselves without worrying about state subsidies and their justification: What was the good of it? Not just for us, but for society? The communal experience? Sitting shoulder to shoulder in the auditorium, occasionally baffled when your neighbor laughs or doesn't laugh, fortifying your attention against coughers, occasionally isolated in rapture, at other times disgusted by an actor who's sweeping your right- and left-hand neighbors off their seats; sad and nervous and then, the moment the curtain falls, abruptly rebuked by thundering applause; and then standing in the lobby, smoking all by yourself or struggling shoulder to shoulder for a cup of coffee, anxiously adding your part to the intermission chatter so as not to hurt anyone's feelings, or else maintaining a deferential silence while listening to someone pontificating his judgment . . . It seems to me that communal experience is not the right word for it.

And yet something is happening that's different from reading: something public. A demonstration that takes place every evening. At the very least what's being demonstrated shows what our fellow citizens want and do not want to know, what they consider sacred, what makes them mad and what consoles them. For example, when a state of affairs they've put up with year in and year out outrages them on the stage, you can see (more clearly in the dark of the auditorium than in the light of everyday life) their relationship to reality outside the theater. Let's put it this way: theater as a testing ground. That it is. If I were a politician, I would often sit in the front loge with a view of the orchestra and the balconies, so I could recognize my *polis*. Even the poetry of the absurd, which seems to escape them, confirms the political nature of the theater; a public that finds satisfaction in absurdity would be a dictator's delight: such a public does not seek to be enlightened about the causes of fearful disorder, it wants to enjoy it instead, take a vacation in an apocalyptic gazebo . . . But what do the other plays accomplish, the plays of the enlighteners?

That's my other question.

Looking for a classical example to show that the theater has an effect beyond that of artistic enjoyment, my favorite one is *Hamlet*: the way the murderer-king, when the traveling players perform his crime for him, finds their art unendurable, leaps up, and rushes off, unmasked. A truly consoling example, but it's theater in the theater. "The play's the thing / in which I'll catch the conscience of the king": that's the way Hamlet defines his program as theatrical producer. But this presumes that the murderer has a conscience; in reality, for example in the Gallus Hall[2] in Frankfurt, such an effect cannot be expected. Granted, when we entrust the theater with a political function, we do not intend this direct Hamlet-effect; it would be quite enough for us if the theater entertainingly opened the eyes of the viewer in the audience, the citizen in his leisure time, so that at some point he toppled the murderer-king, or at least didn't re-elect him. This, again, presupposes that people's actions are guided by reason.

Brecht hoped that without him those in power would rule more securely. A modest hope, a very bold hope. Millions of people have seen Brecht performed and will see him again and again; but I venture to doubt that anyone has ever changed his political viewpoint or even examined it as a result. I can remember a not very far-off time when literary historians who are now writing about Brecht considered it a delusion to speak of this agitator as a poet; today he is a genius, we know it, and he has the sweeping ineffectuality of a classic. Art, insofar as it isn't miserable, just happens to have something culinary about it. Guernica, the name of a Spanish city which was bombed before all the others, made us enthusiastic about Picasso. What remains is art. And Franco. Now to stay with the theater: is there a fascist play of any stature (assuming we don't include a force like Genet)? I don't know of any; but fascism does exist, even though its vocabulary has been modernized. What does this mean? The theater, I'm afraid, deceives us with regard to the modern world situation. The left is simply more talented: in the theater, which doesn't mean the world. Hence my question, whether we don't tend to overestimate the theater.

Let's assume the following:

As we're sitting on the stoop, conversing, and having just noticed that the key which magically shut down all the theaters has inadvertently turned up in my left pocket—all I'd have to do would be to take it out and we'd have our theater back: theater tomorrow as it was yesterday—a third person arrives, a man of serious demeanor, he steps out of a black car with a governmental emblem and comes right up to us. A minister of culture. He is more upset than we are, and my suggestion that we should let moss grow over the state theaters so that other theaters can spring up elsewhere will hardly persuade him. What's at stake here is culture. And I don't have to mention that we are no longer sitting down, that we have risen to our feet, as honored as we are frightened. Theater as a point of honor for the state. Now, we know: every state (at least in Europe) has the strict need to possess culture, and even though we theater people live off this need for culture and want to be thankful for it, we should not be bemused by the fact that the state demands and supports culture where it is relatively inexpensive, namely, in the theater.

I hope the minister doesn't misunderstand me! We are in favor of this state, it seems to me, and hope it will succeed in realizing its constitution more and more; in fact we're very much in favor of it. How on earth shall I put it? The collective urge to sit there as a cultural nation, and the individual urge to write or to act or to paint or to dance, are two things. Speaking as a democrat, I say: Art is no substitute for political culture. Or to say it straight out: The state should demonstrate culture where it's directing its own show, from the administration to the army barrack. As citizens, we would like to help the state achieve this, but art can't shoulder this particular burden. And as for the key I'm magically keeping in the pocket of my trousers: I would not hand out this key just because the state is showing itself to be munificent. And this, as I said, not out of enmity toward the state; on the contrary. I earnestly hope that the minister will understand me and my shrugging at the theater of culture-manifestation, and I hope we will part in agreement that the culture we desire for our nation and all nations is not a category separate from politics and the economy.

We don't want to overestimate ourselves.

Now to speak of theater as theater:

(*after the minister has left us*)

Let's talk about whether the world of today can still be depicted on the stage; it was Dürrenmatt who formulated this question, and you know the equally well-known answer of Brecht's, that the contemporary world can be reproduced on the stage, but only if it is conceived as something alterable. The question is more upsetting than the answer—upsetting because of the supposition that it was once possible to portray the world. When? What Aeschylus and Sophocles put on the stage was not a depiction of Greek society but a mythological design. In the case of Aristophanes we might speak more accurately of a depiction of the given, actual world; but he too can only do it by mirroring it in a designed world, via the grotesque; he raises people from the actual world into an imagined one, be it only to drop them and show the length of the fall. Is he depicting them? It's not the right word. Calderón? I suspect the theater never depicted the real world; it always altered it. Shakespeare? His work is universal; but is it a depiction of the world of his time? That world, I imagine, was already more pluralistic than is evident in any of his plays; his plays have survived for us, not the actual world of his time, and the fact that we now regard his plays as a depiction of something that no longer exists is an understandable illusion, but still an illusion. Schiller? Kleist? Büchner? Chekhov? Strindberg?

The closer we come to the present—the more we're acquainted with the actual world—the more obvious it becomes how impossible it is to depict this complex reality; a theater piece, even a great one, is always just a piece: a narrowing-down, and precisely for that reason a release for a few hours. No matter how the theater presents itself, it is art: play as an answer to the world's undepictability. What becomes depictable is poetry. Brecht, too, does not show the world as it is. His theater pretends to show it, and Brecht invented ever new means of showing that it's being shown. But outside of the gesture of showing: what is being shown? A great deal, but not the world as it is; instead, models of the Brechtian-Marxist thesis, the desirability of another, nonexistent world: poetry. It is no accident that his plays, with the exception of the fragmentary scenes from *Fear and Misery in the Third Reich,* are not set in contemporary Germany but in China, in the Caucasus, in Chicago, in the Thirty Years' War, in Galileo's Italy; not one of them in East Germany. Why not? Shakespeare did the same thing;

his plays are set in ancient Rome or distant Denmark or in Illyria, and when they're set in England, it's historical England. Because of censorship? That may be part of it, but it's not the only and not the essential reason for taking up residence outside the world that happens to be there at the moment.

Anyone who writes will soon discover the reason; you have to alter things in order to depict them, and whatever can be depicted is already a utopia. "It will hardly surprise you," writes Brecht in that reply, "to hear me say that the question of describing the world is a social one," and we know what Brecht means by that; but it can also be read the other way around, namely like this: that the political creed that demands a transformation of the world is secondary, an elaboration of the problem of representation. Even if the playwright does not commit himself politically, does not believe that the theater contributes to the transformation of society; even, that is, if we do not restate the question of the world's describability as a social question; the fact remains that the undepictability of the world can only be answered with utopia, that every scene, by being playable, surpasses the world as it is and, with some luck, succeeds in depicting what is called a vision.

The greatest play in the German language since Brecht is not based on a political ideology, its vision does not present itself as a program, it does not show society as something that can be changed; nevertheless it is a great play. I am speaking of *Der Besuch der alten Dame*.[3] There not only exists a place called Szechuan, there is also a place called Güllen; both exist only on the stage, both refer to our world, but they are not representation of it, they interpret it, and in Dürrenmatt's case the question whether this will change the world does not arise. . . .

I don't know to what extent Brecht actually believed in the didactic effectiveness of his theater; when you asked him, his yes was definite, and the same goes for his writings. Watching him at his rehearsals, I had the impression that even if it were proven that the theater contributes nothing to the transformation of the world, his need for the theater would be undiminished. I'm not saying this to cast doubt on his political attitude, but to inquire after the impulses underlying artistic creation. What is it that impels us to undertake the difficult labor of writing a play, and all the subsequent labors involved in putting it on the stage? We are not producing a better world on the stage but rather a playable, transparent world, a world that allows for variants, and to this extent a changeable world, changeable at least in the realm of art. We know that Brecht was an indefatigable experimenter, that is to say: a transformer, and full of joy at that and everything but a dogmatist, a world-educator. He used the word "beautiful" more frequently than I expected. Or "ugly." Even the expression: "a more elegant solution." And in a letter, the phrase: "to produce beauty." As if the solutions strived for were all in the realm of art. Every scene, every story, every picture, every sentence involves change: not of the world, but of the material we derive from the world; it is changed in order to make it performable. Brecht's opinion that "the contemporary world can be described in the theater as well, but only if it is conceived as something that can be changed" looks like the translation of a simple artistic experience into a political program transcending the artistic act. The will to change the world as an extension of the artist's creative urge? Our play, understood as an answer to the unrepresentability of the world, does not change this world, but it does change our relationship to it: for one, it produces enjoyment even of tragic subjects, and this enjoyment does not need to be justified by didactic considerations; it is a self-assertion of man against historicity. But that's not always all there is to it; just by attempting to reconstruct a piece of life into a theater-piece, we are revealing a certain alterability, transformability in the historical world, which is our material: a raw datum, unsought for, but henceforth inescapable. Peter Suhrkamp,[4] who still knew the pre-Marxist Brecht, possibly meant the same thing when he said: Brecht became a Marxist because of his experience as an artist. That would mean that political commitment is not the impulse but a result of artistic work, secondary but not irrelevant, at least not insofar as a work of art is genuine at all; and it would also mean that the customary attempt to cultivate Brecht as a poet by subtracting the Marxist is not only idle but philistine.

Let's leave the subject of Brecht.—

Our question whether the theater furnishes a contribution to the shaping of society has not been answered; but at any rate we can see how this question (which some people, Benn for example, don't ask) can present itself, and not only to Salvation Army types who seek to buttress their artistic impotence with lots of "Message . . ."

I am speaking here, as announced, about the author and the

theater, and you might ask me: do you as an author wish that the theater were effective in some way? That would be the first question. Do I, when I write plays, want to change society? Do I want this (to put it another way:) for the sake of society or for the sake of the play? The question contains a suspicion that can not be ignored. Do I as a playwright really want to contribute to a political utopia, or (and here's the suspicion) do we love the utopia because it's the more productive position for us? What's called nonconformism may also be no more than a gesture; not false, but a gesture for the benefit of our work. Is that the case? There's a commitment; does it enter art because we're concerned for the world, or is it the other way around? I'm asking myself. Not that the political commitment isn't a serious one, oh no; we are prepared, it seems to me, to take a stand outside the theater as well—otherwise we may be forced into a position we do not like, perhaps very roughly some day; these are the consequences even when we don't write as agitators and are aware that we need our commitment as a source of productivity. Of course as writers we occasionally take pleasure in leaping up from our desk and signing a manifesto in a standing position, as it were, unconcerned whether this is an opportune thing to do and proud of this unconcern, in a dare-devilish mood, as if the puny personal reputation which everyone's pledging with his signature were equivalent to the arduousness of political activity which we then, returning to our desks, leave to others. This makes me uncomfortable. I suppose we're thinking of Emile Zola who mobilized his nation with his *J'accuse*[5]; that can happen. But the prerequisite is not Zola's fame; that's a mistake, to think that a writer's fame could be put into action like a manual fire-extinguisher in response to a political alarm. The prerequisite is the authority of the intellectual as *citoyen,* opposition out of civic consciousness, not contempt for the state or literary cleverness. The writer and politics . . .

The question whether one really wishes to contribute to the shaping of society or whether the appearance of political commitment in one's work is merely a productive gesture—this is something everyone has to answer for himself. Even when our sort proposes a political idea: let the Federal Republic help the German Democratic Republic in this and this way! the question remains open; that idea redounds to the speaker's honor even if it is never realized and even if he never again lifts a finger toward its realization. I'm not objecting to the expression of ideas! I'm only asking myself: am I, who distinguish myself before other fellow citizens by the work I perform at my desk, am I called upon or even entitled to present statesmen with a problem, in writing, to the practical solution of which I myself will contribute nothing? Of course I am entitled, even though I don't have the calling; everyone is entitled. But what's the result? At the very best, if the product differs significantly from a soap-box harangue by the quality of its formulation and hence of its thought, the result will be literature; but to suppose that writers make politics by making political statements would be self-deceptive. Politics is a labor of Sisyphus. Who among us has ever subjected himself to it? Not I; once for barely a year, and then I wanted to get back to writing, too lazy for the power that was attainable, satisfied with the formulation of my idea; a writer.

There once was a man named Henri Dunant who also had an idea, the Red Cross. He sacrificed his profession and his time and his strength to it, his life. To us (to most of us) literary success is enough, and this success is more easily attained than the most modest change in the world—and then, reading the paper, I'm amazed by this world: riots in Harlem, explosions in the South Tyrol, bombs in Cyprus, and wherever I read, armies ready to shoot for peace; and sports reports in between: the language of chauvinism, which is still being avoided by the ministers (except for one), is back in full bloom in the sports pages: the folk-myth for the time being in sport-terms; good news as well: Maunz,[6] sometimes a man can't be held back after seven years after all; on the same page: Swiss industry, outside the European Common Market, supplying Nasser with war materials against Israel; I switch to another section: literature, Germany's back in the world league, literature as a sandbox for the opposition; Franz Josef Straus at work; Goldwater. Is it too late, once again? The editorials: the way what's written between the lines is silently changing; and letters from the readers: a swarming of unsuspected vermin, like turning over a rotting plank, and this is the plank we stand on and walk on. I'm frightened. Yes. Sometimes I'm frightened:—that we might be overestimating the theater . . .

Now we can also say:

(*feeding the pigeons*)

We are making theater out of love for the theater, nothing more, and, artists that we are, we do not let ourselves be confused by the day, art is absolute, and whatever the world wants to make or not make of our theater is its affair, not ours, and society is our material but not our partner, we are not here to educate the public, we play because we like to (as long as society permits it) without a partner and in full consciousness of the inutility of art. We can say this. And basically it's even true; but only basically. We play in public, and this public, which we evidently need for our pleasure, is something we can never quite get rid of. Even if we answer the intrusive interview question: "Why do you write?" in a less than serious fashion, it's true: the public proffers itself as a partner whether I want it or not. When I see the people in the lobby, I have to admit I'm always pretty upset, as if, despite my hope for a full house, I hadn't counted on one thing: the public. Why do I write? I would like to reply: it's an urge, an urge to play, it gives me pleasure. And also, there's vanity involved; after all, we're vain, too. But that's not enough for a life's work; that much gets used up by one's failures, and if you succeed, it gets burned up by the realization of how insufficient a lot of things are. So why do I keep writing? What doesn't get used up is the need for communication (which is as primal as the urge to play); otherwise you could leave your efforts in the drawer of your desk.

So I write to satisfy my own needs, not those of society. And possibly out of the fear which the cave-dwellers already turned into images: you paint demons on the wall of your cave so that you can live with them, they don't have to be buffaloes; or else you paint your joy on the wall of your cave (as in the tombs of Tarquinia), your otherwise so perishable joy. All this begins in a thoroughly naive manner, even if it eventually leads to artistic insights. I admit: a responsibility of the writer to society was not envisioned; it tends to sneak in after a certain amount of success, and some may roundly reject it while others are unable to do so. The self-misunderstanding, later on, that led me to believe I was writing out of a sense of responsibility ruined many a work at its inception; but realizing that this is a misunderstanding doesn't change the fact that a sense of responsibility has subsequently established itself as an unjoyful consciousness; it has nothing to do with any sort of "mission" when a writer considers the possible effect of his work from the point of view of his values and convictions. But this value system is not something you deliberately set out to perform in your writing; it's constitutional and remains largely unconscious while you write. That's not what writing's about, we say. But to conclude from this that because the literary product is originally without didactic intention, it will have no effect on society, would be not naive but unrealistic. Inadvertently, at the latest when the confrontation with the audience takes place in the theater, not at your desk, where you're alone, but when I'm sitting in the lighting technician's box and see the faces in the orchestra, I'm no longer sure that we are free of responsibility for the effects of our work; it might at the very least make the fatal contribution of inciting to misdeeds or inducing sleep in a time of misdeeds; the latter is the more common, the usual . . .

So, do I suddenly believe after all that the theater has something like a political function?—I believe this is not a postulate but a perception; from the vantage of the lighting technician's box, so to speak; an experience you can't so easily forget once you're back at your desk. I'm speaking as a playwright; the same certainly holds for the director and the actor. I don't know anyone who became a director or an actor out of responsibility to society. But having become what they are, responsibility has overtaken them, I believe, no differently from the way it catches up with the playwright, and we have to speak of a responsible or irresponsible performance. I'm not talking about responsibility to one's work, artistic responsibility; I mean social responsibility.

Performing the classics is no vacation in this respect. Take *Hamlet,* for example. However apolitically this play is commonly interpreted, Hamlet is a young prince in the luxurious house of a murderer, and whether this is made evident by the performance or blurred for the sake of the audience in the auditorium is surely more than a matter of taste and style, more than an aesthetic decision. Why does Hamlet not act in the house of the murderer? He is bound to his mother: that is one reason, the uncle, whom he recognizes as a murderer, has relieved him of his Oedipus-deed, and unconsciously Hamlet feels he is an accomplice; he sees the blood-guilt of a world of power, but it is a world his father (and others before him) belonged to; what Hamlet could do in order to put an end to crime would merely be a suicide *en famille,* an option he understandably hesitates to carry out, and this is what happens nevertheless, while young Fortinbras with his fanfares hardly represents a higher moral order; he's just sturdy enough to start the tragedy all over again. Isn't this something that will affect us rather directly, assuming the style of the performance doesn't cover it up? Hamlet hears the call to action from the fourth scene of the first act on, but he intellectualizes and abstracts himself in the intangible complicity of the inactive; or rather, it is tangible only as nausea and melancholy. Let's say our director shows a Hamlet— and maybe he'll succeed in making it the performance of the year— who cannot act because a man of intellect is always too noble for action: even then the slogan is true that Germany is Hamlet! But in a sarcastic sense . . .

I'm speaking of the style of performance. Hamlet is just an example. Of course I'm not demanding that classical texts be brought up to date, on the contrary: I'm asking that what is all too close to us become transparent by means of classical distance. The promise of the repertory plastered on the wall can only be fulfilled by the style of performance—if that's not the case, it would really be better if we remained sitting on the stoop feeding the pigeons while the poster yellows on the wall . . .

So what's the upshot of our conversation on the stoop?

A dilemma—which you are acquainted with, but which we must remain conscious of: as a dilemma, not to be resolved by this or that postulate; a question: does theater exist for its own sake or are we, players for the fun of it, liable for the society we entertain?— this question seems to me to be posed by the very location of our meeting today. St. Paul's Church in Frankfurt holds a special place in German history. The fact that we theater people were welcomed here is an honor and possibly even an assignment to a mission; at the very least a challenge to respond to the question whether the theater can furnish a contribution to the shaping of society and thereby of history. Not until entertaining the playful hypothesis that all the theaters were shut down did I manage to regard my own skepticism skeptically. If literature didn't exist, the world would perhaps be no different, but it would look different: it would look the way the beneficaries of the status quo would like it to be seen: unquestioned. The verbal transvaluation accomplished by every literature for its own sake, namely for the sake of the vitality of words, is in itself a contribution, a productive opposition. Certain attitudes of the recent past, though they are still with us, are no longer respectable, because literature has renamed them in accord with their quotient of reality, and this affects not only the consciousness of the small group of literary consumers; the remodeling of our vocabulary reaches all those who employ a borrowed language, including the politicians. Whoever uses certain words today gives himself away by doing so: thanks to literature, which determines the currency value of words. I know: what Karl Kraus[7] once accomplished in this sense didn't save Vienna from anything. But perhaps we are too modest. Perhaps literature deserves credit for the fact that a word like *war* (to pick one among many) can no longer be proffered with seductive intent, at least not in Europe. Ministers of war are called ministers of defense. This too, of course, is turning into empty phraseology; that's why literature has to keep up with the times; if it's alive, it brings language back to reality again and again; this is true even and especially of literature that doesn't commit itself programatically. "Go and follow your phrases through to the point where they take on fleshly form!" says Büchner in *Danton*: "Look around you, these are all things you have spoken." That is what literature says, insofar as it deserves the name; the rest is belles-lettres. Just the fact that the Hitler regime, which depended on passionate stupification, could not tolerate the literature of its time would be sufficient proof of the power of language, albeit a negative proof. My question, whether we don't overestimate the theater when we expect it to contribute to the everlasting transformation of society, now seems to be obviated, and I could close with the hope that the theater would assume an Inner Leadership—if we didn't happen to be sitting in St. Paul's Church, an important place in German history, which all in all has taken very little guidance from Germany's great literature from Schiller to Brecht.

So: are we back to being skeptical?

Yes.

Resigned, then?

No.

As for the key to the theater, ladies and gentlemen, I'm releasing it; I don't dare to bury it; I herewith ceremoniously place it upon the table of this your beginning conference.

1964   *Translated by Joel Agee*

Notes

1. Pauluskirche in Frankfurt am Main: site of the national assembly of 1848, which attempted to write a constitution for all the German states.
2. Special courtroom where the Auschwitz trial was being conducted just then (1963–1965).
3. *The Visit* (1956), the play by Friedrich Dürrenmatt that takes place in Güllen. "Szechuan": a reference to Brecht's play *The Good Woman of Szetchuan* (1943).
4. Peter Suhrkamp (1891–1959), German publisher.
5. Reference to Emile Zola's open letter to the French president in 1898 on behalf of the unjustly condemned Captain Dreyfus.
6. Gerhard Maunz, court reporter of the news magazine *Der Spiegel*.
7. Karl Kraus (1874–1936), Austrian satirist, editor of *Die Fackel*.

From a Correspondence with Walter Höllerer

... I can already see that I have to watch out now, conceptual porcelain all around me, I can just barely manage carefully to set it aside: the concept of coincidence, my dramaturgical bricks, General de Gaulle and the accident-coincidence involving armored state vehicles, from Grabbe[1] to Handke and the concept of divine dispensation ... So I'll simply say something about my temperament, and in consideration of this sunny day I'll keep my remarks as brief as possible:

First of All

I find myself getting bored in the theater more and more frequently (and not just at performances of my own plays), while rehearsals nearly always fascinate me, especially early rehearsals in which the scenes are still being worked out and variations are starting to develop. The variations of a dramatic situation reveal more than the definitive version of that situation, a fanning out of all the possible ways in which one and the same character can behave. It's often nearly impossible to decide which version is more believable; there's never just one that's right. But then the finished performance; that's how it goes and that's that. It's just like life: a one-track course instead of this fanning out. Granted, it's all "merely" in play, but no matter how unnatural every one of the dialogues may be, the one-track line of the action makes the dialogue historical; so, what we have here is an imitation of life, which, as we know, does not ever allow more than one of all the many possibilities to be realized, and not necessarily the most probable one either, but once it's happened, it's irrevocable, that is to say historical . . . First of all, therefore, the need to preserve the fascination of the rehearsal in the performance, by including the variations in the design of the play itself.

Second

I believe that the only reality of the stage is that the people on it are *playing*. Play permits what life does not permit. That's why we need it so urgently. For example, life does not let us suspend the dreadful continuity of time, or be in several places at once, or interrupt an action (song, chorus, commentary, etc.) and arrest it until we've understood its causes and possible effects; nor does it allow us to get rid of purely repetitive business, etc. But what life prohibits is permitted by the theater: Kurmann, the protagonist in the play I mentioned earlier[2], can cast his vote again, i.e., he can revoke history. In reality we may be able to redress a past error by a subsequent action, but we can't expunge it, it can't be undone; we cannot choose a different mode of behavior for some past date, we can't try out another way of having acted on this or that day. Life is historical, definitive at every moment, it will not tolerate any variation. But it does allow for play . . . Flight from reality?— The theater reflects reality, but it doesn't imitate it. Nothing is more contrary to reason than this business of imitating reality, and nothing is more superfluous; there's enough reality as it is. Imitation-theater (I think that's a term coined by Martin Walser) is a misconception the theater has of itself; there are directors who cultivate it with masterly skill: theater that puts the viewer in the position of a voyeur and deceives him in that position; in order to get into the embarrassing position of the voyeur, I have to turn off my consciousness and forget that what's happening on the stage is play and make-believe, and if I don't succeed in doing that, it's doubly embarrassing. Of course the original theater (with cothurnus, mask, verse, etc.) was not imitation-theater; the ancient Greek was never deceived about the fact that no gods had been hired to perform in the show . . . All this is well known—Brecht, to combat the prevalence of imitation-theater (influence of mediocre movies?), cultivated the performer's strategic alienation-gesture, the well-known inventory of songs, captions, etc., and Peter Handke . . . does it by strictly transposing the dramatic action into language, or into speechlessness. Others flash documents onto a screen to demonstrate the difference between history and play. Friedrich Dürrenmatt opposes it with the grotesque, Samuel Beckett with radical reduction, etc., Martin Walser speaks urgently of consciousness-theater, and what that means, if I understand him correctly, is: representation, not of the world but of our consciousness of the world. Whatever the particular genre-label may be: what's being sought and also found in various ways is theater that does not pretend to reproduce reality (it's only a certain kind of acting that cultivates this particular skill; the playwright's job is to exclude any possibility of imitation-theater before it gets to the stage)—a different means, a way that's perhaps more compatible with my temperament, seemed, as I said, available to me at rehearsals.

Third

The parable form is making me increasingly uncomfortable. (In order to avoid making imitation-theater, I used to try out allegories, then morality plays, then travesties, Don Juan as costume-citation, in order to let the theater present itself as theater right from the start; and later I worked exclusively with parables.) My discomfort: a parable is a play on meanings; a series of events is shown that would be very unlikely to occur in reality, at least not in the manner in which they are shown; the relationship to reality is not established by imitating reality; what's being shown is quite artificial, and it's only the meaning distilled from this artifice that combines in our consciousness with a particular reality—which as such cannot be imitated or reproduced—simply because it appears to be applicable to it. A well-tested method, it certainly excludes imitation-theater, but: the parable tends to the *quod erat demonstrandum,* it implies a teaching, it tends unavoidably to the didactic. It doesn't help if I add as a subtitle: a didactic play with a lesson. At the very most, this indicates that I'm not really concerned with the lesson in the parable, or not mainly concerned with it, or perhaps not concerned with it at all—perhaps I just chose the parable to get away from imitation-theater . . . As you said in our radio program, *Galileo* may be Brecht's most convincing play because among all his parables it's the one that least adds up in the end. That's just it: the parable usually adds up. It tends to mean something. It gives a pretense of explicability, or at least inevitability. It claims to be valid by simultaneously remaining vague. The parable, by forcing me to teach, hedges me in, and finally:

Fourth

I am an ego-maniac, I don't write in order to teach but in order to explore my temperament by depicting it—my temperament: my doubts about what?

1969   *Translated by Joel Agee*

Notes

1. Christian Dietrich Grabbe (1801–1836), early realist playwright.
2. *Biography* (1967) by Max Frisch.

MAX FRISCH, born in Zurich in 1911, is equally known as a novelist and playwright. His *I'm Not Stiller* (1954) and *Homo Faber: A Report* (1957) developed new trends in the German novel. Together with those of his compatriot Friedrich Dürrenmatt, his plays such as *Graf Öderland* (1951), *Don Juan or the Love of Geometry* (1953), *Biedermann and the Firebugs* (1958), and *Andorra* (1962) had a major impact on the German stage immediately after the war.

Peter Weiss

Notes on the Contemporary Theater

Realistic topical theater, which has gone through numerous transformations since the time of the *Proletkult* movement and agitprop, Piscator's experiments and Brecht's didactic plays, can now be found under various labels such as Political Theater, Theater of Protest, Anti-Theater, etc. Beginning with the difficulty of finding a classification for this kind of theater's various forms of expression, we shall attempt here to examine one of its variants, the one that exclusively deals with the documentation of a particular subject-matter and which might therefore be called Documentary Theater.

1

Documentary theater is a theater of reportage. Trial records, dossiers, letters, statistical tabulations, stock market bulletins, closing reports of banking corporations and industrial concerns, government declarations, speeches, interviews, statements by public personalities, newspaper and radio reports, photographs, journalistic movies and other documents of contemporary life provide the foundation of the performance. Documentary theater abstains from any kind of invention, it adopts authentic material and presents it on the stage without any modification of its content, but with definite formal modifications. In contrast to the random character of the news material that flows in upon us from all sides every day, a selection is presented on the stage which concentrates on a particular subject, usually of a social or political nature. It is this critical selection, and the principle determining the assemblage of the excerpts from reality, that make up the quality of documentary drama.

2

Documentary theater is a component of public life as it is brought to our attention by the mass media, and its distinguishing characteristic is the criticism it performs in various degrees.

a. A critique of cover-ups. Are the reports of the press, the radio, and television being manipulated by dominant interest groups? What information is being withheld from us? Whose interests are served by these expurgations? Which circles are benefited when certain social phenomena are hushed up, altered, idealized?

b. A critique of falsifications of reality. Why is a historical figure, a period or epoch erased from our consciousness? Whose position is strengthened by the elimination of historical facts? Who profits from a deliberate distortion of trenchant and significant events? What social strata are interested in hiding the past? How are these falsifications expressed? How are they received?

c. A critique of lies. What are the effects of a historical deception? What is the appearance of a contemporary situation that has been built on lies? What difficulties are likely to arise when the truth is discovered? Which influential organs and power groups will do everything they can to prevent the truth from being known?

3

Although the means of communications have been distributed to a maximal degree and provide us with news from all parts of the world, the most important events that determine our present and our future remain concealed from us in their causes and their interconnections. The information banks of the responsible parties, material that could provide us with insight into activities of which we only see the results, are made unavailable to us. A documentary theater that wants to treat subjects like the murders of Lumumba, Kennedy, Che Guevara, the massacre in Indonesia, the secret agreements during the negotiations on Indochina in Geneva, the latest conflict in the Middle East, and the preparations of the government of the United States to wage war against Vietnam, finds itself faced at the outset with the artificial obscurity behind which the powerful conceal their manipulations.

4

A documentary theater that opposes those groups that have an interest in pursuing a policy of obscuring and obliterating the truth;

that opposes the tendency of the mass media to keep the population subject by enclosing it in a vacuum of narcotization and stupefaction; such a theater finds itself at the same point of departure as any citizen who wishes to conduct his own research, has his hands tied, and finally resorts to the only means available to him: public protest. Like the spontaneous rally with posters, banners, and chants, the documentary theater demonstrates a reaction to contemporary conditions and a demand that they be revealed to the public.

5

Demonstrating in the streets, distributing leaflets, marching in rows, interacting with a broad public—these are concrete and immediately effective actions. They are strongly dramatic in their improvisation, their course is unpredictable, at any moment they might be intensified by a clash with the police and thereby bring out the contradiction in the social conditions. A documentary theater offering a summing up of latent tendencies in society tries to present its material in such a way that it doesn't lose any of its topical import. But the very process of putting together the material for a closed performance on a predetermined date in a limited space involving actors and audience, confronts the documentary theater with conditions that are different from those that apply to direct political action. Instead of showing reality in its immediacy, the documentary theater presents an image of a piece of reality torn out of its living context.

6

Documentary theater, insofar as it does not choose to perform its spectacles in the street, cannot achieve the same degree of reality as an authentic political manifestation. It can never be as dynamic as the opinions expressed in the public arena. Confined to the stage and the auditorium, it cannot challenge the authorities of state and government in the same way that a protest march to government buildings and military and industrial centers does. Even when it tries to free itself from the framework that defines it as an artistic medium, even when it renounces all aesthetic categories, when it refuses to be anything fixed and finished, so as to present nothing more than clear opposition and militant action, even when it pretends to have been born of the moment and to have acted spontaneously, it will be an art product, and it must become an art product if it is to have any justification.

7

For a documentary theater that wants primarily to be a political forum and renounces artistic achievement, calls itself into question. In such a case, practical political action in the outside world would be more effective. Not until the factual material gathered by probing, examining, scrutinizing reality has been transformed into an artistic tool, can the documentary theater attain full validity in its struggle with reality. Such a theater makes it possible for a dramatic work to become an instrument of political persuasion. But close attention must be given to the documentary theater's special forms of expression, which differ from traditional aesthetic concepts.

8

The strength of the documentary theater resides in its ability to arrange fragments of reality into a usable model, a sample of real processes as they actually occur. It is not situated at the center of the event but assumes the position of the observer and analyst. With its cinematic cutting technique it isolates perceptible details from the chaotic materials of external reality. By juxtaposing contradictory details, it focuses attention on an actual conflict and then, on the basis of the data it has collected, offers a recommendation for solving that conflict, or issues a call to action, or poses a radical question. Unlike open improvisation and unlike the politically coloured Happening, which produce a diffusion of tension, emotional participation, and an illusion of political involvement, documentary theater treats its subject in a conscious, attentive, and reflective manner.

9

Documentary theater submits facts for the audience's appraisal. It shows the various ways in which an event or a statement is received. It shows the motives of that reception. One side is benefited by an event, the other is damaged by it. These two parties stand opposed to one another. A light is cast on their mutual dependence, and on the bribery and blackmail that are supposed to keep this dependence intact. Losses are tabulated next to lists showing gains. The ones who are winning defend themselves. They present themselves as the keepers of public order. They show how they administer their possessions. In contrast to them, the ones who are losing. The traitors in the ranks of the losers who hope for a chance to rise. The others who are trying to avoid losing more than they already have. A constant collision of inequalities. Glimpses of inequality shown so concretely that it becomes intolerable. Injustices so convincing they cry out for immediate redress. Situations so twisted they can only be changed by force. Controversial views of the same subject are aired. Assertions are compared with actual conditions. Avowals and promises followed by actions that contradict them. The results of actions initiated in secret planning centers are examined. Whose position was this meant to strengthen, who was affected by it? The silence, the evasions of those involved are documented. Circumstantial evidence is submitted. Corollaries are drawn from a recognizable pattern. The representatives of certain social interests are identified by name, but the point is not to depict individual conflicts, but patterns of socio-economic behavior. Documentary theater is only concerned with what is exemplary, in contrast to the quickly exhausted external constellation; it does not work with stage characters and depictions of milieux, but with groups, force-fields, trends.

10

Documentary theater is partisan. Many of its themes cannot be treated in any way other than as an indictment. For such a theater, objectivity is a concept that under certain circumstances can serve to justify the activities of a power group. The appeal for moderation and understanding is shown to be the appeal of those who don't want to lose their advantages. The aggressions of the Portuguese colonists against Angola and Mozambique, the South African government's assaults on the African population, the aggression of the United States of America against Cuba, the Dominican Republic, and Vietnam, cannot be presented as anything other than unilateral crimes. There is nothing wrong with depicting genocide and predatory war in black-and-white terms, denying the butchers any endearing traits whatsoever and resolutely siding with their victims in every possible way.

11

Documentary theater can take the form of a tribunal. Here, too, it does not pretend to approach the authenticity of a Nuremberg trial, an Auschwitz trial in Frankfurt, a hearing in the American Senate, a session of the Russell tribunal; but it can make a new kind of testimony out of those questions and points of attack that were voiced in the context of a real inquest. Having gained some distance, it can look back on the proceedings from a point of view that did not present itself at the time. The original protagonists are transposed into a new historical context. At the same time that their actions are portrayed, we are shown the development of which they are the product, and attention is directed to those repercussions and consequences which are still with us. By showing their activities, the performance reveals the mechanism that continues to impinge on reality. Everything tangential, every kind of digression, can be cut in favor of a clear statement of the problem itself. This entails a loss of surprise value, local color, sensationalism; what is gained is universality. Documentary theater, unlike an actual trial court, can include the audience in the proceedings, put the audience in the position of the accused or the prosecution, invite it to collaborate with an investigatory commission; it can contribute to the understanding of a complex issue or challenge a resistant attitude to the point of extreme provocation.

12

Some more examples of the formal use of documentary material:

a. Reports and parts of reports, rhythmically arranged in precise intervals. Brief moments consisting of a single fact or exclamation followed by longer, complicated units. A quotation followed by the portrayal of a situation. The situation abruptly changes into another, opposite one. Individual speakers stand opposite a majority of speakers. The composition consists of antithetical pieces, of related examples in sequential order, of contrasting forms, of alternating scales of dimension. Variations on a theme. Intensification of a process. Introduction of disturbances, dissonances.

b. Linguistic elaboration of the factual material. Stressing what is typical in a quotation. Making caricatures of certain personages, drastically simplifying situations. Speeches, commentaries, summaries are delivered in the form of songs. Introduction of chorus and pantomime. Use of gesture to indicate action. Parodies, use of masks and decorative attributes. Instrumental accompaniment. Sound effects.

c. Interrupting the report by reflections, monologues, dreams, retrospections, contradictory behavior. These breaks in the action, which produce an insecurity that can have the effect of a shock, show how an individual or a group is affected by the events. Portrayal of inner reality as a response to outer events. However, such brusque displacements should not produce confusion but should draw attention to the many-layered complexity of the event; the means employed, instead of being ends in themselves, should always provide a verifiable experience.

d. Dissolving the structure. Not a calculated rhythm, but raw material, compact or else flowing without restraint, to show social struggles, to depict revolutionary situations, to report on a war. Conveying violence in the clash of opposing forces. But here, too, the upheaval on the stage, the expression of fear and outrage, must not remain unexplained and unresolved. The more urgent the implications of the material, the greater the need for an overview, a synthesis.

13

A documentary theater's effort to find a persuasive form of expression is closely related to the need to find an adequate place to perform in. If the performance takes place in a commercial theater with its high price of admission, it will be caught in the system it wants to attack. If it sets itself up outside the establishment, it will be limited to locations that are usually visited only by a small and like-minded crowd. Instead of having an impact on society, it often merely succeeds in showing its impotence with regard to the status quo. Documentary theater must gain access to factories, schools, stadiums, meeting houses. Just as it detaches itself from the aesthetic canons of traditional theater, it must put its own methods in question again and again and develop new techniques that are adequate to new situations.

14

Documentary theater can only be sustained by a firm, politically and sociologically educated group of collaborators who are supported by an extensive archive and are capable of scientific investigation. A documentary dramaturgy that shrinks back from defining a condition, that only shows a condition without revealing its causes and pointing out the necessity and the possibility of its removal, a documentary dramaturgy that freezes in a gesture of desperate attack without ever striking the enemy, devalues itself. For this reason, documentary theater opposes the kind of drama that uses its own rage and despair as its main theme and clings to the notion of a hopeless and absurd world. Documentary theater argues for the alternative view, according to which reality, however impenetrable it tries to be, can be explained in all its details.

1968   *Translated by Joel Agee*

Conversation with Peter Weiss

INTERVIEWER: Mr. Weiss, many thanks, first of all, for your willingness to discuss current problems of dramatic art.—About five years ago I had the opportunity to discuss this same subject with Friedrich Dürrenmatt, and we arrived at the question whether the so-called historical drama is still viable in our time. Dürrenmatt was very skeptical and said among other things: "Historical drama was only possible in a naive era. The imagined world, the 'model' in the form of a parable, has a much better chance today of 'compelling' the viewer, of creating a disturbance. Yes, only such a theater, a theater that transforms reality, is capable of revealing changes in reality . . ." And in his book *Problems of the Theater* he wrote: "Caesar is no longer a pure and simple subject-matter for us; rather, for us, Caesar has become an object of scientific scrutiny. By attacking not just nature but the mind and the arts with increasing intensity, science has turned into literary scholarship, history of ideas, philosophy, and who knows what else, and has created facts that can no longer be ignored (for there is no conscious naiveté that could steer clear of the conclusions of science), depriving the artist of his subject-matter by assuming tasks that ordinarily would have been the tasks of art." He said further: "If Shakespeare had known Mommsen,[1] he wouldn't have written his Caesar, because at that moment he would necessarily have lost the sovereignty with which he wrote about his subjects." According to Dürrenmatt, the attempt to write a drama about a subject that has been scientifically elucidated amounts to "a tautology; a resumption, with an unfit instrument, of a work already accomplished, a mere illustration of scientific insights: which is precisely the way science looks at it." This strikes me as a rather peremptory, not to say *excessively* peremptory exclusion of the possibility of making a dramatic adaptation of historical material for our time.— You, Mr. Weiss, have furnished the refutation of Dürrenmatt's view in your two-act play *The Persecution and Murder of Jean Paul Marat, Presented by the Theater Group of the Hospital of Charenton Under the Direction of M. de Sade*. And now you have presented the theaters with a play, *The Investigation*, that deals with a horribly significant event of our recent history, the mass annihilation of the Jews by the Nazis. Perhaps you could explain how you came to terms with this material; that is, how, in your opinion, can history be adapted for the present-day stage?

WEISS: When I take up a historical theme, I am mainly interested in its contemporary relevance. While I was writing *Marat*, the encounter with its material struck some very strong chords that are quite topical and are even more relevant now than they were when I wrote the play two years ago; the whole conflict between these two historical figures, Marat and de Sade, was really a contemporary conflict. In the new Auschwitz play it's very obviously a historical process. It is German history that is coming to life in the play and is being judged from a present point of view, so it is not simply a description of the past but a description of the present in which the past comes alive. I think that when I select a historical subject I am particularly concerned with making it relevant to the present, transferring it into the present, perhaps revising it. I have plans to make a dramatic adaptation of Dante's *Divine Comedy*, and this is exclusively a matter of revising Dante. In my opinion, historical themes always work very well as a typical basis for present-day conflict . . .

In *Marat* I adopted a completely modern dramatic form in which the historical material is constantly transformed and constantly exposed to influences from various directions; the contemporary aspects enter into it again and again. But I think that basically the way Brecht, too, worked with historical materials aims at a very topical and immediate statement; for Brecht wasn't writing *Coriolanus* in order to depict ancient Roman history, but to reflect a modern world in it . . .

This preoccupies me again and again: how to present the interconnections between themes that have been expressed before and themes that have some current significance, and thereby reveal a unity in history. We can see the causes of things that took shape long ago, and we see how they developed. So, from our present view-point, we can always control, always revise our history, our past. I find this so very interesting. When I take a theme that is altogether contemporary, it often turns out to be very one-sided, for all I have is the world that immediately surrounds me, and this limits me. But of course that too, is dramatically viable . . .

I believe that in order to adapt a very large and comprehensive subject for the theater, you have to simplify it, concentrate it, and of course you also have to strongly modify reality in accordance with the dramatic scheme. This is what Hochhuth did, and I believe there is no other way to go about it if one is not completely convinced that this raw material, which in our present world is so enormously complicated, can only be represented in well-made plays, or "pre-fab" plays, if you will.

1965   *Translated by Joel Agee*

Notes

1. Theodor Mommsen (1817–1903), German historian. In 1902 he received the Nobel Prize for Literature for his five-volume *History of Rome*.

PETER WEISS (1916–1982), born near Berlin, lived in England, Czechoslovakia, and Switzerland before finally settling in Sweden. First known as a painter and experimental film maker, he started writing in 1952; first fiction (*Abschied von den Eltern*, 1961), then plays (*Marat/Sade*, 1963; *The Investigation*, 1965; *Vietnam*, 1968; and *Hölderlin*, 1973). His last novel was the monumental *Ästhetik des Widerstands* (3 volumes, 1975–1981).

Peter Hacks

Interview

INTERVIEWER: Mr. Hacks, what playwright has made the most lasting impression on you?

HACKS: Pocci.[1]

INTERVIEWER: Is your artistic development representative of something?

HACKS: I'm afraid I am extraordinarily representative of the development of the theater in our country.[2] During a period of epic-sociological theater, all the good people here learned to depict social processes on the stage and can now go beyond that. They can now tell great stories about people without neglecting the fact that these people are members of a society.

INTERVIEWER: What role did the theater of the Storm and Stress play in this development?

HACKS: You see, we have quite literally recapitulated the development of early bourgeois drama. We, too, insisted on reinventing the theater. Like the dramatists before Lessing—people like Lillo, Pfeil, Brawe—we began with plays that were completely satisfied with just putting the new class on the stage; they portrayed them at their most silly and banal, and the only message was that this new class had a monopoly on virtue. The next higher level in bourgeois theater was the Storm and Stress drama, where the class, having become more self-confident, went and started to insult the conventional forms of society and of art. This corresponds to the fifties in our time, to *Dorfstrasse*,[3] *Schlacht bei Lobositz*[4] and *Lohndrücker*.[5] Analogies never prove everything; but the Storm and Stress was followed by the Classical period, where the way

304

playwrights dealt with the great creations of the past was not to ignore them but to improve them. I suspect that's where we want to get to. Of course it's difficult to talk about the latest developments in our theater as long as the three most important plays of the GDR, Müller's *Umsiedlerin*,[6] Lange's *Marski*[7] and my *Tassow*[8] are not available to the public.

INTERVIEWER: You have written that "the classical attitude has greater possibilities than the attitude of the innovator." What do you mean by that?

HACKS: What I mean by an innovator is someone who is so deeply stuck in a progressive idea that it makes him pig-headed. A classic, on the other hand, would be someone who has so thoroughly understood the laws of social and economic development that he can recognize all the highways of progress and stand on the shoulders of his predecessors and even of his enemies. An innovator scorns tradition. A classic improves it. People who do things differently are honorable folk, but the people who do things better are the right ones. The innovator's mistake shows itself in the aesthetic realm primarily as a confusion between art and science; the so-called new ideas are generally new scientific ideas. But a scientific idea is out of date as soon as a newer one is invented, while a work of art is never out of date. Anyone who intends his work to say something about today and today only will be disappointed after a short while when he learns that today has become the day before yesterday. And nowhere do things change as fast as they do in our country.

INTERVIEWER: What role can science play in a writer's work?

HACKS: A subordinate role. A slave's role. Science must dwell in the writer's consciousness but it must not appear in his method. Of course there is nothing more horrible than a stupid poet, but scientific poets are hardly less horrible. The entire modern movement in the West claims to be scientific. The theater of the absurd justifies its theatrical failure with the "scientific" impossibility of roundly judging anything that's going on. No doubt it's a particularly miserable science that's being practiced there—positivism; no doubt our science is better and the same mistake is more excusable when we commit it. But it's still a mistake.

INTERVIEWER: What is the difference between scientific and artistic method?

HACKS: The difference results from their different fields of investigation. Science tries to separate subject and object, to give a perfectly pure description of the object; the object is its field of investigation. But for art, it's the peculiar unity of subject and object, of that which is grasped and the grasp itself. The artist shows the world in his own highly personal manner. We might say that art deals with reality as it is experienced through an attitude. An example: if you see a piece of Parisian architecture, a bridge or a church, painted by a realistic, an impressionistic, and an expressionistic painter, you will find that the object, which is always the same one for science, is different for each of the three artists. A subjective attitude has flowed into it. In the first instance, the attitude of a contented bourgeoisie, in the second of a skeptical bourgeoisie, and in the third, of a bourgeoisie that is in revolt against itself. Naturally art deals with objective matters as well, and to the extent that it does, it yields something like objective knowledge. But the purpose of art is not to deliver information about reality. The purpose of art is to provide information about an attitude that can be assumed with regard to reality. Portrayal of reality is the means; the end, the purpose (which gives rise to the artistic method), is to present an attitude; at this point it all turns into politics.

INTERVIEWER: How does a dramatic work come about?

HACKS: Two productive ideas are usually needed for a play. The first one generally has to do with issues of the stage and of dramaturgy—in other words, an idea that provides the meat for a play. The second one is generally a poetic moral which one considers worthwhile. The two ideas hardly ever come up simultaneously; usually one of them lies around for three years, and then you find the other one and say: yes, this is the one I needed for that one. The rest is electronics.

INTERVIEWER: What else can you tell us about those two basic ideas? Which comes first, or is there no rule?

HACKS: There is no rule, there is an example. I had the idea of writing a comedy about a man who is ahead of his time; he is placed in a concrete social situation and acts as if he were living a hundred years later. After an interval of at least six years, I heard a story about a man who in 1945 had forced some peasants at gunpoint to set up a commune. From these two components came the idea for *Moritz Tassow*.

INTERVIEWER: Do you have what is called a basic theme?

HACKS: Three. At first, in West Germany, my basic theme was to refute class society, and this seemed sufficient to me. A while later I discovered that others had done this before me. My next plays—I'm simplifying—dealt with man's duty to emancipate himself, they were stories about people who are ridding themselves of barriers, *Die Schlacht von Lobositz* for example, and *Die Sorgen und die Macht*, or about people polemicizing against unemancipated souls, against servile and opportunistic attitudes, as in *Der Müller von Sanssouci* or *Die Kindermörderin*. My last plays no longer find this question to be of current importance; we've moved ahead. They are about emancipated people who are in contradiction with a society that is not emancipated or not completely emancipated. All my recent plays deal with this theme: *Frieden, Tassow, Polly, Helena*, yes. They're about emancipated humanity, about the attitude of human beings who have been restored to their own nature.

INTERVIEWER: When do you think you'll be able to start working on a contemporary play again?

HACKS: If you remember the example of the Parisian building and the three schools of painting, you might permit yourself to be convinced that one really doesn't need any special sort of material in order to say anything new. Those works of art that caused the great scandals—that had a big impact, in other words—were usually the ones that were novel because of their formal means, rather than because of a new political content. Of course you might ask: why don't you apply your new form to a new subject? I would reply that new subject-matter tempts an author to be satisfied with the novelty of his subject and to forget that he must treat it in a truly new manner, that he must propose truly new attitudes. Someone who takes a neutral subject, as the ancient Greeks did, sets himself only one task: How to treat this old subject in a new way? But someone who takes a new subject might end up treating it in a conventional manner and yet be convinced he's created something new. There's more to be said about this question, but this is the danger of new subjects and the advantage of old ones.

INTERVIEWER: What do you demand of a subject?

HACKS: It must be important. It might be of great social importance; in that case it would deal with people in positions of power. Or a play of great ideological importance—i.e., about people whose inner life is worth knowing about.

INTERVIEWER: In each case, then, the subject involves a hero?

HACKS: Yes. A play must have a hero. I justify this assertion by the laws of the theater and by the laws of our epoch.

INTERVIEWER: Does this mean that ours is a favorable time for dramatic art?

HACKS: Enormously favorable. Theater is just beginning. In the historical time that we can survey, art had the function of dealing with the faults of the world: by portraying them, or by delivering a utopian counter-idea. We might translate "faults" as: antagonistic contradictions. Antagonistic contradictions no longer exist; we have arrived at a period where the contradictions have ceased to be antagonistic; it isn't just a phrase any longer. Now, I believe that only in a time when the contradictions are no longer antagonistic is the dramatist capable of the freedom, the daring, and the objectivity to write a truly contradictory play.—Permit me to digress a little. From various places in our country one hears the bizarre demand that art must be for all the people, not just some. This is the demand for a homogeneous art and a homogeneous population; it's a demand for the absence of contradictions. This would simply mean the end of art and the end of human evolution altogether (for there is no development without contradictions). Now anyone can see that this is nonsense. There obviously have to be factions, including factions in matters of taste.

INTERVIEWER: That brings up the public. What audience are you writing for?

HACKS: I won't say I have no audience at all in mind, but neither do I write for any particular audience. I create the audience I'm writing for in my own head. Presumably this is a room full of people who are rather like myself.

INTERVIEWER: Thinking observers?

HACKS: For heaven's sake, no. A theater with the thinking observer as its premise must have the intention of boring its audience. Art addresses all the human capacities; sensibility, sensuality, political interest. And of course reason, too.

INTERVIEWER: Do you recognize your projected audience in reality?

HACKS: Ask the cashier.

INTERVIEWER: Did you once say that a quantitatively large work was better than a small one?

HACKS: A big work is better than a small one. A play that has included a lot of the world is better than one that has only included a limited segment. Quantity, artistically mastered quantity, is an expression of strength. I believe that strength is one of the distinguishing characteristics of a modern socialist writer.

INTERVIEWER: This leads to the question of artistic means. Can one distinguish between major and minor forms and techniques?

HACKS: The means are provoked by the contents. If the contents are important, the means become great. Anyone who tries to write in verse will notice that verse can effortlessly accommodate great ideas, great feelings and passions, but is enormously resistant to describing the way a coffee table is set. It can't be done. There is no correspondence between the means of blank verse (despite a few experiments of my own and many by other people, I have not found another dramatic verse form that's appropriate for the German language) and naturalistic contents. That's why I welcome the renaissance of verse drama in the GDR as a very refreshing development.

INTERVIEWER: Do you believe that such means might have a controlling effect on the choice of material?

HACKS: On yes. Great form unmasks whatever's miserable in the content by becoming miserable itself. I learned this seven years ago.

INTERVIEWER: But is it permissible to select materials according to their suitability for one's formal means?

HACKS: It is not permissible, it is one's duty. Art doesn't give a damn about what's considered important in other fields of knowledge. Art has its own conceptions of what is important, what is topical. If there are means important to art, they are important. This applies to art's relationship to science, and to the relationship between the various art forms. A subject that is good for one art form might be useless for another. And it applies, last but not least, to the personality of the individual artist. For you can only do a good job at something you're able to do in the first place. And in

art there is no other criterion than that a job be well done—
otherwise it's not art.

1964   *Translated by Joel Agee*

Notes

1. Franz Pocci (1805–1876), Bavarian author of puppet plays.
2. The German Democratic Republic.
3. Play by Alfred Matusche (1955).
4. Play by Hacks (1954).
5. Play by Heiner Müller (1956).
6. 1956–1961.
7. Play by Hartmut Lange (1965).
8. *Moritz Tassow* (1961).

PETER HACKS, born in 1928, wrote his first plays in Munich. Upon the invitation of Bertolt Brecht, he went to East Berlin in 1955, where he has been living since. His most important plays are *Die Schlacht bei Lobositz* (1956), *Moritz Tassow* (1961), and *Das Jahrmarktsfest zu Plundersweilern* (1975) after Goethe.

Peter Handke

Street-Theater and Theater-Theater

Brecht is a writer who has given me something to think about. He took certain functional possibilities of reality that once seemed as unarguable as an algebraic equation and arranged them in such a way that they now represented a model of mutually contradictory ideas. By means of these Brechtian models of contradiction, it was now possible conclusively to contradict those functions of reality that used to appear as a smoothly working mechanism. At last the condition of the world, which before had seemed simply given and natural, appeared as something *made* and precisely for that reason makeable, changeable: not natural, not ahistorical, but artificial, capable and under certain circumstances needful of transformation. Brecht helped to educate me.

The central conceit of reactionary conservatism concerning groups of people living in *untenable* conditions is that they "don't want it any different." In his theater of contradiction, Brecht has exposed the colossal stupidity and meanness of this notion: people whose will has been regimented by social conditions to leave social conditions as they are—people, that is, who are *unable* to want life to be different—do not in fact want it to be different; but do they *naturally* not want it to be different? No, they quite artificially don't want it to be different, for the conditions under which they live have been purposely *created* in such a way that the people remain unconscious and are not only incapable of wanting anything different but of wanting anything at all.

It is of these contradictions that Brecht made his plays—*plays:* for in this regard the commune in Berlin with Fritz Teufel[1] as its

311

chief hero is Brecht's only successor, a Berliner Ensemble[2] of an effectiveness that is diametrically opposed to that of the legitimate Berliner Ensemble: the legitimate Ensemble sets up contradictions only to demonstrate their possible resolution by the end of the play, and it presents contradictions that, at least formally, no longer exist in the social order that sustains the ensemble, and therefore cannot give rise to any objection: but the commune has ventured to think things anew, and has transferred its theater of contradiction from the accepted places of contradiction (theaters) to (as yet) unaccepted places of contradiction; it has abstained from adding on to the end of its plays some readymade recipe for social renewal, since the plays themselves, the *form* of the playacting, already presented itself as a recipe for renewal. Just as a soccer team "plays" the ball into an opportunity for a goal-kick, Brecht used his parables to "play" contradictions into positions propitious for transformation, though of course he did it in the wrong place, with the wrong sociological means: he was infinitely far away from the reality he wanted to change, using the hierarchical order of the theater hierarchically to disturb other hierarchic orders: he never unsettled anyone who was settled, but he did give countless people a few lovely hours. Granted, he changed the attitudes of actors, but not directly the attitudes of the audience: and the notion that the viewer's attitude was at least indirectly changed by the attitude of the actors is historically false. Despite his revolutionary intentions, Brecht was so dazzled and captivated by the given theatrical canons that his revolutionary will always remained within the limits of taste, for he considered it tasteful that the audience should let itself be entertained without suffering any disturbance, simply by remaining an audience: his final concern, almost a worry, was that a play should be "entertaining." Others would perhaps characterize this attitude as a "stratagem of reason": but it would seem to me to have been the stratagem of a rather self-serving reason.

Furthermore, Brecht does not content himself with the arrangement of contradictions: the Marxist model of the future always comes into play at the end, proffered as solution and resolution: comes into *play,* I say: the viewer, who has been made insecure by the play, is supposed to be reassured: the Marxist model of a possible solution is stated or at least recommended in the play. What disturbs me is not that the Marxist model is presented as a solution, but that it is presented as a solution in the *play* (I myself would at all times support Marxism as the only possible solution of the dominant contradictions—"dominant" in every sense of the word; but I would not support its announcement in a play, in the theater: that is about as false and untrue as a group of people chanting for freedom in Vietnam or against the Americans in Vietnam when this chant is being performed in a *theater;* or as when "regular working guys" get up in a *theater,* as happened in Oberhausen recently, and sing a protest song in unison: the theater as a meaning-making space is determined in such a way that whatever is serious, committed, definite, and final outside the theater, turns into a *play*—so that earnestness, commitment, etc., in the theater are hopelessly subverted by the play-ful and meaning-making context in which they are presented—when will people finally notice this? When will the mendacity, the disgusting falseness of serious matters presented as plays be recognized? This is not an aesthetic question but a question of truth, i.e. an aesthetic question after all). So that's what upsets me about Brecht's plays: the unambiguous definiteness with which everything is resolved in the end (even though Brecht acts as if all contradictions were wide open) appears as a form of play because it is occurring in the *play*- and *meaning*-making space of the theater. Any kind of message, or to put it more simply: any suggestion for a solution of the contradictions previously presented is *formalized* on the stage. A chant that is intended to be *effective,* not on the street but in the theater, is nothing but kitsch and mannerism. The theater as a social institution strikes me as a useless instrument for the transformation of social institutions. Theater formalizes every movement, every insignificance, every word, every silence: therefore it cannot propose any solutions; what it can offer is at best a play with contradictions.

Today, politically committed theater does not take place in theater rooms (in those falsifying art rooms that render all words and all movements vacuous), but for example in lecture halls when a microphone is taken from a professor's hand, when professors blinkingly peer through smashed doors, when leaflets flutter down from the balconies to the assembled crowd, when revolutionaries take their small children with them to the speaker's podium, when the commune, by "terrorizing" reality, turns it into a theatrical and no doubt deservedly ridiculous event, and beyond that, reveals, by the reactions it provokes, the potential dangerousness, unconsciousness, and falseness of this reality, its pretense of idyllic composure, its terror. In this way, theater becomes immediately effective. We now have street theater, lecture hall theater, church theater (more effective than 1000 Masses), shopping mall theater, etc.: what we no longer have is theater theater—at least not as a means for an immediate change of conditions: it is itself a condition. What it could be used for (and what it has been used for until now) is to provide play-room for the creation of hitherto undiscovered room for play within the viewer, to provide means by which consciousness can be made more *exact* rather than more expansive, means to produce sensitivity: irritability: reaction: a way to come into the world anew.

The theater, then, does not copy the world, but the world shows itself to be the replica of the theater. I know this is a contemplative position; but I would not let anyone tell me that the alternative to contemplation is action. Now, whether the more precise consciousness of the viewer or listener can by itself produce the impetus to change conditions in the Marxist sense (which would accord with my own intentions)—this I doubt, even though I hope for it; that is, I doubt it the more I hope for it: theater in the theater seems to be capable only of producing the preconditions, the linguistic leap that anticipates new possibilities of thought; but because it is play, it does not immediately and unambiguously present the actual *leap,* the new possibility of thought itself that would signify the solution. Brecht of course includes the *leap,* the solution, in the play and thereby deprives it of its effect, its reality. But the commune in Berlin, no doubt influenced by the theater, but certainly not influenced by Brecht (though, for all I know, they revere him), is, one might say, playing the leap in reality. It will, we hope, play it until reality itself has become a single space dedicated to play. That would be beautiful.

1968   *Translated by Joel Agee*

Notes

1. One of the leaders of the student demonstrations of 1968.
2. Name of Brecht's theater company in East Berlin.

PETER HANDKE, born in Austria in 1942, was first known for his plays *Offending the Audience* (1966) and *Kaspar* (1968); he then turned to prose and film making.

Martin Walser

A Further Daydream about the Theater

There is no vocabulary as degenerate as the one that refers to art. The going jargon would have made a shambles of any other discipline long ago. Imagine the theoretical physics of today having to employ the concepts of 1805. But the leading German art vocabulary—the one that goes back to Weimar[1]—commended itself from the start as something suprahistorical. And what's more, those guys got away with it. For this reason, divisions like those between Art and Life, Art and Reality, and Art and Nature persist to this day. I much prefer the statement of the Westphalian mental patient Erich Spiessbach: "Art cannot be separated from all other human feats of skill and intelligence."

But once art had been isolated from everything else in its own elite domain, it went without saying that no outsiders could be permitted to have any say-so: Art was answerable only to its own laws. Finally the equally blasphemous and phony term "creativity" was brought in to explain it all. And that put the lid on it.

Goethe's sentimental and quasi-atavistic regression, his flight from the beginnings of bourgeois history to Weimar and into a Greece of his own imagination, had some sad consequences. But elsewhere in Europe, too, the Greek rule was adopted like a law around which you then had to navigate as well as you could, since it proved completely useless for one's own practical purposes.

Goldoni, in his memoirs, describes the setting of his play *The Coffeehouse* and then remarks with a sigh of relief: "Here, undeniably, is Unity of Place. This time the stern judges will be pleased with me in this respect—but what about Unity of Action?

316

Will they not find the play convoluted and the suspense intermittent?"

The Marxists were probably the first to investigate this tradition without being paralyzed by fear of sacrilege. But that comical division was not overcome by Marxism either, nor by Brecht: the division into Art and Life, Art and Reality, Art and Nature. This convention, born in the land of idealism, still messes up the works. True, Brecht made plays that are no longer worthy exercises in reproduction for the purpose of creating an illusion; his plays are pure products of the stage, of purely exemplary character; what happens in them can only happen on the stage; all the decisions are made of theatrical material and could only occur on the stage (though of course they're intended to strike sparks across the footlights and give the audience a piece of their mind); but still the play's supposed to be a distorted image of reality, some verisimilitude of an enlightening sort is intended: this is how it is, that's how it's done, but it's not the way it should be, kindly do something about it. Brecht thought he could achieve his goals without iconism. His alienation effect is still in the service of representation, which is nourished by the idealistic axiom that art and life are made of different materials, and that art imitates nature for some purpose or other. Yet the agreeable difference between Brecht's tradition and Goethe's is that Brecht subordinated and adapted the rules to the end, while before him art was allowed to pursue its elitist chitchat for the propagation of a particularly useless image of man without any further terrestrial interference: on the hither side Art (into this heaven ye shall never come!), on the thither side Reality (go on, now, strive a little!). It will always remain remarkable and worthy of study how the glorious Schiller had the marrow removed from his bones to Weimar.

But back to the complicated present: theater is more than ever in the service of representation. Documentary theater is a theater of illusion, it conjures up reality with the materials of art. The viewers are supposed to be made witnesses of imitations of moral decisions, are supposed to be stimulated to participate in these always easy-to-follow moral-political calisthenics. Brecht, who by now has turned into the prize morsel of the theater festivals, is the documentarists' theoretical godfather, and indeed they can claim him on the basis of his theories. This is less true of his practice.

He was insurmountably averse to reproducing on the stage the reality that he knew. He preferred exotic images as vehicles for his message. Some among his posterity are proceeding along his lines (Hacks, Lange, Weiss in *Marat/Sade*) but they are showing signs of nervousness, they can no longer bring themselves to preserve their earthly experience in such pure packaging materials (Kipphardt, Weiss, Hochhuth), so they stage the real process almost faithfully and as revealingly as possible. They produce exact imitations, using the stage as a means of transportation; the audience's trust is gained by the most direct means: look here, you can see for yourself, this is how it is, we're not cheating, we can back up every word.

This most recent theatrical practice, which no longer insists on art for itself, has, in my view, only apparently overcome the ridiculous distinction between art and reality. These shows are always running after reality without ever getting close to it. The stage can be made to resemble the place where the story once actually happened, but this tremendous effort at imitation doesn't let you forget for an instant that what we're dealing with is a harmless reproduction of reality. The viewer is enjoined to become a voyeur or a witness; but since the play's imitative character is supposed to be left intact, since the illusion is supposed to remain transparent, the viewer remains a voyeur who isn't being offered enough and a witness who hasn't seen anything. Or rather, he has seen something: a substitute. A substitution for a reality which fortunately he didn't have to participate in. He has seen art that pretended to be reality.

This sounds more polemical than I intended. After all, the viewer is accustomed to ersatz fare. He has a well-trained sensory apparatus, he knows how to deal with a substitute: how to let himself be informed and stimulated to pass judgment. An alien world has been set up and brought into play for his benefit: now he can have a say. He was there, in a manner of speaking. But just in a manner of speaking. If there existed a cinematic record of the same event that is being imitated on the stage, it would surely be more informative and more reliable. But since our culture educates us to consume theatrical productions as representations of real life, it is conceivable that this kind of substitute could create a lasting impression. I'm saying this because I have a high regard for the authors of these documentary plays and because I believe that we live in a time when everything must be tried. In view of the cavalier manner in which the bourgeois press treats the news, the theater will have to serve as a newspaper as well. Nevertheless, I believe that these documentary plays and the parable plays (the other branch of Brecht's heritage) lead to a misunderstanding of the nature of theater; a misunderstanding which, however, can be justified politically. The misunderstanding, in my view, lies in the fact that the stage is once again being separated from reality. After all, it's art that's being made on this documentary and parable stage, and art, once again, is the other world. The other material. In other words: on this stage, too, nothing real is happening. Here too, there is really nothing happening.

And now I suppose I should declare my opinion, which is more of a need than an opinion, more a wish than a theory.

But it's an old wish, frequently tested, and rejected again and again by the ruling theatrical practice. A need that has been intimidated again and again by dramatists and dramaturgies, by the administrators of theory and the watchmen of tradition, and by myself.

I would like to see the theater liberated from the strictures of art and the burdens of representation. Not necessarily the whole theater; I'd just like to see a part of the energy of play-makers directed toward the future again. There should be an effort to make the theatrical event independent of all real events. In other words: what's happening on the stage is itself a reality; but it's a reality that exists only on the stage. So it's not a copy made of different material. No more ideological separation between art and life. *Et hic vita est*; and not just imitated life, but original life.

What kind of light would such a theater of consciousness shed? We would have to find out. It might be an incomparably sharper light than the kind that results from refraction, from purposive imitation. Intimidated by both tradition and current practice, I hesitate to describe this need at greater length, at least at this point. I don't want merely to have reacted to documentary theater. Before I unfold my theater dream, I want to consider our entire theater life: the new houses and the old traditions.

So: for a while, every time I saw a picture of a new theater in the newspaper, I was embarrassed. How much of the gross national product was being invested in the monumental grace of these concrete bandboxes! And I felt responsible. Not out of megalomania, but out of a kind of solidarity. It's the duty of all of us text deliverers, gesture drillers, grimace makers, administrators of public expression, to see to it that these heart-stirring sums don't wither away in Alexandrian stripped concrete. Those were my thoughts. I eventually overcame this phase of unrequested empathy with the fate of the gross national product. I slept soundly again, for I had realized: these theaters were built for the past and not even for the whole past but just for that skein of tradition that least concerns me. Why, I said to myself, these are nothing but bourgeois foster homes for a tradition which in the final analysis is all Goethe's fault; he started it, and that's why to this day he's played more frequently in these houses than, say, Kleist, one of Goethe's exemplary victims in his own lifetime; these pretty bandboxes are more for Gerhart Hauptmann than for Sternheim, more for plaster than for nerves, so what the hell! Let them foster their asocial humanism and spend their theatrical evenings washing each other's ears out with a super-refined nobility, the ineffectuality and social irrelevance of which may be safely considered guaranteed after 150 years of bourgeois history. Then this self-sufficient polemical view of our theater died away in me as well. Today I hope I'm a little more capable of understanding. Today I suspect that the city councils and the cooperating theater directors would like nothing more than to place the lovely new houses in the service of bourgeois self-adoration, and that they don't do it against their better knowledge. And the mitigating circumstance: our theaters are placed in every sense of the word at the center of our society, and this society has been suspicious of progress for the past 150 years, self-adoration is practiced and routinely drilled from top to bottom, self-assurance turns into charisma, and doubt is regarded as something to be ashamed of; under these circumstances, how could the theater not turn into a place where a beautiful semblance of movement is enacted? Those solemn theater houses are not laboratories crackling with futurity, they are pieces of municipal heraldry or retreats for the conscious mind, leisure time churches, saunas for the soul, come on and tickle us! You know where we like it. And where we don't.

It's been this way for a long time. And everywhere. A society going to the theater to enjoy the experience of being blandished. We have heard, however, of societies that still had plans for the future and where something new could be shown on the stage. And where, when it wasn't shown, you still expected to see it. It was that way here too. In the fifties, for example. And in the early sixties. Many believed we were moving in the direction of an ever greater democracy. We simply believed this to be a trend. And we expected a new theater. A theater of our own. Suited to us. It may be that we were seduced by Brecht's exaggerated demands. The things he thought possible! At least he acted that way.

And now: our social development stagnated and our theaters were built as sites for the celebration of immobility. There are an increasing number of people among us who are more than suspicious of the origins of the aesthetic according to which our art is performed. But we don't liberate ourselves. We continue to fiddle around with art works in which life is cautiously imitated, satisfying the old demands for packaging and resolution. For that's what it's about, ultimately: reality is resolved by art. Art within, life without. My demand, my need would be for life within as well. And this is not a requirement I've invented, I owe it to the theater. A great many plays (both good and bad) from all the dramatic literatures have shown me that while the authors submitted to an already threadbare convention (the laws of the theater) and set their characters loose in an imitated world, the characters themselves lead me to suspect that they are protagonists of the author's consciousness. Allegedly, Franz and Karl Moor[2] used to be played by a *single* actor. Schiller decided that they would never appear together on the stage. We can be sure that he was enough of a dramatist not to forego the explosive effect of this meeting of brothers without some good reason. He could only address these two sides of his consciousness, these two characters, in succession. Karl and Franz are the unfolding of a consciousness. They are a drastic example of the fact that dramatic characters are made of the stuff of consciousness. That's a highly real material, even though it's not available in a drugstore. Puntila and Matti[3] are a pair that expresses the movements of Brecht's consciousness. While they can't be played by a single actor, they could be played as a set of consciousness-twins, as Brecht's unsolvable problem, as his personal embarrassment, as a class-struggle idyll which doesn't represent anything that happens in the social world, but that brings into play a conversation of Brecht with Brecht concerning Brecht, or a conversation of the irritated burgher with the one who's irritating him, on the subject of his irritation. The greatest of Shakespeare's plays are the ones most purely established on the stage of consciousness: *Othello, Hamlet, Lear,* and *The Tempest.* And: *Romeo and Juliet.* Freud had no problem deriving his consciousness-analytical tags from Greek tragedy. But this doesn't mean that we should regard all plays in line with Freud's historical procedures. Psychoanalysis is merely the first (and by now replaceable) scientific attempt to speak concretely about our consciousness. It would be enough if we spoke of the plays at hand as attempts on the part of their authors to give expression to their consciousness. Toward this end, they use all sorts of subjects and characters. Only in recent times, under the influence of bourgeois ideology, which so fatally separates art and life, are subject-matters and characters hedged in by increasingly strict standards of imitation; more and more, a dramaturgy is coming to the fore whose ideal it would be to fabricate one-to-one replicas of reality.

Beckett is the first great interruption of this new, already victorious tradition of imitation. True, Beckett is still putting together parables, but these parables no longer betray themselves so easily; they even point to their origin in consciousness and turn the theater back into a place where acts of consciousness can occur. And I believe there is a need for this. If a number of people were willing to declare their need, the desired theater would take shape before long. I'll take the risk and set down a few key words:

1. The stories or plots; it is hard to imagine that our consciousness, nourished as it is by our society, would still express itself in representational sequences, in a unified plot, in constellation and disturbance and the resolution of that disturbance. We know the old course of events by heart. All this ceaseless significance has long become a bother to us. Everything that happens is part of it. An actor can't cross the stage without the meaning of this walk bursting through all the seams. And the productions do their best to emphasize the imitative character of the plays.

No matter what happens, it will be revealed. Everything is set up with an eye to its consequences. And to its broadly emphasized implications. If an accounting error should creep into the swift unwinding of the plot, any critic can tote up the bill and point up the author's or the director's miscalculation. The laws of the theater are sufficiently well known. After all, we're dealing with art.

But: a theater that would supply the site for independent, autonomous actions would express our unhappy consciousness more exactly. That is my hope. Our social situation, our political lethargy, our groundless vocabularies—all these demand a different kind of action than this elaborate parroting. The degeneration of the American world mission cannot be recreated on the stage. But it might be possible to express what it feels like to be the observers and accomplices of this decadence of a policy that was once rich in hope.

But our theater events are ritualized, very much in the sense in which the biologist Julian Huxley described the ritualization of the movements of great crested grebe; gradually, in the course of the history of the species, these movements lose their original function and turn into symbolic ceremonies. And Konrad Lorenz has described the similarity between rituals of cultural-historical and phylogenetic origin. Theater plots, i.e., the sum of all the dramaturgies, both traditional and currently in vogue, amount to a ritualized sequence which is routinely laden with gently imitative functions, brought up to date and thus presented to a long specialized audience. How can we break out of these thoroughly rehearsed sequences? We could begin the way Handke did, by *Offending the Audience* and by *Self-Accusation*. But we should not cease wanting to continue to perform stories. Not, of course, stories that are so ritualized that they can only be consumed as a kind of moral-gymnastic spectacle guaranteed to be totally ineffectual. If our task were to present the consciousness of a fellow-citizen, i.e., our own consciousness—this spectator's consciousness artificially rendered innocuous, this consciousness trained by newspaper and government, eager to be deceived and self-deceived—then "action" would be undesirable. Stagnation, discontinuous stases, blind alleys, mortally dangerous idylls, montages of ragged contrasts—all these would be more suitable than any kind of "action." In a play dealing with contemporary consciousness, nothing can change. At best, there can be an increasing insight into a state of affairs. Whoever wants change should go to the magician's stall in the fair: there he will see a rabbit disappearing from a hat. Nowhere else.

2. Characters: Beautiful though the great characters of the traditional stage are, they are too well known. We know them by heart.
And the bad thing about that is that the law of the theater
apparently forces authors to make their characters compete with
the glaring familiarity of those grand old characters. That's why,
when one goes to the theater, one gets the impression that nothing
is better known than human nature. That character on the stage—
he's made of glass. The part fits. It's a corset. The part, I say: It's
more like a vehicle for this or that quality. And please not too
pale, gentlemen! And please, keep it close to life. These aren't
supposed to be figments of a consciousness but imitations of
"lifelike" human beings! Author, be creative! Your predecessor
could do it. Granted, he limited himself to Adam and Eve. But
please, you can follow his example, you don't have to be quite as
creative as he was. Whereupon the author, forced by these rigid
conventions, pads his characters, which perhaps were conceived as
burningly fragmentary creatures, into perfectly lifelike puppets.
Now they have everything a real person needs, including a tic and
the death-mask of a problem. Characters that have been limited to
the requirements of imitation usually come equipped with an
opinion and a biography. The impenetrable thicket of human
consciousness has been cleared and cropped so that the sun of the
easiest comprehension can shine through unimpeded. That's probably why Doderer[4] contemptuously refused to follow a colon with
words. It would be a pleasure to encounter a stage character that
was as difficult to understand as any real human being, any real
consciousness is. The audience is much more obscure than the
plays they go to watch. In so-called reality, i.e., in the normal
traffic conditions of our society, a consciousness has to go through
all sorts of contortions just to get by: and then its intra-cranial
existence, filled as it is with unacceptable excess, is practically
illegal. It could find an outlet on the stage, in the stage character.

3. The actors: why do they act? Isn't the actor involved above all
with imitation? No doubt it is a joy and a great delight to watch
an actor engaged in the work of imitation. But is it just that? Here
are two pertinent experiences: Goldoni[5] tells us that every actor
has "his own native character; if the poet has him play a character
that corresponds to his own, success is virtually assured." Stanislavski[6]:

"Everyone knows about this peculiar tendency of actors: the ugly one wants to embody a radiant beauty on the stage, the short one wants to appear tall, the clumsy one dexterous and nimble . . . Just ask an amateur what part he would like to play . . . People always strive for what they lack, and actors seek to represent on the stage the qualities they have been denied in life. But this is a dangerous and misleading path. This failure to comprehend one's own craft and profession is the greatest obstacle to an actor's development." Two truly competent but completely different men of the theater, and yet they are of one opinion. Nevertheless I don't like to think of an actor's need to play a part that isn't himself as merely a dangerous, wrong turn in his career. Even though he can only succeed with parts which he can back up with his own character, the experience of his own lack may well be the necessary condition for an actor's power. Only someone who can't put up with his own limitations will want to play the part of another; no, more than that, to play himself as another. Not just to be the one you have to be under the merciless constrictions of the environment. A human consciousness always has a notion of itself that is not confirmed by the surrounding world. From this disparity arises the need to show off, to put on a show, to act.

The actor observes, takes measure, garners expressive material by experience, but this capacity for imitation is secondary. The real source of his magnetism, of his infectious power, is his unadaptable consciousness. The actor is frequently overwrought. He is less accepting than others. He acts up. He often remains unhappy. He has very little self-reliance. He is very dependent. And he wants to be loved more than anything. He is, in other words, an especially typical human being.

The roles that require the necessary capacity for mimicry don't satisfy him. He wants to play Franz and Karl Moor, because he is always being given just one part. He wants to act out of his consciousness, wants perhaps to play a part that suits his make-up, but always with the mad hope of getting rid of his secrets, his unconfessed and suppressed and aborted claims which the world would refuse to acknowledge. That is his real wealth.

4. The author: no doubt plays, too, are the products of an endogenous or exogenous scarcity. A play is a fragment of re-

nounced life or festering hope or fear striking back. It should be possible for as much to happen in a play as happens in a human consciousness. A play built to the measure of a consciousness would be able to accommodate more politics than one following the path of imitation. However: a play evincing an intimate connection with its author's consciousness must have a more important occasion than an opinion or a will. I believe that consciousness does not require expression until it has experienced too much. And then, consciousness does not imitate itself, it expresses itself.

But the author would have to put up with being temporarily classified as an unrealist by the administrators of the traditional vocabulary, who will grant the term "realism" only to a particular brand of recognizability and *déja vu*. And: the public might object as well.

I'd like to stop here.

Just one more thing: the fact that younger authors are showing a preference for the movies is alarming. Theater as a holy terror. Theater, a sacred land with laws that are carried out by the unbelieving. A public accustomed to consuming its ritual: a beautiful make-believe world that purports, for the audience's sake, to resemble their own.

I can't imagine that theater will ever cease to exist. We simply can't do without it. Our situation necessitates it. And consciousness should play the main part. After all, it's our one and all. And there is no public place other than the stage where it is allowed to show itself. And consciousness needs publicity. Consciousness needs society or it gets sick. And society needs consciousness, otherwise it is a horde: ritual alone isn't enough. Besides, it would be a shame to waste all those expensive buildings.

1967   *Translated by Joel Agee*

Notes

1. I.e., the classical period of Goethe and Schiller.
2. Main characters in Schiller's *The Robbers*.
3. In Brecht's *Puntila and His Servant Matti*.

4. Heimito von Doderer (1896–1966), Austrian novelist.
5. Carlo Goldoni (1707–1793), Italian playwright.
6. Konstantin Stanislavski (1863–1938), eminent Russian director and theoretician.

MARTIN WALSER, born in 1927, writes novels, short stories, and essays as well as plays. His most noteworthy plays are *Eiche und Angora* (1962), *Der schwarze Schwan* (1964), and *Das Sauspiel* (1975).

Heinar Kipphardt

Theater and Reality

INTERVIEWER: You are considered one of the fathers of the documentary drama, Mr. Kipphardt. Some people object that the theater is getting the shorter end of the stick.

KIPPHARDT: That may be the case. It doesn't have to be. There is no such thing as theater in and of itself, it's always the theater of a particular time. The more important question for me is whether in our contemporary theater the world isn't getting the shorter end. If the theater isn't put in the position of dealing with the key political questions of our time, it won't be taken seriously for very much longer. It will sink to the level of other instruments for the manipulation of false consciousness, a game for relaxation, a public bath for the emotions. Not a worthwhile occupation. An eater wants a steak, and a person who goes to the theater wants to see something that's worth thinking about.

INTERVIEWER: The question is, how can these key questions be vividly represented on the stage? Theater is a sensual business.

KIPPHARDT: Certainly. There is no art without sensuality. But thinking is sensual too. Brecht counted it among his greatest pleasures. If a dramatist succeeds in vividly portraying a complicated reality with all its contradictions, if he succeeds in making this reality transparent, he will be providing thoroughly exciting aesthetic pleasures and quite enough entertainment.

INTERVIEWER: Why do you consider the new techniques of documentation—the ones you use in your plays, the ones Weiss or Hochhuth use—to be particularly suited for this purpose?

KIPPHARDT: I think I should only speak for myself. The authors you have named, though they have all based their work on factual material, have developed very different types of plays, different with regard to their way of viewing the world and with regard to the dramaturgical techniques they employ. What they have in common is perhaps the feeling that in our time of slogans and ideologies where everything turns into an instant thesis, a prejudice, one should be exact, one should be able to furnish testable evidence for what one is expounding on the stage. For this reason, a scientific component is adopted in one's artistic work, the writer assumes the attitude of a researcher. We can find this same trait in other art forms. Interestingly enough, the authors of the so-called documentary drama developed these techniques independently of each other as they were working on the adaptation of great political subjects to the stage. I'm not saying that these techniques are the only way to treat great political subjects, but there seem to be subjects that can't be written about in any other manner than that of documentation, they demand a factually authentic treatment. There are subjects of which one cannot have a vision; to get at their characteristic essence, you have to go into the fullness of the facts with all their contradictions.

INTERVIEWER: Didn't Brecht discover in the parable a poetic form in which political subjects could be treated?

KIPPHARDT: Oh, I wouldn't dispute the parable's ability to treat many subjects in a satisfactory way. But I don't think the parable form suits every kind of subject. I don't know whether you could think up a meaningful parable about Auschwitz or Hiroshima or Vietnam. It would strike me as slightly obscene.

When I began working on *Oppenheimer,* I tried out several techniques. At first I was thinking of an epic form reminiscent of Shakespeare's historical plays, with the hearing as the last act. This didn't satisfy me; it wasn't exact enough. I found that the questions of the contradiction between the spectacular development of recent natural science and the retarded development of our knowledge of society could not be treated either parabolically or in the form of a historical play, but only with this attitude of documentation.

INTERVIEWER: I am in complete agreement with your doubts concerning the possibilities of the parable, Mr. Kipphardt. A parable may succeed in prettifying a subject, making it more enjoyable, but at the same time it renders it less demanding and less exact. On the other hand, I ask myself whether your documentary play, *Oppenheimer,* hasn't turned into a new kind of parable after all, a parable of the scientist's role in our time?

KIPPHARDT: Surely not a parable, but naturally I wanted to use the extreme case of Oppenheimer to depict the contradictions and conflicts of the scientist in our time. And this example was intended to be applicable to other areas of activity. The wealth of facts is the basic material from which the dramatist draws what is characteristic for his subject, and he has to do a few things in order to end up with an enjoyable product.

A mere montage of facts will never be enough, no matter how good or how pure it is. It would be sad if a play were to descend to a mere collection of facts without any essence of meaning. You'd have the facts, but where's the play? The play will of course be as good or as bad as the brain and the talent of its author.

1972   *Translated by Joel Agee*

HEINAR KIPPHARDT, 1922–1982. His documentary plays include *The General's Dog* (1962), *In the Matter of J. Robert Oppenheimer* (1964), *Joel Brand—The History of a Business Deal* (1965), and *Brother Eichmann* (1982).

Tankred Dorst

A Conversation with Rudolf Vogel

VOGEL: In the mid-fifties you founded a marionette theater, *Das kleine Spiel*, and wrote marionette plays for it. Then, in 1957, you published an essay, "The Secret of the Marionette." In this essay you said, for example: A good marionette play should always be slightly fragmentary. In this essay you were already speaking of the open form. Fifteen years later, concepts like open theater reappear in your remarks on *Toller* and on *Kleiner Mann—was nun?* and *Eiszeit*. When you were still writing marionette plays, had you already developed a dramaturgy that still holds true for you today?

DORST: I have to say, first of all, that I didn't found the theater, it already existed when I was studying here. And one day I went in and found it interesting, so I wrote my first plays for this theater, for *Das kleine Spiel*. And I do think that this experience of the marionette theater influenced the way I wrote my plays later on.

VOGEL: What made you decide to write for the marionette theater first, instead of for the regular theater?

DORST: Well, for one thing, I was a very inhibited person and simply didn't dare to come out with something. And the psychological advantage of the marionette theater was that you disappeared behind it. It's a kind of mechanical theater, and for that reason it's of course very useful for someone who lacks self-confidence; and also because it was a group. It gave me the courage just to come out with something. And then of course I had fun working in this medium, and it suited me, or else I or my kind of imagination or whatever you call it was suited to *it*. And then, because you're

331

already kind of in a theater, sort of, you want to go with it, develop it. And the more you get to know a medium, the more you enjoy it, normally. But you can't make a living with it, and I think you can't do it all your life, otherwise it starts getting sectarian . . .

VOGEL: You said you wanted to write a play for the theater in Bochum, a play that would have a chance of being popular, that would draw people to the theater. What has your experience with the public been? Do you have an audience for which you write?

DORST: Well, my first plays, that is, *Die Kurve* and also *Die Freiheit für Clemens,* which was a failure, were three-character, four-character plays, one-act plays, and they were mostly performed in small theaters like factory theaters and student theaters. At any rate, they were never meant for a large audience, but always really for a more or less intellectual audience, and probably they were written for them too. And there comes the time when you get tired of that, at least that's the way it was with me, and also with Zadek, incidentally. And this coincided with a general crisis situation in Germany, which still exists. You had the feeling that theater's finished, nobody's interested in it any longer. Young people aren't interested, all that's left is this old bourgeois public, an audience nurturing its education—I don't think that's something that should be excluded—but it's not a real live audience, so there's no real communication, no real excitement. And we were kind of tired of writing and putting on plays for a studio audience, an intellectual audience. And now Zadek became a director and suddenly he had this big theater house, and that house had to be filled somehow, and when he took over there wasn't much of an audience left, and we thought: we ought to make a theater for a large public, sort of a new popular theater. That's how we came up with *Kleiner Mann,* and the results were very good. At any rate, that success justified *Kleiner Mann* and several other plays.

VOGEL: You were tired of writing for an intellectual audience. You wanted to reach many people, and you did reach many people. So you wanted to create a new form of folk-theater, a theater for the great majority.

DORST: Yes, I mean, if the theater still has any sort of appeal, any sort of attraction, it's that it creates a kind of communication that isn't possible through any other art form. Television can't do it, you're just sitting at home watching it in a little room, and the movies, too, are reeled off mechanically, what happens on the screen doesn't depend on any immediate tension between the actors and the audience. But theater, particularly a theater that's watched by many people, has a special sort of excitement. It's the struggle with the audience that takes place every evening, something every actor's acquainted with, and of course it has a lot to do with the play, too, with whatever is provocative about the play. The audience as an enemy who is conquered or won over in the course of an evening. And that, I think, is the essential and vital appeal of the theater, which I believe will always exist, and which will see to it that the theater doesn't die out. I think it'll always be interesting to take part in this kind of communication; but of course this again has something to do with the theater having an audience. You can have the most interesting and exciting plays for just a few people, but if no one wants to see them, if no one comes into the theater, your message and its intellectual caliber won't serve any purpose. So the first thing is having an audience, and in my opinion the audience is basically more important than the critics.

VOGEL: Does this communication, this struggle with the audience also serve to change the audience in some way, to influence it?

DORST: I don't believe that an author sits down and says: Now I want to move people in this or that direction. I believe that an author who writes plays will first of all have a need to express something, to express himself, to tell his own story, the story that interests him. And if he is a good author, it will be a good story and an interesting story, and it will also have a meaning that could possibly change the audience in a certain way. But there are limits to this kind of change. I think people overestimate the theater when they say: O.K., today's theater could start revolutions or even great political upheavals. I don't believe that. Revolutions have something to do with economic conditions, not aesthetic conditions. And let's face it, *Mother Courage*[1] didn't prevent a war and it didn't make history either, it just made theater history. I think people had an exaggerated view of these things for a while. But what theater can do, if it's good theater, it can have an effect on people. Because in the last analysis it's a reflection on society, and people reflect on themselves in the theater, and theater can move the audience, can move or teach or stimulate people to think about their situation in a more complex and discriminating fashion. And that of course is an effect that can reach beyond the theater. I think that's very beautiful, and I also think it's no small thing when a theater can achieve this.

VOGEL: Mr. Dorst, you have only written plays. Why haven't you written any prose?

DORST: I don't know. For one thing, I don't think I have the patience to write a fat book. When I think of colleagues of mine, friends who sit for years writing a single book—that would make me very restless, for one; and also, I like to work together with other people.

VOGEL: What is this collaboration like? Tell us a little about the way you work on one of your plays.

DORST: That varies a lot. Different plays have taken various amounts of time. It took me a long, long time to finish *Toller*. That is: I didn't work on it for years on end without interruption, but I had a conception of it which I wrote down years before the premiere: I think I started with it in 1963. But at first it was still a tight, closed sort of story, and a regular parable too, and then I cut it apart and rearranged it, added new things, etc. So it was a long, long process. And I think that has something to do with the nature of the material. I don't mean the fact that I had to collect the material but that this play, *Toller*, didn't have any real story in the narrow sense. If you've got a story, as in *Kurve* and in the sort of parable play that depends a lot on the basic idea, and if that idea is a good one, the play practically writes itself, and that doesn't take long at all; but it's something I no longer want to do. I want to see people in a more complex way, and I want to give up this closed form. That does make things difficult in some respects, because the criteria of whether something is working or not are harder to find. You always have the feeling that you're swimming, and the only criterion by which I can judge whether this scene or this conception is good now is really myself. And since I am always very suspicious of myself, I always end up feeling unsure of myself in my work. I would say: there's a vacillation between hubris and annoyance at what you're doing, and you always want to throw it away. This is not good . . .

VOGEL: And the people who work with you, let's say the director . . .

DORST: I've noticed in recent years that there are directors, especially star directors, particularly in Germany but not just here, Cherreau in France is one of them, who have the ambition and the intention of putting on a very good show, but it's supposed to be the only performance. That is, they're not really very interested in helping the play to get twenty or thirty or 100 performances and becoming popular, what they're really interested in is that this performance get a good reputation and that it be talked about in the press; and this is a development which in Germany has something to do with the fact that our theaters are heavily subsidized, so they're not operating under a financial, economic risk, and the image of a director doesn't depend on popular success but on his critical reception by the press. In my opinion, this development, the fact that an evening of theater can be conducted without any sort of risk as far as the public is concerned, has some great disadvantages, to put it mildly. And the result is that the evening in the theater lacks tension and excitement. That is why Zadek and I, working together in Bochum, intended from the start to write plays for the public—not exactly against the press, but mainly for the public, and perhaps we'll succeed in diminishing if not eliminating altogether the great discrepancy that exists in Germany between the judgment of the press and the judgment of the public.

VOGEL: How do you find your materials?

DORST: Basically, I think you always want to write the same play, and yet people have frequently said of me that I always wrote a new and different play, that I never stayed in the same place: O.K., I guess you might say that.—The earlier plays were model plays, and my current ones no longer are; my way of writing has changed. That's partly due to my own developments. But the fact is basically—and I notice this by the kinds of materials that appeal to me or the conflicts that fascinate me—I always have the same theme: the actor, the intellectual, and gambler.

VOGEL: Toller for instance—

DORST: Toller for instance. I arrived at Toller by a strange detour. I wanted to write a play about an actor, a sort of paraphrase of an early Christian legend about an actor who during the time of the persecution of Christians plays a Christian, and who goes into hiding while the persecution persists—that is, he plays a different part. And the theme was for me always a moral theme, the question of our accountability: to what extent are we responsible, to what extent can we play; it's the same thing I've always found interesting about the Don Juan theme. And I notice that all my plays have something to do with the theater, without my actually intending it: actors, theater, accountability, nonaccountability, and therefore also "theater" as a moral theme. Just to play-act, or to be who you are—in a way it's existence reduced to a role, to a single denominator.

VOGEL: This brings us to the question: reality and theater. Is the reality of the theater the only legitimate reality for you?

DORST: No, I don't think so. I think so less and less. Of course when you write a play, the theater, and play itself, has its own laws. You're moving within the confines of a play. And it's happened to me at various times, for example in the case of *Toller,* that somebody calls me in the morning and says: here is Leviné on the phone—I was just working on the play and wondering who Leviné was—and there's Leviné's widow on the phone. I didn't even know there was a relative still alive. The same thing with *Hamsun.* Suddenly I get a letter from the son of Hamsun, who doesn't exactly play a part in *Eiszeit,* since it's not a play about Hamsun in that sense, but the old man has a son in the play, and now I'm getting a letter from the Hamsun family. I was really always surprised, because I was so involved with the play that I'd completely forgotten that these same people existed in a different form. I mean: you have to, and I want to do this more and more in my plays, you have to start with reality. I think that a theater without realism, completely without realism, in other words a completely artificial theater, gets very uninteresting, at least for me. And what fascinates and preoccupies me is always a quasi-objective reality. I use this reality, but in the context of the play its meaning and its value change. Mrs. Leviné of course thought of her husband, and I thought of my character, whose importance in the play was relative to that of the other characters. That's the basic difference.

1973   *Translated by Joel Agee*

Notes

1. Play by Brecht.

TANKRED DORST, born in 1925 in Sonneberg, Thuringia, lives in Munich. His major plays are *Toller* (1968) and *Eiszeit* (1973).

Heiner Müller

Fatzer +/− Keuner

I shit
on the order of the world
I am
lost

The fact that the bourgeois revolution did not take place in Germany both facilitated and forced the emergence of the Weimar classic period as a neutralization of the positions of the Storm and Stress. Classicism as a substitute for revolution. Literature of a vanquished class, form as adjustment, culture as a set of formal manners for intercourse with the ruling power, and as a vehicle for false consciousness. Goethe's conscious choice against the starving weavers of Apolda[1] and in favor of the iambs of *Iphigenie*[2] is paradigmatic. Of all the misfortunes of recent history the one with the most far-reaching consequences was perhaps the failure of the proletarian revolution in Germany and its strangulation at the hands of fascism, its worst effect being the isolation of the socialist experiment in the Soviet Union under conditions of underdevelopment. The results are well known and they have not been overcome. The amputation of German socialism by the division of the nation is not among the worst consequences. The GDR can live with it.

Brecht's expulsion from Germany, his distance from the German class struggles, the impossibility of continuing his work in the Soviet Union meant: emigration into classicism. His *Versuche 1–8* contain the vital part of his work, as far as its potential for immediate political impact is concerned—its theological core of

338

fire, in the sense of Walter Benjamin's conception of Marxism. Hollywood became the Weimar of the German anti-fascist emigration. The need not to talk about Stalin—because his name stood for the Soviet Union so long as Hitler was in power—compelled the exiles to resort to generalities: hence the parable form. The Svendborg[3] conversations edited by Benjamin tell us something about that. The GDR's situation during Brecht's lifetime, nationally and internationally, did not offer him any way out of the classical dilemma.

One of the subjects discussed in Brecht's and Benjamin's Svendborg conversations was Kafka. Reading between the lines, we can hear Benjamin asking whether Kafka's parable isn't more capacious, more capable of taking in (and giving out) reality than Brecht's parable. And this not despite but because of the fact that it describes/portrays gestures without any system of reference, without taking its bearings from a movement (praxis), without being reducible to a single meaning; because it is alien rather than alienating; because it makes no moral point. The avalanches of recent history have done less damage to the model of the "Penal Colony" than they have to the ideal dialectical structure of the didactic plays. The blindness of Kafka's experience is proof of its authenticity. (Kafka's gaze as a gaze into the sun. The inability to look history in the eye as the basis of politics.) Only the increasing pressure of authentic experience—provided it "takes possession of the masses"—can develop the ability to look history in the eye, which could mean the end of politics and the beginning of human history. The author is wiser than the allegory, and the metaphor is wiser than an author.

Gertrude Stein, in a text on Elizabethan literature, explains its power by the speed of the transformation of meaning in language: "Everything moves so much." The transformation of meaning is the barometer measuring the pressure of experience at the dawn of capitalism, which is just beginning to discover the world as a market. The speed of the transformation of meaning constitutes the primacy of metaphor, which serves as a kind of optical diaphragm to scale down the bombardment of images. "The pressure of experience drives language into poetry" (Eliot). The fear of metaphor is the fear of the material's independent mobility. The fear of tragedy is the fear of the permanence of revolution.

I remember a remark Wekwerth[4] made when he was preparing

a performance of *St. Joan of the Stockyards*. He said it was important to obscure what Brecht had clarified, so that it could be seen anew; Hegel: what is well known is not recognized. The history of the European Left suggests that here, too, Hegel needs to be stood from his head onto his feet. On every territory that has yet been occupied by the Enlightenment, unknown zones of darkness have "unexpectedly" opened up. Again and again the alliance with rationalism has exposed the Left to back-stabbing by the powers of reaction, with daggers that were always forged in these zones of darkness. What has been recognized is not well known.

Brecht's insistence, in his last conversations with Wekwerth, on naiveté as the primary category of his aesthetics, illuminates this state of affairs.

Brecht's effort not to understand or at least to misunderstand Kafka can be inferred from Benjamin's record of the [Svendborg] discussions.

Around 1948, North German Radio broadcast a program on two representatives of politically committed literature, the Catholic T.S. Eliot and the Communist Brecht. A sentence of Eliot's was used to staple the whole thing together: "Poetry doesn't matter." I remember another sentence from the interview with Brecht: continuity, keeping on with it all, brings about destruction. Brecht explained this in some detail later on, in a text that starts out from the theater situation in post-war Germany: the basements haven't been cleared out yet, and already new houses are being built on top of them, etc. This is obviously parallel to Thomas Mann's remark that not a single epoch in German history has been lived to the end because none of its revolutions were successful, and that this can be seen in the construction of German cities. Which doesn't mean that Brecht must have read Mann's *Dr. Faustus*. The Germanist Gerhard Scholz tells of a conversation with Brecht at the time of their common exile in Scandinavia, concerning the future of socialism in Germany. Brecht polemicized at least half seriously against the Popular Front conception with its "Fatzer"-dream[5] of setting up a communist dictatorship (a cell), in Ratibor or elsewhere, in order to set an example.

In the same year, 1948, in a discussion with students in Leipzig, Brecht formulated the goal of his work in the Soviet-occupied zone

of Germany as follows: twenty years of counter-ideological dem-
olition work and his need for a theater of his own, dedicated to
the "scientific production of scandals," aiming at a political division
of the audience instead of its illusory "unification" in an aesthetic
make-believe. In other words: his hope for a political theater
independent of market pressures. A theater that finds its *opportunity*
in the contradiction between success and effectiveness, not its
dilemma, as in capitalist society. That was an anticipation, a
projection of a future which as yet, twenty-three years after Brecht's
death, has not been realized. The scandals, the sparks initiating a
larger discussion, did not take place in the theater but instead, as
an obstacle to discussion, on the cultural pages of the press. The
new houses had to be built faster than it took to clear the basements.
The GDR, beleaguered as a result of the cold war—which still
continues, as far as the total German situation is concerned—
needed and continues to need ideology. Between the Leipzig
statement and the sentence in the late foreword to the early plays,
which formulates his renunciation of the ideal of the tabula rasa,
of the pure example: History may make a clean sweep, but she
doesn't like to leave the room empty ... between these two
statements lies Brecht's GDR experience. An essential aspect of this
experience is the discovery of friendliness as a political category.
Brecht's theater work: a heroic effort to clear out the basements
without endangering the stability of the new buildings. (This
formulation contains the fundamental problem of the GDR's
cultural policy.) In this context, his treatments of classic plays were
not escapes from the demands of the day, but a revision of the
revision of the classics, or, in some cases, of their traditional
interpretation.

Brecht's difficulty in coming to grips with a GDR subject is
evidenced by the history of his "Büsching"-project. The first draft
aims at a historical play, the worker (Garbe) as a historical character.
With one epochal distinction from Plutarch-Holinshed-Shake-
speare: this hero was his own chronicler. (Brecht had Käthe Rülicke
assemble a collection of materials from tape-recordings of stories
told by Garbe.) What that difference means is: the petroleum
refuses to fit into the five acts, the unconscious hero is not dramatic,
or else a different drama is needed. Brecht had developed his
arsenal of forms in response to a different reality, starting out from

the class situation and the interests of the European proletariat before the revolution.

After the decimation of the avant-garde, the depraving of the masses, the destruction wreaked on eastern Germany and the Soviet Union during World War II, the revolution in the GDR could only be made *for* the proletariat, not by it. The job of catching up in consciousness had to be accomplished under the conditions of the cold war, in an occupied and divided country, under the drum-fire of daily advertisements for the miracle of capitalism in the other German state, legal successor to the German Reich, shrunken into health after two world wars. This reality cannot be grasped with the classical Marxist categories: they cut into the flesh.

The "Büsching"-project was temporarily abandoned with the comment that the whole thing wouldn't amount to more than a one-act play and that he, Brecht, saw no way of giving his hero the range of expression he would need to write a play. This recalls Plekhanov's thesis of the (positive) uninterestingness of the proletarian hero in contrast with the negative interestingness of the bourgeois hero, the first quality of the proletariat being its quantity, etc. . . . Brecht resumed the project, this time as a didactic play "with choruses, in the style of *The Measures Taken*," after the uprising of June 17, 1953, where, for the first time since his exile, he had heard "the class" speak out and perform, depraved and manipulated though it was by its enemies. Confrontation as an opportunity for opening up the Big Discussion which is the precondition of production. The play remained a fragment.

The net of his (Brecht's) dramaturgy was too widely meshed for the microstructure of the new problems: the very notion of "the class" was a fiction, for actually it was a conglomerate of old and new elements, and this was particularly true of the construction workers who initiated the first strike on what was still called the *Stalinallee* in Berlin, most of them being members of a declassé middle class: former *Wehrmacht* officers, officials of the fascist state apparatus, assistant principals, etc., and also failed bureaucrats of the new order; the Great Design effaced by the sandstorm of reality, impossible to discern or reveal by means of the simple alienation effect, which is based on/derives from the negation of the negation. In this connection, Brecht's reaching for Gerhart Hauptmann and his failed treatment of *The Beaver Coat/Red*

Rooster might be of some interest: the power of tribalism and the terrors of the province.

The Days of the Commune[6] written with a conscious lowering of the "technical standard" for the repertory of a socialist theater, has the same relationship to real socialism that *Don Carlos*[7] has to the bourgeois revolution. Its beauty is the beauty of opera, its pathos that of utopia. Until his death, Brecht himself could evidently see no way to perform the play without any loss of reality (effectiveness). The timing of the premiere at the Berliner Ensemble, in 1961 after the closing of the border, was the first possible occasion. The application of the model to the given circumstance, which could only have been accomplished by the subsequent production of new plays, never happened. As an isolated event, the production of *Days of the Commune* came both too late and too early: too many opportunities had been missed, too many problems had been postponed.

Turandot, Brecht's last attempt to use a parable to shovel away the old shit he saw rising up again, is a genuine fragment. Its forced ending by recourse to anti-fascism—which, applied to conditions in the GDR, has the character of an alibi—destroys the structure/ the play. Under other circumstances, e.g. military dictatorships of the Third World, the fissure that runs through the play may permit/ facilitate the penetrating perception that is the precondition of insurrection. Brecht: What gives works of art their permanence is their mistakes.

The name Büsching, like other names in the Garbe project, refers to the Fatzer material, Brecht's greatest draft and the only text in which he gave himself the freedom to experiment, as Goethe had with the Faust material; freedom from the compulsion to perfect and complete the work for any contemporary or future elite, freedom from the need to package and deliver it to an audience, to a market. An incommensurable product, written for self-knowledge only.

The text is pre-ideological; instead of formulating the results of thought, his language scans the process of thinking. It has the authenticity of a first glimpse at something unknown, the shock of seeing something for the very first time. Along with the topoi of the egoist, the mass man, the new animal, we see, beneath the dialectical pattern of Marxist terminology, laws of movement that have punctured this pattern in recent history. The gesture informing the writing is that of a research scientist, not a scholar who interprets the results of research, or a teacher who transmits them. In this play Brecht is less of a Marxist—that ultimate nightmare of Marx's—than in all the others. (Why should this truth not apply to Marx: that the first appearance of the new is terror, the first shape assumed by hope, fear?) With the introduction of the Keuner character (Transformation of Kaumann/Koch into Keuner) the design begins to dry up into morality. The shadow of Leninist party discipline, Keuner the petty-bourgeois dressed up in the Mao-look, the adding machine of the revolution. "Fatzer" as a battle of material, Brecht vs. Brecht (= Nietzsche vs. Marx, Marx vs. Nietzsche). Brecht survives it by shooting himself out of it. Brecht vs. Brecht vs. Brecht with the heavy artillery of Marxism/Leninism. Here, on the dial from anarchist to party official, Adorno's derisive critique of the pre-industrial traits in Brecht's work seems judicious. Here, from a revolutionary impatience with undeveloped conditions there arises the tendency to substitute the proletariat which culminates in paternalism, the sickness of the communist parties. In the resistance against the anarchic-natural matriarchy begins the rebellious son's remodeling along the lines of the father image, a development that accounts for Brecht's success and hinders his effectiveness. His recourse to the folkloric by the reintroduction of the culinary (into his theater) in his late work was made to seem prophetic in the stupefying whirl of media hype and in view of the posthumous cementing of the father-image by socialist cultural politics. What dropped out was the present; wisdom, the second exile.

Brecht, an author without a present, a work between past and future. I hesitate to say this critically: the present is the time of the industrial nations: the history of the future will, I hope, not be made by them; whether that future is something to be feared, depends on their politics. The categories of right and wrong don't apply to a work of art. Kafka's statue of liberty holds a sword instead of a torch. To use Brecht without criticizing him is to betray him.

1980   *Translated by Joel Agee*

Notes

1. Town near Weimar, within the administration of Goethe, who was chief minister of state.
2. *Iphigenie in Tauris* by Goethe.
3. Town in Denmark, first station of Brecht's exile in 1933.
4. Actor and stage director at Brecht's Berliner Ensemble.
5. Unfinished play by Brecht on which he worked from 1927 to 30.
6. Play by Brecht (1948–56).
7. Play by Schiller (1787).

Reflections on Post-Modernism

1

Orpheus the singer was a man who could not wait. He had lost his wife by sleeping with her too soon after she gave birth to a child, or by giving her a forbidden glance too soon during their return from the underworld after his song had liberated her from death. Thus she was turned back into dust before becoming flesh anew whereupon Orpheus invented pederasty which excludes childbirth and is closer to death than is the love for women. Those he scorned hunted him with the weapons of their bodies, branches and stones. But the song protects the singer: what he had praised with his song could not scratch his skin. Farmers, scared by the noise of the hunt, ran away from their plows for which there had been no place in his song. So his place was under the plows.

2

Literature is an affair of the people. (Kafka)

3

Writing under conditions in which the consciousness of the asocial character of writing can no longer be repressed. Just talent in itself is a privilege, but privileges have their price: the way one contributes to one's own expropriation is one of the criteria of talent. With the rise of free enterprise the illusion about the autonomy of art, a prerequisite for modernism, begins to fall. The planned economy does not exclude art. It endows art with a social function again. Until art ceases to be art (that is, a narrow-minded activity in the way Marx described it) it cannot be relieved of this function. In the meantime this activity is practiced—in my country as well—by specialists who are more or less qualified for this. The level of culture cannot be raised if it is not expanded. This expansion occurs at the expense of the cultural quality—in my country as well—and this is due to the smog of the media which prevents the masses from seeing the real situation, blots out their memory, and makes their imagination sterile. In the *realm of necessity,* realism and popular culture *(Volkstümlichkeit)* are two separate things. The split goes through the author.

In regard to the conditions under which I work, I find myself at odds with the notion of post-modernism. My role is not that of Polonius, the first comparatist in dramatic literature, last of all in his dialogue with Hamlet about the shape of a certain cloud which demonstrates the real misery of power structures in the very misery of comparison. Nor is my role unfortunately that of the gypsy in Lorca's one-act play who turns a police investigator into a screaming bundle of nerves by giving senseless, surrealistic answers to official questions about birthplace, date, name, family, etc.

I cannot keep politics out of the question of post-modernism. Periodization is the politics of colonialism as long as history has as its prerequisite the domination of elites through money or power and does not become universal history which has as its prerequisite *real* equal opportunity. Perhaps that which predated modernism will reappear in other cultures in a different way, albeit enhanced by the technological progress of modernism influenced by Europe: a social realism which helps close the gap between art and reality, *art without strain addressing humankind intimately*—Leverkühn's dream before the devil comes to fetch him, a new magic for healing the rift between humankind and nature. The literature of Latin America could stand for this hope. Yet, hope guarantees nothing: the literature of Arlt, Cortázar, Marquez, Neruda, Onetti does not amount to a plea in defense of the conditions on their continent. Good writing still grows from tainted soil. A better world will not be achieved without bloodshed; the duel between industry and the future will not be fought with songs which allow one to feel at ease. Its music is the cry of Marayas springing the strings of his divine torturer's lyre.

4

The seven major characteristics of modernism or their post-modernistic variation as formulated by Ihab Hassan described New York just as well as the Orpheus myth in Ovid or Beckett's prose. New York constitutes itself out of its decay. A system which is composed from its own explosion. The metropolis of dilettantism: art is what one wants, not what one can do. An Elizabethan city: the impression of free choice is an illusion of freedom.

Warhol in Basle, Rauschenberg in Cologne are major events. In the context of New York they dwindle to symptoms. Robert Wilson's theater—as naive as it is elitist, infantile toe-dance and mathematical child's play—does not distinguish between amateur and professional actors. A prospect of epic theater as Brecht conceived it but never realized it, making a profession out of the luxury. The murals painted by minority groups and the proletarian art of the subway, anonymously created with stolen paints, occupy an area beyond the commercial market. Here the underprivileged reach out of their misery and encroach upon the *realm of freedom* which lies beyond privileges. A parody of the Marxist vision where art assumes a new function in a society whose members are all artists and have other vocations as well.

5

As long as freedom is based on violence and the practice of art on privileges, works of art will tend to be prisons; the great works, accomplices of power. The outstanding literary products of the century work toward the liquidation of their autonomy (autonomy = product of incest with private property), toward the expropriation and finally the disappearance of the author. That which is lasting is fleeting. Whatever is in flight remains. Rimbaud and his escape to Africa, out of literature into the desert. Lautreamont, the anonymous catastrophe. Kafka, who wrote to burn his works because he did not want to keep his soul as Marlowe's Faust did. And he was denied the ashes. Joyce, a voice beyond literature. Mayakovsky and his crash-dive *out of the Heavens of poetry* into the arena of class struggle. His poem *150 Million* bears the name of the author: *150 Million*. Suicide was his response to the signature which never came. Artaud, the language of torment under the sun of torture, the only one which illuminates all continents of this planet simultaneously. Brecht, who saw the new creature which was to replace humankind. Beckett, a life-long attempt to silence his own voice. Two figures of poetry who fuse into one in the hour of incandescence. Orpheus singing under the plows, Daedelus lying through the labyrinthic intestines of Minotauros.

6

Literature participates in history by participating in the movement of language first evident in common language and not on paper. In this sense literature is *an affair of the people* and the illiterates are the hope of literature. Work toward the disappearance of the author is resistance against the disappearance of humankind. The movement of language shows two alternatives: the silence of entropy or the universal discourse which omits nothing and excludes no one. *The first shape of hope is fear, the first appearance of the new arouses a feeling of horror.*

1978   *Translated by Jack Zipes, with Betty Nance Weber*

HEINER MÜLLER, born near Chemnitz in 1929, is generally considered East Germany's most important, certainly most prolific playwright since Brecht. His main plays are *Der Lohndrücker* (1956), *Geschichten aus der Produktion* (1974), *Zement* (1975), *Die Hamletmaschine* (1977), *Gundlings Life Frederick of Prussia Lessing's Sleep Dream Scream* (1977), *Der Auftrag* (1981).

Franz Xaver Kroetz

I don't write about things I despise.
I find myself very interesting.

INTERVIEWER: Mr. Kroetz, all of your plays, from the first to the most recent, provide a close up view of a narrow social segment, usually a family. Yet in an interview in the *Kürbiskern* you yourself spoke of the need to expand the scope of this view of society. With the exception of *Münchner Kindl*[1] this hasn't happened. Why don't you experiment with mass scenes or venture into historical drama? Why did you give up the project *KPD lebt!*?[2]

KROETZ: The characters in my early plays are proletarians and petty bourgeois, for example well-to-do innkeepers in *Hartnäckig,* newly rich petty bourgeois in *Maria Magdalena,* and a still higher stratum in *Agnes Bernauer.* So the scope of my lens isn't narrow at all. A broad spectrum of characters appears in my plays, from the proletariat to the petty bourgeoisie and the peasants.

INTERVIEWER: You once expressed the intention of presenting antipodes in your plays, industrialists like von Siemens, even though you don't know him personally.

KROETZ: I no longer know what it was that made this sort of idea attractive to me. For a while I wanted to make theater in the grand style. But it's absurd to have two hundred people standing on the stage, when all they represent sociologically is an amorphous mass. If you could characterize them individually, it might make sense. It already drives me up the wall when just five extras stand around on the stage, because it's just childish, one is more than enough. The *Nest* is a mass play, *Oberösterreich* is a mass play with two characters; a lot more mass than if you had three hundred

349

extras crawling all over the stage. Mass as such is a meaningless thing, it's just a multiplication: *Mensch Meier* times ten. The large-scale play, the mass play, is a flight into formalism.

The older I get, the more clearly I see that I'm not the communist writer who's capable of coming up with a politically necessary subject by thinking in an ad hoc manner. Even in my plays about unemployment, I treat unemployment as a condition that involves a certain existential ruin, something which I myself have experienced fairly often without being unemployed. No matter what plays I'm dealing with, the subject is always some kind of existential social damage. No matter whether I'm writing about children or grand-pas—and this is something I didn't admit for a long time—a lot of it's about me. There's more of me in these characters than there is of the manager or director of the A and B companies or Mr. von Siemens. I wouldn't know what to do with characters like that; I find their milieu unexciting; I'm completely uninterested in these puffed up guys with their little attaché cases. I don't write about things I despise. If I did I might end up with plays like Hochhuth's, but I'd rather go to the jungle than write as badly as he does. What he's after is something very important; Hochhuth is a political writer in the truest sense of the word. But I'm more and more interested in my own inherently biographical, existential ruins, which I'm trying to understand and depict as social phenomena. In this sense, my writing is more like Handke's. I find myself very interesting, more interesting than Filbinger.[3]

INTERVIEWER: Why do you avoid showing up objective social contradictions by the interaction of characters that are represent-ative of different classes or interests? Why do you only show the effects of these contradictions on the consciousness of the individual?

KROETZ: What's the use of having the boss appear in person in the *Nest*? The only thing that matters is what Kurt knows about him. The contradiction is in Kurt. This is more dramatic than having the characters attack each other bodily in the old Schiller-like manner. This would be old-fashioned theater with embodied ideas instead of characters. I'm proud of not having to personify the contradictions.

If the contradictions aren't present in the individual, the artistic method of the theater is useless.

INTERVIEWER: Do you ever think of writing a play about a group's learning process, instead of just about individuals?

KROETZ: There are no groups in the theater. Runge[4] tried it once with a *Mannesmann Cantata,* but this kind of thing has to fail because the theater needs individuals. The direct class struggle between the printing industry and the typesetters, for example, considered as a general process, is something I can't see working on the stage. I can only see it as an individual possibility ("Shall I participate or not?"), with the hope that this filtered individual fate will some day help develop a mass base.

INTERVIEWER: Aren't there some interesting group processes that could be used in a play? In labor cooperatives for instance, or at work among colleagues, or in communal homes? Why do your plays always stop where a group process might begin; for example, in the *Nest* when the union shows up? Might this not be a chance for you to avoid the danger of a repetition compulsion? You could come down from your family trip!

KROETZ: But the family is so much more interesting! Most people can identify with a family situation better than with any other. Of course a play can just as well be set in a factory lunchroom. But I'm completely uninterested in putting the union on the stage. Union membership by itself is meaningless, it has no influence on the way the members think and feel; their commitment is absorbed rather than activated by the act of joining. In many companies you're just automatically part of the union, and you can be sure the great class struggles don't take place there!

What remains an unsolved question for me is whether I myself am not caught up in a process that's leading me in a petty-bourgeois direction, with the result that I'm incapable of giving my characters a proletarian utopia. This is something that really preoccupies me. A writer just can't cover more than a limited area. I don't know the communal scene and the intellectual and student milieus as well as Botho Strauss[5] does. So the scope that's available to you as an author is not very large: you're not in a position of making a free choice, of saying, today I'll write this and tomorrow that.

The theater has its laws too. Theater consists of suffering, pain, killing, life, tears; it consists of this whole, huge, stupid misery. Peter Stein[6] once said to me: "Death is uninteresting on the stage, but not sufferings and torments!" Theater always needs an active process: Dying is beautiful, deadness is boring. The theater also needs this fundamental contradiction between fear and hope. "Do I dare?" is a program for 3000 years of theater. Then there are problems of craft, like the question of the number of characters. If at all possible, a play should have three or four people in it and no more. You can't write complicated parts for people who only speak five minutes worth of text, because no decent actor will go along with that. On television you can show twenty, thirty, or more people at a time, but not on the stage. The rule of the theater is: the fewer characters the better.

INTERVIEWER: Only a very few interpreters mention the comedy and the wit in your plays. Despite the fear that often maintains a latent grip on the dialogues, it seems to me that the humorous effects can't be overlooked!

KROETZ: But that's a misunderstanding that goes back to my early plays. Take, for example, the latest one, *Mensch Meier*: there is a sense in which the character is gotten rid of, he falls apart in the course of the play. Hence the scene with the jolly guessing of professions. No matter how careful the actor is—as soon as he gives himself over to the character, he falls apart, he bursts at the seams. And that introduces some very comical and interesting moments. All the good productions of even the early plays have elements of this. Those dense, dull, debilitated characters were never there in the first place. In this sense you're absolutely right: humor, situation comedy, the pleasure in playing, exhibiting, exaggerating, in short, comedy—this has always been part of my work. Even *Wunschkonzert*, for example, can be an extremely amusing play; and it can stay amusing to the end. My better plays, at any rate, all have an active tendency to take pleasure in exhibiting various sorts of behavior and attitude, various linguistic contents that have ceased to be the contents of a personage, and trying them on for size, juggling with them. There's a scurrilous, contrary sort of humor rather like Valentin's.[7] When language takes off on its own, the way it does in Nestroy[8] and Valentin, it gets interesting; when language grabs the characters by the scruff of their necks and picks them up off their feet.

INTERVIEWER: Do you think that political shifts in the Federal Republic might affect your future dramatic work—let's say, if Strauss[9] should become chancellor? Wouldn't you have to relocate your characters in a somewhat different political climate? Would this impair your possibilities of expressing yourself as a communist author?

KROETZ: No. The problems that interest me would remain the same. Otherwise I might as well vote for the Social Democrats now. *Münchner Kindl* and *Sterntaler* have never been performed anywhere even under the Socialist government. How could Strauss react very differently to, say, NATO questions, than Schmidt or Genscher?[10] Of course I'd rather have "Schmidt on my ass than Strauss on my face," as the Bavarians put it.

INTERVIEWER: A number of left-wing authors have run into problems of censorship on TV. You've hardly had any difficulties. Why is that?

KROETZ: I see no contradiction in a communist author's being successful in a capitalist country. For the past ten years, Brecht has been the most widely performed author in the Federal Republic with 12–13,000 performances a year. Neruda sells very well too. The flourishing bourgeois-capitalist cultural industry has an enormous belly and has no trouble at all digesting the five or six communist artists we have.

Also, my plays aren't limited to West German conditions. They are being successfully staged in Scandinavia, England, New York, recently in Calcutta, in Brazil, and Venezuela. It's exciting to see the changes that come about there!

INTERVIEWER: Probably lots of changes. They must rewrite the plays quite a bit!

KROETZ: Not necessarily! Of course for me, my characters primarily live here. Nevertheless, and strangely enough, they're exportable. The translations should, if at all possible, introduce the specific conditions of the country where the play's being performed. It's best not to follow a West German blueprint. The Brazilians put *Mensch Meier* in a Saõ Paolo setting, among the industrial proletariat. In England they speak Cockney and use the great industrial belt around London as the setting.

INTERVIEWER: Is the reception of your plays in the GDR different from the way they're received here?

KROETZ: You'd have to examine that play by play. In the case of *Oberösterreich,* the question of "a Golf or a child" or "a Wartburg or a child"[11] arises in the same way on both sides.

Actually, they're probably more consumerist over there. But in the case of *Heimarbeit, Stallerhof,* and *Nest* the conditions in the East are different. Basic problems like the isolated position of the woman in *Wunschkonzert* continue to exist in a developed socialist society. Or take *Weitere Aussichten*: old houses are torn down over there too; the rent situation is different, but the problem of enforced separation, of seeing something being torn down that once was yourself, this remains as a contradiction for them. If I were an East German writer, I'd be drawn to a particular kind of problem: in the course of industrializing their country, they leveled entire villages; the people just had to get out. Those kinds of conflicts make theater exciting.

1980   *Translated by Joel Agee*

Notes

1. Play by Kroetz (1972).
2. "KPD lives": Initials stand for Communist Party of Germany.
3. H. G. Filbinger, controversial minister-president of Baden-Württemberg, who eventually had to step down
4. Erika Runge, born 1939, West German writer.
5. Botho Strauss, born 1944, West German writer and playwright.
6. Director of West Berlin's Theater am Halleschen Ufer.
7. Karl Valentin (1882–1948), Bavarian actor and humorist.
8. Johann Nestroy (1801–1862) wrote seventy-six comedies, mostly in Viennese dialect.
9. Franz Joseph Strauss, leader of CSU party, minister-president of Bavaria.
10. Helmut Schmidt, Social Democrat, then West German chancellor; Hans Dietrich Genscher, Liberal Democrat, vice-chancellor and foreign minister.
11. "Golf" is the name of a West German car; the "Wartburg" is its East German equivalent.

FRANZ XAVER KROETZ, born in 1946, has written over thirty plays so far, many in Bavarian dialect. Most often performed are *Stallerhof* (1972), *Münchner Kindl* (1973), and *Mensch Meier* (1978). The interview was conducted by M. Beetz and members of the MSB Spartakus Saarbrücken.

ACKNOWLEDGMENTS

Every reasonable effort has been made to locate the parties who hold rights to previously published translations reprinted here. We gratefully acknowledge permission to reprint the following:

BERTOLT BRECHT: excerpts from *Brecht on Theatre: The Development of an Aesthetic*, edited and translated by John Willett. Copyright © 1957, 1963, and 1964 by Suhrkamp Verlag, Frankfurt am Main. This translation and notes © 1964 by John Willett. Reprinted by permission of Hill and Wang, a division of Farrar, Straus and Giroux.

GEORG BÜCHNER: "Letter to His Family," from *Georg Büchner: The Complete Collected Works*, translations and commentary by Henry J. Schmidt. Copyright © 1977 by Henry J. Schmidt. Reprinted by permission of Avon Books.

TANKRED DORST: "Gespräch zwischen Tankred Dorst und Rudolf Vogel," from *Werkbuch über Tankred Dorst*. Suhrkamp Verlag, Frankfurt am Main, 1974.

FRIEDRICH DÜRRENMATT: "Friedrich Schiller. Eine Rede." © 1960 by Verlags AG Die Arche, Zurich. Speech delivered on 9 November 1959 at the National Theater in Mannheim on the occasion of the awarding of the Schiller Prize to Friedrich Dürrenmatt. Translated by permission of Arche Verlag.

FRIEDRICH ENGELS: "Letter to Ferdinand Lassalle," from Karl Marx and Friedrich Engels, Selected Correspondence, translated by I. Lasker, edited by S. Ryazanskaya. Progress Publishers, Moscow, 1965. Reprinted by permission of VAAP.

MAX FRISCH: "Der Autor und das Theater," from *Öffentlichkeit als Partner*. © Suhrkamp Verlag, Frankfurt am Main, 1967. Translated by permission of Suhrkamp Verlag. —*Dramaturgisches: Ein Briefwechsel mit Walter Höllerer*. Literarisches Colloquium, Berlin.

FRANZ GRILLPARZER: "Über das Wesen des Dramas," from *Sämtliche Werke*, vol. 3, edited by Peter Frank and Karl Pörnbacher. © 1964 Carl Hanser Verlag, Munich/Vienna. Translated by permission of the publisher.

PETER HACKS: "Interview," from *Die Massgaben der Kunst: Gesammelte Aufsätze*. Henschelverlag, Berlin, 1977. Translated by permission of the author.

PETER HANDKE: "'Strassentheater' und 'Theater,'" from *Prosa, Gedichte, Theaterstücke, Hörspiele, Aufsätze*. © Suhrkamp Verlag, Frankfurt am Main, 1969. Translated by permission of the publisher.

GERHART HAUPTMANN: selection from *Sämtliche Werke*, vol. 6 Propyläen Verlag, 1963. Translated by permission of Verlag Ullstein GmbH.

ARNOLD HAUSER: "The Origins of Domestic Drama," from *The Social History of Art*, translated by Stanley Godman. Reprinted by permission of Random House, Inc., and Routledge & Kegan Paul, Ltd.

FRIEDRICH HEBBEL: "Ein Wort über das Drama!" from *Werke*, vol. 3. Carl Hanser Verlag, Munich, 1965. Translated by permission of the publisher.

GEORGE WILHELM FRIEDRICH HEGEL: selection from *The Philosophy of Fine Art*, translated by F. P. B. Osmaston. G. Bells & Sons, Ltd., 1920.

WOLFGANG HILDESHEIMER: "Über das absurde Theater," from *Theaterstücke/Über das absurde Theater*. © Suhrkamp Verlag, Frankfurt am Main, 1966. Translated by permission of the publisher.